MULTIPLE CRITERIA ANALYSIS

Multiple Criteria Analysis

Operational Methods

Edited by
PETER NIJKAMP
Free University, Amsterdam
and
JAAP SPRONK
Erasmus University, Rotterdam

Gower

Published by
Gower Publishing Company Limited,
Gower House, Croft Road, Aldershot,
Hampshire GU11 3HR, England.

British Library Cataloguing in Publication Data

Multiple criteria analysis.
1. Decision-making
I. Nijkamp, Peter II. Spronk, Jaap
658.4'03 HD30.23

ISBN 0-566-00412-7

Contents

Chapter 16 Postefficient Sensitivity Analysis in Linear Vectormaximum Problems

T. Gal

Preface

The field of multiple criteria analysis is a rapidly expanding area. A great variety of papers, articles and books are devoted to this subject. Multiple criteria analysis appears to becoming a new mode of thinking for decision-making, planning theory, choice analysis and conflict management.

This volume is composed of a set of operational contributions to multiple criteria analysis. The major part of the articles in this book consists of papers which were presented at a meeting of the European O.R. Working Group on Multiple Criteria Analysis held in Amsterdam. In addition, some new articles have been included so as to make this volume a more integrated set of contributions to multiple criteria analysis.

We want to express our gratitude towards Mrs. Ann O'Brien and Mrs. Mary Tan, who carefully typed out this manuscript.

Amsterdam/Rotterdam, August 1980

Peter Nijkamp

Jaap Spronk

Contributors

D.J. Ashton	School of Management, University of Bath, England.
D.R. Atkins	University of British Columbia, Vancouver, Canada.
B. Bona	Instituto Meccanica Razionale, Politecnico Torino, Italy.
C. Carlsson	Abo Swedish University, School of Economics, Abo, Finland.
D. Deshpande	School of Management, State University of New York at Buffalo, U.S.A.
L. Duckstein	Systems and Industrial Engineering Department, University of Arizona, Tucson, U.S.A.
J.R. Fayette	Université Jean Moulin, Lyon, France.
T. Gal	Fernuniversität, Hagen, Germany.
Y.Y. Haimes	Case Western Reserve University, Cleveland, U.S.A.
J. Kempf	Systems and Industrial Engineering Department, University of Arizona, Tucson, U.S.A.
S.M. Lee	College of Business Administration, University of Nebraska, Lincoln, U.S.A.
D. Merighi	Instituto Meccanica Razionale, Politecnico Torino, Italy.
P. Nijkamp	Free University, Amsterdam, Netherlands.
A. Ostanello-Borreani	Instituto Meccanica Razionale, Politecnico Torino, Italy.
P. Rietveld	Free University, Amsterdam, Netherlands.
B. Roy	LAMSADE, Université de Paris IX Dauphine, France.

L. Seiford	School of Business, University of Kansas, Lawrence, U.S.A.
J. Spronk	Erasmus University, Rotterdam, Netherlands.
K. Tarvainen	Case Western Reserve University, Cleveland, U.S.A.
E. Werczberger	Center for Urban Studies, Tel-Aviv University, Israel.
A.J. Wynne	Information Systems Department, Virginia Commonwealth University, Richmond, U.S.A.
P.L. Yu	School of Business, University of Kansas, Lawrence, U.S.A.
M. Zeleny	European Institute for Advanced Studies in Management, Brussels, Belgium.
S. Zionts	School of Management, State University of New York at Buffalo, U.S.A.

1 Multiple Criteria Analysis: Theory and Reality

P. Nijkamp and J. Spronk

1.1. GENERAL

Henry Ford's statement that his customers could get their T-Ford in any colour they liked provided it would be black, is often being quoted by marketing analysts as an example of a peculiar but mistaken marketing concept. In this view, the existing product with its given attribute(s) is adopted as a datum in a sales policy oriented to a maximization of the number of products sold. In modern marketing policy, however, the existing and potential set of customers and their varying needs are addressed [1] by means of a coherent and differentiated set of production and marketing activities with the primary aim to fulfil the customers' needs.

It is surprising that the lessons of modern marketing theory are so poorly understood or applied by analysts and experts in the field of normative decision and choice techniques. It occurs too often that those designing new techniques (for example, in the area of multicriteria techniques) are hardly aware of the varying needs and desires of the potential users of these techniques. Sometimes it seems as if the market for new techniques is oriented to scientific journals publishing theoretical articles instead of to the real world applying these techniques. There is indeed a real danger that real-world decision and choice problems do not lead to satisfactory incentives for scientific research.

In our view, the best way to avoid a situation where decision and choice techniques are being developed in an abstract wonderland of no realistic dimensions is to place more emphasis on their operational nature. It is indeed disappointing that so many methods (either simple or sophisticated) have found so little application. Apparently, the lesson taught by modern marketing theory that a product (or a decision technique) has to be in agreement with the needs of the user (or decision-maker), has been too often neglected. The usefulness of a certain method in a practical choice situation should be emphasized as a judgement criterion of major importance (see also Sinden and Worrell (1979)).

1.2. DIVERGENCE BETWEEN THEORY AND PRACTICE

The above-mentioned disagreement between the theory of new policy and choice techniques on the one hand and its practical use on the other hand, holds true in almost all areas of decision and policy analysis. In macro-economic policy-making and planning, the achievements and results of recently developed programming models have only found limited application. In micro-economics (for example, consumer choice theory), the behaviour of individuals is still badly understood, despite some progress made in multi-attribute theory and in logit or probit analysis.

The same holds true for entrepreneurial behaviour, with an exception perhaps for marketing analysis. Also at the meso level (for example, urban planning, project evaluation, institutional planning) the results of applications of new decision and choice techniques are not at all impressive, despite the abundant number of scientific contributions in this field.

The above-mentioned divergence between theory and practice may be caused by several factors:

- the premises of the methods are not valid;
- the abstraction level of the methods is too high;
- the methods do not fit into the decision-maker's mind due to lack of training in employing such methods;
- the data necessary for applying the methods are not available;
- the results of the methods are not translated as concrete or applicable solutions.

In addition to these factors, during the last decade some new developments in society have taken place which have even enlarged the gap between theory (supply of techniques) and practice (demand for techniques). In the first place, many decision problems have to be placed in a much broader framework than covered by the interest of the decision-maker. Examples of such externalities in a decision and choice situation are: environmental preservation, conservation of energy and natural resources and the interest of the Third World. Entrepreneurs, governments and individuals are increasingly faced with the need to place their own priorities in a much broader perspective. Such a multidimensional view of normative decision-making requires the assumption of a single objective to be abandoned in order to take better account of the pluriformity and heterogeneity of aspirations and priorities in a social context. Secondly, the awareness of political power - often via informal channels -, the process of emancipation and democracy, the occurrence of many social spillover effects and the emergence of so many conflicts among individuals or groups have favoured a situation in which divergencies in choices are more likely to occur. 'The decision-maker' is very often only a fiction, and the assumption of a single (unidimensional) denominator for including and reconciling all these divergent interests is far beyond reality.

Traditional attempts to transform all aspects of a complex decision problem into the same dimension (for example, money, utility or wealth) are most likely to fail, since they do not reflect the heterogeneity and the conflictual nature of many decision problems. Only in a fully operating market and price system such attempts may be valid, but as the existence of such a system is normally only fictitious, such methods do not contribute very much to the real frictions inherent to any decision and choice problem. In general, the occurrence of externalities, risks, uncertainties, unreconciliable interests and soft information preclude the application of such unidimensional decision and choice techniques (see Nijkamp (1979), Rietveld (1980) and Spronk (1980)). Therefore, the search for new and better adapted methods for decision and policy analysis is a prerequisite for dampening the gap between theory and practice.

1.3. MULTIPLE CRITERIA ANALYSIS

The awareness of the above-mentioned divergencies between the theory and practice of policy analysis, the changing social views on the nature of decision and policy problems and the need of a multidisciplinary approach to complex problems, have induced the development of more appropriate decision techniques which are capable of reflecting the heterogeneity and conflictual aspects of choice situations. The field of *multiple criteria* analysis is nowadays being considered as a major contribution to more satisfactory techniques by representatives from several disciplines (economics, operations research, management science, mathematics, psychology, sociology, organisation theory, planning, etc.).

Multiple criteria analysis has proved to be an important mode of thinking in policy and choice analysis, both by taking account of the wide variety of aspects inherent in any decision problem and by offering an operational framework for a multidisciplinary approach to practical choice problems. In this way, much more attention can be paid to the specific requirements of decision-makers, decision processes and the practice of decision-making. Clearly, traditional paradigms such as utility maximization or profit maximization are becoming less important (or at least less dominant) in such multiple criteria techniques, but the resulting gain is a much higher degree of operationality and a closer agreement with the practice of decision-making.

Although the field of multiple criteria analysis has had several early initiators, its drive to maturity did not take place until the end of the seventies. During the last decade an enormous number of articles and books in the area of multiple criteria decision techniques have been published. Despite this great number of publications, the description of empirical illustrations by means of these techniques still forms a minority.

The present volume aims at bringing together a set of operational methods in the field of multiple criteria analysis. The focus of these methods is not on the development of new theories *per se*, but on the empirical aspects of the use of these methods. Therefore, almost all articles in this volume contain one or more illustrations demonstrating the frictions, but also the richness when one wants to apply these techniques. Rather than a compilation of the existing body of knowledge, this book contains many new methods which have not been applied hitherto. As a whole, this volume aims at demonstrating the usefulness of a wide variety of recently developed multiple criteria decision and choice methods.

The origin of this book can be found in a conference of the EURO Working Group on Multiple Criteria Decision Making held in April 1979 in Amsterdam, which was organised by the editors of this book and which was devoted to the same subject as the theme of this book. A compilation of the contributions to this conference extended with contributions from some outstanding authors in the field forms the ingredients of this volume.

1.4. ORGANISATION OF THE BOOK

The book is subdivided into four main categories of multiple criteria problems:

- micro-economic problems;
- plan and project evaluation problems;
- socio-economic problems;
- specific methods useful for either of the three above-mentioned types of problems.

1.4.1. *Micro-economic problems*

The micro-economic problems discussed in this book concern mainly the field of entrepreneurial decision-making. Ashton and Atkins show that multicriteria programming methods appear to be an appealing tool for financial planning. Two problems which may be faced when implementing multicriteria programming in financial planning are discussed in greater detail. One difficulty is that these kinds of planning problems often result in a large number of objectives. Another problem is the phenomenon that objectives may have been formulated in ratio form, which may cause non-linearities. The authors offer satisfactory solutions for these two problems, which apparently stem from the specific nature of financial planning.

In his paper, Spronk discusses several motives to treat both capital budgeting and financial planning as decision problems involving a multiplicity of goals. One of these motives is that even the well-established discounting rules (both in its more traditional and in its modern form) are based on a number of assumptions, some of which are often violated in practice. A sample of financial planning models dealing with multiple goals is discussed by the author. For the solution of these models, a new method (interactive multiple goal programming) is proposed.

An important friction - often faced in financial planning, but also in many other kinds of problems - is the assumption of the optimization of a given system, characterised by an externally determined set of alternatives. Zeleny attacks this assumption by introducing the concept of 'De Novo Programming'. The question is 'how to design a new system of available resources in a satisfactory way', rather than optimizing the given systems. This new tool is fully compatible with linear multiple objective programming, so that - according to the author - a further integration may be very fruitful. This approach is illustrated by a case-study in production planning.

In practice, many decision problems are complex, i.e., they are composed of interdependent subproblems and interdependent goals. Carlsson discusses three principal types of interdependences. He develops the basis for a methodology for solving complex and ill-structured problems. With the help of a production planning problem, the relative merits of this non-conventional approach are compared with the merits of more traditional approaches.

1.4.2. *Plan and project evaluation*

Plan and project evaluation problems are study areas in which the existence of multiple goals has already since long been recognized. Methods like cost-benefit and cost-effectiveness analysis have been very popular in the past, but are now increasingly being substituted for methods which explicitly deal with multiple goals, without translating all aspects of a choice problem into one common denominator.

Duckstein and Kempf present a new method for plan evaluation, labelled 'Q-Analysis'. Its applicability is demonstrated by means of a case-study for the Tosza River Basin in Hungary. This case-study had, in earlier studies, already been tackled by four other multicriteria techniques, so that their merits could be compared with those of Q-Analysis.

Although the field of multiple criteria analysis is fairly young, the number of applications to plan evaluations is steadily growing. A very interesting application is the case of the financial resource allocation of an Italian metropolitan area, described by Bona, Merighi, and Ostanello-Borreani. The aim of their study was to improve the effectiveness of public intervention in social services and to reduce the disparities between zones of the area concerned. The implementation of the study has brought about results judged as satisfactory by the decision-makers.

Lee and Wynne present a separable goal programming algorithm based on the piecewise linear approximation technique for nonlinear goal programming problems. The purpose of this paper is to extend the capabilities of the well-known goal programming technique to include a class of multi-criteria decision problems that are subject to nonlinear systems and goal constraints. An example illustrates this new approach.

The appraisal of investment projects, especially in the developing countries, includes numerous and diverse criteria. Fayette considers this appraisal problem first from the standpoint of the theory of decision-making. Attention is paid to the precise nature of the criteria for evaluating investments. An important problem is that many projects are not mutually independent. The author formulates some ideas about how to allow explicitly for project interdependences.

1.4.3. *Socio-economic problems*

The contributions brought together in this part are related to socio-economic problems.

The paper by Zionts and Deshpande describes the implementation and application of a multiple criteria decision-making method, viz. the well-known interactive procedure developed by Zionts and Wallenius. This method was implemented via a systematic use of several criteria in the energy planning models used by the U.S. Department of Energy. The main conclusions about the feelings of the users of the interactive system are also summarised by the authors.

An integrated planning framework for a system of regions has to take into account *inter alia* the *intra*regional conflicts among the set of relevant regional objectives and the *inter*regional conflicts due to diverging interests of the regions within the system. Nijkamp and Rietveld provide an analytical framework for integrated regional planning for a spatial system. In this framework, the authors combine interactive multi*level* planning methods with interactive multi*objective* decision methods. This new approach is illustrated by means of an application to a multiregional model with economic and environmental objectives.

Werczberger presents a model for decision-making when there is uncertainty with respect to constraint values and to aspired values (targets) of the multiple objectives. By means of the 'versatility' criterion the feasible policy, which maximizes the probability that a set of linear constraints is satisfied, can be found. The model's potential application is illustrated by an example of a planning agency in Israel faced with the task to compare alternative plans for the physical rehabilitation and renewal of a residential neighbourhood.

A hierarchical-multiobjective framework, which recognizes that most large-scale systems are characterised *inter alia* by multiple objectives and several levels of decision-making, is developed by Haimes and Tarvainen. They combine the 'hierarchical approach', which is based on the decomposition of large scale systems into independent subsystems, with the multiobjective approach which is widely known as surrogate worth trade-off method.

1.4.4. *Specific methods*

In the last part of this book, some specific methods are presented. However, all of them may be quite attractive tools for decision-making in practice.

An example of a finite stage decision problem is the optimisation of a serial production process in which the input of one production division is the output of its previous division. Yu and Seiford address themselves to the finite stage multicriteria problem, which occurs in the above example if, for instance, both cost and quality are important issues for management. The authors focus on domination structures and non-dominated solutions. Furthermore, a dynamic programming scheme is proposed and illustrated by an example of a three-stage production process.

The decision aid procedure presented by Roy has been designed for so-called 'trichotomic segmentation problems' (decision problems with three possible answers: yes, no, don't know). For example, in credit-granting, the decision-maker has to assign his clients to one of three classes: accept, reject, or delay to gather additional information. As Roy points out, in this and similar problems (e.g., adopting a medical treatment, launching a new product or research project, etc.) the decision-maker has to account for diverse factors which are not always quantifiable and even sometimes rather subjective. Roy illustrates his technique by means of a numerical exercise.

In reality, decision-makers are seldom interested in 'the' optimal solution provided by one or another decision method. Normally, they are more interested to know what happens if some of the initial data change. Likewise, in multiple criteria decision problems, the decision-maker wants to know whether (and under which circumstances) optimal and Pareto-optimal (efficient) solutions change. These questions are answered by Gal for the linear vector maximum problem, which has already had many applications in the past.

1.5. CONCLUDING REMARKS

The contributions to multiple criteria analysis, brought together in this book, demonstrate the perspective of new normative decision methods. Multiple dimensions of a decision and choice problem can be taken into account, while also socio-psychological and organisational aspects can be dealt with. It is also clear that a fruitful application of these methods requires a good understanding and adequate description of the decision situation at hand. The successive chapters of this book show also that, apart from the institutional structure of a given decision problem, also much attention has to be paid to the collection of appropriate data (including their level of measurement) and the presentation of the output to the decision-maker. Several crucial characteristics of decision situations are included in Figure 1 (see Despontin and Spronk (1979)).

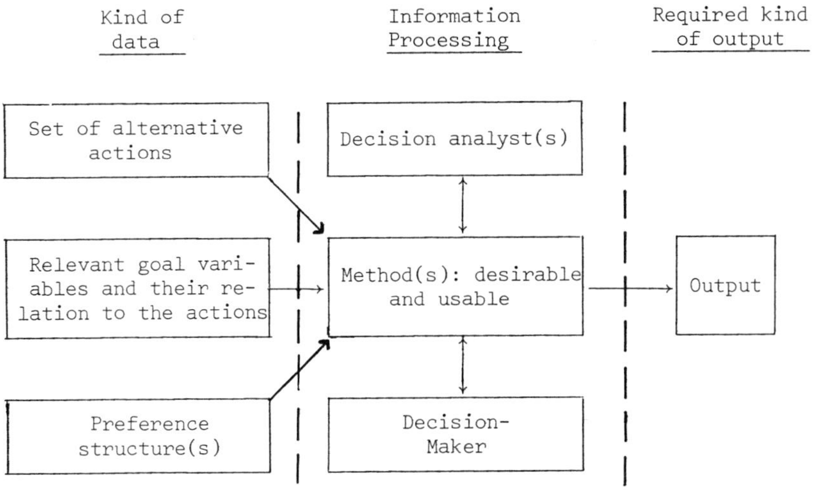

Figure 1.1. Features of a decision problem

Figure 1.1. demonstrates quite clearly that the attitude of the analyst in a decision problem - through his active involvement in the whole decision process - is becoming more modest. He is no longer the expert in the ivory tower who knows the precise answer to every choice problem. In the past, the analyst often played the role of a doctor who removed an ill patient from his bed and took his place, while he next proudly told what he would have done when he would have been ill (cf. Diepenhorst (1974)).

The multiple criteria decision methods have taught that there is no simple and unambiguous answer to a decision problem. The analyst can never be a substitute for a decision-maker or a decision-committee. His task is much more limited: he has to define a decision problem in a coherent and consistent way, he has to collect the necessary data on all relevant aspects, he has to show the impacts and trade-offs of the various policy options and he has to structure the output in a surveyable manner. In this respect, multiple criteria analysis may contribute substantially to an improvement of the practice of decision-making by rationalizing its conceptual and empirical basis. We hope that this volume will provide a new stimulus for a further operationalization of multiple criteria analysis.

1.6. NOTES

[1] Kotler (1972), for example, states: 'The marketing concept is a customer orientation backed by integrated marketing aimed at generating customer satisfaction as the key to satisfying organisational goals'.

1.7. REFERENCES

Despontin, M. and Spronk, J., Comparison and Evaluation of Multiple Criteria Decision Methods, Report 7923/A, Centre for Research in Business Economics, Erasmus University, Rotterdam, 1979.

Diepenhorst, A.I., Een Bedrijfseconomisch Model voor de Problemen van Waarde en Winst, *Jubileumbundel 50 Jaar MAB*, Muusses, Purmerend, May

1974, pp.179-190.
Kottler, P., *Marketing Management: Analysis, Planning, and Control*, Prentice-Hall, Englewood Cliffs, 1972.
Nijkamp, P., *Multidimensional Spatial Data and Decision Analysis*, Wiley, New York, 1979.
Rietveld, P., *Multiple Objective Decision Methods and Regional Planning*, North-Holland Publ. Co., Amsterdam, 1980.
Sinden, J.A. and Worrell, A.C., *Unpriced Values*, Wiley, New York, 1979.
Spronk, J., *Interactive Multiple Goal Programming for Capital Budgeting and Financial Planning*, 1980 (forthcoming).

A. MICROECONOMIC PROBLEMS

2 Multicriteria Programming for Financial Planning: Some Second Thoughts

D. J. Ashton and D. R. Atkins

2.1. INTRODUCTION

The capital investment decision implicit in medium term financial planning is largely concerned with exploring and choosing that set of investment and financing opportunities which, while ensuring the highest possible degree of future profitability, will still maintain adequate cover for the suppliers of short-term credit and long-term capital. The efficiency with which financial management is able to fulfil these typically conflicting objectives will be judged, retrospectively, by the analysis of the published financial statements of the company. While in carrying out their analysis the financial community may compute and use many indicators of performance, certain key indicators or ratios are universally accepted as of particular significance. These include measures of current and future profitability such as return on capital, sales growth, dividend and earnings per share and measures of the underlying certainty in the plans to short-term creditors, shareholders and suppliers of fixed interest capital, the current ratio, dividend cover and times interest covered respectively. As a result it has become one of the accepted skills of financial management to maintain a good or at least satisfactory score on all these indicators. Consequently, consideration of these indicators constrains the possible investment and financing strategies of the firm and provide a set of policy targets for the guidance of financial planners.

A major contribution of operational research to the problems of financial planning has been the development of integrated financing and investment models of the organisation. These have taken two different and distinct forms. One form has been the development of simulation models or rather financial statement generators in which the data processing power of the computer has been used to project and analyse the impact of alternative strategies of the firm (see Boulden and Buffa (1970), Schreiber (1970) and Grinyer and Wooller (1975)). The other has been the formulation of the investment and financing opportunities into a mathematical programming model (see Carleton (1970), Chambers (1967, 1971), Hamilton and Moses (1973) and Weingartner (1962)). In this approach the model is used to maximise one particular financial criterion, usually a valuation of the firm at a chosen horizon, subject to a constraint set which imposes minimum levels of performance on other indicators in the period upto the planning horizon. The survey work by Grinyer and Batt (1974) and by Higgins and Finn (1977) in the U.K. and by Naylor and Schauland (1976) in the U.S.A. has shown that while the managerial acceptance of the simulation approach has been good, the instances of successful implementation of the corresponding mathematical programming approach are very few.

Mathematical programming models for financial planning are distinguished from simulation models in the nature and structure of the information inputs and outputs, as well as in the search procedures employed. Thus the characteristic feature of simulation models is that they examine the consequences of a decision by producing a series of financial performance indicators. These indicators range from projected profit and loss accounts together with balance sheets and sources and uses of funds statements to just a few financial ratios. Simulation models require inputs in the form of decisions from the user and respond by analysing the impact of these decisions on selected policy variables. As such the computer is merely used to carry out computations previously performed by accountants, albeit with far greater speed and accuracy. Although their high degree of managerial acceptability may well stem from this emulation of traditional accounting methodologies it does impose a severe limitation upon their power. In particular they provide little or no guidance to alternative and possibly better solutions. Thus the search is unstructured and proceeds on a trial and error basis. As Myers (1978) states in an overview of the strengths and weaknesses of financial planning models: 'The trial and error process of financial planning often bogs down in the face of the sheer complexity of the problem. The number of alternative strategies that could be examined is practically infinite. It would be nice to endow a simulation model with some intelligence, so that it could automatically sift through alternative strategies, throw away the obviously undesirable ones, and perhaps come up with ones the manager would not even have thought of trying.'

In contrast, mathematical programming provides a very powerful search tool. Its main limitation is that before the search is commenced it is necessary to specify the minimum set of conditions which any plan must satisfy together with a scalar measure of the value of any plan. In this case the information input is the data relating to the benefits and costs of various alternatives together with minimum achievement levels for financial policy variables. The output is an optimal set of decisions. This prior specification of minimum conditions and a single criterion introduces an unnecessary and possibly unacceptable rigidity into the planning system.

Hence, as currently used, mathematical programming models search through decision space for a plan that maximizes a scalar measure of company performance whereas simulation models are used to search, even though that search is unstructured, over a vector of policy variables. The obvious question here is whether an intermediate methodology could be developed in which the search procedures in linear programming were used to 'structure' the search over the vector of policy variables, yet still retaining the more acceptable input-output format of the simulation approach. Our own particular interests in this problem arose from discussions with an operational research group who had a very successful record of implementation of simulation models and were actively considering the next stage of development. They were tentatively experimenting with fairly conventional LP formulations of the capital investment decision, but had not entirely convinced themselves, or indeed anyone else, of the appropriateness of such models. In such a situation it seemed natural to try to enhance the power and facilities of the existing systems rather than to resort to a completely fresh system. Hence the idea was to try to endow a simulation model with sufficient intelligence that it could search through and screen out the non-efficient financial strategies. Multicriteria programming appeared to afford such a possibility. As it turned out, it rapidly became clear that the existing multicriteria methods were just not sufficiently flexible to cope with the complexities of financial planning. We first had to develop a methodology. As a consequence we were not able at that time to involve senior management in our research. Thus the case-study as presented in Ashton and Atkins (1979) is a 'laboratory' reconstruction using some company financial data, where the role of the decision-maker was played by our university colleagues in finance. The purpose of this reconstruction was to try to identify the practical and procedural issues which needed to be solved prior to any serious attempts at implementation. With hindsight though it is clear that the case-study actually raised many more questions than answers, and procedures which seemed comprehensive at the time can now be seen as rather ad hoc solutions related to the idiosyncracies of the particular data under scrutiny. This was partially recognised in the conclusion to the earlier paper where it was stated: 'Clearly there remain many weaknesses in the methods outlines, the objective function structure devised are frequently cumbersome, though here a matrix generator would have helped considerably. In the absence of any coherent and comprehensive framework the methods developed were of an ad hoc nature.'

This current paper discusses two of the most problematic of these weaknesses in some detail in the sections which follow a brief description of the actual model used. The two weaknesses arise respectively from the large number of criteria typically encountered in financial models, and the use of linear approximations to the fractional forms which follow from the adoption of ratios as criteria.

The model as originally developed was a linear programming representation of the investment opportunities over eight years together with a set of financing alternatives facing an organisation. Briefly, it contained four groups of variables representing accounting quantities, financing and investment opportunities together with variables associated with goals and targets, plus two groups of constraints. The constraints consisted of a technological set relating to cash balances and accounting definitions and a policy variable set relating to various financial criteria. The intention of the model was to explore methods of identifying the optimal set of investment and financing decisions with respect to the policy variables of return on capital employed, sales, profits, earnings per share, dividend per share, liquidity, times interest covered and dividend cover. In all, the model consisted of some 200 variables connected by 105 defining equations and the eight policy variables in each of eight years constituted 64 criteria against which the performance of the organization was assessed. More detailed information about the actual model used can be found in the case-study presentation (see Ashton and Atkins (1979)).

2.2. THE PROBLEMS ASSOCIATED WITH A LARGE NUMBER OF CRITERIA

The actual numbers involved here are not the point, our choice of eight criteria over each of eight years, making 64 individual criteria in all, was perhaps relevant only to the case-study under scrutiny. What is typical though is that, for medium term financial planning, analysts need the criteria identified on a year by year basis. Even though much of their analysis is carried out using aggregated data, they seem to need this bedrock of individual figures for continued reference. Now whether the number of individual criteria, that is each criteria in each year, is 64 as in our case, or 20 or 200, most methodologies for multicriteria optimization are ill-suited to handle such problems.

The difficulties associated with such a large number of criteria is paradoxically both simplified and compounded by the observation that the criteria are meaningful and familiar to the financial community. It is simplified because management is used to considering and interpreting these criteria and is likely to have a fairly clear idea of achievement levels at which to aim. Thus even prior to any formal planning procedure, management will probably be able to describe the gross characteristics of the desired plan. Typically this might include a steady and stable growth in sales and earnings per share together with acceptable minimum levels for the current ratio and times earnings covered ratio. The problem is compounded because all the targets are individually important. This is not to say that the manager considers all the (sixty-four) criteria simultaneously but rather that at various stages in the planning process he will examine particular features in aggregate as well as in detail. Hence, although at any one time he will consider only a few criteria or more likely summary statistics of these criteria, he will need to be able to make the assumption that these are not at variance with the other criteria not included in the summary statistics or the individual criteria comprising these summary statistics. Unfortunately prior to the actual exploration of the alternatives it will be extremely unlikely that the manager will be able to detail a precise and exhaustive list of the way in which he will view or wish to examine individual and aggregate features of the plan. It is thus essential therefore that the search procedure should be sufficiently flexible to be capable of exploring both aggregate and individual criteria as desired and that the information inputs and outputs should accurately reflect this search process.

It is natural in financial planning to speak in terms of targets or goals. In this sense many of the constraints typically used in the mathematical programming formulations are more goal-like than binding limits on possible courses of action. Hence an obvious style of methodology was one based essentially on a goal programming formulation.

To introduce some convenient notation we may say that in goal programming our intention is to 'minimize' the matrix elements Z_{it} of target underachievements defined by

$$\gamma_{it}(x) + Z_{it} \geq T_{it} \quad \text{all } i,t \quad x \varepsilon \Gamma = \{x \geq 0 \,|\, Ax \leq b\} \tag{2.1}$$

In this formulation Γ is the set of vectors x representing the feasible production, investment and financing decisions, γ_{it} are the criteria $i = 1,\ldots,8$ over each year $t = 1,\ldots,8$ and T_{it} is the target or goal for criterion i in year t. For the moment the criteria γ_{it} are assumed linear, and throughout our work target overachievements being a minor extension if required, are ignored. The problem of how to organise such 'minimization' of all the Z_{it} simultaneously forms the substance of the theory of multicriteria optimisation.

The particular problems involved in our approach are best illustrated by describing the intended organisation of the search procedure and then highlighting the consequent difficulties encountered. The search procedure was originally envisaged as taking place over three distinct phases.

The purpose of the first phase was to obtain rapidly a region of the efficient surface over which a more detailed search could be carried out. It was intended during this phase to explore only overall tradeoffs between some 'average' value over time of each criterion. If we denote this 'average' shortfall from target for criterion i by $\bar{Z}_i$ then this would appear to be achieved by minimizing the weighted average of these $\bar{Z}_i$ with an objective function of the form

$$\text{Minimize } \sum_i w_i \bar{Z}_i \tag{2.2}$$

Even better, a sequence of trial efficient points could be generated by defining an objective function where u_i is a change vector and λ is a parameter used with objective function parametrics. If we delay for the moment the definition of 'average' over time for a particular criterion and concentrate first on the most important properties of the families of solutions generated by this parametric, then we can make the following two observations. Only vertices in criteria space will be generated as trial points and as the solution jumps to the next vertex, the solution is extremely sensitive to small changes in the values of w_i. Now as this first phase was rather exploratory it was anticipated that these properties would not cause any serious problems. That this was not the case became apparent when an attempt was made to explore dividend policy by a parametric study of a tradeoff between dividend per share and dividend cover. The objective function was a sum of weighted 'average' deviations from target and the relative weights on the two dividend policy variables were being changed using objective parametrics. It was found that a 2 per cent variation in the weights caused a 500 per cent change in the dividend cover and a 200 per cent change in the dividend per share. Again further details can be found in the case-study. Now while it is fairly clear much of this particular difficulty arises because the residual nature of dividends in financial models usually results in a strong inverse relationship between dividend per share and dividend cover, it does not excuse the failure of the methodology to be able to explore this relationship more adequately.

An alternative to the adoption of the goal formulation of minimizing the weighted average of deviations from targets is to use the Tchezycheff metric which gives rise to a minimax programming formulation. The objective function in this formulation is the minimization of the maximum deviation. Dropping the time index for ease of illustration we have

$$\text{Minimize } Z \quad \text{such that } \gamma_i(x) + Z/w_i \geq T_i \text{ all } i \text{ and } x \varepsilon \Gamma \tag{2.3}$$

While this has the advantage of 'smoothing' deviations from targets by steering a balanced course between the criteria it has the disadvantage that once the maximum deviation is minimized it is indifferent to the actual deviation on all the other criteria. It can thus only guarantee weakly efficient points. For minimax programming the parametric exploration is best done on the right-hand side or target which now becomes $T_i + \lambda\delta_i$ where δ is a change vector.

When a minimax formulation was adopted to continue the search over the dividend policy variables a second difficult was immediately encountered. The previously acceptable levels for the times interest cover and liquidity ratios fell to unacceptable levels as the dividend per share was increased. The cause was that the dividends in the early years were partly paid for by additional borrowing. The need at this stage was to explore the dividend policy in relative isolation and a little reflection shows that this could be achieved by using the minimax method with right-hand side parametrics only on the two criteria that make up the dividend policy and leaving the other six criteria with the simple weighted average of goal programming.

In the case-study something similar to this was done, but a slight modification was used. This modification also partially overcame the problems of weakly efficient solutions with minimax programming and the instability of goal programming. The deviation from target is split into two parts. Then these sub-deviations are each treated by one of the two metrics already discussed and recombined as a simple weighted sum. This hybrid formulation is thus

$$\text{Minimize } \alpha Z + \sum_i Z_i$$

$$\text{such that } \gamma_i(x) + (Z+Z_i)/w_i \geq T_i \qquad \text{for all } i \text{ and } x \varepsilon \Gamma \qquad (2.4)$$

With $\alpha \geq N$ the variables $Z + Z_i$ can be replaced by Z_i and we have goal programming again, while with $\alpha \leq 1$ we have a minimax formulation. As α varies between these extremes the isoquants associated with each value of α varies also. The effect of this is to 'smooth' the solution towards the minimax solution as α decreases.

This technique is particularly useful when dealing with one criterion over several time periods and it is instructive at this point to return and consider the definition of $\bar{Z}_i$, the 'average' value over time of criterion i. What definition of 'average' is most appropriate? A simple weighted sum, such as discounting, which is typically used in financial models will not do because of the instability properties already mentioned. Financial management requires smooth or steady changes rather than erratic swings from year to year. Thus a natural choice would be the minimax method over years and indeed our first choice for Phase I of the study was minimax over years and goal programming between criteria. It might be constructive to illustrate this formulation here even though as recounted above it did not really perform as required. Note that the $\bar{Z}_i$ is now simply replaced by Z_i.

$$\text{Minimize } \sum_i w_i Z_i$$

$$\text{such that } \gamma_{it}(x) + Z_i \geq T_{it} \qquad \text{for all } i,t \text{ and } x \varepsilon \Gamma \qquad (2.5)$$

However using the minimax method over years means that if within a criterion there occurs a particular lean year and consequently a large deviation from target in that year, then for that criterion the performance in the other years is largely ignored. We have the problem of weak efficiency in its most serious form. A natural response would be to control the years with the hybrid method above, but consider now the stage which we reached. By asking for quite a simple set of experiments on these criteria to explore, as a first pass, some efficient solutions we now had the deviations partitioned into three, the overall Z and Z_i specific to criteria, and the Z_{it} for each year. In addition we had an overall α and a separate α_i for the hybrid over years within each criteria. We had already created a monster and we still had two phases in front of us, one to compare average values and growth rates and the other to check whether management would wish to weaken the plan for any year in order to seek improvement on balance elsewhere. The case-study goes on to document these other phases but it is more appropriate here to re-examine the purpose and philosophy behind our choice of methodology.

It is clear from the above description that we are already in danger of losing one of the prime motivations and attractions behind the design of the system, that of being able to be responsive to management's need for a flexible search procedure. With such elaborate objective function structures, experimenters would be unwilling to abandon their preprogrammed sequence of experiments or respond positively to management requests to explore particular features of alternatives. Management would discover that the promised new flexible tool for the investigation of alternatives has turned into a Leviathan of its own. The problem is that simple objective functions are not adequate and, as has been demonstrated, the need for quite complex structures arises quickly. What is needed therefore is a method of systematically developing models of adequate complexity using just a few basic building blocks. The next section outlines a proposal for such a methodology.

2.3. A PROPOSED FRAMEWORK FOR ALTERNATIVE OBJECTIVE FUNCTION STRUCTURES

The principles guiding our design for a framework were that we would only use the basic linear building blocks of goal and minimax programming with which we had already become familiar. Combinations of these should then be used to generate a wide range of alternative objective function structures suitable for processing through a matrix generator. The part of the LP giving the constraints $x \varepsilon \Gamma$ would thus not be affected and by defining the deviations from target as $d_{it} = T_{it} - \gamma_{it}(x)$, we need only consider the equations relating d_{it} to the objective function. It was found that a suitable framework needed only five operators, viz. S,T, +,o and o'. From various concatenations of these, a remarkably wide range of structures could be generated.

If we assume that the operators S,T map a vector of deviations $d = (d_1,\ldots,d_n)$ to the real line according to the following definitions, then we have the simple weighted sum of goal programming and the minimax (or Tchebycheff) metric respectively.

Definition 1

$$S_w(d) = \sum_i w_i d_i \text{ for suitable weights } w_i \tag{2.6}$$

Definition 2

$$T(d) = \underset{i}{\text{Min}}\ d_i \tag{2.7}$$

The third definition, that of the operator 'o' is a composite product relation. This enables us to use either S or T on a row (criterion) or on a column (year) of $[d_{it}]$ in any order. Note that d now resumes both its indices and is a matrix of deviations.

Definition 3

Let f and g be either S or T or indeed the hybrid still to be defined. By d_i we mean a row vector of $[d_{it}]$ and y_i is the i-th component of y

$$f o r(d) = f(y) \text{ where } y_i = g(d_{i.}) \tag{2.8}$$

The use of this definition is perhaps better understood by taking a simple example. Thus if we take f and g as S_w and T respectively then we have

$$S_w o T(d) = S_w(y) = \sum_i w_i y_i \text{ where } y_i = \operatorname*{Min}_t d_{it} \tag{2.9}$$

or to write it out in full

$$\operatorname{Min} \sum_i w_i y_i \qquad \text{such that } y_i \geq T_{it} - \gamma_{it}(x) \text{ for all } x \varepsilon \Gamma \tag{2.10}$$

which is the minimax over years and weighted average between criteria that we aimed for in our Phase I experiment above. The properties follow from the notation. Thus $S_w oT$ is interpreted as minimize the weighted sum of the maximum deviation over time for each criteria. On the other hand ToS_{w_i} or in its longer form

$$\operatorname{Min} Z \text{ such that } Z \geq \sum_t w_{it} \, d_{it} \quad \text{for all } i \tag{2.11}$$

is not one we have used to any extent. This is because this form minimizes the maximum weighted average deviations over criteria for a particular year and has no obvious immediate application to financial planning.

Definition 4

This is merely convenience and is the transpose product which operates first on columns (years) and then on rows (criteria). Thus

$$fo'g[d_{it}] = fog[d_{ti}] \tag{2.12}$$

Only one more definition is needed, that of an operator corresponding to addition. It is not one which is quite so intuitively appealing at first sight but is suggested by the form of the hybrid method. Again f and g refer interchangeably to T and S and α is just any positive constant. Just for this definition, d reverts once more to a single index vector, as also are Z and U and we must also bear in mind the fact that T and S are linear operators.

Definition 5

$$(\alpha f+g)(d) = \operatorname{Min}(\alpha f(Z) + g(U)) \text{ where } Z_i + U_i \geq d_i \text{ for all } i$$
$$\text{and } Z_i \geq 0 \quad U_i \geq 0 \tag{2.13}$$

To motivate this definition take f and g as T and S respectively, then we find that $\alpha T + S$ is just the hybrid form.

$$\begin{aligned} &\text{Min } (\alpha T+S)(d) = \text{Min } \alpha Z + \sum_i w_i U_i \\ &\text{where } Z + U_i \geq d_i = T_i - \gamma_i(x) \text{ for all } i \end{aligned} \qquad (2.14)$$

The hybrid form can also be seen as a method of "mixing" the properties of the goal programming and Tchebycheff metrics using the constant α. We are now in a position to generate a wide range of objective function structures. Thus if with the form SoT above, we were worried about weak efficiency occurring between years within a criterion then using the hybrid method within a row might be useful to give the form $S_w oT + S_w oS_v$. In expansion this gives

$$\begin{aligned} &\text{Min } \alpha \sum_i w_i y_i + \sum_{i,t} w_i v_i Z_{it} \\ &y_i \geq U_{it} \text{ all } i,t \\ &U_{it} + Z_{it} \geq d_{it} \text{ all } i,t \end{aligned} \qquad (2.15)$$

Again the notation suggests the likely solution properties of such a structure. We are minimizing the weighted sum (S_w) of deviations over time for each criteria, where the deviations over time are a mix, determined by α, of the goal and minimax programming forms.

A very different structure is given by $S_w oT + S_v o'T$. This splits each deviation into two and minimizes the sum of the weighted (w) sum of row maxima and the weighted (v) sum of column maxima. In expanded form we have

$$\begin{aligned} &\text{Min } \sum_i w_i Z_i + \sum_t v_t Y_t \\ &\text{such that } Z_i + y_t \geq d_{it} \text{ all } i,t \end{aligned} \qquad (2.16)$$

This form experiments on all 64 criteria with only 16 weights w and v and turns out to be superior to the somewhat similar form $S_w oS_v$ which also has 16 weights. This is because the latter form reintroduces all the problems associated with the instability of goal programming but this time associated with the relative sizes of $w_i v_t$.

Our experiments are still continuing but we have found so far that a remarkably wide range of interesting structures (see Ashton and Atkins (1978)) can be generated from just these five symbols and that it lends to the search process a framework and coherence that was lacking before.

So far the discussion has concentrated on using notation to suggest alternative objective function structures. However, it also facilitates the translation via a matrix generator into an operational form. Full details will hopefully become available shortly when this particular aspect of the research is completed.

2.4. THE PROBLEM OF RATIO CRITERIA

In Section 2 it was assumed that the criteria were linear. With financial models this is unhappily seldom the case. More likely is that they are ratios or linear fractional functions such as

$$\gamma(x) = \frac{cx + \alpha}{dx + \beta} \tag{2.17}$$

where c, d are vectors of appropriate dimension and α and β are constants. Thus in our case-study, six of the eight basic criteria were ratios; dividend per share, dividend cover, earnings per share, liquidity, earnings cover and return on capital employed. This makes 48 of the 64 criteria linear fractionals. The approach which we adopted was the one which is typically used in financial optimisations models. A linear approximation to the fractional forms was made by initially estimating the magnitudes of the denominators and the values of the denominators were updated as the search progressed. It should be noted that in our approach errors in the predicted value of the denominator merely affected the solution points and the intervals at which these solutions were filed for further analysis by the report writer, since the report writer computed the value of the criteria from the actual value of the denominators and not their expected value. It must also be noted however that no attempt was made to prove that such a procedure 'converged' or more important perhaps that the solutions generated in this way were necessarily efficient solutions. There is clearly a need to investigate these points much more carefully.

Some of the problems associated with using ratios in multicriteria formulations can readily be illustrated by the following simple example.

$$\text{Maximize } \gamma_1 = \frac{x_1}{x_1+x_2+1} \text{ and } \gamma_2 = \frac{x_2}{x_1+1} \tag{2.18}$$

$$\text{such that } \Gamma = \{(x_1,x_2) | x_1+x_2 \leq 1,\ x_1 \geq 0,\ x_2 \geq 0\}.$$

It can easily be seen that the image of Γ in criteria space is bounded by the efficient frontier as shown in the diagram below.

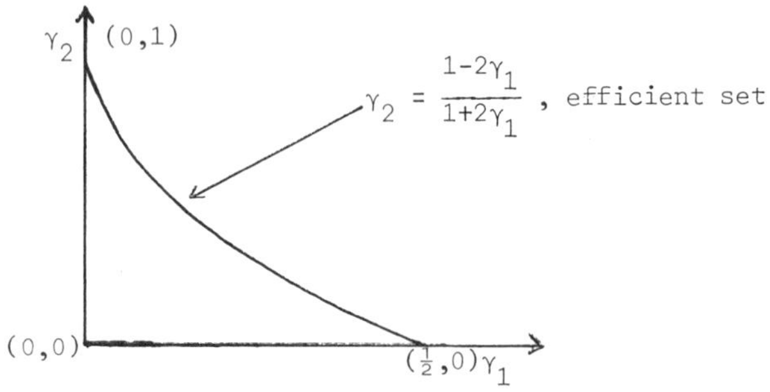

Figure 2.1. An efficient frontier

From this simple example the two most unpleasant properties are clearly apparent, that the image of the feasible region in criteria space is no longer convex and that the efficient region is no longer piecewise linear. From the first property we deduce that methods that rely on simple weighted sums of the criteria, even though such an expression is nonlinear in this case, would not give the entire efficient region. In the example above, only the two extreme points could be generated in this way. From the second property we deduce that methods that rely on enumerating only efficient extreme vertices of Γ are also of little use as neither linear combinations of these are necessarily efficient nor are efficient solutions necessarily linear combinations of such vertices. Other properties worth mentioning but not illustrated by the diagram are that portions, not necessarily all, of the unconstrained interior of Γ might be efficient and that the efficient set need not be closed. It is usually made bounded by demanding that no denominator can drop to zero in Γ.

To know what properties actually remain with ratio criteria that can usefully be exploited has proved to be a thorny theoretical problem and here we can just report on progress so far. One rewarding special case, that of just two linear fractional criteria, has been extensively studied by Choo and Atkins (1979a). It turns out in this case that the efficient region is path connected and is the finite union of convex (possibly open) polytopes. They show that even though the efficient region can still be quite a complex set it can be easily scrutinized by the use of a single row parametric applied to a linear program.

Unhappily these properties do not carry over into the three or more criteria case and counter examples have been found to show this. It does though seem likely that the weakly efficient region is still path connected. The proof of this important property is to be published shortly and will ensure that the (weakly) efficient region is not composed of disjoint areas. Choo and Atkins (1979b) have also developed an algorithm for the multiple linear fractional case which proceeds by basically maximizing one criterion at a time holding the others to a minimum level. Applying the Charnes and Cooper (1962) transformation ensures that this subproblem is equivalent to a linear program. Extensive testing of this algorithm on a model equivalent in size to that used in the case-study is still underway.

To date no work has been done on attempting to integrate the material of Sections 2 and 4.

2.5. CONCLUSIONS

In this paper, further consideration has been given to one particular approach to the use of a multicriteria programming methodology for financial planning. It has been argued that unlike many other potential application areas of multicriteria programming, there already exists a widely used and accepted set of models built by operational research scientists. Thus the emphasis, here as in the earlier paper has been on the development of existing systems rather than the presentation of a new or alternative methodology. In this context, multicriteria programming is seen not as a method of extending the flexibility of linear programming but rather as a means of enhancing the power and search procedure of simulation models. While such an aim provides considerable guidance in the design and development of a suitable methodology, it is not without a cost. The need to employ search procedures which fitted in with the existing input-output formats of simulation models considerably restricts the choice of multicriteria methodology and made the parametric programming approach the most attractive of those available.

When attempting to use such a methodology on a realistically sized financial planning model, two major problems were encountered. In an earlier paper which detailed this attempted implementation, the problems were mentioned and solved in a rather ad hoc way. Removed from the pressures of the actual case-study, this paper has taken a more careful look at the two issues and reported on progress to date on work towards comprehensive solutions.

The first of these was work carried out in developing an algebra of classification of the properties of objective function structures. This was a response to the problem of maintaining an acceptable overall balance to the solution while exploring selected features of that solution. The algebra developed appears to fulfil the need for characterizing the likely solution properties of alternative objective functions and to facilitate their translation into an operationally viable form using a matrix generator, though clearly there is a need for much greater computational experience with these structures.

The second was the problem of ratios as criteria and it has been shown that most of the attractive properties of the multilinear model are lost in this case. It was reported that the two criteria case is however amenable to simple investigation and that a trial algorithm is now being tested for the multiple fractional case. These form the content of two recent papers (see Choo and Atkins (1979a), (1979b)).

Much however remains to be done. Neither the work on objective function structures nor the multiple fractional algorithm have been subjected to sufficient computational trials. More seriously though, almost no thought has been given as to how these two procedures can be combined, which would seem essential if an effective tool for investigating multicriteria financial planning is to be developed.

2.6. REFERENCES

Ashton, D.J. and Atkins, D.R., Criteria Structures for Goal Programming, Working Paper no. 568, Faculty of Commerce and Business Administration, University of British Columbia, 1978.

Ashton, D.J. and Atkins, D.R., Multicriteria Programming for Financial Planning, *Journal of the Operations Research Society*, vol.30, no.3, 1979.

Boulden, J.B. and Buffa, E.S., Corporate Models: On Line Real Time Systems, *Harvard Business Review*, vol.48, 1970, pp.65-83.

Carleton, W.T., An Analytical Model for Long Range Financial Planning, *Journal of Finance*, vol.25, 1970, pp.291-235.

Chambers, D.J., Programming the Allocation of Funds Subject to Restrictions on Reported Results, *Operational Research Quarterly*, vol. 18, 1967, pp.407-431.

Chambers, D.J., The Joint Problem of Investment and Financing, *Operational Research Quarterly*, vol.22, 1971, pp.267-295.

Charnes, A. and Cooper, W.W., Programming with Linear Fractional Functionals, *Naval Research Logistics Quarterly*, vol.19, 1962, pp.181-186.

Choo, E.U. and Atkins, D.R., Bicriteria Linear Fractional Programming, Working Paper, University of British Columbia, 1979a.
Choo, E.U. and Atkins, D.R., An Interactive Algorithm for Multicriteria Programming, 1979b. (To appear in *Computers and Operations Research.*)
Grinyer, P.H. and Batt, C.D., Some Tentative Findings on Corporate Financial Simulation Modes, *Operational Research Quarterly,* vol.25, 1974, pp.149-167.
Grinyer, P.H. and Wooller, J., *Corporate Models Today,* The Institute of Chartered Accountants, 1975.
Hamilton, W. and Moses, M., An Optimisation Model for Corporate Financial Planning, *Operations Research,* vol.21, 1973, pp.677-692.
Higgins, J.C. and Finn, R., Planning Models in the UK: A Survey, *Omega,* vol.5, no.2, 1977.
Myers, S.C., Financial Planning: Putting it all Together, *Modern Developments in Financial Management* (Myers, S.C. ed.), 1978, p.562.
Naylor, T.H. and Schauland, M., A Survey of Users of Corporate Planning Models, *Management Science,* vol.22, 1976, pp.927-937.
Schreiber, A.N. (ed.), *Corporate Simulation Models,* University of Washington, 1970.
Weingartner, H.M., *Mathematical Programming and the Analysis of Capital Budgeting Problems,* Prentice-Hall, Englewood Cliffs, 1962.

3 Capital Budgeting and Financial Planning with Multiple Goals

J. Spronk

3.1. INTRODUCTION

In this paper we will consider capital budgeting and financial planning as decision problems involving a multiplicity of goals. Furthermore, we will investigate the usefulness of a number of multidimensional optimization methods for the solution of these problems [1].

Capital budgeting and financial planning both deal with the selection of capital investment proejcts. Capital budgeting can be described as follows (cf. Lorie and Savage (1955) and Weingartner (1966)): 'Given the net present value of a set of independent investment alternatives, and given the required outlays for the projects in each of the time periods of the planning horizon, find the subset of projects which maximizes the total net present value of the accepted ones while simultaneously satisfying a constraint on the outlays in each of the periods.' This formulation has been adapted and extended in various ways. Other - for instance liquidity and manpower - constraints have been added, different objective functions have been proposed, uncertainty has been explicitly dealt with, and so on. Financial planning can be seen as an extended capital budgeting problem too. In financial planning, capital investments, financing and dividend options are considered simultaneously (see e.g. Myers and Pogue (1974)). A typology of models for capital budgeting and financial planning models will be given in the second section.

There are several motives to treat capital budgeting and financial planning as decision problems involving a multiplicity of goals. First of all, by undertaking (capital) investments one is offering income in one period in order to receive (hopefully more) income in a future period. Income in each of the periods can thus be seen as a separate and mutually conflicting flow of goal variables. Second, in an uncertain world, investing involves taking risks. Clearly, apart from its (expected) income characteristics, an investment project should be described by some measure of its riskiness. The decision-maker, having the possibility to choose different subsets from the set of all of his investment opportunities, can influence both expected income and total risk involved. Thus 'risk' can be viewed as another goal variable. Obviously, this holds true both for investments in the public sector and for those in the private sector. However, in the latter case, modern capital market theory provides tools to aggregate all future and uncertain income flows in one measure, being the market value of the firm. This subject will be dealt with in more detail in Section 3. Third, in general, objectives different from those mentioned above influence decisions concerning the selection of investment projects. This is especially true for the public sector, where the existence of multiple goals in project selection has long been recognized, as is witnessed by the widespread use of cost-benefit and cost effectiveness analyses [2]. But also the private enterprise is, and should be, dealing with a complex of multiple goals, which changes over time (cf. Easton (1973)). In consequence, private project selection should be seen as a decision problem involving multiple goals. Several authors recognized this fact and presented a variety of capital budgeting and financial planning models, which explicitly deal with multiple goals. A sample of these models is discussed in Section 4. In Section 5, we focus on some of the merits and demerits of these models. This will be done from two points of view. One concerns the properties of the multidimensional optimization methods used, i.e. their technical possibilities and shortcomings in this field of application. The other viewpoint is whether, and to what extent, results of modern finance theory are being used. A subsequent paper will be devoted to an originally single-objective financial planning model, which has a sound basis [3] in the modern theory of finance (Myers (1974)). We show how such a model can be translated into a multiple objective programming model. For the solution of the thus modelled problem, we are proposing a new, interactive procedure, called Interactive Multiple Goal Programming (see Nijkamp and Spronk (1980)).

3.2. THE SELECTION OF CAPITAL INVESTMENT PROJECTS: A TYPOLOGY

In this section we present a typology of investment selection problems when only one objective is strived for. Knowledge of this typology and of the concepts described may be helpful in understanding the following sections. However, because of limited space, this exposure can only be rudimentary. We refer to others for further details (see e.g. Bromwich (1976) or Bierman and Smidt (1975)). Throughout this paper we assume K_{tj}, the cashflow in period t (t=1,...,T) associated with project j (j=1,...,n), to be concentrated at the end of period t, so that we assume discrete instead of continuous time. When the sign of K_{tj} is positive, the cashflow should be considered to be a cash-inflow. A negative sign indicates a cash-outflow. All cashflows are assumed to be determined according to the 'with-or-without' principle, which means that the incremental effects of the project on the firm's total cashflow are being measured. An import element in project selection is the possible interdependency between projects. Generally, a distinction is made between economic and stochastic dependence. Economic dependence occurs if acceptance of one project influences the (possibly random) cashflows of another project.

A special case is offered by mutually exclusive projects, which means that the acceptance of one project prohibits the other project's acceptance. Two projects are said to be stochastically dependent if the covariance between their respective cashflows is non-zero. In reality, all conceivable combinations of economic and stochastic dependence may occur.

According to Lorie and Savage (1955), three distinct selection problems can be formulated:

(i) given the cost of capital, should a given project be accepted or not?
(ii) which project from among a set of mutually exclusive projects can best be selected?
(iii) what is the optimal set of investment projects to be undertaken if the available funds are limited?

Originally, these problems were formulated under the assumption of certainty. Under this condition, and further assuming perfect capital markets and perfect divisibility of investment projects, it is readily seen (cf. also the next section) that the net present value of the cashflows of a given project forms a correct yardstick for measuring the project's desirability. If the latter assumptions are being relaxed, this criterion can be used with some reservation only. In particular, problems may arise while answering the third question, to which we will return in more detail at the end of this section. If the assumption of certainty is being dropped, the three problems become much more difficult. Most, if not all, decision rules for this situation either suffer from theoretical deficiencies or are not very practical. Nevertheless, in reality project selection involves uncertainty, which means that a decision procedure has to be found which is practical and does not violate the theoretical requirements very seriously. As will be shown in the following sections, this may be found by using, within a multidimensional optimization procedure, decision rules provided by modern capital market theory.

Both capital budgeting and financial planning (as an extended capital budgeting problem) deal with constraints on the required outlays for the projects in each of the time periods of the planning horizon. This phenomenon is commonly called *capital rationing*. However, in the literature this term has not always been used in the same way. As was clearly shown by Weingartner (1977), various authors have made different assumptions about the phenomenon of capital rationing. Not surprisingly, these differences have led to series of controversies, concerning questions such as which discounting rate should be used in computing present values, what does this rate stand for, and whether it does measure the firm's [4] opportunity cost of capital properly. According to Weingartner (ibid), most participants in the controversies have interpreted capital rationing as a market-imposed limitation on the expenditures a firm may make. Within this interpretation, which will be denoted by *external* capital rationing, a further subdivision can be made. One manifestation of external capital rationing is called *pure* (or hard), defining the situation in which neither the firm nor its owner have access to financial markets. More often, the firm is thought to exist apart from its (possibly) many owners. In this case only the firm is supposed to be rationed by the financial markets.

One may rightly wonder whether external capital rationing, in one form or another, exists for the private enterprise in reality. One may argue, that for a good project, funds will always be available. Indeed, modern capital market theory learns how a given claim on a future and uncertain income stream is being valued by the capital market. In this market, the expected returns and the riskiness of a claim constitute important determinants of its value. When the expected returns are low and/or the riskiness is high, the value of the claim will be low, but it *will* have a value [5]. The value of such a claim, at the time of issuance, can be considered as the amount of funds the form can get in exchange for the claim concerned. Thus for any project, funds can be obtained. As such, there are no *a priori* reasons for external capital rationing. Obviously, the firm may consider the claim 'price' offered by the capital market to be too low, in which case the funds are not acquired and the project is not undertaken. In our opinion, the firm in this case limits itself (because of cost considerations), rather than being rationed by the market.

This brings us to another interpretation of rationing: the so-called *internal* (or *self-imposed*) capital rationing. A firm may refuse to attract additional funds, because it thinks the conditions offered by the market to be unfavourable. A factor causing this refusal may be that there is an important disagreement between the firm and the market with respect to the prospects of the firm. Another reason for a firm to impose itself limits to its expenditures may be that its current owners do not want to lose their control over the firm.

Capital budgeting models incorporating capital rationing constraints can also be used in situations quite different from those described above. Indeed, Weingartner (ibid, p.1404) states that his 'contributions have been directed at utilizing the information content of the programming formulation as an aid to decision making and not as a positive theory of financial markets'. In the managerial process of capital budgeting within firms, frequently limits are set on *plans* for expenditures on capital account. According to Weingartner (ibid, p.1428), this is done for planning and control purposes, and consequently, it is not properly a case of capital rationing. As we will show later on, it is better not to treat the expenditure limits in this case as 'hard' constraints as in most of the current programming formulations, but rather as 'soft' constraints as provided for instance by the goal programming formulation.

The first mathematical programming formulation of the capital budgeting problem has been provided by Weingartner (1963). The model can be written as:

$$\text{Max} \sum_{j=1}^{n} b_j \cdot x_j,$$

$$\text{s.t.} \sum_{j=1}^{n} c_{tj} \cdot x_j \leq C_t \qquad \text{for } t=1,\ldots,T;$$

$$0 \leq x_j \leq 1 \qquad \text{for } j=1,\ldots,n;$$

where b_j denotes the net present value of project j, and where c_{tj} is the outlay required for project j in period t. The maximum permissable expenditure in period t is given by C_t. The fraction of project j accepted is given by x_j. This fraction can be required to be either zero or one, by which the linear programming problem turns into an integer programming problem. Both problems have been dealt with in detail by Weingartner (1963, 1967). Many authors, assuming one form of external capital rationing or another, have concentrated on the 'correct' discount rate(s) to be used for calculating the coefficients b_j in the objective function. However, this problem and its proposed solutions are irrelevant, as soon as capital rationing is considered to be self-imposed, which agrees with the private firm's reality.

Obviously, these capital budgeting models can be, and have been generalized, e.g. by introducing other constraints on investment. These may stem from capacity, manpower, liquidity and other considerations. As noted by Jääskeläinen et al. (1975), this development is highly desirable, because the business practice itself is moving towards the joint consideration of operating and capital budgets.

3.3. RATIONALES FOR DISCOUNTING

Discounting can perhaps be regarded as the oldest, and certainly the most widespread used multiple objective decision method. In this view K_t, the sum of the cash-flows in period t (t=1,...,T), is considered to be a separate goal variable which should be maximized. By assigning *a priori* weights (i.e. discounting factors) to each of these goal variables, the desirability of a given investment plan can be expressed in a single-valued measure. This measure, the discounted value of the investment plan, is defined as the sum of the discounted values of the cash-flows K_t. Unlike in many other multiple objective decision problems, the use of *a priori* weights (i.e. discounting factors) in this case can be theoretically justified through the existence of a price mechanism. The latter, which in fact is the capital market, determines 'prices' (i.e. discounting factors) for lending and borrowing money. To give a simple example: if the discount factor is 10 percent, a sum of 110 dollars to be received in exactly a year, values 100 dollars at this moment. The sum of 110 dollars to be received in a year is called the 'future value' of the present 100 dollars. Equivalently, the 100 present dollars form the 'present value' of the future 110 dollars. Thus, in order to measure an investment plan's desirability, the present value (or analogously: the future value) of the plan is used as a yardstick. We shall refer to this as the 'present value criterion'.

Most theories which deal with the correctness of the use of the present value criterion, start with the *a priori* assumption that the firm is (and should be) maximizing its owners (stockholders) wealth. Then the firm, which is supposed to be confronted with a set of economically independent investment opportunities, cannot make its investment independently of its owners' consumption decisions. In this view, investment is 'not an end in itself but rather a process for distributing consumption over time' (cf. Hirshleifer (1958) for a more detailed discussion). To reach an optimal solution, both the firm and its owners can (and should) also consider the exchange opportunities as offered by the capital market.

For the certainty case, Hirshleifer (ibid) has shown 'that the present-value rule for investment decisions is correct in a wide variety of cases'. One of these cases occurs when investment opportunities are independent and the capital market is 'perfect' (a perfect capital market is one in which the lending rate equals the borrowing rate, where this rate is independent of the amount of borrowing or lending, and where no capital rationing exists). In some cases, the present-value rule is only correct in a formal sense, because 'the discounting rate used is not an external opportunity but an internal shadow price which comes out of the analysis' (ibid, p. 362) [6]. Unfortunately, there are also cases for which the present-value rule fails to give correct answers. According to Hirshleifer (ibid, p.352), this is only true 'for certain cases which combine the difficulties of non-independent investments and absence of a perfect capital market'.

In an uncertain world the analysis becomes much more complicated. The main problem [7] is the description of the capital market, valuating uncertain future income streams. Some authors have tried to avoid the need for a detailed market equilibrium model. Others have used a very general uncertainty model, the time-state preference approach. For both approaches it is difficult to derive meaningful decision rules for capital budgeting within the firm. An intermediate approach uses the capital asset pricing model (CAPM), as developed by Sharpe, Lintner and Mossin [7]. The CAPM, which essentially is a one-period model [8], has produced results which have shown empirically to be reasonably close approximations of the valuation of uncertain income streams by capital markets. This theory says, that in market equilibrium, the value of each uncertain income stream $\tilde{X}$ is determined by the riskfree interest rate, $\tilde{X}$'s covariance with the income stream generated by the total market and the market price of risk. Because investors have the possibility to diversify their portfolios, the competitive capital markets assigns no value to the 'unsystematic risk' of $\tilde{X}$, which is associated with the part of $\tilde{X}$, which is stochastically independent of the market. The same kind of reasoning can be applied to the valuation of the firm's capital investment projects. Given an economically independent project (cf. Section 2), and given the firm's objective to maximize its stockholders' wealth, the firm does not have to worry about the unsystematic risk of the projects, because 'it is of no value to its owners'. Accordingly, the discount factor to be used can be expressed in terms of the risk-free interest rate, the market price of risk, and the project's covariance with the market (its 'systematic' risk) - (cf. Ballendux and van Vliet (1978)). In consequence, different projects will require different discount factors.

Clearly, there are very good theoretical reasons to use some variant of the present value rule in evaluating investment plans. Nevertheless, the theoretical justification of its use is certainly not complete. As mentioned above, this even holds for the relatively simple certainty case [9]. For the world of uncertainty, very promising results have been provided by the development of the capital asset pricing model. As noted already, this is a one-period model. To our best knowledge, a generally accepted multiple period version of this model does not exist yet. Besides these apparent theoretical shortcomings, there are also some practical problems in applying the present value rule [10]. The most notorious of them is the requirement of economic independence, both between the projects to be evaluated and the existing operations of the firm and between the projects themselves. Within the same firm, such independence is of not very frequent occurrence. Another important problem is the determination of the 'correct' discounting factor. Obviously, in an uncertain world, where interest rates may change over time, this is not a very easy task.

Another important point is that the justification of the present value rule is conditioned by the *a priori* assumption that the firm should be maximizing its owners' wealth. These owners are assumed to have unlimited access to the capital markets. Furthermore, their only interests in the firm are the risk-return characteristics of the income streams generated by it. Under these assumptions, the owners' interests are best served if the firm maximizes its market value. However, the present value rule does not discriminate between projects having the same present value but with different time patterns of their cash-flow streams. If one project has a very equally distributed pattern and the other a very erratic one, not all owners will be indifferent. Neither will other participants of the firm. The same kind of argument holds for the firm's unsystematic risk. The capital market is insensible for this risk, because of its described ability to diversify it.

Owners and other participants of the firm do not always have the possibility to compensate for the unsystematic risk factor. This alone is an important reason to treat this factor as another criterion in the evaluation of projects.

Additional problems arise if, besides the net present value of the cash-flows associated with the investment plans, also other goal variables are considered to be important. Within the given multi-period framework, most of these goal variables will have to be defined for each of the time periods separately. For example, assuming that the size of the labour force in one of the goal variables to be considered does not make sense if it is not clear which period or point in time is concerned. Moreover, there are generally no procedures to aggregate these time-indexed goal variables, in a theoretically sound way, to a single goal variable (this in contrast with the discounting procedure, which has - as was shown above - a number of roots in the financial theory). This being so, one would have to accept, besides each other, time-indexed goal variables together with goal variables which themselves are aggregates of other goal variables. As far as we can see, there are two alternative ways out. Neither of which is without complication, however.

The first possibility is to replace a set of analogue time-indexed goal variables by some kind of aggregate. Although the choice of such an aggregate is to some extent arbitrary, there are several possibilities, which may be useful in practice. To mention just a few of them, one could could use the goal variables' average over time, or only the goal variable defined for the end of the planning horizon, or the maximum growth of the goal variable, or the minimum growth, and so on. Of course, it is necessary that the chosen aggregate has some practical meaning to the decision maker. A clear advantage of using aggregates is that it reduces the number of goal variables, thus facilitating the weighing process.

The second way out is to disaggregate the net present value and to treat the sums of the cash-flows in each of the periods as separate goal variables. In symmetry with the above argument, the increase of the number of goal variables is certainly a disadvantage. On the other hand, each of the goal variables defined in this way, certainly has a clear and indisputable meaning. Furthermore, tradeoffs may be recognized in a much more precise way. For example, one may learn that the goal to maximize a given time-indexed goal variable in period t is in conflict with maximizing the cash-flow in period t+1. By using aggregates, one learns at most (if it is learned anyhow) that one aggregate is in conflict with another.

3.4. A SAMPLE OF MULTIPLE OBJECTIVE DECISION MODELS

In this section we discuss a sample of capital budgeting and financial planning models, which explicitly deal with multiple goals. These models will be characterized both by their technical and by their (financial) economic properties.

One of the easiest ways to deal with multiple goals is to single out one of them which then has to be maximized, while requiring minimum values for the other goal variables. Such an approach was followed e.g. by Robichek, Ogilive and Roach (1969), who extended the capital budgeting problem by imposing constraints on each period's level of earnings induced by the accepted projects. The objections against such a procedure are clear. It assumed that all goals formulated as constraints are equally important and moreover, that they have absolute priority over the goal variable which is being maximized.

Already during very early stages of the development of goal programming, it was suggested several times that this technique could be an important means to deal with capital budgeting and financial planning involving multiple objectives. For instance, Ijiri, Levy and Lyon (1963) argue that their linear programming model for budgeting and financial planning could be combined with goal programming approaches to break-even budgeting. Indeed, a considerable number of authors have used goal programming in financial planning and goal programming models (an extensive list of references can be found in Nijkamp and Spronk (1979b)). Its use in these fields corresponds with the decision-maker's reality. With this respect, Ashton and Atkins (1977) state that: 'it is natural in financial planning to speak in terms of targets and goals; many of the indicators of company performance such as dividend cover, liquidity, or return on capital employed have target ratios adopted by customs and practice'. Nevertheless, the employment of goal programming is not without difficulties. Notably, its need of a considerable amount of *a priori* information to be given by the decision-maker should be mentioned. This shortcoming of goal programming clearly paved the way for interactive procedures. Also in the realm of capital budgeting and financial planning, as the following examples will show.

Candler and Boehlje (1971) describe a two-period capital budgeting model in which the alternative activities consist of (a) two investment projects, to be undertaken either in period 1 or in period 2, (b) the 'opportunity to put cash in the bank', (c) net tax-free cash at the end of the planning horizon, (d) the value of the assets at the end of the planning horizon, (e) dividends paid to shareholders, and (f) pollution. At the same time, the latter four activities have been defined to be goal variables, each of which has to be maximized or minimized. Moreover, dividends have been restricted to maintain at least its current level. Furthermore, the dividends have been restricted to increase at a given (linear) rate. The outcomes of the existing operations have been assumed to be given and fixed and consequently, to be independent of the investment projects.

This problem has been formulated as a deterministic vector maximum problem. The feasible region of the activity vectors $\underline{x}$ is described by linear (in-)equalities in $\underline{x}$. Some of the elements of $\underline{x}$ are integer. Because the goal variables $g_j(\underline{x})$, $j=1,\dots,4$; are at the same time activity variables, they can be expressed on a linear scale only. Candler and Boehlje aim at efficient (Pareto-optimal) solutions. The ultimate solution is to be found by an (unstructured) iterative and interactive approach.

Chateau (1975) gives a numerical example of a capital budgeting problem with multiple goals [11]. The problem is to choose from a set of investment projects, some of which are indivisible. Internal capital rationing is assumed to have the highest priority. Furthermore, three other goals are assumed (an acceptable level of cash, a desired level of dividend disbursement, and a minimum target asset value). These goals are expressed entirely in present values.

This problem has been formulated as a deterministic, mixed-integer goal programming model, employing pre-emptive priority factors. Chateau shows the results for a variety of objective functions, including the one originally used by Weingartner. Although Chateau finds merit in the goal programming model's flexibility, he also mentions a number of its disadvantages. In his opinion, 'the ordering and weightings on *a priori* ground and in absolute or relative terms may constitute a rigidity factor of the goal programming approach' [12]. Not surprisingly, he proposes an interactive procedure. However, for this he has chosen an approach which also requires very detailed information from the decision-maker, i.e. marginal rates of substitution for multiple criteria.

With regard to multiple objective decision models, many interactive procedures have shown to be a very powerful tool in the process of searching for a final (compromise) solution. However, as mentioned above, financial planners are used to express their preferences in terms of goals and targets. Therefore it seems useful to search for interactive procedures which correspond to this use. An attempt in this direction was made by Ashton and Atkins (1977). They describe an interactive procedure based on goal programming, in which both weights and targets are changed parametrically. Two important technical problems they have met are the choice of the distance metric in the goal program and the considerable number of goals which are being used in their financial planning model. They developed a three-stage methodology which could deal with these problems in an ad hoc way. In their opinion (with which we wholeheartedly agree), a specific methodology is necessary for financial planning problems involving multiple objectives. Moreover, in view of the possible applications in this field, the efforts to find such a methodology seem to be justified.

Ashton and Atkins describe an eight-period financial planning model incorporating a set of investment opportunities and financing alternatives available to the firm. Furthermore, it contains a number of accounting variables which correspond with the UK tax law and accounting standards. For each of the planning periods, eight goal variables are defined (six of which are ratios). Thus the problem contains a total of 64 goal variables. In connection with this model, a number of characteristics of financial planning are mentioned, which constitute a source of difficulties in using multiple objective programming methods.

3.5. CONCLUSIONS AND DISCUSSION

In the literature, many examples of capital budgeting and financial planning models involving multiple objectives have been given, which are solved by means of a multiple objective programming approach. Although there are a lot of differences between those examples (both from a technical and a financial economic point of view), it seems that for these kind of problems, an interactive procedure in which goals (targets) are being shifted in a systematic way, may prove to be a good approach. The use of goals, instead of goal variables which are being weighted, is in close correspondence with financial planning in reality. Of the advantages of this 'goal approach', we mention the possibility to deal with the capital rationing problem described in Section 2. Moreover, within such an approach, one might also consider to deal, in an interactive way, with chance constraints. Obviously, an additional provision is then needed to translate chance constraints (and deviations from them) into the corresponding probabilities. This causes no very big problem if the underlying probability distribution is assumed to be normal. Finally, within such an approach one can assure efficient (Pareto-optimal) solutions, although *if* the decision-maker for one reason or the other prefers interior points of the feasible region, these may be found in a straightforward way also (see Nijkamp and Spronk (1980)).

Financial planning and capital budgeting problems with multiple objectives generally cause a number of difficulties, which - to our knowledge - are hard to solve by any of the existing multiple objective programming models. We mention the widespread use of goal variables defined by ratios - causing non-linearities, the indivisibility of investment projects - which can only be modelled by means of (0,1)-variables, and the often impressive number of goal variables - which obviously calls for special treatment.

As mentioned above, the examples on multiple objective financial planning and capital budgeting found in the literature show a lot of differences, also from a financial economic point of view. In many cases, the results of modern finance have not been included in the models. Although this theory has its shortcomings, one should recognize that the firm's outcomes are being valued on financial markets. To take this fact into account, the sum of the market values (as defined in Section 3) could be used as one of the goal variables.

A method which, in our opinion, is reasonably well suited for capital budgeting and financial planning involving multiple objectives, is Interactive Multiple Goal Programming (IMGP), as described by Nijkamp and Spronk (1980). In Spronk (1980a, 1980b) it is shown how this method can be used to solve financial planning model incorporating a multiplicity of goals.

3.6. NOTES

[1] We assume the reader to be familiar with the theory and terminology of multidimensional optimization methods. An overview can be found in Nijkamp and Spronk (1979).

[2] In spite of the merits of these techniques, it is our opinion that other techniques are better suited for the selection of public projects (cf. Nijkamp et al. (1979)).

[3] One cannot say that this model has been generally accepted. However, given the considerable number of reactions on this model published so far, it can be said that it has drawn much attention and that many researchers have recognized its merits.

[4] In the following discussion we mainly deal with the private enterprise, although capital rationing obviously also exists in the public sector. However, the problem of capital rationing in the public sector is, to some extent, similar to one of the private sector's problems to be described below.

[5] This value also depends on 'capital market conditions', which may change over time. Consequently, the firm's cost of capital is not constant. This should be taken into account within the discounting procedure.

[6] Although not providing a theoretical answer to this problem, interactive procedures may be helpful in the search for such an internal shadow price.

[7] For obvious reasons, the following discussion can only be very brief. The interested reader is referred to Hamada (1969), Rubinstein (1973) and Stapleton (1971).

[8] In order to make the CAPM-analysis suitable for multi-period capital budgeting, additional assumptions should be made. See e.g. Hamada (1969).

[9] Surely this was recognized by Hirshleifer (1958). For further discussion on possible theoretical shortcomings, we refer to Adelson (1970).

[10] See also Derkinderen (1978).

[11] According to Chateau, this example is an adopted version of the two-period Lorie and Savage problem as presented by Weingartner (1973, Section 3.2).

[12] Furthermore, Chateau seems to suggest that goal variables should be expressible in monetary terms. In our opinion, this is not generally true for the goal programming formulation.

3.7. REFERENCES

Adelson, R.M., Discounted Cash Flow: Can we Discount it?, *Journal of Business Finance*, vol.2, no.2, 1970, pp.50-66.

Ashton, D.J. and Atkins, D.R., Multicriteria Programming for Financial Planning, Paper presented at the XXIII International Meeting of TIMS, Athens, 1977.

Ballendux, F.J. and van Vliet, J.K., Firm Effects and Project Values, Report 7815/F, Centre for Research in Business Economics, Erasmus University, Rotterdam, 1978.

Bierman, H. and Smidt, S., *The Capital Budgeting Decision*, MacMillan, New York, 1975.

Bromwich, M., *The Economics of Capital Budgeting*, Penguin, Harmondsworth, Middelsex, 1976.

Candler, W. and Boehlje, M., Use of Linear Programming in Capital Budgeting with Multiple Goals, *American Journal of Agricultural Economics*, vol.53, no.2, 1971, pp.325-330.

Chateau, J.P.D., The Capital Budgeting Problem Under Conflicting Financial Policies, *Journal of Business Finance and Accounting*, vol.2, no.1, Spring 1975, pp.83-103.

Derkinderen, F.G.J., Investeringsproblematiek Financieel Strategisch Bezien: Enige Consequenties van Imperfecties, in Jonkhard, Schuit and Spronk (1978), pp.94-104.

Easton, A., *Complex Managerial Decisions Involving Multiple Objectives*, Wiley, New York, 1973.

Hamada, R.S., Portfolio Analysis, Market Equilibrium and Corporation Finance, *Journal of Finance*, 1969, pp.13-31.

Hirshleifer, J., On the Theory of Optimal Investment Decision, *Journal of Political Economy*, 1958, pp.329-352.

Ijiri, Y., Levy, F.K. and R.C. Lyon, A Linear Programming Model for Budgeting and Financial Planning, *Journal of Accounting Research*, 1963,

pp.198-212.
Jääskeläinen, V., Nummijärvi and Saarela, P., A Generalized Corporate Model for Small and Medium Sized Industrial Firms, Working Paper 75/27, European Institute of Advanced Studies in Management, Brussels, 1975.
Jonkhart, M.J.L., Schuit, J.W.R. and Spronk, J., *Financiering en Belegging: Stand van Zaken Anno 1978*, Stenfert Kroese, Leiden/Antwerp, 1978.
Lorie, J.H. and Savage, L.J., Three Problems in Rationing Capital, *Journal of Business*, Oct. 1955, pp.229-239.
Myers, S.C., Interactions for Corporate Financing and Investment Decisions - Implications for Capital Budgeting, *Journal of Finance*, vol.XXIX, no.1, 1974, pp.1-25.
Myers, S.C. and Pogue, G.A., A Programming Approach to Corporate Financial Management, *Journal of Finance*, vol.XXIX, no.2, May 1974, pp.579-599.
Nijkamp, P., Rietveld, P., Spronk, J., van Veenendaal, W. and Voogd, H., *Multidimensional Spatial Data and Decision Analysis*, Wiley, New York, 1979.
Nijkamp, P. and Spronk, J., Analysis of Production and Location Decisions by Means of Multi-Criteria Analysis, *Engineering and Process Economics*, Spring 1979 (1979a).
Nijkamp, P. and Spronk, J., Goal Programming for Decision-Making, *Ricerca Operativa*, Winter 1979 (1979b).
Nijkamp, P. and Spronk, J., Interactive Multiple Goal Programming, An Evaluation and Some Results, in Fandel, G. and Gal, T. (eds.), *Multiple Criteria Decision Making - Theory and Application*, Springer Verlag, Heidelberg, 1980, pp.278-293.
Robichek, A., Ogilive, D. and Roach, J., Capital Budgeting: A Pragmatic Approach, *Financial Executive*, 1969, pp.26-38.
Rubinstein, M.E., A Mean-Variance Synthesis of Corporate Financial Theory, *Journal of Finance*, 1973, pp.167-181.
Spronk, J., Interactive Multiple Goal Programming as an Aid for Capital Budgeting and Financial Planning with Multiple Goals, in Crum, R. and Dekinderen, F. (eds.), *Capital Budgeting under Conditions of Uncertainty*, Martinus Nijhoff, Boston, 1980a.
Spronk, J., *Interactive Multiple Goal Programming for Capital Budgeting and Financial Planning*, 1980b (forthcoming).
Stapleton, R.C., Portfolio Analysis, Stock Valuation and Capital Budgeting Decision Rules for Risky Projects, *Journal of Finance*, 1971, pp.95-117.
Weingartner, H.M., *Mathematical Programming and the Analysis of Capital Budgeting Problems*, Prentice-Hall, Englewood Cliffs, 1963.
Weingartner, H.M., Capital Budgeting of Interrelated Projects: Survey and Synthesis, *Management Science*, vol.12, no.7, March 1966, pp.213-244.
Weingartner, H.M., Capital Rationing: n Authors in Search of a Plot, *Journal of Finance*, vol.XXXII, no.5, 1977, pp.1403-1431.

4 A Case Study in Multiobjective Design: de Novo Programming

M. Zeleny

4.1. INTRODUCTION

It is quite interesting to note that linear programming, after the decades of relatively minor modifications, is now undergoing major *qualitative* changes in response to the challenges of both the theory and practice.

First, it was almost a conventional wisdom until the sixties that models ofconstrained optimization, such as mathematical programming, should provide improved solutions to problems with respect to a *single* 'figure of merit', an objective function or a criterion. In the last ten years, however, *multiple* objective functions, different and noncommensurable, have been incorporated within mathematical programming; see for example Cohon (1978) and Zeleny (1974, 1980a). A special issue of *Computers & Operations Research* on Mathematic Programming with Multiple Objectives has also appeared recently (see Zeleny, (1980b)).

Second, most of the linear programming methodology, single- or multi-objective, assumes that the set of constraints, describing an orderly arrangement of resources and their availabilities *is given a priori*. Only very little methodology exists for designing such systems *de novo*, starting from the organizational needs and yet undifferentiated and uncommitted resources. Most of the previous efforts and knowledge were spent on redesigning and improving the functioning of the *existing* systems. The *de novo* design of systems is to meet the changing social needs and priorities. These questions were initially considered and formulated in Zeleny (1976).

Third, the simplex method is being superceded by a more efficient approach of Khachian (see e.g. *Science*, 1979). This technique involves the construction of a sequence of *ellipsoids* in a multidimensional space that close in *directly* on the optimal solution. No inefficient movement from vertex to vertex of a polyhedron is necessary anymore. The smallest ellipsoid envelope that would encompass all feasible solutions determines the optimum.

There are some other challenges to LP. For example, *interaction*. The traditional LP lacks any sort of decision-maker's involvement in the formulation, solution and evaluation process. Now the decision-maker becomes an integral part of the loop of solution process iterations. This 'interactive' philosophy strives to enhance the role of men in decision-making, *not* the role of computers; see for example the articles in Zeleny (1980b).

In this paper we shall analyze the second of the challenges listed above: the design of systems *de novo*.

In the traditional LP, the analyst accepts a given system, even if possibly sub-optimal, badly conceived and inherently wasteful, and then accepts to 'optimize' it. Although the outcomes may be referred to as 'optimal' solutions, there is probably nothing optimal about them. Although a (single) criterion of some kind has been improved a little, the system itself stays sub-optimal and as badly designed as before.

One can recall a useful analogy about the futility of performing exact computations on a set of inexact or approximate numbers. Why do we try to impose the precision of optimization on a system which was put together by intuition, habit or chance?

The supreme problem of the optimization theory, mostly neglected or avoided in the past, is *to design optimal systems, not to optimize given systems*. Only the former process can be designated as optimization; the latter (and more traditional) notion leads only to an improvement and could be quite unrelated to the optimal conditions of any kind.

We can ask the following question: 'Given a set of available manpower, machine capacities, warehouse limitations, raw materials, market potentials, etc., what choice of decision variables would satisfy these constraints and conditions while maximizing a given figure of merit?'. That is the traditional problem of mathematical programming.

Or, we may ask: 'In order to optimize a given figure of merit, how much and what kinds of resources should be acquired so that we can realize such a system?'.

It is the second type of these questions which represents the subject of inquiry for *de novo programming*.

In the world of increasingly limited resources and their steadily climbing costs, we cannot leave the specification of the 'given' to purely experiential, capricious and habitual-intuitive approaches. No amount of subsequent 'optimization' efforts would remove the inadequacies of an inherently inferior design. But, if we directly and initially design the system so that it would provide the largest return per unit of committed resources, no further 'optimization' would be required.

Before proceeding with our arguments and *de novo programming* formalizations, we shall discuss these main concepts through a practical case-study of production planning issues.

4.2. ISSUES IN DE NOVO DESIGN: A CASE-STUDY

We shall demonstrate the *'problem of the given'* through the following, simplified linear programming case. A small company has been producing a highly profitable decorative material for the last several Christmas seasons. This decorative material came in two versions, x and y. Five different component ingredients were needed: golden thread, silk, velvet, silver thread and nylon. The prices of these inputs and their technological contributions to both x and y are given in Table 4.1.

Observe that in order to produce one unit of x, one needs 4 units of golden thread, 2 units of silk, 12 units of velvet and 4 units of nylon;

silver thread is not used in x. Similar interpretation holds for the technological conditions concerning the production of y.

Table 4.1.
Data for linear programming model

resource	x	y	Price: $ per unit
golden thread	4	0	30
silk	2	6	40
velvet	12	4	9.5
silver thread	0	3	20
nylon	4	4	10

Specialized machinery and skilled operators are available for the production run but no plans for expanding the activity are being considered by the top management. The profit margins are $400 per unit of x and $300 per unit of y. In order to maintain these margins, the company does not allow more than $2600 to be spent on the purchase of the components. Although the prices have been stable over the past several seasons, and the company always managed to sell all it had produced, the overall profits often fluctuated as different managers figured out different ways of organising the production.

1. Manager A, who introduced the whole operation, used some inventory cost analysis and established that 20 units of golden thread, 24 units of silk, 60 units of velvet, 10.5 units of silver thread and 26 units of nylon should be purchased. That exhausted the budget, 20($30) + 24($40) + 60($9.5) + 10.5($20) + 26($10) = $2600, and established the available resources for the season. Manager A then used a simple strategy: produce as much of x as possible. This meant producing 5 units of x, i.e. x=5, and producing no y. This would bring in profits of $2000 but also leave him with $560 worth of unused silk. He got some raised eyebrows about spending all this money on silk and then not using it; he decided to change the strategy: produce as much of x as possible while utilizing *all* the silk. He finally figured that x=3.75 and y=2.75 would not waste any of the 'precious' silk and could be produced within all the available constraints. To his surprise, the realized profits were $400(3.75) + $300(2.75) = $2325. While he tried to figure out why he made more by producing less of a more profitable product and more of a less profitable product, his good performance was noticed and he was promoted to a higher executive position.

2. Next year, new Manager B had to take over the operation. This was a younger MBA, with a good training in linear programming. He soon got tired of listening to the stories about how the 'old man' increased profits, utilized all the silk, etc. He decided to check the optimality of the ongoing system by formulating it as a linear programming problem and by solving it mathematically. His problem was stated as follows:

$$\text{Max } 400x + 300y$$

subject to

$$\begin{aligned} 4x \quad\quad\; &\leq 20 \\ 2x + 6y &< 24 \\ 12x + 4y &< 60 \\ 3y &< 10.5 \\ 4x + 4y &< 26 \end{aligned}$$

By solving the above problem by the simplex method (see Appendix (4.1), Manager B obtained $x=4.25$ and $y=2.25$. The corresponding profits were even higher than previously: \$400(4.25) + \$300(2.25) = \$2375. He received some comments about the unused silk and the 'old man', but he countered: 'If you want to maximize profits, don't worry about the underutilization of resources; this is a maximizing solution and we can't do any better unless they give us more money'. He was also promoted; his high profits and high confidence impressed even the 'old man'.

3. Manager B hired Manager C for the next season. He wanted somebody who would continue in his footsteps and thus Manager C was a true expert in linear programming. He immediately found that *shadow prices* of velvet and nylon were 12.5 and 62.5 respectively. That is, he explained, if we increase the available amount of nylon by one unit, *ceteris paribus*, our profits will be increased by \$62.5. Similarly, by increasing the availability of velvet by one unit the profits would be increased by \$12.5. So, Managers B and C both asked for an increased budget. They argued that by raising the amount of nylon to 27 they could increase profits to \$2437.5 and, since a unit of nylon is only \$10, realize a net gain of \$52.5. Top management did not want to increase the budget and there was no way to get rid of the two young men and their shadow prices. Old Manager A argued that the same profits should be attained within the current budget limits. He did increase the nylon to 27 but then he tried to rearrange the availability of the remaining resources and arrived at the following system:

$$\text{Max } 400x + 300y$$

subject to

$$\begin{aligned} 4x \quad\quad\; &\leq 16.5 \\ 2x + 6y &\leq 24 \\ 12x + 4y &\leq 60 \\ 3y &\leq 7.875 \\ 4x + 4y &\leq 27 \end{aligned}$$

He had it solved on the computer (he became familiar with the linear programming by now) and found that he can produce $x=4.125$ and $y=2.625$ and realize the profits \$400(4.125) + \$300(2.625) = \$2437.5. This was the same as the two young managers proposed to achieve. Manager A then checked his budget: 16.5(\$30) + 24(\$40) + 60(\$9.5) + 7.875(\$20) + 27(\$10) = \$2452.5 ! That is, not only that no budget increase was needed, but the same profits were attainable by actually saving \$147.5 from the current budget. Both Manager B and Manager C were fired and the days of linear programming seemed to have been numbered. Manager A had to look for a replacement but he also had to prepare the production for the upcoming season himself. He ended up with the following:

$$\text{Max } 400x + 300y$$

subject to

$$\begin{aligned} 4x &\leq 16.25 \\ 2x + 6y &\leq 25 \\ 12x + 4y &\leq 60 \\ 3y &\leq 8.4375 \\ 4x + 4y &\leq 27.5 \end{aligned}$$

Thus, he was producing x=4.0625 and y=2.8125 and realizing profits of \$400(4.0625) + \$300(2.8125) = \$2468.75 - the highest profits ever! And with the budget of only 16.25(\$30) + 25(\$40) + 60(\$9.5) + 8.4375(\$20) + 27.5(\$10) = \$2501.25. Everybody was saying: 'The old man did it again!'

4. Manager A was further promoted but they asked him to find a suitable replacement for both Manager B and Manager C. This time they tried to avoid MBA's and do without their shadow prices and requests for higher budgets. The 'old man' finally came across a young Ph.D. in systems, or something like that. The young man complained about his difficulties: there are no systems courses in most business schools and the industry does not want him because he is 'overeducated' and wants to make changes all the time. The 'old man' decided to try him and briefed the new Manager D about their experience with the production of the decorative material. The young man said: 'If you want to maximize profits, then your system is no good. It is actually a very bad, suboptimal system. You should produce the version x only. Forget about y and get 29.4 units of golden thread, 14.7 units of silk, 88 units of velvet and 29.4 units of nylon.' The 'old man' was not ready for that kind of talk: Manager D was fired the next day.

5. Over the weekend, on his personal minicomputer, he tried Manager D's suggestion. As he could recall, its linear programming expression would be as follows:

$$\text{Max } 400x + 300y$$

subject to

$$\begin{aligned} 4x &\leq 29.4 \\ 2x + 6y &\leq 14.7 \\ 12x + 4y &\leq 88 \\ 4x + 4y &\leq 29.4 \end{aligned}$$

And, as the young man said, forget the silver thread! Well, first he checked the budget: 29.4(\$30) + 14.7(\$40) + 88(\$9.5) + 29.4 (\$10) = \$2600. At least the budget constraint is respected by this new generation! Let us then solve the problem: x=7.34 and y=0; the profits \$400(7.34) = \$2936! That is \$467.25 more than my best solution! I shall remember my promotion when I squeezed \$2325 of profits out of this budget!

4.3. CASE DISCUSSION AND FORMALIZATION

As we have seen in the previous case, the level of utilization of resources is potentially significant. The underutilization of resources does matter: it decreases the *productivity* of the system. If the same level of profits can be achieved with a smaller amount of resources, such 'higher-productivity' systems would be preferable. Let us assume that two systems can provide the same value of an objective function while consuming different amounts of the necessary resources. Then the system using smaller levels of that particular resource (measured in physical or monetary units) attains higher productivity with respect to that resource. If we measure the total value of resources used, for example in terms of their current or future market prices, then the system requiring smaller total investment attains higher total productivity. For each value of the objective function, the highest-productivity system is the one achieving that value with the lowest total investment in necessary resources.

If we denote the available amounts of resources by b_i, $i=1,\ldots,m$ and their prices by p_i, then $p_1b_1 + \ldots + p_mb_m$ represents the total valuation of resources. Individual b_i's are not 'given' constants but rather decision variables affecting the values of the objective functions involved.

Suppose that W indicates the amount of money available (budget) for the purchase of the resources. We want to maximize profits, $c_1x_1+\ldots+c_nx_n$, by solving the following problem:

$$\text{Max } 400x + 300y$$

subject to

$$\begin{aligned}
4x \quad & -b_1 &= 0\\
2x + 6y \quad & -b_2 &= 0\\
12x + 4y \quad & -b_3 &= 0\\
3y \quad & -b_4 &= 0\\
4x + 4y \quad & -b_5 &= 0\\
& 30b_1+40b_2+9.5b_3+20b_4+10b_5 &= 2600
\end{aligned}$$

Our solution to the above problem was: $x=7.34$, $y=0$, $b_1=29.4$, $b_2=14.7$, $b_3=88$, $b_4=0$ and $b_5=29.4$

Our formulation produces a 'tight' system design with no or minimum slack resources. It is recognized that operating a system under such conditions could be quite risky and that some 'safety' levels of spare or additional resources are desirable. These safety 'buffers' should be added *a posteriori* to the optimally designed system; they should not be a capticious outcome of the mathematical properties of a system's model. Safety reserves can be determined either as experimental percentages of the actual usage or as distinct managerial policy operators. Observe that the budget limitation W can be relaxed and the system analyzed for a series of alternative budgets, W_1, $W_2,\ldots$, or parametrically, for λW, where $\lambda \geq 0$.

4.4. GENERAL TAXONOMY OF LINEAR PROGRAMMING

In order to promote further research and applications of *de novo programming*, we should establish its relationship to the existing body of knowledge and show its proper place in the existing taxonomical map.

4.4.1. *Basic formulations*

The traditional, *single-objective LP model* can be stated as follows:

$$\text{Opt } f \equiv \sum_{j=1}^{n} c_j x_j$$

$$\text{subject to} \quad \sum_{j=1}^{n} a_{ij} x_j \leq b_i, \quad i=1,\ldots,m \qquad (4.1)$$

$$x_j \geq 0, \quad j=1,\ldots,n,$$

where 'Opt' stands for either maximization or minimization (or both).

Formulation (4.1) is a special case of a more general mathematical programming formulation involving optimization of several objective functions. Let

$$f_k = \sum_{j=1}^{n} c_{kj} x_j, \qquad k=1,\ldots,l.$$

The linear *multiobjective programming* model is then characterized by 'optimizing' a *vector* of objective functions, f:

$$\text{Opt } f \equiv (f_1,\ldots,f_l)$$

$$\text{subject to} \quad \sum_{j=1}^{n} a_{ij} x_j \leq b_i, \quad i=1,\ldots,m \qquad (4.2)$$

$$x_j \geq 0, \quad j=1,\ldots,n$$

In expressions (4.1) and (4.2), the constants b_i indicate the maximum available amounts of m kinds of resources that can be used in n activities, characterized by n decision variables x_j, and related through structural (technological) coefficients a_{ij}. A graphical representation of formulation (4.1) for n=2 appears in Figure 4.1.

In order to be able to model the level of utilization of each particular resource, we shall introduce slack variables y_i in (4.2) as follows:

$$\sum_{j=1}^{n} a_{ij} x_j + y_i = b_i \qquad (4.3)$$

$$x_j \geq 0, \quad j=1,\ldots,n$$

$$y_i \geq 0, \quad i=1,\ldots,m$$

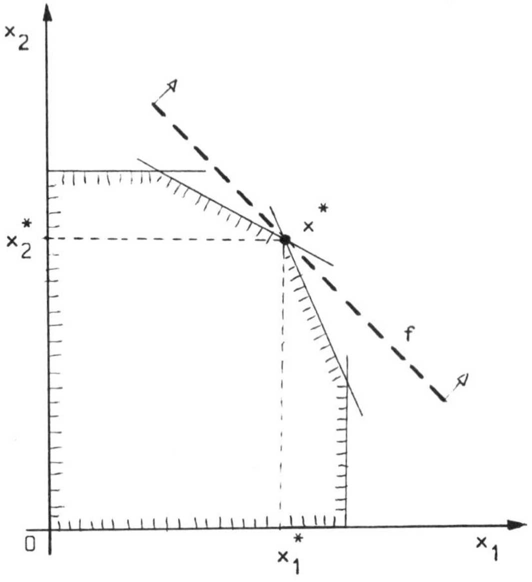

Figure 4.1. Feasible area

Observe in (4.3) that $y_i > 0$ implies $\Sigma\, a_{ij}x_j < b_i$. There are no other stipulations imposed on y_i, and thus both formulations (4.1) and (4.2) can be designated as *wasteful or low-productivity systems*: the actual values of y_i are of no interest.

Let us incorporate the slack variables y_i within the objective function:

$$\text{Opt } f \equiv \sum_{j=1}^{n} c_j x_j + \sum_{i=1}^{n} c_i y_i$$

subject to

$$\sum_{j=1}^{n} a_{ij}x_j + y_i = b_i \tag{4.4}$$

$$x_j \geq 0, \qquad j=1,\ldots,n$$
$$y_i > 0, \qquad i=1,\ldots,m$$

In expression (4.4) observe that the traditional LP model is obtained by setting $c_i=0$ for all i. A *goal programming* formulation is derived by setting all $c_j=0$ and at least one $c_i \neq 0$.

More generally, we can replace the objective function in (4.4) by the following system of objectives:

$$\text{Opt} \begin{cases} f_k \equiv \sum_{j=1}^{n} c_{kj} x_j, & k=1,\ldots,l \\ \text{and} \\ f_r \equiv \sum_{i=1}^{m} c_{ri} y_i, & r=1,\ldots,s \end{cases} \tag{4.5}$$

subject to the same constraints as in (4.4). Observe in (4.5) that functions f_k represent conventional objective functions, while functions f_r measure the utilization of resources.

Even though the values of y_i are now controllable through f_r, we still cannot talk about optimization. Even model (4.5) is of a resource-wasteful and low-productivity type because of being based on independently and externally determined levels of resources b_i.

4.5. INCREMENTAL SYSTEM REDESIGN

A more traditional approach to controlling the stipulations b_i was investigated earlier in Charnes and Cooper (1962, 1964). The indices i are decomposed into subsets I_1 and I_2, according to whether the associated b_i's are being varied or not. Then:

$$\text{Opt } f \equiv \sum_{j=1}^{n} c_j x_j$$

subject to

$$\begin{aligned} &\sum_{j=1}^{n} a_{ij} x_j \leq b_i + \Delta b_i, && i \in I_1 \\ &\sum_{j=1}^{n} a_{ij} x_j \leq b_i, && i \in I_2 \\ &x_j \geq 0, && j=1,\ldots,n. \end{aligned} \tag{4.6}$$

The above evaluation of the alterations in the available resources is a well-known *sensitivity analysis* and should not be confused with a systems design.

Consider the following problem:

$$\text{Max } f \equiv \sum_{j=1}^{n} c_j x_j - \sum_{i=1}^{m} c_i y_i$$

subject to

$$\sum_{j=1}^{n} a_{ij} x_j < b_i + y_i$$

$$0 \leq y_i < d_i, \qquad i=1,\ldots,m \tag{4.7}$$

and

$$\sum_{j=1}^{n} c_j x_j - \sum_{i=1}^{m} c_i y_i \geq f^* \, (1+\Delta)$$

$$x_j \geq 0, \qquad j=1,\ldots,n.$$

In formulation (4.7), value f^* indicates the maximum of $f = \Sigma\, c_j x_j$ attained subject to $\Sigma\, a_{ij} x_j \leq b_i, x_j \geq 0$. Observe that $f^*\,(1+\Delta)$ requires that an increment of at least $\Delta\, f^*$ be realized in calculating a new solution. See Charnes and Cooper (1962, 1964) for further details.

Another approach would be to consider a set of discrete changes in the levels of b_i, occurring within prespecified ranges. This means that we allow different, *a priori* known combinations of resources to be tested against a set of objectives. Consider the following problem:

$$\text{Opt } f_k \equiv \sum_{j=1}^{n} c_{kj} x_j, \qquad k=1,\ldots,l$$

subject to

$$\sum_{j=1}^{n} a_{ij} x_j \leq B_p \tag{4.8}$$

$$x_j \geq 0, \qquad j=1,\ldots,n$$

Observe in (4.8) that $B_p = (b_1,\ldots,b_i,\ldots,b_m)$ is a column vector of a $(m \times p)$-dimensional matrix B, where $p=1,\ldots$. The disadvantage of this approach is that instead of one set of b_i's, there are now p of such sets to be specified *a priori*.

4.6. HIGH-PRODUCTIVITY SYSTEMS

Assume that there are two systems providing the same value of an objective function while consuming different amounts of the necessary resources. Such systems are then comparable in terms of their productivity: the system consuming a smaller amount of a particular resource, *cetetis paribus*, attains higher productivity with respect to that resource (in physical or monetary units of measurement). If we then measure the total value of the resources used, for example in terms of their current or future market prices, then the system requiring smaller total investment in order to achieve the same value of the given objective function can be characterized as having higher productivity. For each value of the objective function used, the *highest productivity system* is the one which requires the lowest total investment in the necessary resources.

Some operations researchers still insist that one should not care about the utilization of resources as long as the objective function is optimized. This is of course a bad management advice. It ignores the possibility that the same or higher value of the objective function can be obtained with lower levels of the committed resources. Nor does it appreciate the fact that with some types of resources (e.g., labour, rented equipment) the low or haphazardly determined utilization levels are politically or economically undesirable (unemployment). Further, such an attitude tends to establish the minimum safety levels of idle resources only as simple derivatives of the mathematical model structure and not in direct response to a careful analysis of actual environmental conditions. Finally, the optimization of objectives without including those of the best utilization of resources among them, is a precept and result of another era, with very little appeal to a modern manager. Its short-sightedness, wastefulness and diseconomy are now becoming painfully obvious.

Let us denote the prices of m resources as p_i, i=1,...,m. Then a given system can be evaluated by:

$$\sum_{i=1}^{m} p_i b_i, \qquad i=1,\ldots,m,$$

where b_i are the actual amounts of resources ultimately employed within the system. One can see that b_i, instead of being treated as 'given' constants, should stand for *resource variables* with their values to be determined through the analysis.

Consider that a resource $W > 0$ is to be divided into parts $w_1,\ldots,w_m$. where $\Sigma\, w_i = W$ and $w_i = p_i b_i$, $i=1,\ldots,m$, as follows:

$$\text{Opt } f_k \equiv \sum_{j=1}^{n} c_{kj} x_j, \qquad k=1,\ldots,l$$

subject to

$$\sum_{j=1}^{n} a_{ij} x_j - b_i = 0 \tag{4.9}$$

and

$$\sum_{i=1}^{m} p_i b_i = W, \qquad i=1,\ldots,m \text{ and } j=1,\ldots,n.$$

Formulation (4.9) specifies the following problem: find $(x_1,\ldots,x_n)$ and $(b_1,\ldots,b_m)$ such that a set of k objective functions f_k, $k=1,\ldots,l$. are 'optimized', while all resources, including W, are fully utilized. That is, all y_i should be 0.

Remark. Formulation (4.9) results in a 'tight' system design with no slack resources. It is recognized that operating a system under such conditions would be risky and that 'safety' levels of spare or additional resources are desirable. These safety reserves should however be

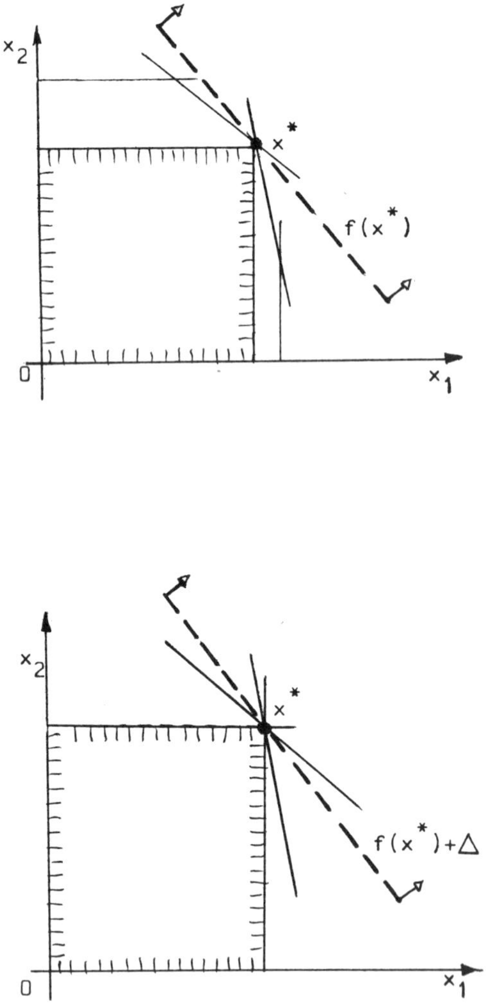

Figure 4.2.   Feasible area

added to the optimally designed system; they should not be a capricious by-product of the mathematical properties of a system's model. Safety reserves should be decided *a posteriori*, either as experimental percentages of the actual usage, or as distinct external operators of managerial policy.

Observe that in (4.9), c_{kj}, a_{ij} and p_i are constants, x_j and b_i are variables, and W is a parameter. One can run the optimal design process for a series of alternative budgets W_1, W_2,..., etc., in a way similar to the parametric or multiparametric programming approach.

In Figure 4.2, for k=1, n=2 and m= 4, we assume that $\Sigma\, p_i b_i = W$ is satisfied at all times. Starting with an initial distribution of resources $(b_1,\ldots,b_m)$, a maximum of f_1 is achieved at x*. All the corresponding y_i are then reduced to zero while maintaining the same $f_1(x^*)$. This causes $\Sigma\, p_i b_i < W$ and those b_i that produce the largest increase in f_1 can be expanded until $\Sigma\, p_i b_i = W$ is satisfied again.

Observe that if W is not determined *a priori*, one should solve the following:

$$\text{Min } W \equiv \sum_{i=1}^{m} p_i b_i$$

$$\text{subject to} \quad \sum_{j=1}^{n} a_{ij} x_j - b_i = 0 \qquad (4.10)$$

$$\text{and} \quad \sum_{j=1}^{n} c_j x_j \geq K,$$

where K is a desired minimum value of the objective function. Or, more generally, we can rewrite (4.10) as a multiobjective linear programming problem:

$$\text{Min } W \equiv \sum_{i=1}^{m} p_i b_i$$

$$\text{and} \quad \text{Max } f_k \equiv \sum_{j=1}^{n} c_{jk} x_j, \qquad k=1,\ldots,l \qquad (4.11)$$

$$\text{subject to} \quad \sum_{j=1}^{n} a_{ij} x_j = b_i$$

$$x_j > 0, \qquad j=1,\ldots,n$$

A general problem of the multiobjective system design can be formulated as follows:

$$\text{Max } f_k \equiv \sum_{j=1}^{n} c_{kj} x_j, \qquad k=1,\ldots,l$$

and

$$\text{Min } b_i \equiv \sum_{j=1}^{n} a_{ij} x_j \tag{4.12}$$

subject to

$$\sum_{i=1}^{n} p_i b_i = W .$$

Problem (4.12) consists of m+n objective functions and one parametric constraint. Graphical representation of the problem is given in Figure 4.3.

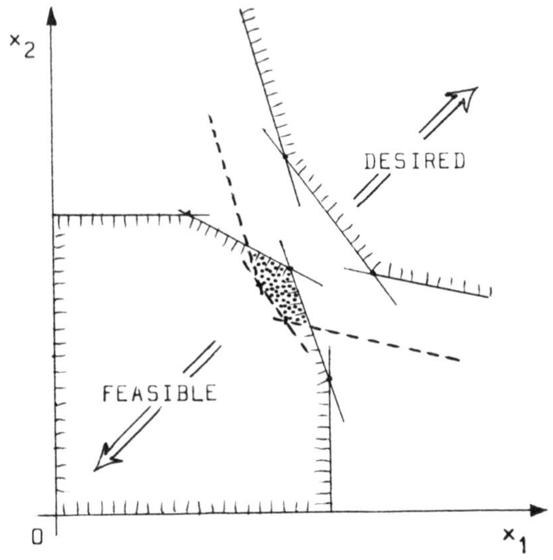

Figure 4.3. Graphical representation of parametric multiple objective problem

Although we do not currently have an efficient method for solving problem (4.12), it seems that the global approach of Khachian (see Kolata (1979)) will be appropriate.

In figure (4.3), observe that two separate convex regions are moving in the opposite directions. The extent of the conflict between the two, i.e., the desired and the feasible, is characterized by their 'distance'. One is looking for the minimum intersection of the two sets at a given level of W. The conflict is fully dissolved if the desired and the feasible regions are both expanded so that they have at least one point in common.

4.7. CONCLUSION

De Novo Programming is still only in its early stages of development. It requires some non-conventional solution procedures but its potential application returns are substantial. There is every reason to believe that the current advances in computer technology and algorithmic methodology will facilitate the consideration of problems as they are needed, not as they are dictated by mathematical conveniences. As we recognize that all of our problems *are* multiobjective, the need for establishing linear multiobjective programming as a rightful area of inquiry will disappear - *it* will become *the* area of inquiry. Then we can proceed with its own development, perhaps along the lines indicated in this paper.

4.8. APPENDIX

Within the case presented in this paper, we have solved the following problem:

$$\text{Max } 400x + 300y$$

subject to

$$\begin{aligned} 4x \quad &\le 20 \\ 2x + 6y &\le 24 \\ 12x + 4y &\le 60 \\ 3y &\le 10.5 \\ 4x + 4y &\le 26 \end{aligned}$$

The solution process traversed the following simplex tableaux:

	x	y	s_1	s_2	s_3	s_4	s_5	
s_1	1	0	1	0	0	0	0	20
s_2	2	6	0	1	0	0	0	24
s_3	12	4	0	0	1	0	0	60
s_4	0	3	0	0	0	1	0	10.5
s_5	4	4	0	0	0	0	1	26
	-400	-300	0	0	0	0	0	0

	x	y	s_1	s_2	s_3	s_4	s_5	
s_1	0	-	1	0	-	0	0	15
s_2	0	5	0	1	-	0	0	14
x	1		0	0		0	0	5
s_4	0	3	0	0	0	1	0	10.5
y	0	2	0	0	-	0	1	6
	0	-166	0	0	33	0	0	2000

s_1	0	0	1	0	-	0		15.75
s_2	0	0	0	1	$\frac{1}{2}$	0	-2	2
x	1	0	0	0		0	0	4.25
s_4	0	0	0	0	·	1		3.75
y	0	1	0	0	-	0		2.25
	0	0	0	0	12.5	0		2375

Optimal solution: $x=4.25$, $y=2.25$, $s_1=15.75$, $s_2=2$, $s_3=0$, $s_4=3.75$, $s_5=0$; the corresponding *dual variables* are: $u_1=0$, $u_2=0$, $u_3=12.5$, $u_4=0$, $u_5=62.5$.

4.9. REFERENCES

Charnes, A. and Cooper, W.W., Systems Evaluation and Repricing Theorems, *Management Science*, vol.9, no.1, 1962, pp.33-49.

Charnes, A. and Cooper, W.W., Constrained Extremization Models and Their Use in Developing Systems Measures, in M.D. Mesarović (ed.), *Views on General Systems Theory*, John Wiley, New York, 1964, pp.61-88.

Cohon, J.L., *Multiobjective Programming and Planning*, Academic Press, New York, 1978.

Kolata, G.B., Mathematicians Amazed by Russian's Discovery, *Science*, vol.206, no.4418, 1979, pp.545-546.

Zeleny, M., *Linear Multiobjective Programming*, Springer-Verlag, New York, 1974.

Zeleny, M., Multiobjective Design of High-Productivity Systems, *Proceedings of Joint Automatic Control Conference*, Purdue University, Paper APPL9-4, ASME, New York, 1976, pp.297-300.

Zeleny, M., *Multiple Criteria Decision Making: A Companion Text*, McGraw Hill, New York, 1980a.

Zeleny, M. (ed.), *Computers & Operations Research*, special issue on *Mathematical Programming with Multiple Objectives*, vol.7, 1980b.

5 Solving Complex and Ill-Structured Problems: an MCDM-Approach

C. Carlsson

5.1. INTRODUCTION

It is almost a truism to state that modern managers have to handle complex and ill-structured problems. Then it is strange to find that modern operations research literature - including modern MCDM literature - almost exclusively deals with well-defined, or well-structured problems (a problem will be well-defined/well-structured if it is possible to formulate a specific problem space and a set of operators for working in that space (cf. Simon (1973)). It is also easy to find precise definitions of the concept 'problem' (cf. Ackoff and Emery (1972), Carlsson (1977b) and Johnsen (1973)), or a list of criteria a problem should satisfy in order to qualify as well-defined/well-structured (cf. Simon (1973)). But definitions are hard to come by: they are often characterized as a rest class of problems which, in some respect, lack in definition. In a real-life management context it is however so, that as knowledgeable and experienced managers tackle their well-structured problems - well-structured because they are pre-processed by assistants and committees - they usually break out of the problem space by making use of (seemingly irrelevant) experience and inside information, and by applying original operators. Usually these managers have considerable success, and usually they cannot formulate any comprehensive methodology which could explain that success. Or, in other words, our methodology for tackling well-structured problems cannot help managers solve ill-structured problems, and they cannot tell us how we should modify that methodology in order to make it operational and relevant for ill-structured problems.

Let us assume that a decision-maker (DM) regards a problem situation as *multigoal* if a set of goals (G), with at least three different elements, should be attained, such that either all the goals are attained simultaneously at some t_i or all of them at least once by some t_i.

With most of our MCDM methods this problem is tackled as a well-structured problem: a problem space is defined, and a set of operators is developed for that space. This is easily verified: (i) mathematical programming approaches delimit a convex set of admissible alternatives, and determine extremum values of a set of objective functions, (ii) multiattribute utility theory approaches delimit a set of utility functions and operators for decomposing and maximizing the functions, (iii) the interactive methods force the decision-maker to compare alternatives in a closed space, and usually have some device to ensure convergence, and (iv) the moving target (and similar) approaches operate with a finite set of alternatives and iterative displacements of an ideal form. It could also be observed that these models in most cases aim at a simultaneous attainment of all the goals and do not explore interdependences among the goals.

Now three interesting questions arise: would it be possible to find other ways for tackling the multigoal problem by treating it as an ill-structured problem? Is there any operational methodology that could be used for that purpose? Would such a methodology also be operational for complex and ill-structured problems in general?

Although the literature deals almost exclusively with well-structured problems, we will try to both tackle the multigoal problem as an ill-structured problem, and to formulate a methodology. For that purpose we will apply the following definitions:

1. A *problem* is a purposeful state a decision-maker (DM) is dissatisfied with, and which he does not know how to change to a satisfactory one (adapted from Ackoff and Emery (1972)).
2. A problem is *multigoal* if the dissatisfactory state represents a non-attainment of at least one goal of a set G of goals, and there are at least three, interdependent elements in G. We will assume that there are three forms for *interdependence* in G: conflict, unilateral support and mutual support.
3. A problem A' is *complex* if it is composed of at least three interdependent subproblems. We will assume that the forms for interdependence are those of definition 1.
4. A complex problem A is *ill-structured* if DM cannot reformulate it as well as a well-structured problem, i.e. formulate a specific problem space and a set of operators. In this context we will, furthermore, assume that A (i) is multigoal, (ii) contains at least two states which cannot be formulated in the same problem space and (iii) has a structure which changes over time, i.e. the interdependences among the goals and the subproblems are allowed to change over time.

The problem A will thus be multigoal, complex and ill-structured, and we will assume that the goals implemented in A are elements of G.

Here we will carry out the following program: in *Section 5.2* a multigoal, complex and ill-structured production planning problem is introduced; in *Section 5.3* a traditional MCDM approach for tackling this problem is given a critical assessment; in *Section 5.4* a non-traditional MCDM approach, based on systems theory and adaptive control, is discussed at some length, and its merits as a basis for a problem-solving methodology are explored; the concluding section *(5.5)* gives a proposition towards the wanted methodology.

5.2. A COMPLEX AND ILL-STRUCTURED PRODUCTION PLANNING PROBLEM

Let us consider the production process we have formulated in Figure 5.1. It is a 9-stage plywood production process, from which we will discuss stages 2, 3 and 4 which are the cutting, turning and drying processes.

A few data can be read from Figure 5.1: (i) the three processes contain 2,4 and 4 subprocesses, (ii) there is a flow of products through the subprocesses, combined with in-process stores in stage 3; the products get new characteristics when passing through a subprocess, (iii) the processes are interdependent through feedback-loops. To that could be added that it is not trivially easy to handle the three processes in practice:

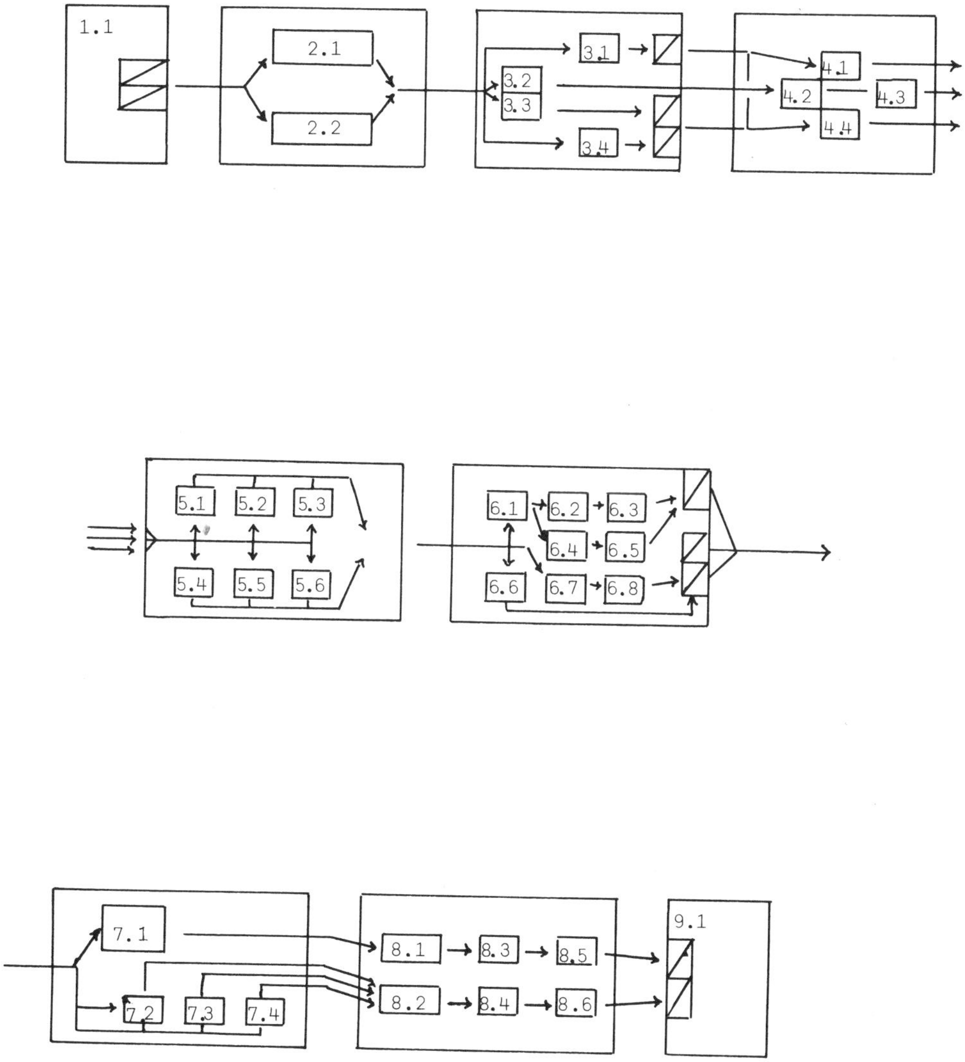

Figure 5.1. A complex and ill-structured production planning problem

they are technically difficult to understand and control; there are several goals to be attained in each process due to the interdependences and the variety of products; hold-ups occur from time to time in all three processes and are amplified through the interdependences; the forms for interdependence change over time according to order requirements, etc.

We will now assume that DM, whom we introduced in Section 5.1, is responsible for the tactical production plans for the plywood process. Then he has three planning problems, which we will denote A_2, A_3 and A_4. Each one of the planning problems can be assumed to be *multigoal*, as the corresponding process is composed of interdependent subprocesses, and at least one goal can be expected per subprocess. Then the problem to find a plan in which A_2, A_3 and A_4 are solved, and the interdependences of A_2, A_3 and A_4 are taken care of, is a *complex* problem (cf. Definition 3). This problem is also *ill-structured* as the products get new characteristics when passing through the subprocesses (cf. Definition 4 (ii)) and the subprocess-interdependences change over time (cf. Definition 4 (iii)).

Then a tactical production planning problem for stages 2, 3 and 4 of the plywood process shown in Figure 5.1 is a multigoal, complex and ill-structured problem; thus it can be denoted A (cf. Definition 4). In Sections 3 and 4 we will discuss two MCDM approaches for tackling a problem of the type A.

5.3. SIMPLIFICATION: A TRADITIONAL MCDM APPROACH

In the Finnish plywood industry it is almost a tradition to use some variant of linear programming modelling for tactical production planning purposes. That is one reason why we will use a mathematical programming model as an example of a traditional MCDM approach; another reason is that it offers a relatively simple structure for modelling the problem shown in Figure 5.1; a third reason is that if offers a good basis for comparisons with the non-traditional approach which will be introduced in Section 5.4.

The mathematical programming model we are going to introduce is, in a sense, not too traditional: it is a scheme for obtaining composite optimal solutions through an interplay of linear-, goal programming- and multiobjective linear programming.

The mathematical details of this approach are given in Carlsson (1979b); here we will confine the presentation to some principles which are sufficient to offer a framework for a formulation of the production planning problem.

Let V, X, Y and Z be convex hulls defined by:

$$\begin{aligned} V &= \{v \in R^{n_1} \mid M_1\underline{v} \leq B_1, \underline{v} \geq 0\}, \text{ where } B_1 \in R^{m_1} \\ X &= \{x \in R^{n_2} \mid M_2\underline{x} \leq B_2, \underline{x} \geq 0\}, \text{ where } B_2 \in R^{m_2} \\ Y &= \{y \in R^{n_3} \mid M_3\underline{y} \leq B_3, \underline{y} \geq 0\}, \text{ where } B_3 \in R^{m_3} \\ Z &= \{z \in R^{n_4} \mid M_4\underline{z} \leq B_4, z \geq 0\}, \text{ where } B_4 \in R^{m_4} \end{aligned} \qquad (5.1)$$

and let them represent fixed, non-empty regions extracted from and defined in A, A_2, A_3 and A_4 respectively (cf. Section 5.2); i.e. V A, X A_2, Y A_3 and Z A_4. Let us furthermore assume that it is possible to capture all the essential features of the cutting, turning and drying processes in mathematical programming models (this is not too rough an assumption, as is shown in Carlsson (1977a)):

$$
\begin{aligned}
MP_2 :\quad & \max \quad c\underline{x} \\
& \text{s.t.}\quad M_2\underline{x} - \underline{F}^+ + \underline{F}^- = B_2 \\
& \qquad \underline{x},\ \underline{F}^+,\ \underline{F}^- \geq \underline{0} \\
MP_3 :\quad & \max \quad d\underline{y} \\
& \text{s.t.}\quad M_3\underline{y} - \underline{G}^+ + \underline{G}^- = B_3 \\
& \qquad \underline{y},\ \underline{G}^+,\ \underline{G} \geq \underline{0} \\
MP_4 :\quad & \max \quad e\underline{z} \\
& \text{s.t.}\quad M_4\underline{z} - \underline{H}^+ + \underline{H}^- = B_4 \\
& \qquad \underline{z},\ \underline{H}^+,\ \underline{H}^- \geq \underline{0}
\end{aligned}
\qquad (5.2)
$$

where MP_2 - MP_4 now are formulated in regions X, Y and Z and are assumed to capture all relevant, internal interdependences of the cutting, turning and drying processes. As A is composed of A_2-A_4, but also contains some specific features, it would be useful to have a model which is a composure of MP_2 - MP_4 - and has some 'free' elements; MP_1 has these features:

$$
\begin{aligned}
MP_1 :\quad & \max \quad f\underline{v} \\
& \max \quad g\underline{w} \\
& \min \quad R_1\underline{F}_1^+ + R_2\underline{F}_1^- + R_3\underline{G}_1^+ + R_4\underline{G}_1^- + R_5\underline{H}_1^+ + R_6\underline{H}_1^- \\
& \text{s.t.}\quad M_1\underline{v} - \underline{F}_1^+ + \underline{F}_1^- - \underline{G}_1^+ + \underline{G}_1^- - \underline{H}_1^+ + \underline{H}_1^- = B_{11} \\
& \qquad M_1'\underline{v} + M_5'\underline{w} \leq B_{12} \\
& \qquad M_5\underline{w} \leq B_5 \\
& \qquad \underline{v},\ \underline{w},\ F_1^+,\ \underline{F}_1^-,\ \underline{G}_1^+,\ \underline{G}_1^-,\ H_1^+,\ H_1^- < 0 \text{ and } B_1 \ni B_{11}, B_{12}
\end{aligned}
\qquad (5.3)
$$

as it is a combined multiobjective linear and goal programming model, formulated in regions V and W, where W is assumed to be a convex hull, and defined by:

$$W = \{\, w \in R^{n_5} \mid M_5\underline{w} \leq B_5,\ \underline{w} \geq 0\} \text{ , where } B_5 \in R^{m_5} \qquad (5.4)$$

The first objective function and the first constraint of MP_1 are linked to MP_2 - MP_4 through the deviation-vectors F_1, G_1 and H_1 (which are transformations to the V-region: $\underline{F}_1 = \gamma_1\underline{F}$, $\underline{G}_1 = \gamma_2\underline{G}$, $\underline{H}_1 = \gamma_3\underline{H}$). The slack- and surplusvectors of MP_2 - MP_4 are thus re-interpreted as deviations from preset goals, which gives the complex of models some favourable properties: (i) it is possible to formulate multigoal problems, and (ii) to represent (linear) goal-interdependences. The preset goals are to be found in the constraints of MP_2 - MP_4; combined with corresponding objective functions it is possible to formulate several, linearly interdependent goals in each model. As all the deviations are brought together in the first constraint of MP_1 we get an overall, linear interdependence among the corresponding goals.

The second objective function and the second constraint can be used to represent 'higher level' goals, which are 'composed' from goals included in MP_2 - MP_4 and cover a 'global interdependence' - as some form for feedback - among the corresponding problems. The interdependence is formulated in the submatrices M_1' and M_5', which connect the V- and W-regions through a linear relationship.

The third objective function and the first constraint is a goal programming model, in which all the goal deviations are minimized; R_1 - R_6 are ordinal, pre-emptive weights which allow a model-user to select those deviations which are most important to minimize.

It is of course a non-trivial problem to find an optimal solution in MP_1, and some fairly restrictive conditions should be satisfied (cf. Carlsson (1979a) for details). But an optimal solution can be shown to exist, and also a decomposition scheme for transforming that solution to partial, optimal solutions - i.e. optimal solutions in MP_2 - MP_4. This composite optimal solution would, consequently, be an operational production plan, as it provides optimal solutions to A_2 - A_4 and an optimal solution in A.

This approach lacks, however, in some respects: (i) other than linear (or approximately linear) interdependences cannot be formulated (ii) interdependences which change over time are represented by reformulations in the models, (iii) other goal-interdependences than those covered by constraints and objective functions cannot be represented; goal conflicts represent non-feasibilities, (iv) any data which does not fit into the V-, X-, Y- and Z-regions must be left out; thus MP_1 - MP_4 will be rather abstract, and represent a high level of aggregation.

In conclusion it should be observed that our complex and ill-structured planning problem is, in fact, transformed into a complex but well-structured problem.

5.4. A SYSTEMS CONCEPT AND ADAPTIVE CONTROL: A NON-TRADITIONAL APPROACH

In this section we will use a conceptual framework which is somewhat different from that of the previous sections: we will conceptualize the problem context A as the hierarchical system, formulate essential aspects of our production planning problems in terms of system elements and find out if we can tackle the complex of problems in any way more efficiently than with the OR-models of the previous section.

5.4.1. *A systems concept*

Let A be a *system*, i.e. a relation on two real-valued sets A_1 and A_2:

$$A = x\ \{A_1,\ A_2\},\ \text{where}\ A_1,\ A_2 \sqsubseteq R \qquad (5.5)$$

Let further A_1 be defined by:

$$A_1 \sqsubseteq x\{A_k^{(h)}\ :\ h \in H\ \text{and}\ k \in K(h)\},\ \forall\ h,\ k \qquad (5.6)$$

where $A_k^{(h)} \sqsubseteq A$ and H, K are finite, numerical sets. And let $A_k^{(h)}$ be defined by:

$$A_k^{(h)} = \{a_{ki}^{(h)} \times b_{kij}^{(h)} \times a_{kj}^{(h)}\ :\ i,\ j \in N(h),\ i \neq j\} \qquad (5.7)$$

where the elements are given by:

$$a_{ki}^{(h)},\ a_{kj}^{(h)} \sqsubseteq A_k^{(h)},\ \text{and}\ A_k^{(h)} \sqsubseteq A^{(h)},\ A^{(h)} \sqsubseteq A \qquad (5.8)$$

$$b_{kij}^{(h)} \sqsubseteq B_k^{(h)},\ \text{and}\ B_k^{(h)} \sqsubseteq B^{(h)},\ B^{(h)} \sqsubseteq B\ \text{where}\ B \sqsubseteq R,\ \forall\ h \qquad (5.9)$$

Then the sets $A^{(h)}$, $B^{(h)}$ contain finite numbers of elements, which further more are organized into some structure (cf. the h-indices). Consider an element $a_{ki}^{(h)}$; we will call it an *activity* and let it represent (i) an action by DM, or (ii) an event caused by such an action or some 'external' source. Clearly (5.7) and (5.8) outline a static description of an activity; a dynamic counterpart would be:

$$a_{ki}^{(h)} = \{a_{ki}^{(h)}(t_1),\ a_{ki}^{(h)}(t_2), \ldots,\ a_{ki}^{(h)}(t_n)\} \qquad (5.10)$$

$$b_{kij}^{(h)} = \{b_{kij}^{(h)}(t_1),\ b_{kij}^{(h)}(t_2), \ldots,\ b_{kij}^{(h)}(t_n)\} \qquad (5.11)$$

if $[t_1,\ t_n]$ is the interval DM has found to be relevant for consideration. Then the counterpart of (5.7) would be:

$$A_k^{(h)} = \{a_{ki}^{(h)} \times b_{kij}^{(h)} \times a_{kj}^{(h)}\} \qquad (5.12)$$

and we would have $A_k^{(h)} \sqsubseteq A^{(h)}$ and $A^{(h)} \sqsubseteq A$. In this case an activity can be taken to represent a process or a series of actions or events. In both cases, however, an activity is something DM could do or observe, in an interval or at some point of time.

We have also assumed that DM considers only a finite number of activities, and has organized them structurally. If it is a fully ordered set with $h_{min} = 0$, and DM applies its elements as indices, he could organize the sets A and B hierarchically. As a hierarchical ordering is an obvious way for sorting out a complex context (cf. Section 5.1), and as a hierarchical structure has some useful properties for the present context, we will make the assumption that DM has organized the sets A and B hierarchically.

The $B^{(h)}_{kij}$-elements will, furthermore, be taken to indicate *interdependence* of the activities. Consider, for instance, $b^{(h)}_{kij}$ which indicates an interdependence of $a^{(h)}_{ki}$ and $a^{(h)}_{kj}$ at some t_i: as a static description of an activity represents an action or an event, the $b^{(h)}_{kij}$-element would indicate that two actions or events are *simultaneous* at t_i. Consider then $b^{(h)}_{kij}$, which is the dynamic counterpart of $b^{(h)}_{kij}$ and indicates an interdependence of $a^{(h)}_{ki}$ and $a^{(h)}_{kj}$ in the interval $[t_1, t_n]$: as the dynamic description of an activity represents a process, or a series of actions or events in the interval $[t_1, t_n]$, it seems convenient to let $b^{(h)}_{kij}$ represent a *temporal dependence* of process-elements, actions or events (so that $a^{(h)}_{ki}(t_i)$ is dependent on $a^{(h)}_{kj}(t_j)$ if $t_i > t_j$, but $t_i, t_j \in [t_1, t_n]$ and $a^{(h)}_{ki}(t_i) \in a^{(h)}_{ki}$, $a^{(h)}_{kj}(t_j) \in a^{(h)}_{kj}$). Clearly, this case is more general and contains the static $b^{(h)}_{kij}$-element as a special case, as $b^{(h)}_{kij}(t_i) \in b^{(h)}_{kij}$ would indicate that $a^{(h)}_{ki}(t_i) \in a^{(h)}_{ki}$ and $a^{(h)}_{kj}(t_i) \in a^{(h)}_{kj}$ are simultaneous at t_i. But $b^{(h)}_{kij}$ provides us with an additional feature: it can be used to describe changes over time in the structure of temporal dependences among actions or events, as all the elements of $a^{(h)}_{ki}$, $b^{(h)}_{kij}$ and $a^{(h)}_{kj}$ (cf. (5.12) may have different values at different t_i in $[t_1, t_n]$.

We will call the $b^{(h)}_{kij}$- and $b^{(h)}_{kij}$-elements *intrarelations* and observe that they are defined for activities with the same h-index. If then the h-indices indicate a hierarchical organization of the activities we will have the same hierarchical organization among the intrarelations (as indicated by the h-indices). There are of course different forms for operationalizing the intrarelations: for instance algorithms, operators or functions may be appropriate in the present context.

From these definitions and assumptions follows that A_1 in (5.6) is a *system* as it is a relation on real-valued sets - of hierarchically organized activities and intrarelations. It is, furthermore, a system of numerical descriptions for some t_i, or an interval $[t_1, t_n]$, of actions and events DM could carry out and/or observe at t_i or in $[t_1, t_n]$. But it should be observed that A_1 is formed through two types of relations: temporal intrarelations and hierarchical organization. The set A_1 would not even be a system if we had only intrarelations (as each activity would not be related to every other activity); on the other hand, using hierarchical organization as a relation represents a somewhat 'weak' systems structure.

Let us then consider A_2 and let it be defined by:

$$A_2 \sqsubseteq x\{A_1^{(h)} : h \in H \text{ and } 1 \in L(h)\} \ , \ \forall \ h, \ 1 \qquad (5.13)$$

where $A_1^{(h)} \sqsubset A$ and L is a finite numerical set. Let $A_1^{(h)}$ be defined by:

$$A_1^{(h)} = \{a_{1i}^{(h)} \times c_{1ij}^{(\bar{h})} \times a_{1j}^{(\bar{h})} : i \in N(h), \ j \in N(\bar{h}), \ \bar{h} > h \text{ but } \bar{h}, \ h \in H\} \qquad (5.14)$$

where the elements now are given by:

$$a_{1i}^{(h)} \sqsubseteq A_1^{(h)}, \ a_{1j}^{(\bar{h})} \sqsubseteq A_1^{(\bar{h})}, \text{ and } A_1^{(h)} \sqsubseteq A^{(\bar{h})} \quad , \ A_1^{(\bar{h})} \sqsubseteq A^{(\bar{h})} \qquad (5.15)$$

for which we have $A_1^{(h)}$, $A_1^{(\bar{h})} \sqsubseteq A$

$$c_{1ij}^{(\bar{h})} \sqsubseteq C_1^{(\bar{h})} \ , \text{ and } C_1^{(\bar{h})} \sqsubseteq C_1^{(\bar{h})}, \ C^{(\bar{h})} \sqsubseteq C \text{ where } C \sqsubseteq R, \ \forall \ \bar{h} \qquad (5.16)$$

As we have assumed that $\bar{h} > h$ we will have that $0 \leq \bar{h}_{max}$ but $0 \leq h < h_{max}$ if h_{max} is the maximum element of H (which is a fully ordered set with $h_{min} = 0$. The sets $A^{(h)}$, $A^{(\bar{h})}$ and $C^{(\bar{h})}$ contain, analogously with (5.8) and (5.9), finite numbers of elements organized hierarchically according to our assumptions and definitions. In the same fashion as we had dynamic counterparts of the intrarelations (cf. (5.11), we have:

$$c_{1ij}^{(\bar{h})} = \{c_{1ij}^{(\bar{h})} (t_1), \ c_{1ij}^{(\bar{h})} (t_2), \ldots, \ c_{1ij}^{(\bar{h})} (t_n)\} \qquad (5.17)$$

for the interval $[t_1, t_n]$. Then the dynamic counterpart of ((5.14) is:

$$A_1^{(h)} = \{a_{1i}^{(h)} \times c_{1ij}^{(\bar{h})} \times a_{1j}^{(\bar{h})}\} \qquad (5.18)$$

and, analogously, $A_1^{(h)} \sqsubseteq A^{(h)}$ and $A^{(h)} \sqsubseteq A$. From this can be concluded that the $a_{1i}^{(h)}$- , $a_{1j}^{(\bar{h})}$- elements are the same activities we defined in (5.7)-(5.12), but that the $c_{1ij}^{(\bar{h})}$- elements represent another type of relation than the $b_{kij}^{(h)}$- elements.

We assumed above that DM has organized the set of activities structurally, and based this organization on a temporal dependence among the activities which, in turn, is represented by *intrarelations* (the $b_{kij}^{(h)}$- elements). We will call the $c_{1ij}^{(\bar{h})}$- and $c_{1ij}^{(\bar{h})}$- elements *interrelations*, and let them indicate a different type of interdependence of the activities. Consider at first $c_{1ij}^{(\bar{h})}$, which show that there is an interdependence of $a_{1i}^{(h)}$ and $a_{1j}^{(\bar{h})}$; as $\bar{h} > h$ this is an interdependence of activities on different hierarchical levels. We will interpret it as an *abstract aggregation/disaggregation*, so that $a_{lj}^{(\bar{h})}$ in some sense 'contains' $a_{li}^{(h)}$ if $\bar{h} > h$, and 'is contained by' $a_{li}^{(h)}$ if $\bar{h} < h$. This means that DM considers an action or event ($a_{li}^{(h)}$) to be 'part of' another action or event ($a_{lj}^{(\bar{h})}$, if $\bar{h} > h$) at some t_i. Consider then $c_{lij}^{(\bar{h})}$, which indicates an interdepen- of $a_{li}^{(\bar{h})}$ and $a_{li}^{(h)}$ in the interval $[t_1, t_n]$: this interdependence is analogously interpreted as an abstract aggregation/disaggregation of $a_{li}^{(h)}$ and $a_{lj}^{(\bar{h})}$. This means that an activity $a_{li}^{(\bar{h})}(t_i)$ (ε $a_{lj}^{(\bar{h})}$) 'contains' another activity $a_{li}^{(h)}(t_i)$ (ε $a_{li}^{(h)}$) at t_i if $\bar{h} > h$, but 'is contained by' $a_{li}^{(h)}(t_i)$ if $\bar{h} < h$. As $a_{li}^{(h)}$ and $a_{lj}^{(\bar{h})}$ represent processes in $[t_1, t_n]$, or series of actions or events DM could undertake or observe in the interval $[t_1, t_n]$, the interrelations will indicate which elements of a process, or actions, events DM has found to be parts of each other at some t_i. This interdependence is not temporal as it is established for t_i, and we have made no assumption that will prevail for t_{i+1}. But we said that $c_{lij}^{(\bar{h})}$ is a dynamic formulation of the interrelation, from which follows that the interdependence will change from one point of time to another; this is a useful feature as it makes it possible to have a variable structure in the set of activities.

Our interrelations are defined for activities with *different* h-indices, and we adopted the rule that the interrelation was given the index $\bar{h}$, if $\bar{h} > h$. As H was assumed to have a hierarchical structure, it follows that also the interrelations will be ordered hierarchically, but they give something more: they can be used to form a hierarchy. It is known (cf. Whyte, Wilson and Wilson (1969)) that a set can be given a hierarchical structure by introducing a dominance rule among its elements: 'aggregation' or 'disaggregation' is such a dominance rule. As an interrelation links two activities it establishes a relation of dominance between them; this holds for all the activities of A_2 which are linked through interrelations, and as the $c_{lij}^{(\bar{h})}$-elements were defined for all h, l (cf. (5.13)-(5.14), it holds for the whole of A_2. We would consequently get a hierarchical structure even if the $c_{lij}^{(\bar{h})}$ -elements were not ordered hierarchically - this seems to be a useful feature.

If we assume that $L(h) = K(h)$, $\forall$ h, it follows that $A_1 = A_2$ - i.e. the two sets contain the same activities, and even have the same structure, as they are organized hierarchically on the basis of the same set H. And A_2 may consequently also be expected to form a system - and that is really the case: the interrelations were defined for all l (cf. ((5.13) -(5.14), and as then each activity is linked with every other activity, either directly or indirectly, A_2 fulfils a necessary and sufficient requirement for a system. The interrelations give A_2 a strong systems structure, but it seems 'incomplete' as the activities are linked over the levels, but not within the levels.

As the intrarelations also the interrelations can be operationalized in different ways: through algorithms, operators or functions, which all may be appropriate in the present context.

We found above that both A_1 and A_2 were represented by systems structures, but that A_1 formed a 'weak' structure and A_2 a structure which was 'strong' but somewhat 'open-ended'. In the same fashion A_1 and A_2 can be expected to form systems structures, which should be somewhat 'stronger' than those found for A_1 and A_2 as there is added a temporal dimension. But we will get an even 'stronger' systems structure through the relation defined by (5.5):

$$A = x\ \{A_1,\ A_2\},\ \text{or}\ A = x\ \{A_1,\ A_2\} \qquad (5.19)$$

i.e. the set A (or A) is a system with a 'strong' structure, as each activity is linked to every other activity both on and over the levels indicated by the h-indices; as A there is, moreoever, the linkage through the temporal dimension. The resulting (static) systems structure can be illustrated as shown in Figure 5.2:

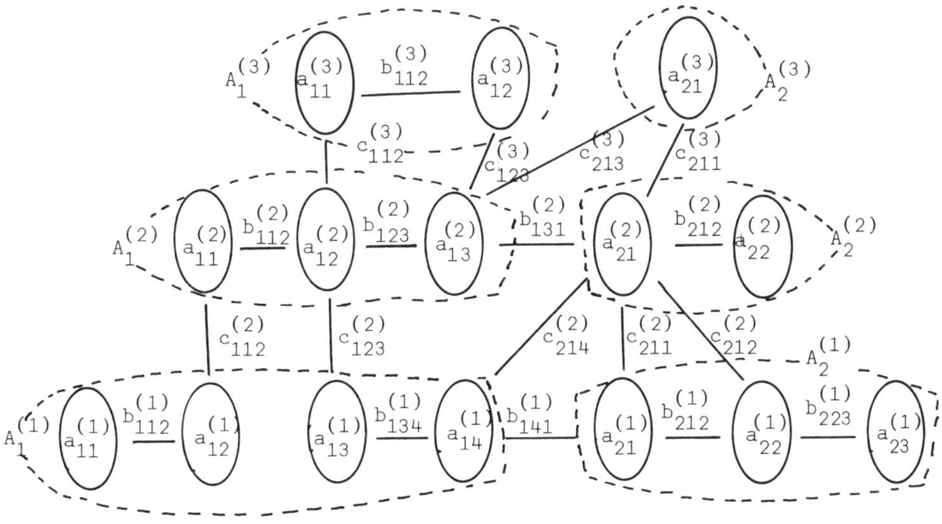

Figure 5.2. A hierarchical 3-level system

In Figure 5.2 activities are represented by $a_{11}^{(1)}$, $a_{12}^{(1)}$, $a_{13}^{(1)}$, etc.; intrarelations by $b_{112}^{(1)}$, $b_{134}^{(1)}$, $B_{141}^{(1)}$, etc. and interrelations by $c_{112}^{(2)}$, $c_{123}^{(2)}$, $c_{213}^{(2)}$ etc.; temporal interdependence is thus indicated with horizontal lines and aggregation/disaggregation with vertical lines. A corresponding dynamic structure could be represented as a series of repetitions of Figure 5.2 in a third dimension, i.e. along a time axis.

5.4.2. *Complex problems in systems concepts*

In the systems concepts introduced through (5.5)-(5.18) we have a useful and - as it seems - fairly powerful tool for modelling even complex problem situations:

(i) a DM could describe simultaneous actions or events at some t_i in terms of activities and intrarelations;

(ii) actions and/or events which form parts of each other at some t_i could be described in terms of activities and interrelations;

(iii) a system of activities, intra- and interrelations was defined as $\sqsubseteq R$, but could as well be $\sqsubseteq R^n$, i.e. activities, intra- and interrelations could be presented by multi-dimensional sets; in this latter case must an aggregation/disaggregation involve a transformation of dimensions;

(iv) a DM could describe processes or series of actions or events in some interval $[t_1, t_n]$ as vectors of activities, intra- and interrelations - even if the actions or events change in shape over time (this can be matched by transforming dimensions through the interrelations);

(v) an operational version of a complex which is a hierarchical 3-level system could, for instance, be a hierarchical system of OR-models, which are linked through algorithms or operators or functions, which form interfaces between the models. In this way it would be possible to have, simultaneously, both precise partial descriptions and sufficiently general total descriptions, either for some chosen t_i or an interval $[t_1, t_n]$.

In order to illustrate this claim for usefulness let us consider the following multi-goal situation: let G be a set of goals adopted by DM for t_i, or an interval $[t_1, t_n]$, and let it contain several goals which have different types of relationships (cf. Figure 5.2):

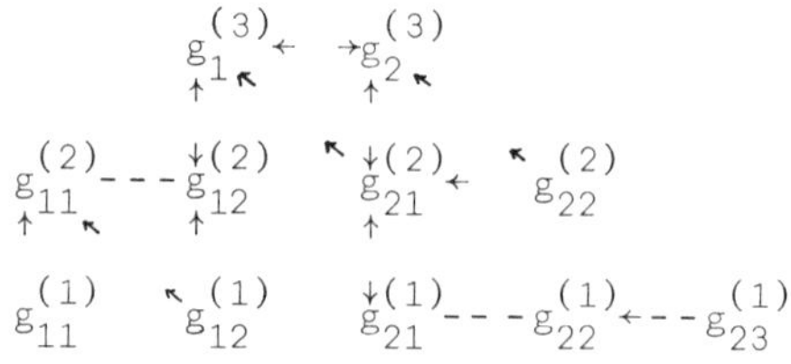

Figure 5.3. A multi-goal situation

Let $g_i^{(h)}$, $g_{ij}^{(h)}$ ε G for i=i,2 , j=1,2,3 and h=1,2,3 , where the h-indices again will be used to indicate hierarchical level; then we assume $g_1^{(3)}$ and $g_2^{(3)}$ to be aggregates of goals of levels 1 and 2. Goals can be linked through (i) *mutual support*, of which aggregation/disaggregation is an example (indicated with ← →); (ii) *unilateral support*, exemplified by temporal dependence (indicated with →), (iii) *conflict*, which is the case when two goals cannot be attained simultaneously (indicated with ---). Goals could, finally, also be defined in such a way that they are *independent* (cf. $g_{11}^{(1)}$, $g_{12}^{(1)}$).

We will assume that $G \sqsubseteq R$ or $\sqsubseteq R^n$, and that every $g_{ij}^{(h)} \sqsubseteq a_{ki}^{(h)}$ or $\sqsubseteq (a_{ki}^{(h)} \cup (a_{kj}^{(h)} \cup \ldots)$, i.e. that we have one- or multidimensional goals, and that every goal is implemented as a subset of one or more activities. Then it is possible to transpose the multi-goal situation described in Figure 5.3 into a hierarchical systems structure (cf. Figure 5.4):

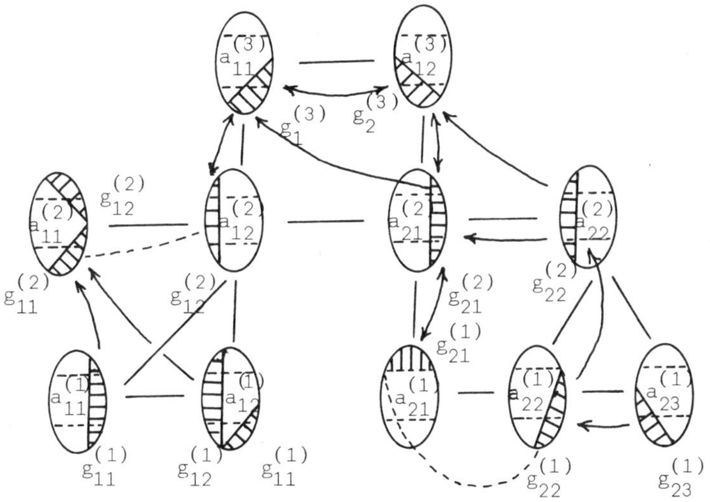

Figure 5.4. A multi-goal structure in a hierarchical 3-level system

From Figure 5.4 it is found that (i) activities are formulated in 3 dimensions and goals in 1, 2 and 3 dimensions, (ii) all the relationships of Figure 5.3 are implemented, (iii) two of the goals $g_{11}^{(1)}$, $g_{12}^{(2)}$ are implemented for more than one activity ($a_{11}^{(1)}$, $a_{12}^{(1)}$ and $a_{11}^{(2)}$, $a_{12}^{(2)}$ respectively), and (iv) the relationships among the goals were (by assumption) given more variety than that given to intra- and interrelations; this should be observed and accounted for when intra- and interrelations are operationalized in some specific multi-goal context.

To this illustration of the usefulness of our systems concepts one point could be added: as we assumed that every $g_{ij}^{(h)} \subseteq a_{ki}^{(h)}$ or $\subseteq$ $a_{ki}^{(h)} \cup a_{kj}^{(h)} \cup \ldots$) we could also assume that $g_{ij}^{(h)} \subseteq a_{ki}^{(h)}$ or $\subseteq (a_{ki}^{(h)} \cup a_{kj}^{(h)}$ ...), which - if we make this assumption for all $g_{ij}^{(h)}$ and all h - will result in a multi-goal structure which can be made to change over time. This property has a useful consequence as changing goal-relationships can be represented and (for instance) goal conflicts can be resolved as activities change over time.

5.4.3. *An illustration of a complex problem*

Let us now move on to a more detailed illustration and discussion of the applicability and usefulness of the systems concept we have introduced; for that purpose we will reformulate and tackle our production planning problem in systems concepts. A closer study of the problem revealed the following - at least tentative - relationships among constitutive sub-problems and goals (cf. Figure (5.5) and Section 5.1; relationships are represented as in Figure 5.3).

In Figure 5.5 we have the following subproblems and goals:

Subprocess 2

A_{21} a cutting problem	g_{20} a rate of return on investment
A_{22} a composition problem	g_{21} optimal cutting
A_{23} a source allocation problem	g_{22} optimal resource allocation
A_{24} a waste minimization problem	g_{23} waste minimization
	g_{24} order fulfilment
	g_{25} minimum production level

Subprocess 3

A_{31} a queuing problem	g_{30} a rate of return on investment
A_{32} a resource allocation problem	g_{31} optimal resource allocation
A_{33} a trimming problem	g_{32} optimal trimming
A_{34} a waste minimization problem	g_{33} waste minimization
	g_{34} minimizing waiting costs

Subprocess 4

A_{41} a resource allocation problem	g_{40} a rate of return on investment
A_{42} a queuing problem	g_{41} optimal resource allocation
A_{43} a composition problem	g_{42} minimizing waiting costs
A_{44} a waste minimization problem	g_{43} optimal lot compositions
	g_{44} waste minimization

among which we have, for instance, the following relationships: *conflict* between the resource allocation problems A_{23} - A_{32} - A_{41}; *unilateral support* between the cutting and resource allocation problems A_{21} - A_{23},

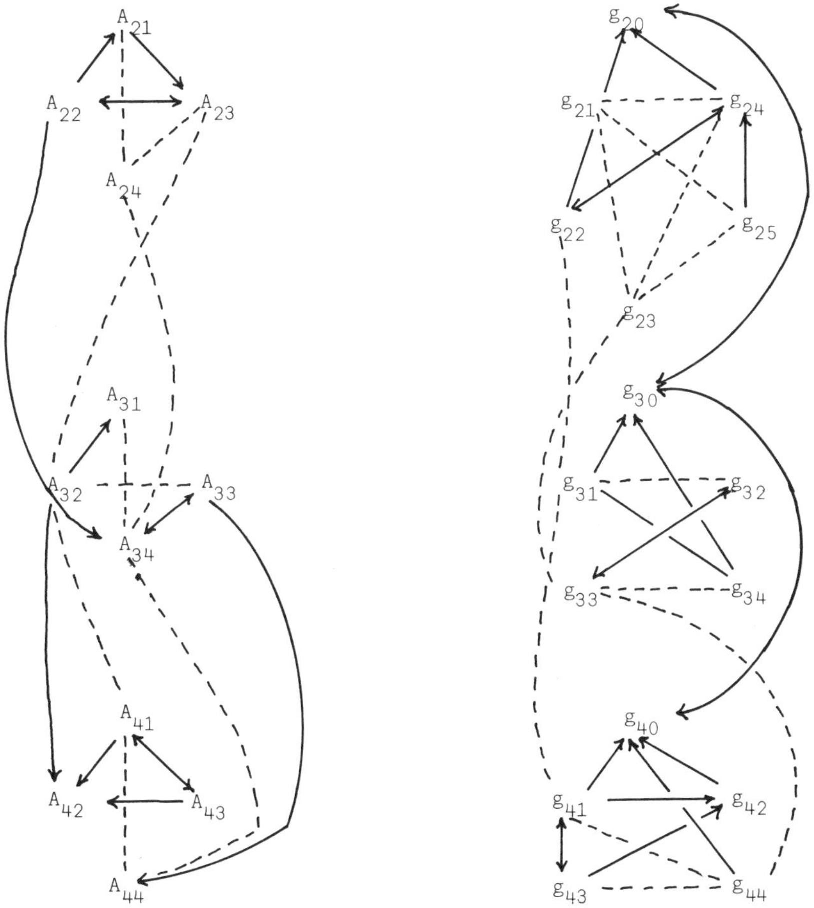

Figure 5.5. Relationships between constitutive subproblems and goals in the complex production planning problem

and the resource allocation and queuing problems $A_{32} - A_{31}$, $A_{41} - A_{42}$; *mutual support* between the composition and resource allocation problems $A_{22} - A_{23}$, the trimming and waste minimization problems $A_{33} - A_{34}$, and the resource allocation and composition problems $A_{41} - A_{43}$. As can be seen from Figure 5.5 we have similar relationships among the goals: we have, for instance, the mutual support of $g_{20} - g_{30} - g_{40}$.

Let us then take one more step towards an application of the systems concept in tackling complex problems; we will try to formulate some of the constitutive problems of subprocesses 2-4 in terms of the systems concepts, show that multiple goals can be implemented and that the relationships between goals and problems can be represented in terms of systems concepts.

The resource allocation problems $A_{23} - A_{32} - A_{41}$ form a complex of conflicting problems; as the product changes gradually - both technically and conceptually - in passing through subprocesses 2-4, and as the problems (A_4) of subprocess 4 include at least some of the problems of subprocess 3 (A_3) - and these in turn some of the problems of subprocess 2 (A_2) - it would be convenient to assume that $A_4 \_ A_3 \_ A_2$, and that these problems form a hierarchical structure. Then follows that we could also assume that $A_{41} \_ A_{32} \_ A_{23}$, i.e. that the allocation problems form a hierarchical structure. In order to comply with this structure we will introduce the following indices: $(A_2, A_3, A_4) \Longleftrightarrow (A^{(2)}, A^{(3)}, A^{(4)})$.

Then the conflicting three resource allocation problems will have the following structure in systems concepts (cf. Figure 5.6):

$$
\begin{aligned}
\underline{A}_3^{(2)} : \quad & a_{30}^{(2)} = b_{30}^{(2)} \, (a_{31}^{(2)}, a_{32}^{(2)}) \\
& a_{33}^{(2)} = b_{33}^{(2)} \, (a_{34}^{(2)}, a_{35}^{(2)}) \\
& a_{36}^{(2)} = b_{36}^{(2)} \, (a_{31}^{(2)}, a_{32}^{(2)}, a_{34}^{(2)}, a_{35}^{(2)}) \\
& g_{2}^{(2)} : a_{36}^{(2)} \ \max \\
& g_{21}^{(2)} : a_{30}^{(2)} \leq \delta_{30}^{(2)} \\
& g_{22}^{(2)} : a_{33}^{(2)} \leq \delta_{33}^{(2)}
\end{aligned}
$$

$$
\begin{aligned}
\underline{A}_2^{(3)} : \quad & a_{25}^{(3)} = c_{25}^{(3)} \, (a_{35}^{(2)}) \\
& \delta_{20}^{(30)} = c_{20}^{(3)} \, (\delta_{30}^{(2)}) \\
& a_{20}^{(3)} = b_{20}^{(3)} \, (a_{21}^{(3)}, a_{22}^{(3)})
\end{aligned}
$$

$$a_{23}^{(3)} = b_{23}^{(3)} (a_{24}^{(3)}, a_{25}^{(3)})$$

$$a_{26}^{(3)} = b_{26}^{(3)} (a_{21}^{(3)}, a_{22}^{(3)}, a_{24}^{(3)}, a_{25}^{(3)})$$

$$g_{1}^{(3)} : a_{26}^{(3)} \ \max$$

$$g_{11}^{(3)} : a_{20}^{(3)} \leq \delta_{20}^{(3)}$$

$$g_{12}^{(3)} : a_{23}^{(3)} \leq \delta_{23}^{(3)}$$

$$\underline{A}_1^{(4)} : a_{15}^{(4)} = c_{15}^{(4)} (a_{25}^{(3)}, a_{35}^{(2)})$$

$$\delta_{10}^{(4)} = c_{10}^{(4)} (\delta_{20}^{(3)}, \delta_{30}^{(2)})$$

$$a_{10}^{(4)} = b_{10}^{(4)} (a_{11}^{(4)}, a_{12}^{(4)})$$

$$a_{13}^{(4)} = b_{13}^{(4)} (a_{14}^{(4)}, a_{15}^{(4)})$$

$$a_{16}^{(4)} = b_{16}^{(4)} (a_{11}^{(4)}, a_{12}^{(4)}, a_{14}^{(4)}, a_{15}^{(4)})$$

$$g_{1}^{(4)} : a_{16}^{(4)} \ \max$$

$$g_{11}^{(4)} : a_{10}^{(4)} \leq \delta_{10}^{(4)}$$

$$g_{12}^{(4)} : a_{13}^{(4)} \leq \delta_{13}^{(4)}$$

Figure 5.6. Three resource allocation problems in systems concepts; $a_{ij}^{(h)}$ = activity, $b_{ij}^{(h)}$ = intrarelation, $c_{ij}^{(\bar{h})}$ = interrelation (where $\bar{h} > h$), and $\delta_{ij}^{(h)}$ = parameter.

This notation is slightly simplified from that introduced in (4.1) - (4.14) : in order to give $A_3^{(2)}$, $A_2^{(3)}$ and $A_1^{(4)}$ a formulation which conforms with a well-known standard (LP-) form, the third index has been omitted in the notations of intra- and interrelations. The intra- and interrelations are linear functions.

The conflict of the three allocation problems is a goal conflict, but we have also other types of relationships involved in the complex (cf. Figure 5.5):

(i) *goal conflict*: if $g_2^{(2)}$ is attained, $g_1^{(3)}$ cannot be attained; if $g_1^{(3)}$ is attained, $g_1^{(4)}$ cannot be attained.

(ii) *unilateral support*: an attainment of $g_2^{(2)}$, $g_1^{(3)}$ and $g_1^{(4)}$ supports an attainment of $g_0^{(2)}$, $g_0^{(3)}$ and $g_0^{(4)}$ respectively. This is represented by:

$$g_0^{(2)} = b_{02}^{(2)} (g_2^{(2)})$$

$$g_0^{(3)} = b_{01}^{(3)} (g_1^{(3)})$$

$$g_0^{(4)} = b_{01}^{(4)} (g_1^{(4)})$$, where the intrarelations are functions or algorithms.

(iii) *mutual support*: an attainment of, for instance, g_0 supports, and is supported by, an attainment of $g_0^{(2)}$, etc. (cf. Figure 5.5). This is represented by:

$$g_0^{(2)} = c_0^{(2)} (g_0^{(3)})$$

$$g_0^{(3)} = c_{01}^{(3)} (g_0^{(2)})$$

$$g_0^{(3)} = c_{02}^{(3)} (g_0^{(4)})$$

$$g_0^{(4)} = c_0^{(4)} (g_0^{(3)})$$, where the interrelations are functions or algorithms.

In this fashion it was thus possible to formulate three conflicting resource allocation problems in systems concepts, to implement four sets of goals and three types of relationships among these goals. The structure shown in Figure 5.6 is static, as it was made for illustrative purposes; a dynamic structure would be more complex, but would be more appropriate for resolving conflicts. A method for obtaining composite optimal solutions in linked MP-models is outlined in Carlsson (1979a).

Let us next consider three pairs of *mutually supportive* problems: $A_2^{(2)} \leftrightarrow A_3^{(2)}$, $A_3^{(3)} \leftrightarrow A_4^{(3)}$ and $A_1^{(4)} \leftrightarrow A_3^{(4)}$. The mutual support means that a solution, when it is obtained for one problem of a pair, supports the solution process in the other problem. Then this support could be on the activities, or the goals, or both.

As we still work with the three subprocesses of the previouw section we are able to apply the same hierarchical structure and the same notation we had in Figure 5.6 (cf. Figure 5.7):

$$\underline{A}_2^{(2)}: a_{21}^{(2)}=a_{20}^{(2)}-b_{21}^{(2)}(a_{22}^{(2)},a_{23}^{(2)},a_{24}^{(2)}) \qquad \underline{A}_3^{(2)}: a_{30}^{(2)}=b_{30}^{(2)}(a_{31}^{(2)},a_{32}^{(2)})$$

$$a_{22}^{(2)}=a_{20}^{(2)}-b_{22}^{(2)}(a_{21}^{(2)},a_{23}^{(2)},a_{24}^{(2)}) \qquad a_{33}^{(2)}=b_{33}^{(2)}(a_{34}^{(2)},a_{35}^{(2)})$$

$$a_{23}^{(2)}=a_{20}^{(2)}-b_{23}^{(2)}(a_{21}^{(2)},a_{22}^{(2)},a_{24}^{(2)}) \qquad a_{36}^{(2)}=b_{36}^{(2)}(a_{31}^{(2)},a_{32}^{(2)},a_{34}^{(2)},a_{35}^{(2)})$$

$$a_{24}^{(2)}=a_{20}^{(2)}-b_{24}^{(2)}(a_{21}^{(2)},a_{22}^{(2)},a_{23}^{(2)}) \qquad g_2^{(2)}: a_{36}^{(2)} \max$$

$$a_{25}^{(2)}=b_{25}^{(2)}(a_{20}^{(2)},a_{21}^{(2)},a_{22}^{(2)},a_{23}^{(2)},a_{24}^{(2)}) \qquad g_{21}^{(2)}: a_{30}^{(2)} \leq \delta_{30}^{(2)}$$

$g_4^{(2)}$: $a_{21}^{(2)}=\delta_{21}^{(2)}\pm\alpha\delta_{21}^{(2)}$

$a_{22}^{(2)}=\delta_{22}^{(2)}\pm\alpha\delta_{22}^{(2)}$

$a_{23}^{(2)}=\delta_{23}^{(2)}\pm\alpha\delta_{23}^{(2)}$

$a_{24}^{(2)}=\delta_{24}^{(2)}\pm\alpha\delta_{24}^{(2)}$

$g_3^{(2)}$: $a_{25}^{(2)}\leq\delta_{25}^{(2)}$

$g_5^{(2)}$: $a_{26}^{(2)}\geq\delta_{26}^{(2)}$

$g_{22}^{(2)}$: $a_{33}^{(2)}\leq\delta_{33}^{(2)}$

$g_4^{(2)}\leftrightarrow g_2^{(2)}$: decreasing α, increasing $a_{36}^{(2)}$ through some function or algorithm.

$a_{26}^{(2)}\leftrightarrow(\delta_{30}^{(2)},\delta_{33}^{(2)}$: mapping through some function or algorithm.

$A_3^{(3)}$: $a_{31}^{(3)}=b_{31}^{(3)}(a_{32}^{(3)},a_{33}^{(3)},a_{34}^{(3)})$

$a_{32}^{(3)}=b_{32}^{(3)}(a_{31}^{(3)},a_{33}^{(3)},a_{34}^{(3)})$

$a_{33}^{(3)}=b_{33}^{(3)}(a_{31}^{(3)},a_{32}^{(3)},a_{34}^{(3)})$

$a_{34}^{(3)}=b_{34}^{(3)}(a_{31}^{(3)},a_{32}^{(3)},a_{33}^{(3)})$

$a_{35}^{(3)}=b_{35}^{(3)}(a_{31}^{(3)},a_{32}^{(3)},a_{33}^{(3)},a_{34}^{(3)})$

$g_2^{(3)}$: $a_{35}^{(3)}\leq\delta_{35}^{(3)}$

$A_4^{(3)}$: $a_{40}^{(3)}=b_{40}^{(3)}(a_{41}^{(3)},a_{42}^{(3)},a_{43}^{(3)},a_{44}^{(3)})$

$g_3^{(3)}$: $a_{40}^{(3)}\leq\delta_{40}^{(3)}$

$g_2^{(3)}\leftrightarrow g_3^{(3)}$: $a_{35}^{(3)}\leftrightarrow a_{40}^{(3)}$ through some function or algorithm.

$A_1^{(4)}$: $a_{10}^{(4)}=b_{10}^{(4)}(a_{11}^{(4)},a_{12}^{(4)})$

$a_{13}^{(4)}=b_{13}^{(4)}(a_{14}^{(4)},a_{15}^{(4)})$

$a_{16}^{(4)}=b_{16}^{(4)}(a_{11}^{(4)},a_{12}^{(4)},a_{14}^{(4)},a_{15}^{(4)})$

$g_1^{(4)}$: $a_{16}^{(4)}$ max

$g_{11}^{(4)}$: $a_{10}^{(4)}\leq\delta_{10}^{(4)}$

$g_{12}^{(4)}$: $a_{13}^{(4)}\leq\delta_{13}^{(4)}$

$A_3^{(4)}$: $a_{31}^{(4)}=b_{31}^{(4)}(\{a_{34}^{(4)}\},\{a_{36}^{(4)}\})$

$a_{32}^{(4)}=b_{32}^{(4)}(\{a_{35}^{(4)}\})$

$a_{33}^{(4)}=b_{33}^{(4)}(\{a_{34}^{(4)}\},\{a_{36}^{(4)}\},\{a_{37}^{(4)}\})$

$g_3^{(4)}$: $(a_{31}^{(4)},a_{32}^{(4)},a_{33}^{(4)})\geq\delta_{30}^{(4)}$

$g_1^{(4)}\leftrightarrow g_3^{(4)}$: increasing $a_{16}^{(4)}$, incresing $(a_{31}^{(4)},a_{32}^{(4)},a_{33}^{(4)})$ through some function or algorithm.

$a_{32}^{(4)}\leftrightarrow\delta_{13}^{(4)}$: through some function or algorithm.

Figure 5.7. Three mutually supportive problems in systems concepts.

Analogously with Figure 5.6 we have applied static rather than dynamic representations of activities and intrarelations; clearly, dynamic representations would have produced interesting patterns of mutually supportive processes, but would also be unnecessarily complex. We have also omitted other relationships than mutually supportive in order to simplify the figure. As the problems forming the pairs are rather complex (resource allocation-, composition-, trimming- and waste minimization problems), and as they refer to a class of products which are gradually developed when passing through the three subprocesses, we could have found many more relationships by going into details; for our present, illustrative, purposes that is not, however, necessary.

Let us then, finally, consider three pairs of *unilaterally supportive* problems: $A_1^{(2)} \rightarrow A_3^{(2)}$, $A_2^{(3)} \rightarrow A_1^{(3)}$ and $A_1^{(4)} \rightarrow A_2^{(4)}$. The unilateral support means that a solution to the first problem supports the solution process in the second problem, i.e. an attainment of goal in the first problem supports a goal-attainment in the second problem, or some state of an activity in the first problem supports some states of activities in the second problem, which support an attainment of one or more goals.

As the three pairs of unilaterally supportive problems still come from the same three subprocesses we had in Figure 5.6 and 5.7 it will be possible to apply the same hierarchical structure and the same notation (cf. Figure 5.8):

$$A_1^{(2)}: a_{11}^{(2)} = a_{10}^{(2)} - b_{11}^{(2)}(a_{12}^{(2)}, a_{13}^{(2)}, a_{14}^{(2)}, a_{15}^{(2)})$$

$$a_{16}^{(2)} = a_{10}^{(2)} - b_{16}^{(2)}(a_{12}^{(2)}, a_{13}^{(2)}, a_{14}^{(2)}, a_{15}^{(2)})$$

$$g_1^{(2)}: (a_{11}^{(2)}, a_{16}^{(2)} \geq \delta_{10}^{(2)}$$

$$A_3^{(2)}: a_{30}^{(2)} = b_{30}^{(2)}(a_{31}^{(2)}, a_{32}^{(2)})$$

$$a_{33}^{(2)} = b_{33}^{(2)}(a_{34}^{(2)}, a_{35}^{(2)})$$

$$a_{36}^{(2)} = b_{36}^{(2)}(a_{31}^{(2)}, a_{32}^{(2)}, a_{34}^{(2)}, a_{35}^{(2)})$$

$$g_2^{(2)}: a_{36}^{(2)} \text{ max}$$

$$g_{21}^{(2)}: a_{30}^{(2)} \leq \delta_{30}^{(2)}$$

$$g_{22}^{(2)}: a_{33}^{(2)} \leq \delta_{33}^{(2)}$$

$$(a_{11}^{(2)}, a_{16}^{(2)}) \rightarrow (a_{31}^{(2)}, a_{32}^{(2)}, a_{34}^{(2)}, a_{35}^{(2)}),$$

through same function or algorithm.

$$A_2^{(3)}: a_{20}^{(3)} = b_{20}^{(3)}(a_{21}^{(3)}, a_{22}^{(3)})$$

$$a_{23}^{(3)} = b_{23}^{(3)}(a_{24}^{(3)}, a_{25}^{(3)})$$

$$a_{26}^{(3)} = b_{26}^{(3)}(a_{21}^{(3)}, a_{22}^{(3)}, a_{24}^{(3)}, a_{25}^{(3)})$$

$$g_1^{(3)}: a_{26}^{(3)} \text{ max}$$

$$g_{11}^{(3)}: a_{20}^{(3)} \leq \delta_{20}^{(3)}$$

$$g_{12}^{(3)}: a_{23}^{(3)} \leq \delta_{23}^{(3)}$$

$$A_1^{(3)}: a_{10}^{(3)} = b_{10}^{(3)}(a_{11}^{(3)}, a_{12}^{(3)}, a_{13}^{(3)})$$

$$a_{14}^{(3)} = b_{14}^{(3)}(a_{11}^{(3)}, a_{12}^{(3)}, a_{13}^{(3)})$$

$$g_4^{(3)}: \text{min } a_{15}^{(3)} = b_{15}^{(3)}(a_{10}^{(3)}, a_{14}^{(3)})$$

$$g_{41}^{(3)}: a_{10}^{(3)} \leq \delta_{10}^{(3)}$$

$$g_{42}^{(3)}: a_{14}^{(3)} \leq \delta_{14}^{(3)}$$

$$g_1^{(3)} \rightarrow g_4^{(3)}: \text{max } a_{26}^{(3)} \rightarrow \text{min } a_{15}^{(3)}$$

$$(\delta_{20}^{(3)}, \delta_{23}^{(3)}) \rightarrow (\delta_{10}^{(3)}, \delta_{14}^{(3)}: \text{increase} \rightarrow \text{decrease},$$

through some function or algorithm.

$A_1^{(4)}: a_{10}^{(4)} = b_{10}^{(4)}(a_{11}^{(4)}, a_{12}^{(4)})$

$a_{13}^{(4)} = b_{13}^{(4)}(a_{14}^{(4)}, a_{15}^{(4)})$

$a_{16}^{(4)} = b_{16}^{(4)}(a_{11}^{(4)}, a_{12}^{(4)}, a_{14}^{(4)}, a_{15}^{(4)})$

$g_1^{(4)}: a_{16}^{(4)}$ max

$g_{11}^{(4)}: a_{10}^{(4)} \leq \delta_{10}^{(4)}$

$g_{12}^{(4)}: a_{13}^{(4)} \leq \delta_{13}^{(4)}$

$A_2^{(4)}: a_{20}^{(4)} = b_{20}^{(4)}(a_{21}^{(4)}, a_{22}^{(4)}, a_{23}^{(4)})$

$a_{24}^{(4)} = b_{24}^{(4)}(a_{21}^{(4)}, a_{22}^{(4)}, a_{23}^{(4)})$

$g_2^{(4)}: \min a_{25}^{(4)} = b_{25}^{(4)}(a_{20}^{(4)}, a_{24}^{(4)})$

$g_{21}^{(4)}: a_{20}^{(4)} \leq \delta_{20}^{(4)}$

$g_{22}^{(4)}: a_{24}^{(4)} \leq \delta_{24}^{(4)}$

$g_1^{(4)} \rightarrow g_2^{(4)}: \max a_{16}^{(4)} \rightarrow \min a_{25}^{(4)}$

$(\delta_{10}^{(4)}, \delta_{13}^{(4)}) \rightarrow (\delta_{20}^{(4)}, \delta_{24}^{(4)})$: increase → decrease,

through some function or algorithm.

Figure 5.8. Three unilaterally supportive problems in systems concepts

As in Figure 5.7 we have applied static representations of activities and intrarelations in order to get a systems representation which is as simple as possible; with a dynamic representation we would have a problem-solving process evolving over time which is generated by several configurations of unilaterally supportive activities and goals. We have omitted other relationships than a few unilaterally supportive in order to simplify the example - clearly we could have found other relationships by going into details as the problems involved are rather complex (resource allocation-, queuing- and a cutting problem). For our present, illustrative, purposes that was however not necessary.

In the fashion shown in Figures 5.7 and 5.8 we could then formulate three pairs of both mutually supportive and unilaterally supportive problems in systems concepts, and implement several sets of goals in these formulations. It should, furthermore, be observed that we have separated the three sets of problems in order to study these relationships; in the complex shown in Figure 5.5 the three sets of problems (and a few more) *interact*. Thus we may now be able to accept our production planning problem as a genuinely complex problem.

As we thus have demonstrated that it is possible - and even useful - to represent complex, multigoal problems in systems concepts, there remains to find a methodology for solving such problems. We will suggest that such a methodology could be based on the principles for *adaptive control*.

5.4.4. *Adaptive control*

Let us then assume given a complex production planning problem of the structure shown in Figure 5.5, with three different forms for relationship between constitutive subproblems (conflict, mutual- and unilateral support) and a set of goals of the structure also shown in Figure 5.5. In this subsection we will now discuss a methodology for tackling the problem in the systems framework we have introduced.

Clearly there are some requirements on such a methodology (cf. Figures 5.5 - 5.8).

(i) It should make it possible for a decision-maker to formulate necessary and sufficient conditions for the existence of genuine, multigoal solutions to a complex problem.

(ii) it should make it possible to obtain genuine multigoal solutions, i.e. combinations of activities which result in a simultaneous attainment of all the goals at some t_i, or an attainment of each goal at least once in an interval $[t_1, t_n]$.

(iii) It should provide a framework for resolving conflicts and utilizing different forms for unilateral and mutual support among the subproblems.

(iv) It should make it possible to formulate problem-solving strategies for as well single subproblems, subcomplexes of subproblems, as the overall complex of problems, and, in the process, to take care of all active relationships among the subproblems and the goals.

These points (i-iv) describe an ideal methodology based on the previous discussion of complex problems, but is also rather close to a description of how an ideal decision-maker would tackle a complex problem (cf. Newell and Simon (1972)). Some key characteristics of human problem-solving are that it is *purposeful*, *adaptive* and based on a *search-learning* process (cf. Ackoff and Emery (1972) and Johnsen (1973)); we will develop and utilize these concepts towards a methodology in the introduced systems framework.

By *adaptation* we will mean a process, involving one or more activities, which reacts or responds to an 'efficiency'-reducing change in the environmental and/on internal state of the system by changing the state of the system, and/or that of the environment, so as to increase that 'efficiency' (adapted from Ackoff and Emery (1972)). A decision-maker is in a *purposeful* state if he wants something and has unequally efficient, alternative ways of obtaining it (cf. Ackoff and Emery (1972)); he may arrive at such a state through a *search-learning process*. This process involves a search for new states of existing activities, and/or one or more new activities, combined with learning their effects on environmental and/or internal states of the system, and on each other.

All these concepts can be synthesized in a definition of *adaptive* control (cf. 1977a): 'A problem-solving decision-maker, or an algorithm, controls a system adaptively if he/it has sufficient capacity to form a process or program, involving one or more activities, which makes the system converge in a finite number of steps to a state of goal-attainment, and this process or program is an efficient reaction (or response) to a change in the internal and/or environmental state of the system, if this change has caused the non-attainment of at least one goal.

As our discussion of the concepts has been more intuitivistic than formalistic we will not try to prove the above-mentioned definition; a formal discussion is given in Carlsson (1977b). We will instead demonstrate the proposition in a simplified version of Figure 5.7:

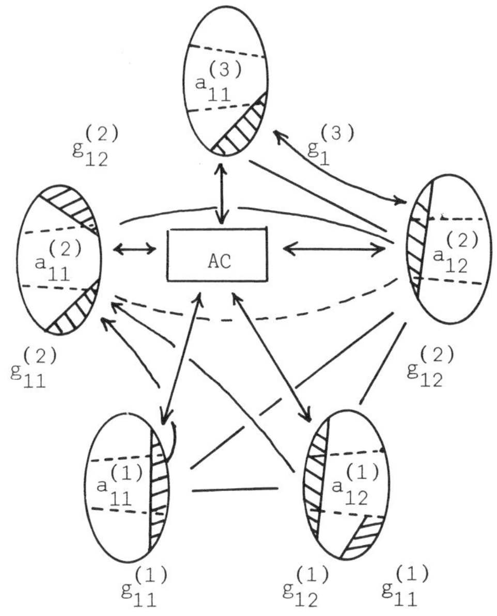

Figure 5.9. An adaptive controller (AC) in hierarchical 3-level, multigoal system

The system shown in Figure 5.12 is a hierarchical 3-level system of 5 intra- and interrelated activities, 5 goals of 3 different levels, which are implemented for one or two activities, and with 3 types of relationships. In order to control the system adaptively, AC should carry out the following program:

(i) Observe and identify a non-attainment of one or more goals (at t_i: $a_{12}^{(2)} \not\subset g_{12}^{(2)}$).

(ii) Determine activities which could produce an attainment of the non-attained goals, through:

- intrarelations (at t_{i+1} : $a_{11}^{(2)}$)
- interrelations (at t_{i+1} = $a_{11}^{(1)}$, $a_{12}^{(1)}$), or
- an influence on the activities for which the goals are not attained (at t_{i+1} : $a_{12}^{(2)}$).

(iii) Find the effects of the activities in (ii) on the rest of the goals by evaluating:

(iii) Find the effects of the activities in (ii) on the rest of the goals by evaluating:

- mutual supports (at t_{i+2} : $g_1^{(3)} \leftrightarrow g_{12}^{(2)}$
- unilateral supports (at t_{i+2} : $g_{11}^{(2)} \leftarrow g_1^{(1)}, g_{12}^{(1)}$)
- conflicts (at t_{i+2} : $g_{11}^{(2)}$--- $g_{12}^{(2)}$)

(iv) Determine an optimal program (at t_{i+3}) to attain all the non-attained goals in a finite number of steps; the criteria for optimality are:

- all goals are attained
- the program converges in a minimum number of steps, by resolving or avoiding goal conflicts, and utilizing mutual and unilateral goal supports.

(v) Carry out the optimal program (at t_{i+4}); if the program causes non-attainment among the goals, return to i.; continue until an optimal program is found, and report unresolved goal conflicts.

We did not specify if AC is an algorithm or a decision-maker, but in the latter case we could expect (i) - (v) to have the characteristics of a human problem-solving proces. If AC is an algorithm we have the following correspondences: if a non-attainment of one or more goals is 'efficiency'-reducing, (i) - (v) is a program for *adaption*; the steps (ii) - (iv) is a *search-learning* process; determining an optimal program (iv) is a *purposeful* process. Thus we have demonstrated that an adaptive controller could be a synthesis of a human problem-solving process; then remains to find out if it works.

The operations of an adaptive controller are demonstrated in Figure 5.10; the situation is an operationalization of the principles shown in Figure 5.9 and the tables show the results of a numerical experiment with the adaptive controller:

$\underline{A}_1^{(3)}$

$(g_1^{(3)})$	$a_{11}^{(3)} = \text{RNORM}\ (a_{13}^{(3)}, a_{14}^{(3)})$
$(g_2^{(3)}, g_3^{(3)})$	$a_{12}^{(3)} = \text{RNORM}\ (a_{15}^{(3)}, a_{16}^{(3)})$
	$a_{13}^{(3)} = a_{11}^{(2)} + a_{21}^{(2)} + a_{22}^{(2)}$
	$a_{15}^{(3)} = a_{21}^{(2)} + a_{23}^{(2)} + a_{12}^{(2)}$

$\underline{A}_1^{(2)}$

$(g_1^{(2)})$	$a_{11}^{(2)} = \text{RNORM}\ (a_{14}^{(2)}, a_{15}^{(2)})$
$(g_2^{(2)})$	$a_{12}^{(2)} = \text{RNORM}\ (a_{16}^{(2)}, a_{17}^{(2)})$
$(g_3^{(2)})$	$a_{13}^{(2)} = \text{RNORM}\ (a_{18}^{(2)}, a_{19}^{(2)})$
	$a_{14}^{(2)} = a_{21}^{(1)} + a_{42}^{(1)}$

$\underline{A}_2^{(2)}$

$(g_4^{(2)})$	$a_{21}^{(2)} = \text{RNORM}\ (a_{24}^{(2)}, a_{25}^{(2)})$
$(g_5^{(2)})$	$a_{22}^{(2)} = \text{RNORM}\ (a_{26}^{(2)}, a_{27}^{(2)})$
$(g_6^{(2)})$	$a_{23}^{(2)} = \text{RNORM}\ (a_{28}^{(2)}, a_{29}^{(2)})$
	$a_{24}^{(2)} = a_{11}^{(1)} + a_{31}^{(1)}$

$$a_{16}^{(2)} = a_{22}^{(1)} + a_{41}^{(1)} \qquad a_{26}^{(4)} = a_{12}^{(1)} + a_{31}^{(1)}$$

$$a_{18}^{(2)} = a_{21}^{(1)} + a_{41}^{(1)} \qquad a_{28}^{(2)} = a_{12}^{(1)} + a_{32}^{(1)}$$

$$g_1^{(2)} = \alpha_{41}\, g_3^{(2)}$$

$$g_2^{(2)} = \alpha_{42}\, g_1^{(2)}$$

$\underline{A}_1^{(1)}$

$(g_1^{(1)})\ a_{11}^{(1)} = \text{RNORM}\ (a_{13}^{(1)}, a_{14}^{(1)})$

$(g_2^{(1)})\ a_{12}^{(1)} = \text{RNORM}\ (a_{15}^{(1)}, a_{16}^{(1)})$

$\underline{A}_2^{(1)}$

$(g_5^{(1)})\ a_{21}^{(1)} = \text{RNORM}\ (a_{23}^{(1)}, a_{24}^{(1)})$

$(g_6^{(1)})\ a_{22}^{(1)} = \text{RNORM}\ (a_{25}^{(1)}, a_{26}^{(1)})$

$a_{23}^{(1)} = a_{23}^{(1)} - \alpha_2\, a_{25}^{(1)}$

$\underline{A}_3^{(1)}$

$(g_3^{(1)})\ a_{31}^{(1)} = \text{RNORM}\ (a_{33}^{(1)}, a_{34}^{(1)})$

$(g_4^{(1)})\ a_{32}^{(1)} = \text{RNORM}\ (a_{35}^{(1)}, a_{36}^{(1)})$

$a_{35}^{(1)} = \alpha_1\, a_{33}^{(1)}$

$\underline{A}_4^{(1)}$

$(g_7^{(1)})\ a_{41}^{(1)} = \text{RNORM}\ (a_{43}^{(1)}, a_{44}^{(1)})$

$(g_8^{(1)})\ a_{42}^{(1)} = \text{RNORM}\ (a_{45}^{(1)}, a_{46}^{(1)})$

$a_{45}^{(1)} = a_{45}^{(1)} + \alpha_3\, a_{43}^{(1)}$

$a_{43}^{(1)} = a_{43}^{(1)} - \alpha_3\, a_{45}^{(1)}$

<u>AC</u>

- determine $\Delta\, g_k^{(h)}$ = deviation from $g_k^{(h)}$
- if $\Delta\, g_k^{(h)} < 0 : a_{\dot{i}\dot{j}}^{(h)} + \Delta\, a_{\dot{i}\dot{j}}^{(h)}$

  $\Delta\, g_k^{(h)} > 0 : a_{\dot{i}\dot{j}}^{(h)} - \Delta\, a_{\dot{i}\dot{j}}^{(h)}$

  $\Delta\, g_k^{(g)} = 0 : a_{\dot{i}\dot{j}}^{(h)} \pm 0$

  where $a_{\dot{i}\dot{j}}^{(h)}$ is the relevant activity,

  and $\Delta\, a_{\dot{i}\dot{j}}^{(h)} = 0.1\, a_{\dot{i}\dot{j}}^{(h)}$
- continue until $\Delta\, g_{\dot{i}\dot{j}}^{(h)} = 0$
- if conflict, modify lower level goals to resolve the conflict

Figure 5.10 A numerical example of an adaptive controller.

In Figure 5.12 RNORM is a random number generator with a normal distribution; as the adaptive controller was simulated on a pocket calculator we aimed at a very simple numerical structure. As can be seen from the tables even this unsophisticated controller is working nicely (other tests with adaptive controllers are reported in Carlsson (1977a)).

It has been necessary to limit this discussion to systems with a static structure, as we-in order to present the principles-needed simple examples. But as we have pointed out frequently: a dynamic systems structure would offer more opportunities to study interactions of subsets of goals and/or activities over time, to resolve goal conflicts, to study the effects of different types of relationships and different forms for interaction. This could, however, not be carried out in the present context.

Thus we have demonstrated that adaptive control might be a viable option for tackling complex problems, and that it could be applied in a methodology for tackling such problems. We found out that adaptive control could be used for tackling multigoal problems which are formulated in systems concepts; we have also found out, in earlier sections, that our initial production planning problem could be formulated in systems concepts; thus it seems reasonable to conclude that also that problem could be tackled with adaptive control. This conclusion ends our discussion of the concepts; we will apply them in the next, final section to formulate a methodology for tackling complex problems.

$A_2^{(1)}$

t	$a_{21}^{(1)}$	$a_{23}^{(1)}$	$a_{24}^{(1)}$	$a_{22}^{(1)}$	$a_{25}^{(1)}$	$a_{26}^{(1)}$
1	2.35	2	1.2	2.10	3	1.3
	1.22	1.67	1.2	3.46	3.30	1.3
	1.88	1.83	1.2			
2	2.18	1.83	1.2	2.41	3.30	1.3
	0.58	1.47	1.2	3.79	3.63	1.3
	3.61	1.61	1.2			
	1.53	1.45	1.2			
	1.67	1.59	1.2			
	1.30	1.75	1.2			
	1.97	1.92	1.2			
3	0.35	1.56	1.2	4.21	3.63	1.3
	1.03	1.71	1.2	3.68	3.27	1.3
	-0.13	1.88	1.2			
	3.98	2.06	1.2			
	2.10	1.86	1.2			
4	2.93	1.53	1.2	3.37	3.27	1.3
	-1.01	1.38	1.2			
	-0.94	1.51	1.2			
	0.05	1.66	1.2			
	1.25	1.82	1.2			
	2.52	2.00	1.2			

$g_5^{(1)} : 1.7 \leq a_{21}^{(1)} \leq 2.8$

$g_6^{(1)} : 2.7 \leq a_{22}^{(1)} \leq 3.8$

$\alpha_2 = 0.1$

$A_1^{(2)}$

t	$a_{11}^{(2)}$	$a_{14}^{(2)}$	$a_{15}^{(2)}$	$a_{12}^{(2)}$	$a_{16}^{(2)}$	$a_{17}^{(2)}$	$a_{13}^{(2)}$	$a_{18}^{(2)}$	$a_{19}^{(2)}$
1	6.00	6.07	1.6	8.99	7.10	1.7	5.08	5.52	1.5
2	5.55	6.65	1.6	9.35	7.57	1.7	7.22	5.75	1.5
				6.12	6.81	1.6			
2'				8.41	7.49	1.7			
3	9.38	6.20	1.6	6.45	6.60	1.6	7.33	5.02	1.5
	5.79	5.58	1.5						
4	7.02	6.95	1.6	6.28	6.88	1.6	6.13	6.03	1.6

$g_1^{(2)} : a_{11}^{(2)} \leq 8.2$

$g_2^{(2)} : a_{12}^{(2)} \leq 9.3$

$g_3^{(2)} : a_{13}^{(2)} \leq 7.8$

$\alpha_{41} = 1.06$

$\alpha_{42} = 1.13$

$A_1^{(3)}$

t	$a_{11}^{(3)}$	$a_{13}^{(3)}$	$a_{14}^{(3)}$	$a_{12}^{(3)}$	$a_{15}^{(3)}$	$a_{16}^{(3)}$
1	22.5	21.81	1.3	28.7	28.50	1.4
2	20.25	20.35	1.3	23.28	22.02	1.4
				28.39	27.16	1.4
3	20.36	21.00	1.3	28.47	25.09	1.4
4	20.71	21.24	1.3	26.44	25.07	1.4

$g_1^{(3)} : a_{11}^{(3)} \leq 22.5$

$g_2^{(3)} : a_{12}^{(3)} \geq 26.0$

$g_3^{(3)} : a_{12}^{(3)} \leq 30.0$

$A_4^{(1)}$

t	$a_{41}^{(1)}$	$a_{43}^{(1)}$	$a_{44}^{(1)}$	$a_{42}^{(1)}$	$a_{45}^{(1)}$	$a_{46}^{(1)}$
1	3.64	3	1.3	4.96	4	1.4
				2.56	3.6	1.4
				3.36	3.96	1.4
				4.19	4.36	1.4
2	2.06	2.12	1.3	4.68	5.11	1.4
	3.78	2.33	1.3			
3	0.42	1.31	1.3	5.62	5.69	1.4
	1.04	1.44	1.3	5.38	5.12	1.4
	0.78	1.58	1.3	5.96	4.61	1.4
	2.92	1.73	1.3	2.71	4.15	1.4
				5.43	4.56	1.4
				2.94	4.10	1.4
				5.04	4.51	1.4
				4.10	4.51	1.4
4	1.30	0.92	1.3	4.43	4.33	1.4
	0.12	1.01	1.3			
	1.27	1.11	1.3			
	0.26	1.22	1.3			
	3.51	1.34	1.3			

$g_7^{(1)} : 2.8 \leq a_{41}^{(1)} \leq 3.8$

$g_8^{(1)} : 3.8 \leq a_{42}^{(1)} \leq 4.9$

$\alpha_3 = 0.2$

$A_1^{(1)}$

t	$a_{11}^{(1)}$	$a_{13}^{(1)}$	$a_{14}^{(1)}$	$a_{12}^{(1)}$	$a_{15}^{(1)}$	$a_{16}^{(1)}$
1	3.09	2	1.2	2.57	3	1.3
	2.36	1.8	1.2			
2	2.11	1.8	1.2	2.44	3	1.3
				4.30	3.3	1.3
				2.81	2.97	1.3
3	1.16	1.8	1.2	3.76	2.97	1.3
	2.96	1.98	1.2			
	2.57	1.98	1.2	3.86	2.97	1.3

$g_1^{(1)} : 1.5 \leq a_{11}^{(1)} \leq 3.0$

$g_2^{(1)} : 2.5 \leq a_{12}^{(1)} \leq 4.0$

$A_2^{(2)}$

t	$a_{21}^{(2)}$	$a_{24}^{(2)}$	$a_{25}^{(2)}$	$a_{22}^{(2)}$	$a_{26}^{(2)}$	$a_{27}^{(2)}$	$a_{23}^{(2)}$	$a_{28}^{(2)}$	$a_{29}^{(2)}$
1	6.07	7.24	1.7	6.07	6.72	1.6	9.77	8.01	1.8
	9.74	7.96	1.7						
2	7.90	6.93	1.6	8.02	7.73	1.7	7.68	7.63	1.7
				10.16	6.96	1.7	8.00	8.39	1.8
				6.90	6.27	1.7			
2'	9.01	7.62	1.7				6.29	9.23	1.9
							9.74	10.15	2.0
3	8.62	6.93	1.6	6.59	7.73	1.7	5.76	7.63	1.7
							10.02	8.39	1.8
4	7.55	5.88	1.5	6.67	7.17	1.7	7.17	8.41	1.8
							11.24	9.25	1.9

$g_4^{(2)} : a_{21}^{(2)} \geq 7.00$

$g_5^{(2)} : a_{22}^{(2)} \leq 7.00$

$g_6^{(2)} : a_{23}^{(2)} \geq 8.00$

$A_3^{(1)}$

t	$a_{31}^{(1)}$	$a_{33}^{(1)}$	$a_{34}^{(1)}$	$a_{32}^{(1)}$	$a_{35}^{(1)}$	$a_{36}^{(1)}$
1	4.15	3	1.3	5.44	4	1.4
	1.86	2.7	1.3			
	2.96	2.9	1.3	2.92	3.86	1.4
				3.97	4.25	1.4
2	0.44	2.9	1.3	4.04	4.25	1.4
	4.21	3.19	1.3			
	4.00	2.87	1.3	2.74	3.81	1.4
				4.05	4.19	1.4
3	3.97	2.87	1.3	3.87	4.19	1.4
4	1.90	2.87	1.3			
	2.60	3.16	1.3			
	3.31	3.47	1.3	4.55	4.62	1.4

$g_3^{(1)} : 2.7 \leq a_{31}^{(1)} \leq 4.0$

$g_4^{(1)} : 3.5 \leq a_{32}^{(1)} \leq 5.5$

$\alpha_1 = 1.33$

Figure 5.11 A numerical example of an adaptive controller

5.5. PROPOSITIONS TOWARDS A METHODOLOGY FOR TACKLING COMPLEX AND ILL-STRUCTURED PROBLEMS

In the previous two sections we have found that the multigoal, complex and ill-structured production planning problem A could be tackled both with a set of four linked mathematical programming models, and with an implementation of adaptive control in a systems formulation of the problem. There were, however, some essential differences between the two approaches:

mathematical programming	*systems concepts & adaptive control*
. models rather abstract, and formulated on a high level of aggregation.	. models formulated on any suitable level of aggragation; aggregation/disaggregation through interrelations.
. static.	. static and/or dynamic.
. only linear, or approximately linear, interdependences.	. interdependences through intra- and interrelations, which may be static or dynamic functions, algorithms, etc.
. many goals, if can be formulated as constraints and objective functions; goal-interdependences indirect; goal conflicts not feasible.	. many goals; any form for implementation which is operational in systems concepts; goal-interdependences direct; all forms for interdependence implementable.
. a static, composite optimal solution; solution vectors in the programming models.	. an optimal, static or dynamic, program which solves the multigoal problems; a human problem-solver or an adaptive, search-learning algorithm (or several interacting algorithms).
. centralized, non-interactive and limited to aspects which can be captured in mathematical programming concepts; readily solvable, mathematically provable optimality.	. decentralized, modular, interactive and limited only by the capacity of the algorithm(s) or the problem-solver; sometimes difficult to find solutions; optimality not always provable.

Figure 5.12. A comparison of a traditional/non-traditional MCDM-approach

Our descriptions of the production planning problem in section 2, and our assumptions on the complex problem A (cf (1.4) - and the (in general) more favorable characteristics of the non-traditional approach - show that an ideal approach to tackling complex and structured problems is closer to the non-traditional than the traditional approach. We will, consequently, formulate the methodology in such a way that it serves the non-traditional approach:

Proposition 1. Problems can be formulated in *systems concepts*, as (for instance) activities, intra- and interrelations.

Proposition 1a. Complex problems can be formulated in terms of hierarchically organized activities, intra- and interrelations, as subproblems can be formulated in systems concepts (cf proposition 1).

Proposition 1b. A multigoal problem can be formulated in systems concepts, as (for instance) activities, intra- and interrelations; complex multigoal problems can be formulated in terms of hierarchically organized activities, intra- and interrelations (cf proposition 1a).

Proposition 1c. Systems concepts consent to static as well as dynamic problem formulations, and to both aggregation and disaggregation.

Proposition 1d. It is possible to formulate an ill-structured problem in systems concepts.; we do not need any common space for systems concepts, and the existence of operators for all the spaces involved in a problem is not self-evident.
Thus it follows, from propositions 1a, 1b, 1c and 1d, that a multigoal, complex and ill-structured problem can be formulated in systems concepts- as the proposed activities, intra- and interrelations.

Proposition 2. If a problem is formulated in systems concepts, it is possible to solve it through an implementation of *adaptive control.*

Proposition 2a. Complex problems can be solved through a hierarchical implementation of adaptive control; adaptive control allows an exploitation of subproblem - interdependencies.

Proposition 2b. Multigoal problems can be solved in a program for either simultaneous or successive attainment of the goals, if that program is an implementation of adaptive control; adaptive control allows an exploitation of goal-interdependencies.

Proposition 2c. Implementations of adaptive control can be both static and dynamic.
Thus follows, from the two sets of propositions, that a multigoal, complex and ill-structured problem could be tackled by implementing adaptive control in a systems representation of that problem.

Proposition 3. Systems concepts can be operationalized as simulation models, as some set of interacting, analytical models, or as a systems model in some appropriate computer language.

Proposition 4. Adaptive control can be operationalized as an (or a set of) adaptive, search-learning algorithm(s), or through a human problem-solver.

Proposition 5. Systems concepts and adaptive control represents a decentralized, modular interactive modelling and problem-solving approach; such an approach is useful for tackling complex and ill-structured problems.

Proposition 6. Complex and ill-structured problems are tackled, but not solved.

The last proposition follows from the definition of an ill-structured problem (cf (1.4)), if a "solution" should be an operationally identifiable state.

This set of propositions does not, of course, form a complete methodology - the propositions have to pass extensive, empirical tests, and should be rewritten in a more rigid form, before they can be accepted as a methodology. But the propositions seem to correspond closely enough to our requirements (cf (4.17)). Then we may conclude, that (i) multigoal problems can be treated as ill-structured problems, when formulated in systems concepts and tackled with adaptive control; (ii) the propositions 1-6 outline an operational methodology for that purpose; (iii) that methodology would be operational also for complex and ill-structured problems in general, as we, by assumption, have been dealing with such problems. Thus we have also answered our initially formulated, interesting, three questions.

5.6. REFERENCES

Ackoff, R.L. and Emery, F.E., *On Purposeful Systems*, Aldine-Atherton, Chicago, 1972.

Carlsson, C., Adaptive Multigoal Control. On the Principles for Operational Problem-Solving in a Complex Environment, Ph.D. Dissertation (in Swedish), Abo, 1977a.

Carlsson, C., An Approach to Adaptive Multigoal Control Using Fuzzy Automata, in M. Roubens (ed.), *Proceedings of EURO II*, North-Holland, Amsterdam, 1977b.

Carlsson, C., On the Multi-Goal Problem and the Linking of OR-Models, in K.B. Hailey (ed.), *Proceedings of the 8th International IFORS Conference*, North-Holland, Amsterdam, 1979a.

Carlsson, C., Linking MP Models in a Systems Framework, *IEEE Transaction Transactions*, SMC-December, 1979b.

Johnsen, E., *Malbevidst Virksomhedsledelse, Nyt Nordisk Forlag*, Arnold Busck, Copenhagen, 1973.

Newell, A. and Simon, H.A., *Human Problem Solving*, Prentice-Hall, New Jersey, 1972.

Simon, H.A., The Theory of Problem Solving, in: Simon, H.A.,(ed.), *Models of Discovery*, 1972.

Simon, H.A., The Organization of Complex Systems, in: Simon, H.A. (ed.), *Models of Discovery*, 1973a.

Simon, H.A., The Structure of Ill-Structured Problems, in: Simon, H.A. (ed.), *Models of Discovery* 1978b.

Simon, H.A., *Models of Discovery*, D. Reidel Publ. Co., Dordrecht, 1977.

Whyte, L.L., Wilson, A.G. and Wilson, D., *Hierarchical Structures*, Elsevier, New York, 1969.

B. PLAN AND PROJECT EVALUATION

6 Multicriteria Q-Analysis for Plan Evaluation

L. Duckstein and J. Kempf

6.1. INTRODUCTION

In this paper, further development of a multicriteria decision technique, called multicriteria Q-analysis one (MCQA1), is described. Quantification of the MCQA1 conclusion process, for which a heuristic approach was described in Kempf et al. (1979), is presented. The methodology is demonstrated on a case-study involving the Tisza River Basin in Hungary, which was originally presented in David and Duckstein (1976). Since four other multicriteria techniques have been used to analyse this case-study, namely ELECTRE, in the original paper, multi-attribute utility theory (Keeney and Wood (1977)), compromise programming (Duckstein and Opricovic (1977)), and another form of multicriteria Q-analysis using utility theory (Armijo et al. (1979)), the conclusions of the present study can be compared with those of the previous studies to demonstrate how MCQA1 differs from other techniques.

A large body of literature on multicriteria techniques exists (see Nijkamp (1977) for a review). The three most widely used as planning aids are multi-attribute utility theory (Keeney (1974)), ELECTRE (Roy and Bertier (1971)), and concordance analysis (Nijkamp and Vos (1977)). Multi-attribute utility theory assesses utility functions for the various attributes or criteria separately; then, provided preferential and utility independence exists, constructs a multi-attribute function. In ELECTRE, pairwise comparisons between the systems are not used to develop a graph from which concordance and discordance indices are calculated, while in concordance analysis, the concordance and discordance indices are calculated without reference to a graph. In both concordance analysis and ELECTRE, the indices are weighed sums of weights associated with the criteria by the decision-maker. MCQA1 was inspired, in part, by ELECTRE and essentially consists of a multidimensional generalization of the two-dimensional graphs of ELECTRE, with a corresponding elaboration of the simple dominance relation which ELECTRE assumes.

Background material on Q-analysis and fuzzy sets, from which MCQA1 was developed, will be presented in the next section. The technique itself is then described in the third and fourth sections, and the case-study is presented and analysed using MCQA1 in Section 5. In the sixth section, the results are discussed in the context of the results obtained through the use of other multicriteria techniques. Finally, conclusions on the usefulness of MCQA1 in planning are drawn in Section 7.

6.2. Q-ANALYSIS AND FUZZY SETS

Q-analysis has been used in a number of different areas to study the structure of systems. In the context of urban planning, Atkin (1974a,

1974b) has used the technique extensively to find new approaches to community design and for structural analysis of existing urban areas. Use of Q-analysis for assignment of parking spaces to apartments in a large apartment complex (Kempf (1977)) has also been reported. Two approaches to multicriteria decision-making using Q-analysis are presented in Kempf et al. (1979), and Armijo et al. (1979), the former being a predecessor of the present study.

Application of Q-analysis requires two finite sets, say P and M, and a binary relation L, which indicates how the elements of P and M interact. One set, say P, is used as the vertices of a multidimensional graph, called a simplicial complex, while the other set, M in this case, contains the faces or simplices of the graph. If:

I = number of elements in M
J = number of elements in P

then an incidence matrix B can be constructed for the relation:

$$(b_{ij}) = \begin{cases} 1 \text{ if } M_i \text{ is related to } P_j \text{ through } L \\ 0 \text{ otherwise} \end{cases} \qquad (6.1)$$

$$i=1,2,\ldots,I \qquad j=1,2,\ldots,J$$

By reversing the roles of the simplex set and the vertex set, the conjugate complex can also be constructed and the conjugate relation examined. Mathematically, the incidence matrix of the conjugate relation is just the transpose of the binary incidence matrix used to represent the relation. The conjugate relation demonstrates how the vertices are related to the simplices. In addition, a relation in which the entries in the incidence matrix are members of some set other than (0,1) can be converted into a 0-1 incidence matrix by using a threshold or indicator function. The binary matrix entry will be 1 if the real relation matrix entry satisfies some numerical criterion, and will be 0 otherwise. Q-analysis can then proceed on the resulting binary matrix.

The property of q-connection is defined in the following manner. Two simplices are said to be q-connected, if and only if a sequence of simplices (M_i, i=1,2,...,p) exists, such that:

1. M_r is a face of M_1
2. M_p is a face of M_s
3. M_i and M_{i+1} have a common face, say M_j
4. The dimension q=min (r,1,2,...,p,s)

A simplex is a face of another simplex if the two simplices share at least one vertex.

Q-connection defines an equivalence relation on the simplices and the structure vector, Q, which results from Q-analysis is a measure of the structural ordering imposed over the set of simplices with respect to the set of simplices (Atkin (1974a)). An algorithm for performing Q-analysis appears in Atkin (1974a).

In applications of Q-analysis to dynamic systems (sometimes called polyhedral dynamics), a pattern consisting of co-simplices (which are members of some subset of the real numbers) is defined on the simplices to indicate the importance of particular simplices to the complex structure, and changes of this pattern with time are examined. Numerous examples of applications exist (Atkin (1974a), Casti (1977), Casti et al. (1977), Atkin and Casti (1977)). In the present context, decision dynamics (Yu (1977)) will not be considered; however, the idea of a pattern will be used to quantify a certain measure of the decision-maker's preferences. The co-simplices can thus be thought of as the 'size' of the simplices in the complex.

Fuzzy sets (Kaufman (1975)) have seen several applications in decision theory (Bellman and Zadeh (1970), Zeleny (1972, 1976)). Briefly, for any set, A, a membership function can be defined which indicates the *degree* to which elements of A are considered to be members of A (i.e. satisfy the membership criterion). If:

$$\mu_A(x) = \begin{matrix} 1 \text{ if } & x \in A \\ 0 \text{ if } & x \notin A \end{matrix} \tag{6.2}$$

then the set is an 'ordinary' set (Kaufman (1975)). If, however:

$$\{\mu_A(x): \mu_A(x) \in \Gamma \} \tag{6.3}$$

where Γ is some totally ordered set, then A is called a fuzzy set. In most applications:

$$\Gamma = [0,1] \tag{6.4}$$

6.3. PREFERENCE STRUCTURE ELABORATION

Define a decision impact matrix as follows:

$$D=(D_{ij}) \qquad i=1,\ldots,I \qquad j=1,\ldots,J \tag{6.5}$$

where:

I = number of projects or systems under consideration

J = number of criteria used to judge projects

d_{ij} = impact of the ith project on the jth criterion.

As pointed out in Duckstein (1978), the matrix D, also called a cost-effectiveness or payoff matrix, is central to every multicriteria decision-making scheme and, although the methods of obtaining the matrix are important, for demonstration of MCQA1, the matrix is considered to be given.

If the decision-maker has some idea of a desirable or satisfying outcome on the criteria (Yu, (1977)), 'linguistic variables' (Zadeh (1973)) can be used to assign membership grades to the matrix entries. Linguistic variables are basically adjectives which the decision-maker can easily use to quantify his feelings about a particular project impact, d_{ij}. For example:

$$\mu_D(d_{ij}) = 1.00\text{-}0.75 \tag{6.6}$$

if d_{ij} is essential to highly satisfactory. In this case, essential and highly satisfactory define qualitative feelings which indicate to what degree d_{ij} is in the decision-maker's set of satisfactory outcomes. The decision-maker's preference structure (Yu (1977)) over the set of project outcomes can thus be assessed.

The resulting preference structure matrix:

$$U(D) = (\mu_D(d_{ij})) \qquad i=1,2,\dots,I \qquad j=1,.,\dots,J \tag{6.7}$$

can be converted into a 0-1 incidence matrix for Q-analysis by defining a threshold function of the following form. If α_k is the kth threshold level, the resulting incidence matrix is:

$$B_{\alpha k} = (b_{ij}) = \begin{matrix} 1 \text{ if } \mu(d_{ij}) \geq \alpha_k \\ 0 \text{ if } \mu(d_{ij}) \geq \alpha_k \end{matrix} \tag{6.8}$$

$$\alpha_k \in [0,1] \qquad k=1,\dots,K \qquad i=1,\dots,I \qquad j=1,\dots,J$$

The incidence matrix thus indicates which project simplices have outcomes on the criteria vertices which are greater than or equal to the decision-maker satisfaction level α_k. The result of this procedure will be K incidence matrices, representing K conjugate complex graphs of the decision-maker's preference structure at K satisfaction levels.

In addition to the decision-maker's preferences on the project impact matrix, a preference structure on the criteria vector will also be assumed. The decision-maker will be asked to assign weights to the criteria, according to his feelings about how important the various criteria are for judging the project. If W is some totally ordered set, then:

$$\underline{c} = (w_1,w_2,\dots,w_m) \qquad w_j \in W \tag{6.9}$$

$\underline{c}$ being the criteria weight vector and w_j the weights.

Q-analysis can now proceed on each of the K complexes. Previously, the complex in which a single project appeared in the high dimensional position of the structure vector was used to judge which project was preferred and to impose a preference ordering over the projects (Kempf et al. (1979)). The threshold level, α_k then gave an indication of the decision-maker's satisfaction with the outcome. However, this heuristic procedure throws out the information available in the other complexes for other theshold levels and also does not provide a definite procedure when no single high Q project appears. A more quantitative procedure is evolved in the next section.

6.4. PROJECT SELECTION

In order to develop a more quantitative measure of the decision-maker's preferences, two different indices will be introduced. The first index grows out of the idea of a pattern on the complex. Given a complex at a particular threshold level α, if M_r is a q dimensional simplex with criteria vertices $p_{j1}, p_{j2}, \ldots, p_{jq+1}$, then define the following co-simplex on M_r:

$$x_{r\alpha} = w_{j1} + w_{j2} + \ldots w_{jq+1} \qquad j_i \epsilon \{1,2,\ldots,m\} \qquad (6.10)$$

where:

w_{ji} = j_ith member of $\underline{c}$

x_r is the sum of the weights assigned to the criteria upon which the project was found to have a satisfactory outcome, at or above the α threshold level.

Define the project satisfaction index (PSI) for project M as follows:

$$PSI_r = \alpha_1 x_{r1} + \alpha_2 x_{r2} + \ldots \alpha_K x_{rK} \qquad (6.11)$$

The project satisfaction index consists of the weighed sum of the project co-simplices across the spectrum of satisfaction thresholds.

What the PSI does is measure how well the decision-maker likes the outcome of a particular project without reference to any of the other projects. Those projects which are satisfying on many criteria or on criteria with high weights or at high overall satisfaction levels will receive a higher PSI rating. Thus the PSI measures how well a decision-maker would like a particular project if that project alone were presented to him.

What the PSI does not measure, however, is how the projects compare with each other. The structure vectors themselves provide this information. A project which appears at a high dimensional position in a structure vector and does not become q-connected until a low dimensional position is, in some sense, preferred to a project which either appears at a low q position or becomes q-connected as soon as it enters the complex. Two projects which are q-connected at a particular dimensional level q satisfy the same q+1 criteria and therefore cannot be differentiated on the basis of those criteria, while those projects which enter at low q levels satisfy very few criteria and therefore are not preferred. Furthermore, a project which stays un-q-connected through a 5 dimensional complex (i.e., is found satisfactory for 6 criteria which other projects do not satisfy) is certainly more preferable than one which only stays un-q-connected through a 2 dimensional complex. The difference between the dimension of a project simplex, q_{max}, and the dimension at which the simplex first becomes q-connected to another simplex, αq_{min}, provides a measure of how the project compares globally with all the other projects, for a particular threshold level, α.

Define the project comparison index (PCI) for a project M_r as follows:

$$PCI_r = \alpha_1 \Delta\ q_1 + \alpha_2 \Delta\ q_2 + \ldots \alpha_K \Delta\ q_K \qquad (6.12)$$

where:

$$\Delta q_k = q_{max} - q_{min} \tag{6.13}$$

for M_r at α_k threshold level. The PCI is the weighted sum of the comparison measures across the spectrum of satisfaction cutting levels.

Note that the two separate measures of decision-maker preference enable one to deal with the problem of intransitivity (Luce and Raiffa (1977)) commonly observed in human decision behaviour. A decision among three choices, A, B and C is transitive if the following occurs:

if A is preferred to B,
and B is preferred to C,
then A is preferred to C.

However, transitivity is not always observed, although it is often assumed for the sake of mathematical convenience (Starr and Zeleny (1977)). If ranking of the projects were to proceed on the basis of the PSI alone, transitivity would be assumed, since the PSI is an ordinal number. The PCI, on the other hand, globally compares all projects, sidestepping the problem by not using pairwise comparisons. However, the PCI does not contain information on the decision-maker's criteria weights.

By normalization of the PSI and PCI and use of an l_p metric (Duckstein and Opricovic (1977)) to calculate an index of decision-maker satisfaction which incorporates both aspects of the decision problem, a final project rating index can be calculated. The PSI and PCI are normalized over the range (0,1) by dividing by the maximum attainable PSI and PCI:

$$PSI_n = \frac{PSI}{PSI_{max}} \quad ; \quad PCI_n = \frac{PCI}{PCI_{max}} \tag{6.14}$$

and the resulting vector norm is calculated as the project rating index (PRI):

$$PRI = \left[(1-PSI_n)^p + (1-PCI_n)^p\right]^{1/p} \tag{6.15}$$

Here, p will be set equal to 2, so that the PRI measures the Euclidian distance between the project vector and the 'ideal' vector. Ranking of projects can be achieved by assigning first preference to that project with the minimum PRI, second preference to the project with second lowest PRI, etc.

6.5. CASE-STUDY

The case-study to be analyzed is the long-range (60 years) planning for the development of a water resource system in the Tisza River Basin in Hungary. A detailed description of the problem, including long-range goals and how measures of effectiveness were developed for the systems can be found in David and Duckstein (1976). The five systems considered are the following:

System I. Both the Tisza and Danube Rivers are developed, with water being transferred from the Danube by a multipurpose canal and reservoir system.

System II. A pumped reservoir system is built in the Sàtoros and Bükk Mountains, supplied from the Tisza River only.

System III. Water from the Tisza is used to fill reservoirs located in the flat land part of the region.

System IV. A mountain reservoir system is developed in the upper Tisza River Basin, outside Hungary.

System V. Tisza water and groundwater are used to supply underground reservoirs in the Debrecen region.

A cost-effectiveness methodology was used by David and Duckstein (1976) to generate the project impact matrix, part of which is shown in Table 6.1. For expository purposes, only eight of the original twelve criteria were retained and the impact entries under the international co-operation criterion were modified from 'easy, very easy,' etc., to the more neutral 'low, none,' etc., to avoid biasing the decision-maker's judgements.

The decision-maker, a professional hydrologist, was asked to fill in the preference matrix according to the following scale:

0-0.25-d_{ij} not satisfactory to slightly satisfactory

0.25-0.50-d_{ij} slightly satisfactory to satisfactory

0.50-0.75-d_{ij} satisfactory to highly satisfactory

0.75-1.0-d_{ij} highly satisfactory to essential.

In addition, he was asked to weigh the criteria by using numbers between one and ten to indicate how important he thought particular criteria were. Different weights for each criterion were not required. The resulting preference matrix and criteria weight vector are shown in Table 6.2.

Before beginning the Q-analysis, it was noted that both systems III and V were completely dominated; that is, the preference matrix entries for projects III and V are all less than the entries for the other projects. Systems III and V were therefore eliminated from further consideration.

A differential threshold level ($\Delta\alpha$) of .25 was used to convert the preference matrix into four binary relations. Q-analysis was performed on the resulting binary relations and the resulting structure vectors are shown in Table 6.3. Calculation of the PSI and PCI for the projects followed. (PSI,PCI) vectors were:

System I : (64.50, 3.75)
System II: (49.50, 0.25)
System IV: (36.75, 1.50).

Calculation of the PRI yielded the following results:

System I : 0.899
System II: 1.121
System IV: 1.131.

The systems can therefore be ranked with I first, II second, and IV third.

As outlined in Kempf et al. (1979), Q-analysis on the conjugate complexes can be used to examine how useful the criteria are, similar to the dual in linear programming. The results of Q-analysis on the conjugate complexes for $\Delta\alpha$ = .25 are shown in Table 6.4. Although no quantitative measures were developed for the criteria complexes, the results of the conjugate Q-analysis will be discussed in the next section.

In order to determine the sensitivity of the results to the choice of differential threshold level, the problem was also analyzed for $\Delta\alpha$ = .1. The structure vectors are not reproduced here; however, the resulting PRI were:

System I : 0.909
System II: 1.123
System IV: 1.157.

Although the numerical values of the PRI changed slightly, the resulting preference ordering is unchanged. Further discussion will proceed on the basis of the results for $\Delta\alpha$ = .25, since a differential of .25 was used in the original assignment of linguistic variables.

6.6. DISCUSSION

In the original paper, David and Duckstein (1976) reported that the non-dominated set selected through ELECTRE consisted of systems I and II and that system II would be preferred as representing a good compromise between costs, shortages, and international co-operation. Keeney and Wood (1977), on the other hand, reported that utilities for the five systems were:

$U(S_1) = .832$
$U(S_2) = .831$
$U(S_3) = .503$
$U(S_4) = .648$
$U(S_5) = .521$,

and concluded that system I was slightly better than system II, which is considerably better than system IV. System IV is also much better than system V, with system III being the least preferred. The results of the present study are similar to those of Keeney and Wood (1977).

In Duckstein and Opricovic (1977) and Armijo et al. (1979), the above dichotomy was resolved. Duckstein and Opricovic (1977), using compromise programming with a surrogate objective function, found that continuous passage from the solution proposed by David and Duckstein (1976) to that suggested by Keeney and Wood (1977) could be obtained by varying the parameter p in the l_p metric equation. Similarly, in Armijo et al. (1979), variation in the observational level (similar to the threshold level in the present study) from 'lax' to 'strict' provided a transition from system I to system II.

The results of the conjugate Q-analysis, displayed in Table 6.4, reveal how the criteria differentiated among the projects and provides some insight into how system I was selected. A criterion simplex of 0 dimension (i.e. one project satisfies the criterion) is more useful in making the decision than a higher dimensional criterion simplex, or a criterion simplex of -1 dimension; since, in the former case, many projects are rated the same on the criterion, while in the latter, no project was found satisfactory and therefore, the criterion is not, in fact, being used.

System I was simply chosen because the decision-maker found it more highly satisfying on more criteria than the other systems. For example, at the α = 1.0 level, three criteria, 2, 4, and 8 enter at the 0 dimensional level and were found satisfactory for system I only, while one criterion, 6, was rated as satisfactory for both systems II and IV, and therefore entered at the 1 dimensional level. Similarly, at the α = .75 level, 2, 3, and 7 enter at the 0 dimensional position of the structure vector, and, again, system I was rated satisfactory for more criteria. System I was satisfactory on criterion 2, while system IV was satisfactory for 3 and 7. Since MCQA1 was designed with optimum decision-maker participation in mind, the results of MCQA1 are dependent upon the individual decision-maker and could vary.

With regard to the conjugate Q-analysis, note that system I and system II share many criteria in common; in fact, all the criteria on which system I was found satisfactory were also satisfactory for system II below the α = .75 level. Also, as mentioned above, criteria 3 and 7 were found satisfactory for system IV alone. This explains why the PSI rating for system II is greater than the system IV while the opposite is true for the PCI rating.

As the preference matrix (Table 6.2) shows, system II was found superior to system I only on criteria 1 and 7, while system IV was rated superior on 1, 3, and 7. Thus systems I and II share many of the same satisfactory criteria, while system I has more. System IV has another satisfactory set of criteria.

The above comments suggest that Q-analysis might serve another function in multicriteria decision-making. The results of Q-analysis separate the set of systems into q-connected subsets, which share the same satisfactory criteria. Using a different threshold function, the project impact matrix could be converted into a binary incidence matrix directly and Q-analysis applied. An example of an appropriate threshold structure would be minimum and maximum requirements on each criterion. Such a procedure would be especially useful as a 'decision aid' (Roy (1977)), when the number of projects and criteria is very high, and would result in the separation of the project set into subsets which share common characteristics. In addition, measures of complex structure introduced from algebraic topology (Atkin and Casti (1977)) might be useful for quantifying the decision.

6.7. CONCLUSIONS

Quantitative measures of decision-maker preferences, which can be calculated from the results of multicriteria Q-analysis, were developed. One measure, the project satisfaction index (PSI) indicates how satisfying the decision-maker felt a particular project was without comparison to other projects and taking into account the decision-maker's criteria weights. The other measure, the project comparison index (PCI) can be used for a global comparison of all projects. The two measures were combined into a project rating index (PRI) by means of an l_p norm. The PRI can be used to develop a preference ordering over the projects, as a sup-

Table 6.1
Modified project impact matrix (from David and Duckstein, 1976, Table 4)

Alternative Systems	1 Total Yearly Costs in 10^9 ft/yr. (a)	2 Probab. of Water Shortage (%)	3 Water Qual. % of Req. Met. (b) I	 II	 III	4 Energy Reuse Factor (c)	5 Recreation (1000 ha. of water surface)	6 Flood Protect. % (d)	7 Land and Forest Use (1000 ha.)	8 Need for Inter. Co-op.
I	99.6	4	90	80	100	.7	60	1.0	90	none
II	85.7	19	80	80	90	.5	50	0.5	80	low to medium
III	101.1	50	70	60	50	0.01	40	1.5	80	medium to high
IV	95.1	50	100	90	90	.1	20	0.5	60	very high
V	101.8	50	100	80	90	0.01	30	2.0	70	medium to high

a) Twenty ft=1 dollar
b) Class Definition: I-domestic, livestock and fishpond; II-irrigation, recreation and industry; III-power cooling
c) Reuse factor: energy produced/energy consumed
d) % indicates the per cent probability of a damaging flood in a year

Table 6.2
Preference matrix and criteria weight vector

Alternative Systems	1	2	3	4	5	6	7	8
I	0.17	1.00	0.60	1.00	0.90	0.75	0.60	1.00
II	0.25	0.50	0.50	0.75	0.75	1.00	0.70	0.80
III	0.10	0.25	0.25	0.10	0.60	0.50	0.70	0.60
IV	0.20	0.25	0.85	0.30	0.30	1.00	0.80	0.40
V	0.09	0.25	0.75	0.10	0.45	0.20	0.75	0.60

Weight Vector:

Criteria:	1	2	3	4	5	6	7	8
Weights :	7	9	6	4	1	6	2	5

Table 6.3
Q-Analysis for $\Delta\alpha = .25$

$\alpha = 1.0$

$q = 2$, $Q_2 = 1$ (I)

$q = 1$, $Q_1 = 1$ (I)

$q = 0$, $Q_0 = 2$ (I), (II,V)

$q = -1$, $Q_{-1} = 1$ (all)

$\alpha = .75$

$q = 4$, $Q_4 = 1$ (I)

$q = 3$, $Q_3 = 1$ (I,II)

$q = 2$, $Q_2 = 2$ (I,II), (IV)

$q = 1$, $Q_1 = 2$ (I,II), (IV)

$q = 0,-1$, $Q_{0,-1} = 1$

$\alpha = .50$

$q = 6$, $Q_6 = 1$ (I,II)

no change through dimension 4

$q = 3$, $Q_3 = 1$ (all)

no change through dimension -1

$\alpha = .25$

$q = 7$, $Q_7 = 1$ (II)

$q = 6$, $Q_6 = 1$ (all)

no change through dimension -1

Table 6.4
Conjugate Q-analysis

$\alpha = 1.0$

$q = 1$, $Q_1 = 1$ (6)

$q = 0$, $Q_0 = 2$ (6), (2,4,8)

$q = -1$, $Q_{-1} = 1$ (all)

$\alpha = .75$

$q = 2$, $Q_2 = 6$ (6)

$q = 1$, $Q_1 = 1$ (4,5,6,8)

$q = 0$, $Q_0 = 1$ (2,3,4,5,6,7,8)

$q = -1$, $Q_{-1} = 1$ (all)

$\alpha = .50$

$q = 2$, $Q_2 = 1$ (3,6,7)

$q = 1$, $Q_1 = 1$ (2,3,4,5,6,7,8)

no change for $q = 0$

$q = -1$, $Q_{-1} = 1$ (all)

$\alpha = .25$

$q = 2$, $Q_2 = 1$ (2,3,4,5,6,7,8)

no change for $q = 1$

$q = 0$, $Q_0 = 1$ (all)

no change for $q = -1$

plement to the qualitative information provided by Q-analysis.

Decision-maker participation in MCQA1 is optimized by allowing the decision-maker to judge directly the project outcomes and the criteria, similar to multi-attribute utility theory; however, problems with preferential and utility independence and intransitivity are avoided, and the preference structure assessment procedure, which uses fuzzy sets, is designed to make translation of the decision-makers feelings into membership grades relatively simple. Results of the case-study were similar to those obtained through multi-attribute utility theory (Keeney and Wood (1977)).

Comparison between projects in MCQA1 is accomplished on a global level, rather than pairwise as in concordance analysis and ELECTRE, so that the set of projects can be separated into subsets, in which the elements share satisfactory criteria. This suggests that Q-analysis might be useful in the pre-decision stage, for simplifying the decision structure of particularly complex problems in which many criteria and projects are involved. In addition, the results of MCQA1 are decision-maker dependent, so that extensions to group decision-making (Kempf et al. (1979)) would be important for actual application.

6.8. REFERENCES

Armijo, R., Casti, J. and Duckstein, L., Multicriteria Water Resources System Design by Q-Analysis, paper presented at the Joint TIMS/ORSA Conference, New Orleans, Louisiana, April 1979.

Atkin, R.H., *Mathematical Structure in Human Affairs*, Heinemann, London, 1974a.

Atkin, R.H., An Approach to Structure in Architectural and Urban Design, *Environmental and Planning Bulletin*, vol.1, 1974b, pp.51-67.

Atkin, R.H. and Casti, J., Polyhedral Dynamics and the Geometry of Systems, IIASA Research Report 77-6, March 1977.

Bellman, R. and Zadeh, L., Decision Making in a Fuzzy Environment, *Management Science*, vol.17, no.4, 1970, pp.141-164.

Casti, J., Connectivity, Complexity, and Resilience in Complex Ecosystems, *Proceedings IFAC Conference on Bio- and Ecosystems*, Leipzig, East Germany, September 1977.

Casti, J., Kempf, J. and Duckstein, L., Lake Ecosystems: A Polyhedral Dynamics Representation, in *Ecological Modelling*, 1979.

David, L. and Duckstein, L., Multi-Criterion Ranking of Alternative Long-Range Water Resource Systems, *Water Resources Bulletin*, vol.13, August 1977, pp.731-754.

Duckstein, L. and Opricovic, S., Multiobjective Optimization in River Basin Development, Working Paper No. 77-41, Systems and Industrial Engineering Dept., University of Arizona, Tuscon, Arizona, 1977.

Duckstein, L., Imbedding Uncertainties into Multi-Objective Decision Making, paper presented at the International Symposium on Risk and Reliability in Water Resources, June 1978, Waterloo, Ontario, SIE Working Paper No. 78-21.

Kaufman, A., *Introduction to the Theory of Fuzzy Subsets - Vol. 1*, Academic Press, New York, 1975.

Kempf, J., Polyhedral Dynamics Applied to the Harbour Landing Problem, SIE Working Paper No. 78-36, 1977.

Kempf, J., Duckstein, L and Casti, J., Polyhedral Dynamics and Fuzzy Sets as a Multicriteria Decision Making Aid, paper presented at the Joint TIMS/ORSA Conference, New Orleans, Louisiana, April 1979.

Kochan, M. and Badre, A., On the Precision of Adjectives which Denote Fuzzy Sets, *Journal of Cybernetics*, vol.4, no.1, 1974, pp.49-59.

Keeney, R.L., Multiplicative Utility Functions, *Operations Research*, vol.22, no.1, 1974.

Keeney, R.L. and Wood, E., An Illustrative Example of the Use of Multiattribute Utility Theory for Water Resources Planning, *Water Resources Research*, vol.13, 1977, pp.705-719.

Luce, R.D. and Raiffa, H., *Games and Decisions: Introduction and Critical Survey*, John Wiley, New York, 1957.

Nijkamp, P., Stochastic Quantitative and Qualitative Multicriteria Analysis for Environmental Design, *Papers of the Regional Science Association*, vol.39, 1977, pp.175-199.

Nijkamp, P. and Vos, J., Multicriteria Analysis for Water Resource and Land Use Development, *Water Resources Research*, vol.13, 1977, pp.523-518.

Roy, B. and Bertier, P., *La Méthode ELECTRE II*, Note de Travail, no. 142, Direction Scientifique, Groupe Metra, April 1971.

Roy, B., A Conceptual Framework for a Prescriptive Theory of Decision-Aid in: Starr, M. and Zeleny M. (eds.), *Multiple Criteria Decision Making*, North-Holland, Amsterdam, 1977.

Starr, M. and Zeleny M., MCDM-State and Future of the Arts in: Starr, M. and Zeleny, M. (eds.), *Multiple Criteria Decision Making*, North-Holland, Amsterdam, 1977, pp.179-210.

Yu, P., Decision Dynamics with an Application to Persuasion and Negotiation, in: Starr, M. and Zeleny, H. (eds.), *Multiple Criteria Decision Making*, North-Holland, Amsterdam, 1977, pp.159-177.

Zadeh, L., Outline of a New Approach to the Analysis of Complex Systems and Decision Processes, *IEEE Transations on Systems, Man, and Processes*, SMC-3, vol.28, 1973.

Zeleny, M., *Linear Multiobjective Programming*, Ph.D Dissertation, Columbia University, Graduate School of Management, New York, 1972.

Zeleny, M., Adaptive Displacement of Preferences in Decision Making, in: Starr, M. and Zeleny, M. (eds.), *Multiple Criteria Decision Making*, North-Holland, Amsterdam, 1977.

Acknowledgements

We would like to thank the Institut Wasserbau III, Universität Karlsruhe and Prof.Dr. E. Plate for institutional support, without which it would have been impossible to conduct this research.

7 Financial Resource Allocation in a Decentralized Urban System

B. Bona, D. Merighi and A. Ostanello-Borreani

7.1. INTRODUCTION

The political problems that rise regarding the choice of different social investments in a metropolitan area are not only complicated by different and often opposed interests, usually large and entangled ones, but also by the presence of technical difficulties. The problem of distributing a given amount of financial resources, assigned by a Public Investment Program, is usually solved through the following procedure:

(a) the technical offices of the municipality evaluate 'sectoral needs' (i.e. needs of services in specific sectors as health care, education);
(b) for every category of service units, qualitative and quantitative standards and costs are identified;
(c) budget percentage for every sector is established in a 'rational way' (here 'rationality' means taking into account 'objective needs', pressures and the ability of every executive administrator to put into evidence the importance of his own sector);
(d) once every sectoral budget has been defined, the subsequent structure localizations are decided by technical and political decision-makers.

In this way, possible heavy difficulties of investments on a structure in some area (due, for instance, to lack of physical space) are surmounted by allocating elsewhere the funds, in the same sector. This kind of procedure hardly permits a balancing of service structures among the metropolitan districts; on the contrary, usually the gap between one zone and another has a tendency to increase. The 'participation' in decisions works only in a negative way, in the sense that in several cases it does not permit the most evident misuse of land by private and public speculators. In this context the 'social demand' can be regarded as a bunch of different group interests, not related to each other and which cannot be compared, mainly because a common 'unit of measure' does not exist. This unit of measure means, above all, a common information basis and also the widespread knowledge of objectives and criteria which are taken into account, when different zonal situations or different sectorial interests are compared.

In a big metropolitan area of northern Italy, the technical staff of the municipality is trying to organize the investment planning and programming on the basis of a 'participative procedure': this means that objectives, criteria and meaning of the used statistical data must be discussed and shared between political administrators and the community; the latter can be in disagreement with the former; in this case the central authority, which has the actual decisional power, assumes all the political responsibilities of a choice. These elements will give rise, however, to a common 'unit of measure' and this latter will be, at least indirectly, accepted by every participating group as far as the information basis is rigorous, and the democratic process, through which the choices are made, is transparent.

The main objective of the Investment Programming Plan (IPP) is to reach 'zonal balancing', officially prescribed by a new regional law, which has been widely accepted. The different phases towards its attainment have been identified. The objective can obviously be reached by successive steps through a process, whose first phase is still experienced (it will be called the 'transition phase').

According to this aim, a first problem is that of sharing a given amount of public financial resources with territorial districts, instead of intervening sectors. This means that the IPP needs availability of data for aggregated zonal needs, which must not be a simple summation of sectorial needs in every district, built up in a traditional way.

Following this objective, a research project, called SBA (Social Balance of Area), has been started. This project is intended as an instrument of knowledge, organically included in the IPP and constructed with the interested community.

The work reported in this paper has been conducted within the SBA activities, during the transition phase of the process. A model for the allocation of public resources has been built, based on a constant and direct connection with the decision-makers, who strongly contribute to its solution. The validity of the model, experienced through its actual application, is tied up with a real participation of the decision-makers, both in the formal setting of the model and in the definition of the decisional parameters. The model is articulated into three parts: 1) analysis of the 'demand', 2) analysis of the 'offer', 3) distribution model, such as described in the following sections, together with the actual application.

The modelling phases have been strongly connected with each other within an interdisciplinary research group: definition of 'needs' (either existing or emerging or latent) was related to the identification of institutional service structures; the choice of the operational model was both a reason for the settlement of the first two models and a consequence of these and of the preference attitude of the central decision-maker (see Figure 7.1).

DEMAND	POPULATION ANALYSIS - Formal definition of a set of indicators, F_h and of their evaluation scales, E_h
OFFER	SERVICES ANALYSIS - Formal definition of a set of criteria, Ω_i and of their evaluation scales, O_i
FUNDS DISTRIBUTION	- Preferences: standards, decisional parameters - Operational model

Figure 7.1. Modelling phases

The structure of the modelling process for the assessment of the demand and offer indicators sets is reported in Figure 7.2.

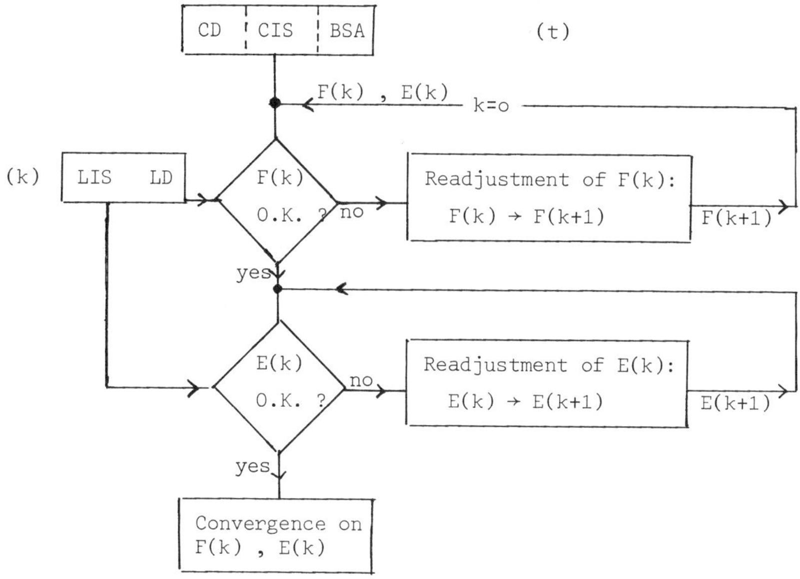

Figure 7.2. Modelling of the demand and offer indicators

Following the IPP, two levels of processes are recognized: a long run process, (t), and a short run process, (k).

Notations

F(k) = indicators set at (k)

E(k) = evaluation scales at (k)

CD = Central Decision-Makers

LD = Local Decision-Makers

CIS = Central Information System

LIS = Local Information System

7.2. ANALYSIS OF THE DEMAND

In this modelling phase, a set of indicators that gives a consistent description of the demand in each district is constructed. The demand must be represented not only quantitatively, but also qualitatively, in order to describe the characteristics of the population which has the most severe and impelling needs. Those needs are referred to the different kinds of services, existing or on the point of being introduced.

It has been assumed, for modelling purposes, that the adopted indicators are to be divided into two sets:

a) those expressing a 'global' demand for zonal services, depending on the social and economical conditions of the local community (sets F_i, F_W of Figure 7.3).

b) those expressing a demand for specific services (set F_C).

A model for the construction of demand indicators is sketched in Figure 7.3.

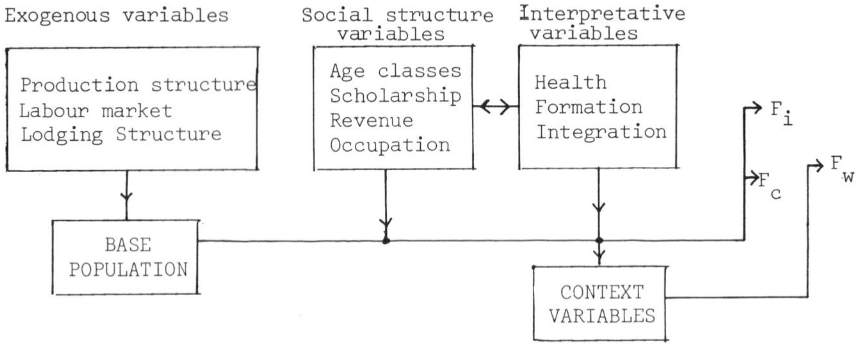

Figure 7.3. Model for the construction of demand indicators

On the basis of such criteria as level of significance, evaluability (qualitative and quantitative) and exhaustivity, a final set of indicators has been actually adopted. This set permits the construction of a 'demand profile' for each zone (see Roy and Bertier (1972)), which can be used as a graphical model of the aggregated evaluation for a multidimensional zonal demand (zones are therefore compared through their profiles).

Such a comparison can be conducted in a formal way by a multicriteria classification procedure; in our case the Electre II method (Roy and Bertier (1972)), has been applied.

In this application, the metropolitan area is divided into 20 districts, with resident population ranging from 35.000 to 100.000 units. The population has been analysed through six classes of age (0-2 years, 3-5 years, 6-14 years, 15-18 years, 19-65 years, more than 65 years); for every class, several subgroups of population with particular socio-economical conditions, and therefore particular needs, have been recognized. The final set of 25 indicators has been assessed; they can be put into four different groups such as:

1) growth indicators, evaluated on forecasted population (7 indicators);
2) birth indicators (2);
3) social indicators (9);
4) indicators for the elderly age (7); (to be found in Comune di Milano (1978)).

7.3. ANALYSIS OF THE OFFERED SERVICES

The analysis has been conducted on public facilities, which are designed for local community, existing in each district. These are described sector by sector with a set of 12 indicators, constructed in

Age	Services											
	1	2	3	4	5	6	7	8	9	10	11	12
0-2	x			x	x		x	x		x		
3-5		x		x	x		x	x		x		
6-14			x	x	x		x	x		x	x	
15-18				x	x	x	x	x		x	x	
19-65				x	x	x		x		x	x	x
>65				x	x	x		x	x	x	x	x

Figure 7.4. Correspondence between age classes and services

order to also take into account some of the qualitative aspects of the supplied services. Each indicator is referred to a class of services addressed to the same group of consumers, as shown in Figure 7.4, with the characteristic that the central decision-maker can assign equal investments to every 'insufficient' service of the same class. In the application, the analyzed sectors are:

- social and health care sector;
- education sector;
- cultural and free-time sector.

The indicators (henceforth called services) have been constructed interactively with sector experts and decision-makers. They have been called respectively: Nidi (crèches: 0-2 years); Scuola materna (nursery school: 3-5 years); Scuola dell'obbligo (compulsory school); Verde Pubblico (public green areas); Sport (sport facilities); Consultori familiari, ostetrici, centri oncologici (family problems advisory centres, osthetrical aid centres, oncological centres); SIMEE (mental care services for the evolutive age); Servizio sociale (social services); Anziani (elderly people); Consigli di zona (zone councils); Servizio socio-culturali (socio-cultural services); Centri civici (civic centres).

Their assessment has been conditioned by the availability as well as the updating of data, and by explicit and particular requests of local decision-makers. Special attention has been devoted to the definition of the scale (see Table 7.1).

For each service, i, a reference level called 'standard' S_i has been defined, which indicates a goal achievement level, equal for every district. This standard can either be defined by laws, national or regional, or by a compromise value, representing a short-term goal. The service standard S_i has been modified into 'local standards' S_{ij}, suitable to represent the particular situation of zone j.

7.4. THE MODEL FOR FUNDS DISTRIBUTION

In each district and for every service, the model evaluates the 'unsatisfaction level' with respect to zonal standards S_{ij}. This level is transformed into an 'investment value' requested to meet the unsatisfied demand.

7.4.1. *Model parameters and notations*

$I = \{i : i=1,2,\ldots,12\}$ index set of services

$J = \{j : j=1,2,\ldots,20\}$ index set of zones

a) 'Objective' parameters:

Ω_i = indicator of the i-th service

$O_{ij} = \Omega_i(j)$ = evaluation of the j-th zone on the i-th indicator

S_i = standard for the i-th service

U_{ij} = units of demand, i.e. global amount of population (from different age classes) potentially asking for the i-th service in zone j.

b) 'Characterizing' parameters:

U^c_{ij} = units of characterizing demand for service i, in zone j; it indicates the amount of potential users who need a higher qualitative level of specific services.

K_i = decisional parameter for the i-th service; it indicates the factor by which the standard S_i ought to be multiplied, if the entire amount of potential users is characterized, i.e. $U_{ij} = U^c_{ij}$.

q_{ij} = 'qualification index'; it depends on U^c_{ij} and K_i and transforms the standard S_i into S_{ij}.

S_{ij} = 'zonal standard'.

d_{ij} = 'unsatisfied demand' for service i in zone j; it gives a conventional amount of people that, potentially asking for a zonal service, would not be satisfied by the present service level.

c) 'Response' parameters:

r_i = 'response standard' for service i. This parameter always indicates a standard for physical structures relative to a given fraction of users, even when the demand implies a different kind of intervention; for this reason it is possible that r_i and S_i will be expressed with different units of measure (see Table 7.1).

c_i = 'unit cost' of the physical structure assumed as a response for the i-th service demand.

$w = (w_j)$, $j \in J$, = 'zonal weights'; decisional parameters defining intervention priorities in zones.

d) Funds shares:

D_{ij} = global demand for service i in zone j; it expresses the amount of funds that should be necessary to assign to the j-th zone in order to build physical structures to meet the unsatisfied demand in zone j.

D_j = global demand of investments in the j-th zone.

7.4.2. *The model*

The model is interactive: the central decision-maker introduces response decisional parameters at different steps, as shown in the flowchart of Figure 7.5.

Step 1. It is assumed that the standard S_i cannot be the same in every district, because of the different characteristics of the community. The value S_i is therefore transformed into S_{ij}, taking into account the qualification index q_{ij}:

$$S_{ij} = q_{ij} S_i \tag{7.1}$$

The qualification index has been defined as follows:

$$q_{ij} = \frac{1}{1 + \left(\frac{1}{K_i} - 1\right) \frac{U^c_{ij}}{U_{ij}}} \qquad i \in I,\ j \in I \qquad K_i > 0 \tag{7.2}$$

where $q_{ij} = 1$ for $U^c_{ij} = 0$ or $K_i = 1$; $q_{ij} = K_i$ for $U^c_{ij} = U_{ij}$.

Step 2. The following formula evaluates the parameter d_{ij} which measures the number of 'unsatisfied potential users'.

$$D_{ij} = U_{ij} \left(\frac{S_{ij} - O_{ij}}{S_{ij}}\right) \tag{7.3}$$

Step 3. An aggregation of d_{ij}'s, in each zone, is searched in order to achieve a global information of the unsatisfied demand. It has to be stressed that: (1) d_{ij} has been calculated in order to assign funds and it must therefore be linked with the intervention costs; (2) this intervention is different from one service to another, both in type and quantity, according to the constraints and the preferences of the central decision-maker (CD). Therefore CD is requested to fix two different paramaters: r_i and c_i.

- r_i represents both type and quantity of the service CD intends to assign for a fraction of unsatisfied users; this being of course a conventional response, because it translates in terms of physical structures a request only partially due to the lack of these ones;
- c_i is the cost parameter; it is fixed in order to take into account the quality of the service, in the sense that it can be implicitly increased in order to satisfy, at least partially, this crucial aspect of the demand.

It is possible to have a local value of r_i by the relation

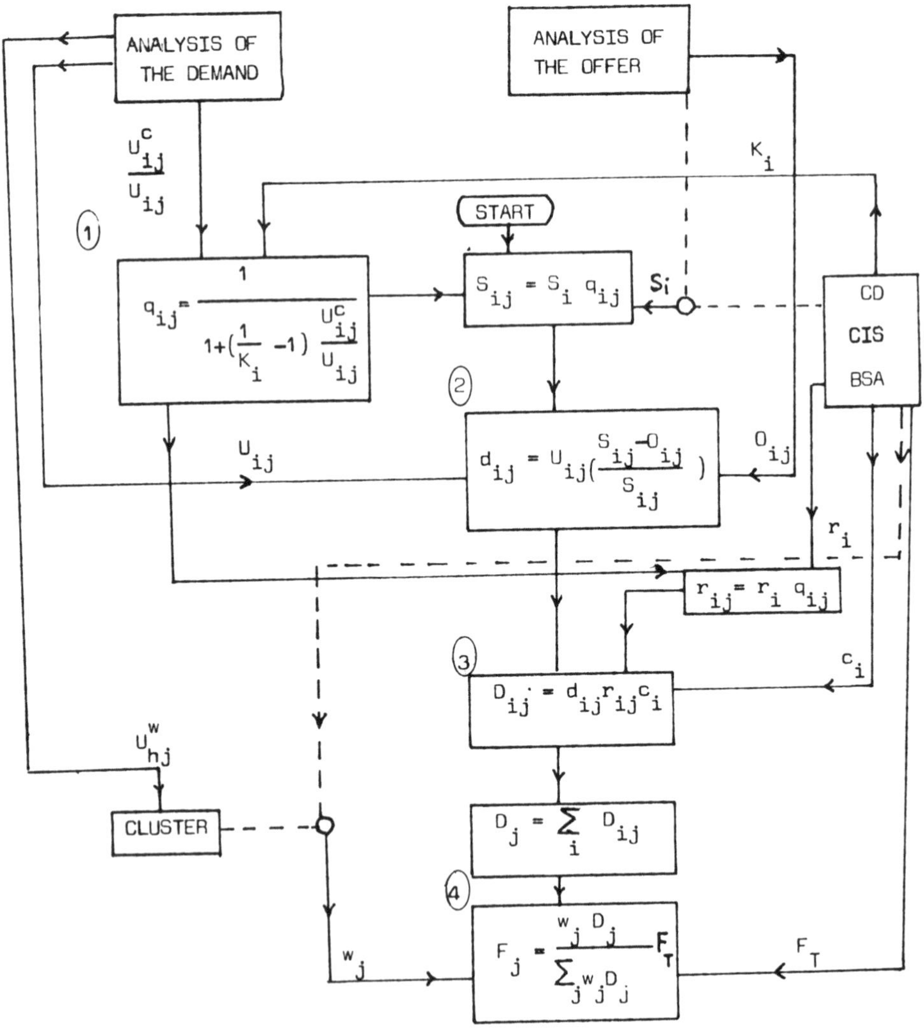

Figure 7.5. Flow chart of the funds sharing model

$$r_{ij} = q_{ij}\, r_i \, . \qquad (7.4)$$

An evaluation of funds, for zone j on service i, can be given by

$$D_{ij} = d_{ij}\, r_{ij}\, c_i \; ; \qquad (7.5)$$

and a global value of investments, by

$$D_j = \sum_i D_{ij}, \qquad (7.6)$$

or better, when the services are at different levels of priority p_i, by

$$D_j = \sum_i p_i\, D_{ij} \; , \text{ where } \sum_i p_i = 1. \qquad (7.7)$$

In Table 7.1 the response values of CD are reported for each service (different units of measure for S_i and r_i can be seen). In Table 7.2, the evaluated values of D_{ij} are reported, normalized to 100, corresponding to the maximal zonal request in that particular service. Rows represent zones, columns represent the assumed services' indicators.

Step 4. As said in Section 7.2, the set of the demand indicators was divided into two groups; the first group, including general discomfort indicators, F_w, is used in this phase to build zonal weights w_j in the following way:

(a) on the basis of the indicators' values, a comparative analysis of the districts is performed (for instance, with a cluster analysis) to identify homogeneous classes;

(b) the results of this analysis are reported to the decision-maker, who is asked to give 'weights' w_j (whose meaning can be defined as the 'priority of intervention recognized to the j-th zone, after having checked its global situation').

Assessment of the zonal weights; the indicators adopted for our analysis are:

- percentage of families, with income lower than a certain level, compared to the number of families in the zone;
- percentage of illiterate people compared to the total zonal population;
- percentage of residents in houses, with more than a certain level of degrading, compared to the total zonal population;
- percentage of workers, having more than 30 minutes' house-work travel.

Two methods of clustering have been applied; a standard non-hierarchical procedure (see Anderberg (1972)), and a fuzzy similarity based procedure (see Bona (1978)). Four classes have been obtained, whose 'mean profiles' are reported in Figure 7.6, together with the mean metropolitan levels. The examination of the data structure has been confirmed through an application of the Electre II method (see Roy (1975) and Bona et al. (1976)), using the same indicators.

The results have been discussed with CD, who decided that the two intermediate classes (class II and III of Figure 7.6) had to be merged.

Table 7.1
Responses of the central decision-maker

Services	S_i	K_i	r_i
1. Nidi	55 places / 100 users	1.82	0.9 unit / 100 users
2. Scuola Materna	70 places / 100 users	1.43	2.3 unit / 100 users
3. Scuola Obbligo	100 places / 100 users	1.0	4.0 classes / 100 users
4. Verde Pubblico	6 mq/user	1.50	6.0 mq/user
5. Sport	25 daily places / 1000 users	2.0	25 daily places / 1000 users
6. Consultori	4 clerk unit / 10000 users	2.0	0.67 unit / 10000 users
7. SIMEE	310 hour service / 10000 users	2.0	1.0 service unit / 10000 users
8. Servizio Sociale	0.67 clerk unit / 10000 users	2.0	0.33 service unit / 10000 users
9. Anziani	-	-	80.0 mc/U^c users
10. Consigli Zona	-	-	400 mq(up to 50000) +20 mq(up to +10000)
11. Servizi Socio-Culturali	455 mq/10000 users	-	455 mq/10000 users
12. Centri Civici	-	-	1 unit / zone

Table 7.2.
Values of D_{ij} (percentage of the maximal value)

	Services											
Zones	1	2	3	4	5	6	7	8	9	10	11	12
1	73.73	11.14	0.0	0.0	86.02	42.86	48.94	88.24	100	66.67	84.55	100
2	69.19	0.0	23.04	70.72	66.36	78.15	54.26	64.71	53.90	88.89	65.45	100
3	53.72	0.0	0.0	59.41	43.67	57.14	0.0	29.41	58.23	22.22	53.64	100
4	63.66	41.55	100	60.33	58.16	40.34	28.72	70.59	62.82	66.67	37.27	100
5	66.40	0.0	0.0	59.41	51.30	73.95	42.87	52.94	57.05	66.67	63.64	100
6	100	100	71.91	100	100	100	71.28	94.12	87.65	44.44	100	100
7	35.94	32.44	0.0	30.69	30.17	31.93	15.96	17.65	21.83	33.33	29.09	100
8	38.05	0.0	0.0	20.02	26.46	7.56	46.81	5.83	18.14	44.44	10.31	0.0
9	98.26	0.0	0.0	45.84	29.47	16.81	12.77	23.53	25.66	55.56	46.64	100
10	97.43	47.25	0.0	86.29	67.45	84.03	100	68.82	58.11	88.89	81.82	50
11	91.47	48.95	21.16	96.63	82.09	91.60	97.87	100	99.55	77.78	97.27	100
12	27.98	0.0	0.0	19.41	30.71	26.89	7.45	11.76	16.48	77.78	80.00	100
13	15.52	0.0	0.0	14.16	11.45	2.52	16.96	0.0	11.84	44.44	23.04	100
14	64.56	0.0	0.0	62.79	44.62	46.22	50.00	41.18	53.37	55.56	47.27	100
15	35.90	0.0	0.0	44.48	30.98	44.54	34.04	17.65	30.95	33.33	33.68	0.0
16	40.86	0.0	0.0	15.26	37.44	31.09	34.04	23.53	20.74	44.44	23.64	50
17	79.51	0.0	24.49	62.07	54.94	62.18	70.21	68.82	57.98	55.56	58.18	100
18	74.44	0.0	0.0	54.08	47.43	52.10	68.09	41.18	32.12	100	30.91	50
19	20.63	0.0	0.0	61.51	55.87	62.10	61.70	68.82	52.30	88.89	57.27	100
20	77.61	0.0	0.0	80.26	72.35	52.10	60.64	47.08	53.92	14.44	36.36	0.0
M.V.	60.25	14.07	12.03	51.67	51.33	49.71	46.33	45.29	48.61	60.00	50.91	77.50

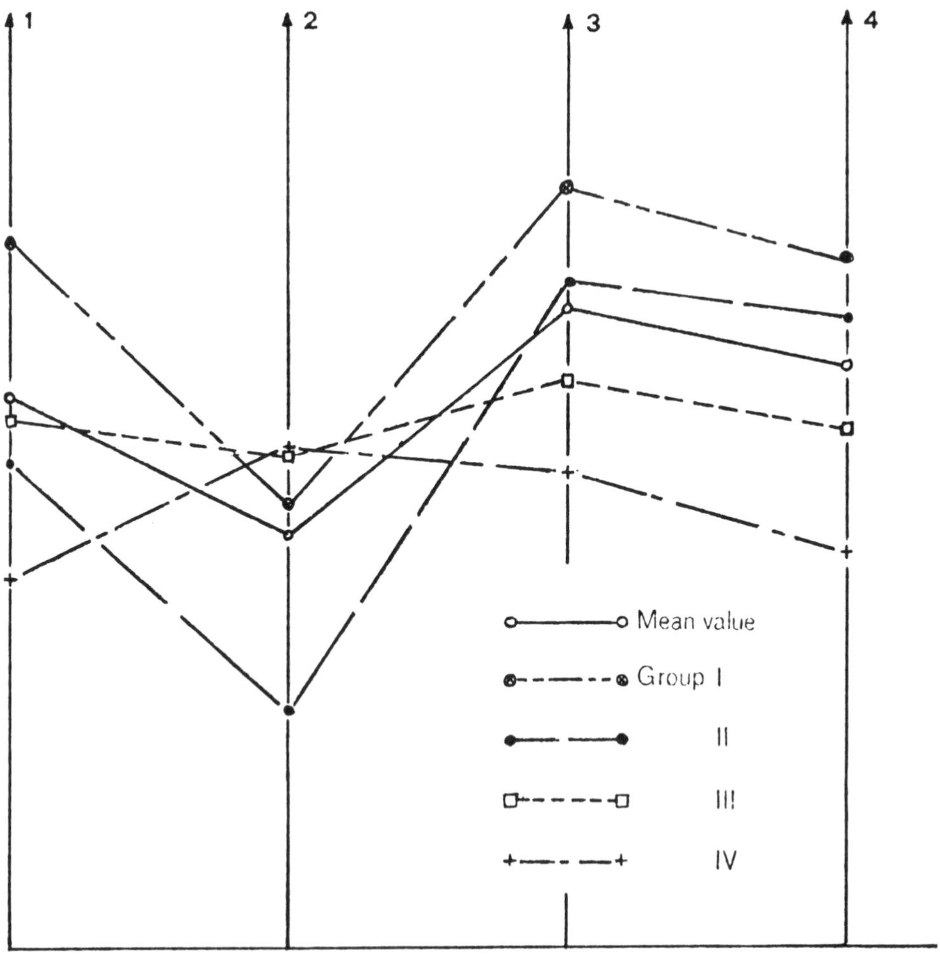

Figure 7.6. Mean profiles of the classes of zones

Table 7.3
Funds sharing between zones (F_T = 50 x 50^9 Italian lire)

zones	F_j	%	per capita
+ 1	1.385	2.77	11˙803 lire
2	2.875	5.75	32˙043
+ 3	1.605	3.21	22˙220
4	2.760	5.52	38˙181
5	2.720	5.44	31˙047
+ 6	3.190	6.38	23˙561
* 7	1.975	3.95	48˙601
* 8	1.795	3.59	34˙036
9	1.335	2.67	21˙998
* 10	5.065	10.13	44˙450
+ 11	3.080	6.16	23˙387
12	1.115	2.23	27˙199
13	.655	1.31	20˙267
14	2.560	5.12	31˙551
* 15	2.140	4.03	33˙884
* 16	2.030	4.06	37˙942
17	3.040	6.08	29˙092
* 18	3.560	7.12	39˙494
19	2.740	5.48	24˙889
* 20	4.335	8.67	40˙457

(+) : zones of the class III

(*) : zones of the class I

Three classes have been retained:

Class I : zones with a high discomfort (7 zones)
Class II : zones with a medium discomfort (9 zones)
Class III: zones with a relatively low discomfort (4 zones)

The decision-maker assigned the following interval values to the w_j:

j=I,II,III : w_I = 75-1000; w_{II} = 50-75; w_{III} = 25-50.

For each class a punctual evaluation of weights, on the above intervals, has then been assigned to each zone, on the basis of two other secondary indicators: a first one, which takes into account the total amount of services, private and public not considered as zonal ones (and therefore not included in the previous analysis), and a second one connected with the presence of those 'cultural centres' not necessarily to be considered as 'services'.

The partition of funds F_j, to be assigned to the zone j, has been actually calculated by (7.6) and (7.8):

$$F_j = \frac{w_j D_j}{\sum_j w_j D_j} F_T \qquad (7.8)$$

where F_T is the global amount of funds to be distributed.

The solution obtained (reported in Table 7.3) has been discussed with the central decision-maker who followed the whole project and in an official public meeting with the local decision-makers (see Comune di Milano (1978)), accepted with only minor criticisms.

7.5. CONCLUSIONS

The method presented in this paper is a result of several approaches of formalization for the funds assignment problem in the transitory phase of the Investments Programming Plan. Other more sophisticated models, with a higher degree of formalism, such as goal programming models, as were proposed initially, have been strongly criticized by the decision-maker: the mathematical formalism, being difficult to understand (see the use of the model as a 'language') would not allow a real and constructive contribution from his part. Other kinds of models, mainly based on subjective evaluations, for the reduction of the difference between offer and demand of services, have been rejected. The method presented here is based on a direct and constant connection between model builders and decision-makers, who give a contribution to the construction of the final solution: the 'objective' data are always elaborated and 'corrected' on the basis of subjective evaluations.

The model validity, proved in the application actually performed, is based on a real participation of the community, or at least on its representatives. They have approved the structure of the model and have developed a critical activity both on the choice of the indicators and their evaluations, and on the definition of the decisional parameters.

7.6. REFERENCES

Anderberg, M.R., *Cluster Analysis for Applications*, Academic Press,

New York, 1973.
Bauer, R.A., *Social Indicators*, MIT Press, Cambridge, 1966.
Bona, B., Town District Classification Using a Fuzzy Multicriteria Similarity Relation, *System Science*, vol.4, no.3, 1978
Bona, B., Giorgi, N., Minini, U., Orlando, E. and Ostanello, A., An Application of a Multicriteria Model to the Diagnosis of Services in Homogeneous Zones of the town of Torino (in Italian), Tech. Report no. 2,3, Politechnico di Torino, 1976.
Charnes, A. and Cooper, W., *Management Models and Industrial Applications of Linear Programming*, Wiley, New York, 1961.
Comune di Milano, I Bilanci Sociali di Area, Rapporto ai Consigli di Zona (in Italian), C. Milano 13/12/1978.
Montgolfier, J. de, and Bertier, P., *Approche Multicritère des Problèmes de Décision*, Edition Hommes et Techniques, Paris, 1978.
OECD, Measuring Social Well-Being: A Progress Report on the Development of Social Indicators, Paris, Jan. 1976.
Roy, B., Vers une Méthodologie Générale d'Aide à la Décision, *Metra*, vol. 13, no.2, 1975.
Roy, B. and P. Bertier, La Méthode ELECTRE II, Proceedings of the VII Conference on Operations Research, Dublin, 1972.
Togsverd, T., Multilevel Planning of Public Services, in M. Thiriez and Zionts, S. (eds.), Multiple Criteria Decision Making, Springer-Verlag, Berlin, 1976.
U.S. Department of Commerce, Report on Statistics for Allocation of Funds-Statistical Policy, Working Paper 1, Office of Federal Statistical Policy and Standards, March 1978.
V.V.A.A., Documentazione BSA (in Italian), Ufficio Studi Decentramento, Comune di Milano, Milano 1977-78.
V.V.A.A., Città Classe - F. Angeli, vol.V, no.18, March 1979.

Acknowledgements

This work has been supported by the Ufficio Studi Decentramento-Comune di Milano, and conducted within the GNAGA-CNR and CENS, Italy.

8 Separable Goal Programming

S. M. Lee and A. J. Wynne

8.1. INTRODUCTION

The simplex-based algorithm developed by Dantzig for solving linear programming problems converges on a solution set in a finite number of iterations. Unfortunately, the nature of general nonlinear programming problems does not allow the direct application of the simplex algorithm for finding optimum solutions. The optimal solution for nonlinear-programming problems can either be any point found by searching along a curved boundary hypersurface of the feasible solution space, or it can be any point within the feasible solution space. According to Simmons (1975; 271), this approach 'requires a complicated parameterization of variables that is likely to be computationally prohibitive'.

Presently, there is no general or universal approach for efficiently solving all general classes of nonlinear-programming problems (see for instance Hillier and Lieberman (1974), Loomba and Turban (1974) and Taha (1976)). The classical solution approaches that utilize calculus provide good results for problems with a small number of variables and second order polynomials. Real-world problems characteristically have a large number of variables and polynomials with third and higher order arguments. Consequently, the classical methods are not adequate for solving practical problems of any great magnitude.

There is evidence that suggests that the most promising approach to solving nonlinear programming problems is the transformation of the original nonlinear programming problem into an acceptable form that permits the application of the linear programming simplex algorithm (see Thierauf (1970; 221)). The simplex algorithm has proved to be the most powerful procedure for solving linearly constrained problems.

Among the various simplex-based algorithms for solving nonlinear programming problems such as geometric programming, quadratic programming and separable programming, the separable programming technique developed by Charnes and Lemke (1954) and later extended by Miller (1963), is of primal importance in the development of this paper. The main reason for the attractiveness of separable programming is that through the modification of the simplex algorithm, the piecewise linear approximation of the original nonlinear problem can be solved fast and efficiently.

Separable programming, in theory, may obtain solutions to any type of nonlinear-programming problem by means of piecewise linear approximations. Essentially, separable programming transforms the original nonlinear function into a linear combination of several single-variable subfunctions to be approximated by a linear function. The problems can then be solved by the standard linear programming simplex algorithm with restricted basis modification.

Separable programming is not without limitations. The limitations of separable programming include such restrictions as: (i) the basic assumptions that are implicit in the standard linear programming model (i.e., linearity, additivity, deterministic, proportionality, divisibility, non-negativity and the single-criteria objective function explicitly expressed in numeric terms), (ii) convexity of the feasible area to ensure global optima, (iii) all nonlinear expressions must be separable functions, (iv) the objective function must be convex in the case of minimization and concave for maximization and (v) the increased number of variables and constraints in the revised formulation.

The one limitation of separable nonlinear programming that has not been fully explored and dealt with is the assumption of a single-criteria objective function of either maximizing profit or minimizing cost. To date, the most effective approach to solving multicriteria decision problems appears to be goal programming. Unlike linear programming where a unidimensional objective function with a single measure of effectiveness is optimized, goal programming strives to satisfice an ordinal system of priorities that are assigned to various goals by the decision-maker. Given a complex array of decision problems, the organizational goals are more often than not found to be incommensurable, multiple and conflicting. Thus, this inability to measure the relative importance of each goal's effectiveness in terms of a commensurable criterion reduces the usefulness of linear programming in solving decision problems with a multitude of objectives.

The purpose of this paper is to illustrate an approach for extending the capabilities of goal programming to include a class of multicriteria decision-making problems that are subject to nonlinear systems and goal constraints. A separable goal programming algorithm is derived by adapting the goal programming algorithm by Lee (1972), to the standard separable nonlinear programming technique with restricted basis entry conditions. The separable goal programming model is based on the pre-emptive priority factors which generalize the model and enable it to effectively analyze multiple conflicting objectives in the decision-making process.

8.2. SEPARABLE GOAL PROGRAMMING (SGP) MODEL

The general SGP model can be expressed as follows:

$$\text{Minimize } A = \sum_{k=0}^{K} \sum_{i=1}^{m} p_k (w_i^{k-} d_i^- + w_i^{k+} d_i^+)$$

$$\text{subject to} \quad \sum_{j=1}^{n} g_i(x_j) + d_i^- - d_i^+ = b_i \qquad i=1,\ldots,m \qquad (8.1)$$

$$x_j,\ d_i^-,\ d_i^+ \geq 0 \qquad i=1,\ldots,m;\ j=1,\ldots,n$$

where x_j are (1 x 1) singular separable decision variables; g_i is a (m_i x 1) vectors of deviational variables for the m goal constraints; P_k

is the $(1 \times m_i)$ vector of pre-emptive priority factors; w_i^{k-} and w_i^{k+} are $(m_i \times 1)$ vectors of differential weights attached to the deviational weights d_i^- and d_i^+ at priority level k, respectively; and b_i is the $(m_i \times 1)$ vector of limited resources for the i constraints.

The general SGP model formulation (2.1) is not readily employable in its present canonical form. Further refinement is needed. First, consideration must be given to the type of linear approximations that should be made to the separable functions $g_i(x_j)$. The approach used in this paper is the piecewise linear approximation, or polygonal approximation. Two piecewise linear SGP models are derived in this paper. The first case derived is the single variable model and the second, the case where more than one variable exists in the model.

(A) Single variable piecewise linear approximation model

The basic concept of the polygonal approximation method is to closely approximate a nonlinear function by a set of linear line segments. Consider the continuous single variable nonlinear function illustrated in Figure 8.1. Define $\hat{f}(x)$ such that $\hat{g}_i(x) \simeq g_i(x)$ for any point along the line segments, and:

$$\hat{g}_i(x) = g_i(x) \tag{8.2}$$

at the end points of any line segment.

Utilizing the analytical geometry relationship in (8.3) below, any straight line segment used to approximate the original nonlinear function can be expressed in algebraic terms if any two points on the line are known:

$$\hat{g}_i(x) = g_i(x_r) + [(g_i(x_{r+1}) - g(x_r)) \;/\; (x_{r.1} - x_r)]\,(x - x_r) \tag{8.3}$$

$$x_r \leq x \leq x_{r+1} \qquad\qquad r=0,\ldots,t$$

The subscripts r and r+1 identify consecutive end points within the domain of interest, and t is the number of breakpoints used to designate the t-1 line segments for approximating the nonlinear function.

To facilitate the representation of $\hat{f}(x)$ as one rather than t-1 subfunctions, a conversion of the expression (8.3) is necessary. Examining (8.3) shows that the fraction $(x-x_r) \;/\; (x_{r+1} - x_r)$ is a real number between 0 and 1 for any value of x between x_r and x_{r+1}. Let us define this fraction as λ such that:

$$\begin{aligned}\hat{g}_i(x) &= g_i(x_r) + \lambda\,[g_i(x_{r+1}) - g_i(x_r)]\\ &= g_i(x_r) + \lambda\, g_i(x_{r+1}) - \lambda\, g_i(x_r)\\ &= (1-\lambda)\, g_i(x_r) + \lambda\, g_i(x_{r+1}) \quad r=0,\ldots,t\end{aligned} \tag{8.4}$$

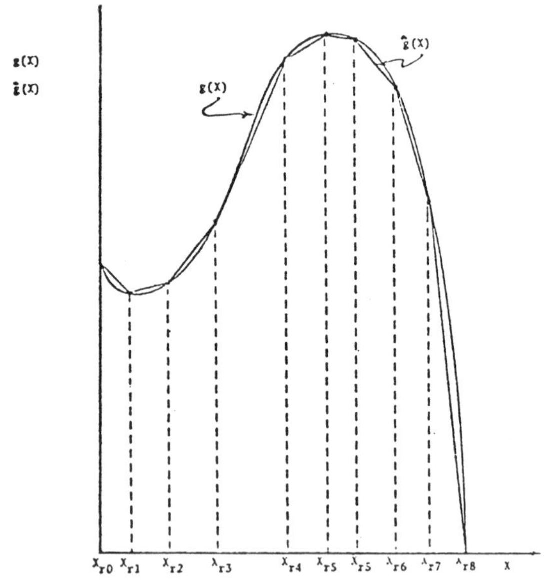

Figure 8.1. Piecewise linear approximation of a single variable continuous function $\hat{g}_i(x) \simeq g_i(x)$

Designating $\lambda = \lambda_{r+1}$ and $1 - \lambda$ as λ_r, expression (8.4) can be rewritten as:

$$\hat{g}_i(x) = \lambda_r g_i(x_r) + \lambda_{r+1} g_i(x_{r+1})$$
$$x_r \leq x \leq x_{r+1} \qquad r=0,\ldots,t \qquad (8.5)$$

where:

$$\lambda_r + \lambda_{r+1} = 0 \qquad r=0,\ldots,t \qquad (8.6)$$

$$\lambda_r, \lambda_{r+1} \geq 0 \qquad r=0,\ldots,t \qquad (8.7)$$

Recalling that $\lambda = \lambda_{r+1}$ and $1-\lambda = \lambda_r$, and furthermore, that $(x-x_r) / (x_{r+1}-x_r) = \lambda$, expression (8.5) can be for x such that:

$$\lambda = (x-x_r) / (x_{r+1}-x_r)$$
$$\lambda (x_{r+1} - x_r) = x - x_r \qquad (8.8)$$
$$x_r - \lambda x_r + \lambda x_{r+1} = x$$
$$(1-\lambda) x_r + \lambda x_{r+1} = x$$

Allowing the equations (8.5) and (8.6) plus the condition (8.7) to take on all values of the domain of interest (i.e., $x_0,\ldots,x_t$), we can express the complete piecewise linear approximation of the separable function as the sum of the individual line functions as follows:

$$g_i(x) = \hat{g}_i(x) = \lambda_0 g_i(x_0) + \lambda_1 g_1(x_1) + \ldots + \lambda_t g_i(x_t) \qquad (8.9)$$
$$\sum_{r=0}^{t} \lambda_r g_i(x_r)$$

with the condition that:

$$\lambda_r + \lambda_{r+1} + \lambda_{r+2} + \ldots + \lambda_t = 1 \qquad (8.10)$$
$$\sum_{r=0}^{t} \lambda_r = 1,$$

and:

$$\lambda_r, \lambda_{r+1}, \ldots, \lambda_t \leq 0 \qquad (8.11)$$

The approximated value for the decision variable x then becomes the sum of the products λ_r and x_r $(r=0,\ldots,t)$ over the entire domain of interest, namely:

$$x = \lambda_r x_r + \lambda_{r+1} x_{r+1} + \lambda_{r+2} x_{r+2} + \dots + \lambda_t x_t$$

$$x = \sum_{r=0}^{t} \lambda_r x_r \qquad (8.12)$$

Incorporating the above relationships with the general goal programming model, the single variable SGP model can now be reformulated as:

$$\text{Minimize } Z = \sum_{k=0}^{K} \sum_{i=1}^{m} P_k(w_i^{k-} d_i^- + w_i^{k+} d_i^+)$$

subject to:

$$\sum_{r=0}^{t} \lambda_r g_i(x_r) + d_i^- - d_i^+ = b_i \qquad i=1,\dots,m$$

$$\sum_{r=0}^{t} \lambda_r = 1 \qquad (8.13)$$

$$x_r, \lambda_r, d_i^-, d_i^+ \geq 0 \qquad r=0,\dots,t \quad i=1,\dots,m$$

This approximation is only valid when the following two restricted basis entry conditions are imposed on the simplex algorithm:

1. at most two λ_r can appear in the basis (i.e., only two λ_r may have positive values);
2. if λ_r is positive then only an adjacent λ_r (λ_{r+1} or λ_{r-1}) is allowed to be positive.

Introduction of any variable λ_r into the basis can take place only if upon entry the remaining λ_r is an adjacent variable. For example, should λ_4 be in the basis, then λ_3 or λ_5 could enter the basis without violating the logical restrictions 1 and 2 above.

(B) Multiple variable piecewise linear approximation model

Expanding the single variable piecewise linear approximation of the SGP model to accommodate more than one variable requires several changes in the model derived in the previous section. The extension of the model (8.13) will allow for the analysis of goal and subgoal constraints with a multiple number of different decision variables.

The first step in the modification procedure assumes that each variable $x_j (j=1,\dots,n)$ is subdivided into K_j intervals. This assumption provides a unique number of intervals for each variable x_j in order to consider the special characteristics of each nonlinear function. An upper bound

S_j is specified such that if x_{jr} is the value of x_j at the rth break-point of subdivision, then:

$$0 = x_{j0} < x_{j1} < \ldots < x_{jr} < x_{jk_j} = S_j \qquad j=1,\ldots,n \qquad (8.14)$$

Special attention must be given on determining the value for each of the upperbounds S_j. These upperbound values are the maximum amount that any real decision variable x_j can assume in light of the pre-emptive priority structure. The pre-emptive priority factor relationships $p_0 >>> p_1 >>> p_2 \ldots p_j >>> p_{j+1}$ $(j=1,\ldots,P)$, implies that higher-order goals can be achieved. This concept is very important in the selection of the upperbounds for SGP problems. The maximum values for x_j are determined by evaluating each constraint in the order of their priority factors and weights. Thus, starting with the system constraints, the maximum and minimum values for the x_j separable variables are determined. Proceeding to the next highest level goal constraint, the new values obtained are compared to the previous priority level goal to determine if the new upperbound further constrains the previous minimum or maximum. The process continues until all the priority factors have been accounted for in the objective function.

In effect, this process of evaluating the upperbound values S_j, yields a 'minimum-maximum' value for each separate variable in the model. For example, assume there are four priority levels, P_0, P_1, P_2 and P_3, assigned to the deviational variables corresponding to constraints I, II, III, and IV, respectively. Beginning with the super priority p_0, we find that x_1 is constrained from being any greater than 100 in constraint I. Calculating the upperbound for the next priority, P_0, we find that x_1 is constrained from being any greater than 100 in constraint I. Calculating the upperbound for the next priority (P_1) constraint, II, the value for x_1 is constrained to 250. Comparison of the new value with the previous upperbound, in light of the pre-emptive priority structure, the maximum value remains 100 for x_1. The following priority (P_2), however, does further constrain x_1 in constraint III from being larger than 75. Since P_0 specified that the maximum value for x_1 was 100, the new maximum, $x_1 = 75$, can now be used as S_1 without violating the higher pre-emptive priority for the goals. Evaluating the last priority (P_3) constraint, IV, we find that the minimum value for x_1 is 125. However, since the previous, higher level priority constraints have constrained the maximum value of x_1 at 75, then x_1 is boxed in with a minimum and a maximum value of 75.

Recalling the approximation $\hat{g}(x) \simeq g(x)$, each function $g_{ij}(x_j)$ can now be approximated as $\hat{g}_{ij}(x_j)$ for $i=1,\ldots,m$ and $j=1,\ldots,n$. The same logical development in the previous section for the single variable piecewise linear approximation method can be used to derive the multiple variable SGP model. The corresponding relationships derived for (8.9), (8.10), (8.11) and (8.12) can be formulated as:

$$g_{ij}(x_j) \simeq \hat{g}_{ij}(x_j) = \lambda_{j0}g_{ij}(x_{j0}) + \ldots + \lambda_{jr}g_{ij}(x_{jr}) \qquad r=0,\ldots,k_j$$

$$= \sum_{j=1}^{n} \sum_{r=0}^{k} \lambda_{jr}g_{ij}(x_{jr}) \qquad i=1,\ldots,m \qquad (8.15)$$

where:

$$\lambda_{jr} + \lambda_{jr+1} + \ldots + \lambda_{jk_j} = 1$$

$$\sum_{r=0}^{k_j} \lambda_{jr_j} = 1 \qquad i=1,\ldots,n \qquad (8.16)$$

and:

$$\lambda_{jr}, \lambda_{jr+1}, \ldots, \lambda_{jk_j} \geq 0 \qquad j=1,\ldots,m \qquad (8.17)$$

Also:

$$x_j = \lambda_{jr}x_{jr} + \lambda_{jr+1}x_{jr+1} + \ldots + \lambda_{jk_j}x_{jk_j}$$

$$\sum_{r=0}^{k_j} \lambda_{jr}x_{jr} \qquad j=1,\ldots,n \qquad (8.18)$$

The complete formulation for the linear piecewise approximation SGP model with more than one variable can now be stated as:

$$\text{Minimize } Z = \sum_{p=0}^{P} \sum_{i=1}^{m} P_p (w_i^{p-} d_i^- + w_i^{p+} d_i^+) \qquad (8.19)$$

subject to:

$$\sum_{j=1}^{n} \sum_{r=0}^{k_j} \lambda_{jr}g_{ij}(x_{jr}) + d_i^- - d_i^+ = b_i \qquad i=1,\ldots,m$$

$$\sum_{r=0}^{k_j} \lambda_{jr} + d_i^- = 1 \qquad j=1,\ldots,n$$

$$\lambda_{jr}, x_{jr}, d_i^-, d_i^+ \geq 0 \qquad r=0,\ldots,k_j; \quad j=1,\ldots,n; \quad i=1,\ldots,m$$

In addition, the restricted basis entry conditions are modified to in-

Table 8.1

Piecewise linear approximation: separable nonlinear goal programming simplex tableau

C_j	V	RHS	λ_{10}	λ_{1k}	λ_{j0}	λ_{jr}	λ_{n0}	λ_{nk}	d_1^-	d_2^-	d_m^-	d_{m+1}^-	d_{m+n}^-	d_1^+	d_2^+	d_m^+
	d_1	b_1	$g_{11}(X_{10})$...	$g_{11}(X_{11})$...	$g_{1j}(X_{j0})$...	$g_{1j}(X_{jr})$...	$g_{1n}(X_{n0})$...	$g_{1n}(X_{nk})$	1					-1		
	d_2	b_2	$g_{21}(X_{20})$......	......	......	......	......	$g_{2n}(X_{nk})$		1					-1	
	.	.	.					.								
	.	.	.					.								
	.	.	.					.								
	d_m	b_m	$g_{m1}(X_{10})$......	......	$g_{mj}(X_{j0})$...	$g_{mj}(X_{jr})$...	$g_{mn}(X_{n0})$...	$g_{mn}(X_{nk})$			1					-1
P_1	d_{m+1}	1	1	1								1				
P_1	d_{m+j}	1			1	1										
P_1	d_{m+n}	1					1	1					1			
$Z_j - C_j$	P_L	U_{L0}	U_{L1}	U_{L2}	....	....	....	....	....	....	....	....	....	....	....	U_{Lh}
	.	.														
	.	.														
	.	.														
	P_1	U_{10}	U_{11}	U_{12}	....	....	....	....	....	....	....	....	....	....	....	U_{1n}

clude all λ_{jr}, such that for each j no more than two λ_{jr}'s can be the basis and only adjacent λ_{jr}'s can be positive. If for a specific j, for example j=4, there is no λ_{4r} in the solution basis, then any λ_{4r} can be a candidate for entry provided that λ_{4r} meets the improvement criterion requirement (i.e., largest Z_j-C_j value). Otherwise, the restricted basis entry conditions must be followed.

8.3. THE PIECEWISE LINEAR APPROXIMATION SEPARABLE GOAL PROGRAMMING (PLA-SGP) ALGORITHM

Now that the PLA-SGP model has been developed, the steps required to formulate the general SGP model in piecewise linear approximation is summarized in the flow chart in Figure 8.2. Utilizing the model formulation procedure outlined, the initial modified simplex tableau can be set up in the format specified in Table 8.1. The column and row headings in Table 8.1 are defined as:

- C_j : pre-emptive priority factors and the differential weights as demonstrated in the PLA-SGP model.
- Z_j-C_j : m x n matrix of simplex criterion, where m represents the number of pre-emptive priority levels and n is the total number of variables (i.e., lambdas plus deviational variables).
- V : m x 1 solution basis vector
- RHS : level of goal attainment
- P_ℓ : the ℓth priority factor in the goal structure
- $U_{\ell 0}$: the underachievement of the ℓth priority
- $U_{\ell j}$'s : the coefficients of the Z_j-C_j matrix
- L : the number of priority levels under consideration
- $g_{ij}(x_{jr})$: coefficient of the jth lambda variable in the ith row evaluated at the x_{jr} breakpoint.

The solution procedure used for the PLA-SGP model is a modified version of the standard goal programming simplex algorithm of Lee (1972). This modification is necessary for invoking the restricted basis entry conditions. The solution algorithm for the PLA-SGP is summarized in the flow chart illustrated in Figure 8.3. The solution obtained in the final tableau can be evaluated for goal attainment.

A computerized version of the PLA-SGP algorithm has been developed. The program can accommodate a total of 250 variables and 100 constraints. Included in the computation of the total number of variables are (i) the number of decision variables, (ii) the number of lambda variables, (iii) the total number of positive and negative deviational variables. The maximum number of priority levels is 10, and the maximum order of any inputted polynomial (exponent) has been set at 10. The program is written in the FORTRAN language and requires approximately 600K of real money to execute. The major transformations that are outlined above in the formulation steps are carried out automatically by the program.

Transparent to the user of the program is the automatic construction of

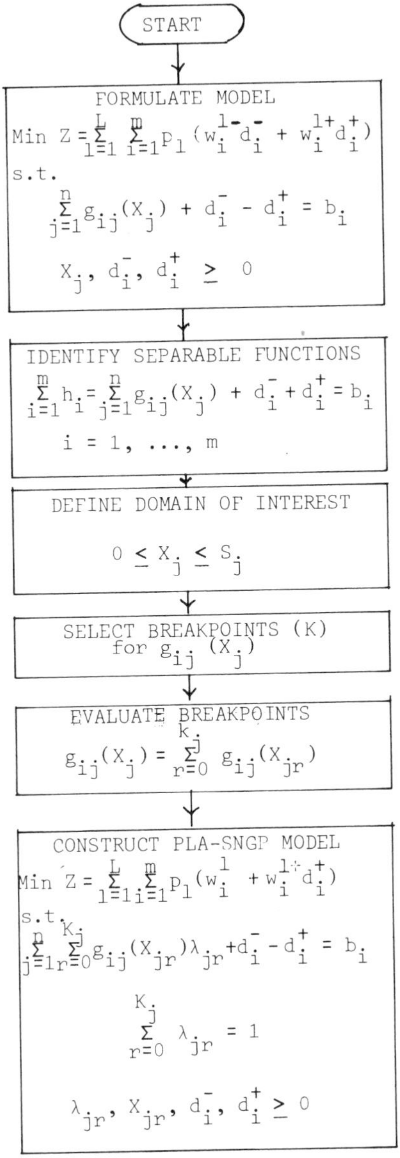

Figure 8.2. Formulation procedure for the PLA-SGP Technique

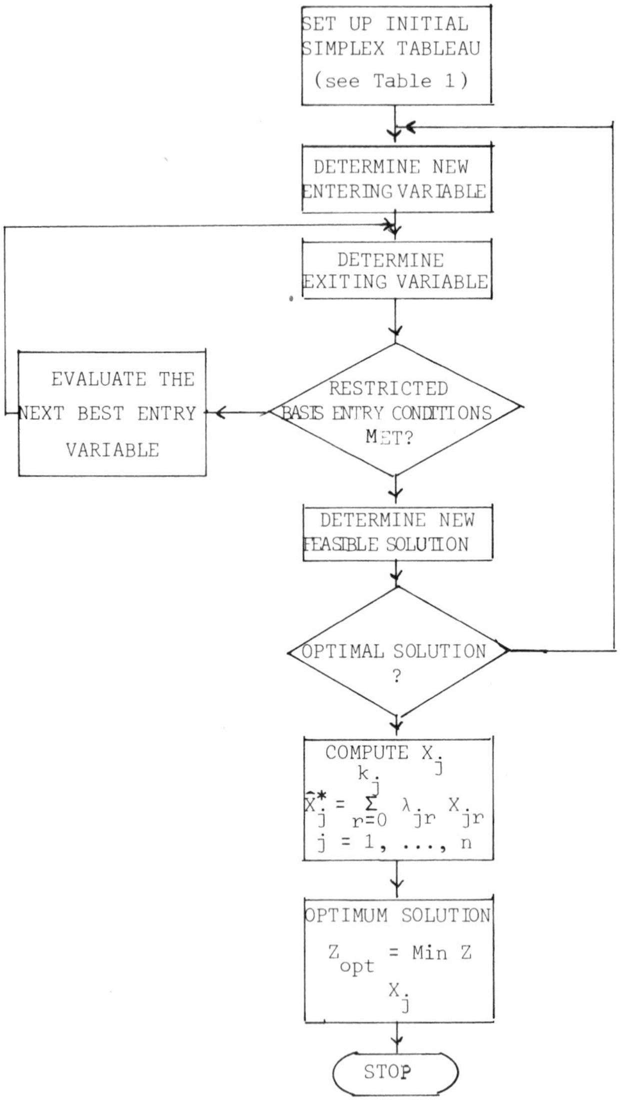

Figure 8.3. Solution technique for the PLA-SGP technique

the lambda summation constraints for each of the separated variables. Reordering of the priority structure takes place, and the lambda summation constraint functions are assigned an artificial priority (P_0) in order to ensure that the restricted basis conditions can be maintained at all times. Reaggregation of the separated variables is computed upon finding the optimal solution. Thus, the user is relieved of any computational effort for determining the optimal solution in terms of the original decision variables.

In most cases, by increasing the number of breakpoints in separable linear programming problems, a resulting improvement in the approximation of the original nonlinear function and hence a better approximated optimal solution closer to the real optimal solution occurs. This phenomenon may not always be the case in separable goal programming. Computational experience with the PLA-SGP algorithm has focused upon some important conceptual considerations. First, the significance of the number of breakpoints for the final solution is dependent upon the feasibility area for the nonlinear functions and the direction of the minimization (i.e. whether d_i^+ or d_i^- is being minimized). Secondly, the importance of this relationship is further magnified as the number of breakpoints more accurately approximate the original nonlinear goal constraints. The intersection of goal constraints with conflicting deviational variables in the objective function further complicates this problem as the modified simplex algorithm consistently searches the extreme corner points. This is especially true when the minimized deviational variables are at different priority levels. If the higher priority goals are related to the nonlinear goal constraints, the more critical the piecewise approximation becomes. The lower the priority, however, the greater the possibility of obtaining a global optimum. The underachievement of the lower order goal constraint will be greater as the approximation improves. Therefore, the structure and ordering of the priority goals in the objective function adds a factor of complexity in deriving a satisfactory solution.

A graphical illustration of this situation is presented in a two-dimensional model in Figure 8.4. The nonlinear convex goal constraint, with its deviational variables depicted in Figure 8.4, represents the total ordering of the storage costs for a quantity Q_j. The linear goal constraint, with respective deviational variables, reflects the desired order quantity for the same Q_j. To demonstrate how the increased underachievement of the total cost goal covaries with the increased number of breakpoints, a series of progressively refined piecewise linear approximations can be utilized. For example, in Figure 8.4 a three breakpoint piecewise linear function represents an approximation of the original nonlinear goal constraint. If the linear goal constraint is to be completely achieved (Min d_{24}^-), then the underachievement of the third goal can be measured as the vertical distance from the extreme corner point defined by the intersection of the two conflicting goal constraints at point C and point B', since point B' is the approximated end point defining the minimum for either line segment AB' or B'D. (Note: point B' is only a local minimum). In reality the true underachievement is more severe as examplified by the measured vertical distance from the point of intersection to the true minimum point (B) as the number of breakpoints progressively increase (see Figure 8.5). The previously defined local minimum (point B') is constantly being redefined (i.e. B'', B''', etc.) and in the process

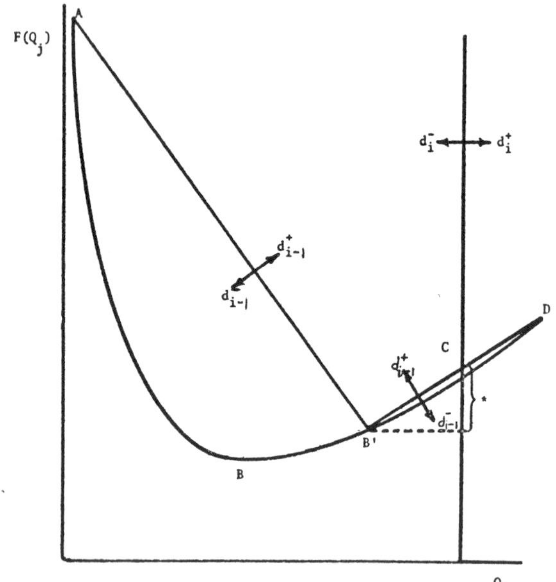

*Amount of underachievement with local minimum at point B'

Figure 8.4. Graphical representation of goal underachievement using three breakpoints for the piecewise approximation of the original nonlinear goal constraint

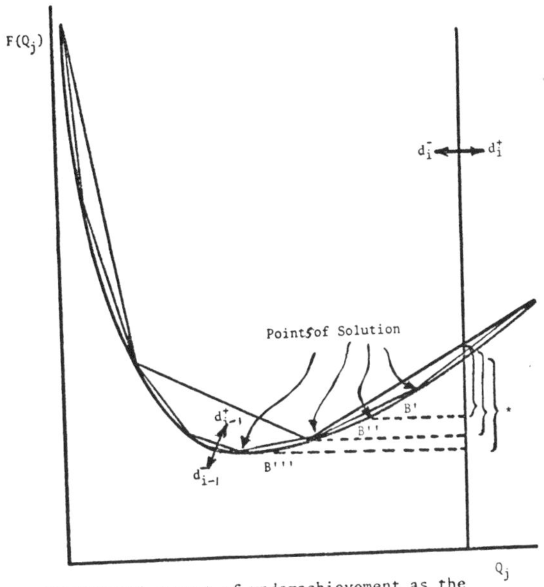

*Additional amount of underachievement as the piecewise linear approximation more closely defines the original nonlinear goal constraint

Figure 8.5. Graphical representation of increased goal underachievement as a result of increased number of breakpoints

the solution moves further away from the linearly constrained order quantity constraint. Consequently, a more realistic, and more costly, underachievement is revealed by the more refined piecewise linear approximation of the nonlinear goal constraint, as the corner points are progressively further removed from the defined local minimum.

The same argument holds true in the case where a positive deviational variable of one goal constraint is minimized at a higher priority level, and the negative deviational variable of a conflicting piecewise linearly approximated concave goal constraint is minimized at a lower priority level. The underachievement of the lower order goal constraint will be greater as the approximation improves. The complexity of the problem is further magnified when multiple nonlinearities and conflicting objectives occur in the model.

8.4. AN ILLUSTRATIVE APPLICATION EXAMPLE

In order to demonstrate the piecewise linear approximation for solving the separable non-linear goal programming problems, let us consider the following illustrative example.

$$\text{Minimize } Z = P_1d_3^- + P_2d_2^+ + P_3d_1^- + P_4d_4^+ + P_5d_5^-$$

subject to:

$$\begin{aligned}
10X_1 - 2X_1^2 + 15X_2 \quad & + d_1^- - d_1^+ = 60 \\
3X_1^2 \quad + 2X_2^2 & + d_2^- - d_2^+ = 42 \\
6X_1 \quad + 4X_2 \quad & + d_3^- - d_3^+ = 24 \\
6X_1 \quad + 4X_2 \quad & + d_4^- - d_4^+ = 30 \\
X_2 \quad & + d_5^- - d_5^+ = \ 5 \\
X_1,\ X_2,\ d_i^-,\ d_i^+ \geq 0 \quad & \quad i=1,2,3,4,5
\end{aligned}$$

By examination, the first two model constraints are nonlinear functions. Further examination reveals that the two constraints can be easily separated into single variable subfunctions of X_1 and X_2. Since both decision variables are also separable variables, all the model constraints must be separated into their respective single variable subfunctions. The list of separated subfunctions is as follows:

$$g_{11}(X_1) = 10X_1 - 2X_1^2$$

$$g_{12}(X_2) = 15X_2$$

$$g_{21}(X_1) = 3X_1^2$$

$$g_{22}(X_1) = 3X_1^2$$

$$g_{31}(X_1) = 6X_1$$

$$g_{32}(X_2) = 4X_2$$

$$g_{41}(X_1) = 6X_1$$

$$g_{42}(X_2) = 4X_2$$

$$g_{52}(X_2 = \quad X_2$$

In this example problem, 9 equally spaced breakpoints are used to provide 8 intervals within the domain of interest for each separable function. Now the model can be reformulated as below.

$$\text{Minimize } Z = P_1(d_6^- + d_7^-) + P_2 d_3^- + P_3 d_2^+ + P_4 d_1^- + P_5 d_4^+ + P_6 d_5^-$$

subject to:

$$\sum_{r_1=0}^{8} g_{11}(X_{1r_1})\,\lambda_{1r_1} + \sum_{r_2=0}^{8} g_{12}(x_{2r_2})\,\lambda_{2r_2} + d_1^- - d_1^+ = 60$$

$$\sum_{r_1=0}^{8} g_{21}(X_{1r_1})\,\lambda_{1r_1} + \sum_{r_2=0} g_{22}(X_{2r_2})\,\lambda_{2r_2} + d_2^- - d_2^+ = 42$$

$$6\sum_{r_1=0}^{8} X_{1r_1}\,\lambda_{1r_1} + 4\sum_{r_2=0}^{8} X_{2r_2}\,\lambda_{2r_2} + d_3^- - d_3^+ = 24$$

$$\sum_{r_1=0}^{8} X_{1r_1}\,\lambda_{1r_1} + 4\sum_{r_2=0}^{8} X_{2r_2}\,\lambda_{2r_2} + d_4^- - d_4^+ = 30$$

$$\sum_{r_2=0}^{8} X_{2r_2}\,\lambda_{2r_2} + d_5^- - d_5^+ = 5$$

$$\sum_{r_2=0}^{8} \lambda_{2r_2} + d_6^- = 1$$

$$\sum_{r_1=0}^{8} \lambda_{1r_1} + d_7^- = 1$$

$$X_{1r_1} > 0$$

$$X_{2r_2} > 0 \qquad i=1,\ldots,5$$

$$\lambda_{1r_1} \geq 0 \qquad r_1=0,\ldots,8$$

$$\lambda_{2r_2} \geq 0 \qquad r_2=0,\ldots,8$$

$$d_i^-,\ d_i^+ \geq 0$$

The optimal solution to this problem is shown in Figure 8.6. Based on the solution, we can easily calculate the value for x_1 and x_2 as below:

Figure 8.6

Optimal simplex tableau

C_j																					P_4		P_2		P_6	P_1	P_1		P_3		P_5	
	V	RHS	λ_{10}	λ_{11}	λ_{12}	λ_{13}	λ_{14}	λ_{15}	λ_{16}	λ_{17}	λ_{18}	λ_{20}	λ_{21}	λ_{22}	λ_{23}	λ_{24}	λ_{25}	λ_{26}	λ_{27}	λ_{28}	d_1^-	d_2^-	d_3^-	d_4^-	d_5^-	d_6^-	d_7^-	d_1^+	d_2^+	d_3^+	d_4^+	d_5^+
	λ_{13}	.205	-2.4	-1.2		1	1.8	2.5	3.1	3.5	3.7	-4.1	-2.5	-1.2	-.4			-.4	-1.2	-2.5		-.1	.5			-2.5	-4.1		.1	-.5		
	λ_{25}	.346	.4	.1			.1	.4	.7	1.2	1.7	-.9	-1.2	-1.1	-.7		1	2.3	3.9	5.8		.1	-.1			.4	.9		-.1	.1		
	λ_{24}	.654	-.4	.1			-.1	-.4	-.7	-1.2	-1.7	1.9	2.2	2.1	1.7	1		-1.3	-2.9	-4.8		-.1	.1			-.4	1.9		.1	-.1		
	d_4^-	6.00																					-1	1						1	-1	
	d_3^-	.634	.4	-.1			-.1	-.4	-.7	-1.2	-1.7	-3.1	-1.8	-.9	-.3			-.3	-.9	-1.8		-.1	.1		1	-.4	-3.1		.1	-.1		-1
	d_1^+	13.7	7.0	2.4			2.4	7.0	14.1	23.5	35.2	35.9	21.5	10.8	3.6			3.6	10.8	21.5	-1	.9	-.3			7.0	35.9	1	-.9	.3		
	λ_{12}	.795	3.5	2.2	1		-.8	-1.5	-2.1	-2.5	-2.7	4.1	2.5	1.2	.4			.4	1.2	2.5		.1	-.5			3.5	4.1		-.1	.5		
$Z_j - C_j$	P_6	.654	-.4	-.1			-.1	-.1	-.7	-1.2	-1.7	-3.1	-1.8	-.9	-.3			-.3	-.9	-1.9		-.1	.1			-.4	-3.1		.1	-.1		-1
	P_5																														-1	
	P_4																				-1											
	P_3																												-1			
	P_2																						-1									
	P_1																							-1	-1							

$$X_1 = (.79487)\ (1.0) + (.20513)\ (1.5) = 1.10256$$

$$X_2 = (.65385)\ (4.0) + (.34615)\ (5.0) = 4.34615$$

The true optimal solution can be found by solving constraints 2 and 3 simultaneously for the common point of intersection and employing the quadratic formula. The true solution is: $x_1 = 1.08$ and $x_2 = 4.38$. This solution can be obtained using the separable goal programming approach with 17 breakpoints and 23 iterations. It should be evident that this algorithm determines a very satisfactory solution (approximate to the true optimal solution) when appropriate numbers of breakpoints are used.

8.5. CONCLUSIONS

This paper presents a simplex-based solution technique for nonlinear goal programming problems. A separable goal programming algorithm based on the piecewise linear approximation is proposed as a viable method for the treatment of nonlinearities that exist in real-world problems involving multiple objectives.

The effectiveness of the algorithm proposed here (PLA-SGP) is based on its ability to approximate the original multiple variable nonlinear functions with combinations of single-variable subfunctions. Computational experience with the PLA-SGP computer-based algorithm provides some interesting results. Varying the number of breakpoints and the 'minimum-maximum' upperbounds for the decision variables, analyses were made with respect to the variances in solutions, the number of iterations required, total execution time, and the degree of goal attainment. In some cases there was an obvious point of diminishing returns when the grid was made finer by increasing the number of breakpoints. Increasing the number of breakpoints poses a particular problem for goal programming, because as the number of breakpoints increase, the total number of lambda variables increase. The significance of the number of breakpoints for the final solution is dependent upon the feasibility area for the nonlinear function and the direction of minimization (i.e., which d is being minimized).

As with the development of any new technique, extensive computational experience is necessary in order to judge the applicability to decision-making. It appears that there exists enormous potential for separable goal programming for application to real-world problems.

8.6. REFERENCES

Charnes, A. and Lemke, C.E., Minimization of Nonlinear Separable Convex Functions, *Naval Research Logistics Quarterly*, vol.1, 1954, pp.301-312.

Hillier, F.S. and Lieberman, G.J., *Operations Research*, Holden-Day, San Fransisco, 1974.

Lee, S.M., *Goal Programming for Decision Analysis*, Auerbach Publishers, Philadelphia, 1972.

Loomba, P.N. and Turban, E., *Applied Programming for Management*, Holt, Rinehart Winston, New York, 1974.

Miller, C.E., The Simplex Method for Local Separable Programming, in Graves, R.L. and Wolfe, P. (eds.), *Recent Advances in Mathematical Programming*, McGraw-Hill, New York, 1963, pp.89-100.

Simmons, D.M., *Nonlinear Programming for Operations Research*, Prentice-Hall, Englewood Cliffs, 1975.

Taha, H.A., *Operations Research*, MacMillan, New York, 1976.
Thierauf, R.J., *Decision Making through Operations Research*, in Grosse, R.A. (ed.), Wiley, New York, 1970.

9 Appraisal of Non-Independent Projects

J. R. Fayette

9.1. INTRODUCTION

For many years now, a great number of articles, books and symposia have been devoted to the appraisal of investment projects, notably in the developing countries. This work has been the product of university economists or of economists working in national or international organisations which finance or study projects, in particular the OECD, the World Bank, the European Investment Bank, the United Nations Industrial Development Organisation (UNIDO), etc.

What characterizes this work and the methods used or advocated is an increasingly complex enlargement of the field of reference and extension of the forward time horizon. Whereas from the standpoint of the investor (public or private) an investment will represent a certain amount of expenditure and returns giving an overall balance sheet and a discounted cash flow rate of return, from the community's standpoint an investment will be seen in terms of effects on income distribution, on prices, on international trade, on growth and so forth. By and large, therefore, the tendency is to incorporate increasingly numerous and diverse criteria into the economic calculation designed to appraise a project from the standpoint of the community.

Because of this emphasis on the field of analysis, the ultimate purpose tends to be lost sight of to some degree. The aim of any project appraisal is to bring about the decision to go ahead or not, or to finance or not, although in the latter case the volume of financing provided by an international organisation, for instance, may constitute one of the variables of the problem.

To analyse an investment project is therefore to include it in a decision-making process of variable length: analysis cannot be an intellectual exercise, it is by nature operational. The first part of this paper will therefore consider investment projects from the standpoint of decision-making theory. Since the decision-making process is bound to involve several points of view or criteria, the second part of the paper will establish what the elements of the multicriteria nature of project decisions are. Finally, some proposals and suggested lines of research will be put forward by way of conclusion.

9.2. INVESTMENT PROJECTS AND DECISION-MAKING THEORY

In all countries, whether developing or economically advanced, the number of investment projects is increasing rapidly as a result of private needs and community needs.

These projects may be directly productive, partially productive or non-productive.

In the case of productive projects, the project initiator may be a national or foreign private body and the community may have to take cognizance of it, either through a procedure of authorization in the context of planning, or because it is asked to participate directly (public financing) or indirectly by way of incentive premiums, tax advantages, special authorizations, etc.

It is quite possible that the nature of the decision to be taken by the authorities (authorization, subsidization, financing) may have some effect on the content of the decision-making techniques used. The tool should therefore be fitted to its end purpose.

In the case of non-productive or non-directly productive projects (infrastructures, social services, etc.), the public authorities are necessarily involved although the social services concerned may come from the public or the private sector depending on the country (hospital services, for example). Consequently, the benefits and costs attached to a project often have to be estimates or approximations. The question is then what decision-making methods to apply in such cases.

In addition to the complexity constituted by all the different types of projects, there is the complexity of the decision-making hierarchy, notably as represented by the different territorial levels of commune, region and state, without forgetting the groups that form, more or less spontaneously, to support or oppose a project, usually once the decision has been taken.

What is striking is that with this complexity of project consequences and diversity of decision-makers, the methods currently proposed for the appraisal of projects, in other words for accepting or rejecting them, are still curiously commonplace and uniform. Generally speaking, the method used is to merge all the criteria into one overall indicator, to calculate an internal rate of return for the project by means of that indicator and to reject the project if the rate of return is less than, say, 12 per cent, or if not, to accept it. The fineness of the equivalances between the criteria and the overall indicator contrasts sharply, therefore, with the bluntness of the decision-making procedure.

As B. Roy (1975) sees it, there are three kinds of situations:

- of several alternative projects, which to choose?
- among several projects, how to tell the good from the bad and decide which need further study?
- how to rank a number of projects in order of overall desirability?

Vis à vis these three types of situations, the position of present appraisal methods is almost always the same. It is to express the sum total of preferences and criteria in one function of utility or value. This poses two problems: (i) choosing the value unit or numerary (ii) measuring impacts with this numerary.

9.2.1. *Choice of the value unit*

The choice of the value unit is fundamental since it will explicitly favour a specific criterion or not. So, in the latest piece of research, done by a team of World Bank staff, the value chosen, a money value, is non-committed government income in terms of foreign exchange.

The choice of a value unit of this type contains at least two value judgements. The first is the importance of budget equilibrium for the government, the second is the amount of incremental value in relation to international trade, hence an implicit affirmation of the optimization function performed by the international division of labour. If the choice of such a unit of measurement is not neutral in its philosophy, it is neither neutral where the choice procedure is concerned. It is wrong to say that this choice has no effect, on the reasoning that it is always possible to switch from one indicator (one criterion) to another by means of a shadow-price for this indicator in terms of another indicator or criterion. This is the same as saying that all objectives are equivalent up to a linear transformation, which is manifestly erroneous, as mathematical programming with multiple objective functions shows.

9.2.2. *Measurement of impacts within the value unit*

Choosing a money value implies two things: first, that all the impacts are measurable and, second, that is is possible to translate the measurement of each type of impact into money terms.

Obviously not all the impacts are measurable, so in using these methods recourse has to be had to 'brave' estimates based on questionable assumptions. For instance, one reads (see Squire and van der Tak (1975)) that a rational government apportions its budget in such a way that 'at the margin, additional expenditure has the same value in all uses'. This is very wise thinking, admittedly, but is it operational to disregard policies and constraints, in short the real world? Might this not cause the countries receiving finance or aid to regard themselves as the wards of international agencies?

To try to assign a measure to all the aspects, all the whys and wherefores of a project therefore seems illusory and dangerous. Moreover, it is pointless since in many cases an appraisal rating of the type 'very good', 'good', 'acceptable' or 'bad' would be quite sufficient for the purposes of a 'yes' or 'no' decision.

Measurement also implies that the measure of each impact can be expressed in money values, for example by means of shadow-prices. The shadow-prices introduced by marginal analysis are becoming an increasingly important part of project appraisal and it seems essential to differentiate between the main types.

(i) Shadow-prices may, in some cases, represent existing prices adjusted to take account of subsidies, taxes, etc. In that case, recourse to shadow-prices is generally accepted by all the theoreticians and practitioners of project appraisal. Even so, attention should be drawn to certain consequences. While a project may be very profitable from the community's standpoint on the basis of the shadow-prices, its financial equilibrium from the operating standpoint will depend on the effective prices, and experience has shown that it is dangerous policy to keep deficit projects going, for when the day of budget austerity dawns, such projects may be dismissed.

(ii) Shadow-prices may result from a process of optimization. It is known that any optimization of use of resources that are scarce and therefore only available in limited quantities, engenders a price system which reflects the scarcity of those resources relative to the objective. This means that there will be as many price systems as there are objectives. For example, in multi-objective linear programming there will be as many dual-variable vectors as there are objectives, i.e. multidimensional dual variables (see Hill (1968)).

But even where there is only one objective, the practitioners of mathematical programming know that a dual price may serve to justify the conclusion that a project is to be rejected but not accepted. Admittedly, the theoreticians systematically argue that it is a matter of marginal transformations, which therefore have no influence on this dual price. But this argument is by no means generally valid since with many projects the transformations are not marginal: this is one of the fundamental principles of the impacts method.

(iii) The shadow-prices may be the result of explicit policy guidelines laid down by the decision-makers but as Roy (1975) points out, a too precise specification of weights creates false certainties, based as this is on reinforcing certain prejudices and exaggerating certain biases. This is especially true when these shadow-prices are established by international bodies having undoubted prestige and equally undoubted means of pressure: the specified value of certain prices becomes sacrosanct, and convicts him who would contest them!

It may be said that these are prices determined by reference to the neoclassical theory of general equilibrium. It seems as though they should be used above all as a means of *a contrario* analysis: if this or that project with characteristics X is preferred by a decision-maker to the project with characteristics Y, it is possible to deduce orders of magnitude among some of the components of these characteristics and bring the original judgement into question. Consequently, shadow-prices of this type can be regarded as backstops, tests of validity, but probably not as principal decision-making criteria.

It therefore seems fundamental to pose the problem of project appraisal as a decision-making problem. Calculating the economic profitability of a project by means of shadow-prices computed to several decimal places, working out from that an equally precise internal rate of return, and then reaching a 'yes' or 'no' conclusion according to whether that rate is above or below a certain threshold (12 per cent, 18 per cent, etc.), seems to be to thumb one's nose at the methods which research on decision-making theory has produced, in particular multicriteria methods.

9.3. THE MULTICRITERIA NATURE OF PROJECT DECISIONS

Investment projects, whether productive or not, whether in developing or economically advanced countries, are by nature projects which have to be appraised from a number of different standpoints. The 'World Bank 'method' basically distinguishes between financial standpoints, economic standpoints and social standpoints deemed commensurable in a single indicator. Economic growth, payments equilibrium, the presence of multiplier effects, development of employment, the contribution of modern technology, quality of life, national independence, and so on, are some of the criteria which may be used in apprasing projects.

The Portuguese code of foreign investment, for example, lists 12 criteria which should determine whether a project is accepted or discarded:

- job creation;
- positive foreign exchange balance;
- enhancement of domestic resources;
- utilization of domestic goods and services;
- location in accordance with regional development programmes;
- production of new goods or services or improvement of goods or services produced hitherto;
- introduction of advanced technologies;
- high value added;
- expected amount of domestic credit needed to form the capital of the undertaking;
- vocational training of national workers;
- reduction of industrial pollution.

Can one accept that such criteria, some of which are correlated, can be reduced to a single indicator? Can one accept the existence of coefficients weighting the numerical values assigned to these criteria so as to make them commensurable?

Some criteria may be purely numerical such as job creation, foreign exchange earnings; others may be quality rankings such as 'very good', 'good', 'average', 'bad'; others may even be bivalent such as 'yes' or 'no'.

Furthermore, investment projects by definition have initiators; private enterprises, regional or national public bodies, etc. There are also decision-makers: development banks, national planning ministeries, regional councils, etc. Any project is therefore the subject of veritable negotiations in which each of the protagonists knows to a greater or lesser extent the avowed or concealed intentions of the others.

It is therefore appropriate to consider the context of project decision-making. This will be done in Subsection 9.3.1. Subsection 9.3.2 will then deal with the way in which decision-aiding multicriteria techniques enable the problem of project appraisal to be modelled. The next section will set out some proposals and suggested lines of research.

9.3.1. *The decision-making context*

Before contemplating any new methods of project appraisal, it is appropriate to consider the implications of the context in which projects are appraised.

The first problem from this point of view is to know whether projects are appraised one by one, or whether a set of projects is appraised and a decision taken accordingly.

With single-indicator methods, appraisal is generally on a project-by-project basis. A project is studied individually, and an internal rate of return computed in more or less complex fashion determines whether the project is accepted or not. In such cases a multicriteria approach is relatively difficult to apply since, with a single project, some criteria will work in its favour, others against, while others will be indecisive. Any decision-making procedure will therefore necessarily involve comparing the 'for' rating with the 'against' rating, and this of course makes it necessary to define terms of equivalence between losses and gains on different criteria (trade-offs).

Basically, what has caused the traditional methods of project analysis to use the single indicator, and therefore shadow-prices, is consideration of a single project. If projects are examined one by one, this is a more or less direct constraint to use a method which amounts to the single-indicator method.

But, in fact, project appraisal is only seldom a matter of an isolated project. If, for example, a 10 per cent internal rate of return is estimated to be insufficient, it is because it is estimated that owing to the scarcity of funds available for the investment there are other projects, known or potential, whose rate of return would be higher. By and large, it can even be said that all shadow-prices considered as opportunity costs imply comparison with other alternative uses of the resource whose scarcity those prices reflect.

Little and Mirrlees (1974) clearly illustrate this aspect of reality by showing how to calculate the rate of discount. Formalizing their approach, one arrives at the following result:

Let n projects $i=1,2,\ldots,n$, let c_i be the cost of project i and r_i its internal rate of return. One establishes a pre-order of purposes as a function of internal rate of return and one retains the k projects, as:

$$\sum_{i=1}^{k} c_i \leq R$$

R being the aggregate amount of financing available for the projects. Any project which subsequently will have a discounted cash flow rate of return of less than r_k will be excluded and r_k will be used as the discount rate.

Thus, the minimum discounted cash flow rate of return will be determined on the basis of a ranking for a set of projects. However, even if this ranking were derived from a multicriteria approach, the decision-making tool that is deduced would necessarily bring one back to a one-criterion procedure: it is as though the available or potential information were being deliberately defaced.

In fact, projects are often presented in sets, but it is necessary to differentiate between two cases: (i) the given set of projects (ii) the flow of projects.

In the case of a given set, a nationa, regional or sectoral plan is involved more often than not; this is also true of a firm which plans its investments over a given period.

Where decisions are submitted to a public body, the following characteristics can be identified:

Origin of projects
public
semi-public
large firm

Scale of projects
generally large to very large

Nature of the decision
approval or rejection
financing

Nature of criteria
financial
economic
socio-political

Nature of the decision-making body
national planning authorities
government

In the case of a flow of projects, it is a question of requests for funding which arrive from day to day without annual budget considerations and decisions have to be taken on a case-by-case basis.

Origin of projects
public or semi-public with private-sector predominance

Scale of projects
Very variable, from the small firm's project to a regional or national project

Nature of the decision
generally financing

Nature of criteria
financial and banking, with subsidies for profitability shortfalls

Nature of the decision-making body
very variable: conventional banks, development banks or central government for inclusion in budget.

The distinction between these two cases is seen in reality to be a distinction of phases in a decision-making process. The investment projects are studied in a relatively overall fashion for approval, and then those that are accepted are studied in more detail and notably against a more specific funding schedule. There are, of course, projects which have been approved and for which the financing is never got together, either because conditions have changed or because funds are not available.

9.3.2. *Modelling the problem*

Reasoning with respect to a set of projects will make it possible, in particular, to discard explicitly the hypothesis of marginality which very largely justified the existence of shadow-prices in the conventional methods. If, for example, one of the objectives of an investment policy is to develop a given region, a project which will create several thousand jobs in that region will, in a sense, resolve the problem. Such a project, once approved, will therefore modify the assessments that may be made of other projects, whether the assessment is made in the course of the same decision-making process or later, in the case of a flow of projects. So it is important to consider the nature of the reciprocal influences of projects and thus their interdependence.

(a) Interdependence of projects

The problem of project interdependence may seem on the face of it to be a classic problem since it has been studied by many authors. Prou and Chervel (1970), for example, study project clusters, i.e. projects which are physically or economically interdependent. The classic example is that of the ore extraction project which cannot be studied without co-appraisal of the project for the railway track which will carry the ore that has been mined. In this context it is commonplace that the two projects should be studied together; even so, it should be pointed out that, in many actual cases, failure to take into consideration certain investments related to a principal investment pay lead to completely false results. A main investment is decided upon and carried out and then it is realized that a related investment has been omitted with the result that the first investment becomes non-operational. The expenditures connected with the first investment are regarded as sunk costs, whereas the related investment is exceptionally profitable since the combined impacts of the two investments are set against the expenditure on the related investment, and the process can thus be continued. Certain major investments have been carried out with this chain procedure, each link presenting a high rate of return and the chain as a whole functioning in a particularly uneconomic way.

This problem really lies more in the sphere of administrative sociology, but Prou and Chervel have the merit of having supplied us with a framework for analysing these multicomponent projects.

The aspect that needs to be stressed here concerns the policy interdependence of projects. By policy interdependence it is meant that two projects entirely separate at the economic level may in fact affect the same group of agents, for instance, and that the cumulative effect of those projects may appear undesirable. Let us take a few examples. A country develops a policy of import substitution and export development. Economic studies show that two industrial projects for import substitution are particularly profitable, only those projects would replace imports from one single country, to which moreover it is sought to export a certain category of products. That country may be expected to take reprisals or, at any rate, to react negatively. This means that only the first substitution project could be accepted; the second would have to be relegated to the advantage of a third project which would perhaps be less economically profitable but which would affect imports from another country.

Two regions simultaneously request the building of a hospital and a university. Studies show that the hospital of region A and the university of region A are the more worthwhile to build, but for financial reasons it is only possible to carry out two projects. It is probable that the fact of having chosen the hospital of region A will cause that region's university to be relegated, to the advantage of either region B's hospital or region B's university.

(b) How to allow for project interdependence

The theory of preferences, notably the contribution of Arrow, usually introduces the principle of independence from third possibilities. This principle is expressed in the following manner: if 'a' is preferred to 'b', the fact of introducing 'c' will not alter the preference relationship between 'a' and 'b'.

Suppose that 'a' is preferred to 'b' and that a third purpose 'c' is introduced, 'a' and 'b' both being investment projects in the same region. The fact of introducing 'c' cannot alter the relationship between 'a' and 'b' at the level of *expression of preferences*, but *at the level of expression of choice* the fact that 'c' ranks as project No. 1 may be what causes 'b' to be below 'a' although individually 'a' is preferred to 'b'.

Principle No. 1

The interdependent ranking of a project in a subset depends on the assessments of that purpose relative to those of the other projects of the subset and on the pre-order of the projects already ranked. It may be, however, that the dependence between 'c' and 'a' is not strong enough and/or that 'a' dominates 'b' to such a degree that the dependence between 'a' and 'c' does not prevent 'a' from being preferred to 'b' in the final choice.

Principle No. 2

The ranking of interdependent projects implies:

- a 'measurement' of interdependence;
- a 'measurement' of superiority as between two projects;
- comparability of the two measurements.

Another approach to the problem may be to reason by reference to plans rather than the projects themselves, a plan comprising a vector of projects. In this approach, each plan is the top of a hypercube in a space which has as many dimensions as there are projects in question. This is the kind of approach taken by van Delft and Nijkamp (1976), who use multi-objective linear programming in totally bivalent variables. However, this approach has a major drawback in that it is highly combinatorial (thus a set of 10 projects will give $2^{10} = 1{,}024$ variables) and it also implies that appraisal of the projects in respect of each criterion is numerical.

The fundamental problem posed by allowance for project interdependence is, on a mathematical level (in the numerical case), the linearity of the impacts. Is the employment created by two projects the sum of the jobs created by the two projects individually? Is the impact on the balance of payments the sum of the impacts of each project, and so forth.

Nijkamp (1975) describes a matrix of interactions between project impacts, which in a way is harking back to the shadow-price theory but without measuring all the impacts in a single indicator. This method also has the advantage of not necessarily supposing symmetry of impacts: if one unit of impact A is worth two units of impact B, one unit of impace B is not necessarily worth half a unit of impact A. In this case, however, there is a limitation in that the impacts are only taken in twos.

Furthermore, the impacts are not in conflict or substitutable in themselves but through the projects which are their actual cause; a matrix of interactions may therefore vary appreciably according to the particular set of projects taken into consideration.

9.4. PROPOSALS AND LINES OF RESEARCH

With a set of projects and a set of criteria one finds that there are always a number of links between the projects. The first link derives, naturally enough, from the cost of the projects and the impossibility in general of financing them all; there may also be global constraints with respect to availability and so forth.

Project interdependence is thus identified at the level of outputs and, generally speaking, this interdependence can be resolved by mathematical programming.

There is, of course, another type of interdependence, which derives from outputs or the effects of projects. Of these effects there are some which are purely economic and can therefore be analyzed with the impacts method (Prou and Chervel (1970)), and there are some which are social and political, as is entirely the case with criteria such as land use, income distribution, good relations with international trade partners, etc.

A project cannot be assessed from the land-use standpoint other than in relation to an objective: it is because project X is in region A (a region with priority ranking) that it will be judged very good from the land-use standpoint.

Even then, this assessment will depend on the fact that project X creates a lot of jobs, a lot of value added, and so on, in region A. There is thus a subset of criteria which we shall call *policy criteria*. For each policy criterion we shall establish a *breakdown* into a set of components by which a project can be appraised. For example, the breakdown of the 'land-use' policy criterion will be all the regions in a programme, that of the 'better social distribution' policy criterion would be all the socio-occupational categories, and so on.

Each project will assign to a subset of each policy criterion components a certain number of numerical values on the basis of evaluators, e.g. employment, value added, CO_2 level , etc.

Suppose we concentrate our attention on the land-use criteria. We get the following matrix:

Table 9.1
Effects of a given project

A	B	C	D	
	200	-20		employment
600	4700	-500		value-added
	5%	-2%	1%	pollution

A given project i will create 200 jobs in region B but suppress 20 jobs in region C because of a substitution in activity. It will increase value added in region A by 600, in region B by 4700 and decrease it in region by 500. The pollution index will increase in region B by 5 per cent, decrease in region C by 2 per cent and increase in region D by 1 per cent. Thus for each project we can attribute different values according to the respective evaluators.

The set of all the projects under consideration will give a global appraisal of the land use consequences if all the projects were to be implemented. This is generally not true because some of the projects may be mutually exclusive projects: factory X in region A or in region B, therefore summing over the effects is seldom meaningful. In a decision process,if a given factory is selected for implementation in region A, alternative locations which increased the number of projects will be disregarded. We therefore have:

- a set of projects P, some of them being possibly incompatible;
- a set of criteria C;
- a set of policy criteria 0;
- $\forall$ k, J $\in$ 0 a breakdown π_j;
- a set of evaluators.

$V_{ijh(\pi jk)}$ means the value of project i according to the j th criteria in terms of h for the h th element of the breakdown of j.

Since different evaluators may be relevant to one policy criteria only, it is hard to imagine that multidimensional scaling methods as presented by Hill and Tzamir (1972) or Nijkamp and Voogd (1978) can be readily used.

If we have three policy criteria, each having a breakdown of ten elements and eight indicators, we get a matrix composed of 240 elements, most of them being zeros.

Table 9.2
A possible project effect matrix

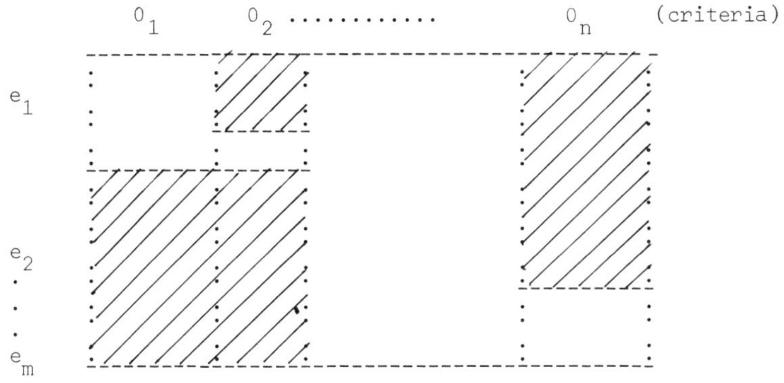

9.3.1. *The set of ideals*

It is common to derive from policy criteria some level of achievements which can be considered as ideals to reach, for instance a target for region A would be the creation of 10,000 jobs to solve the unemployment problem. The relations between goals and achievements are often presented through goal-achievement matrices which can be used as a means to evaluate a set of projects or a plan (see Hill (1968)).

A set of selected projects appreciated according to a breakdown of policy criteria and several evaluators would therefore be as close as possible to a set of ideals. Of course the set of ideals is not usually feasible and this raises once more the question of displaced ideals so as to reach a feasible set (see Nijkamp (1978)).

9.4.2. *Conflicting decision-makers*

Generally speaking, the breakdown of policy criteria will correspond to decision-makers or pressure groups. The interest of region A will be advocated by a governor, mayor etc.; the interests of social group X will be supported by a union or a lobby in the Parliament etc.

Therefore the game-theory approach could also be considered in that case. A region could give up a given project provided another project would be approved. This could be reached either through negotiation between decision-makers of the same level and/or decision-makers of higher levels. As we stated from the very beginning of this chapter, the major defect of present project appraisal techniques is that they completely ignore decision theory, being based on an all-embracing economic calculus.

9.4.3. *Flow of projects*

Generally, projects are not a given set among which to choose. Even in planned economies, however, new projects come up on a regular basis and have to be evaluated and decided upon, consideration being given to already evaluated projects (accepted or rejected ones) and contemplated ones.

An approach of this type of problem has been made by Moscarola. In this approach one has to select or build types of good projects and types of bad projects so that when one has to decide upon a given project, this latter one is compared to the various types of good and bad projects. If the project under consideration overranks a good project it will be accepted; if it is overranked by a bad project it will be rejected. This is done through a fuzzy overranking procedure which makes room for the case when no decision can be reached.

An adaptation of this approach could be considered for solving the case of policy-dependent projects. It will consist in changing through time the set of good and the set of bad projects. For instance a project which which creates n jobs in region A, a balance of payment surplus of x for the country etc. could be considered as a good project, so that any project which overranks it will be considered a good one; but if some projects creating jobs in region A have been accepted, the level n could be raised so that it will become increasingly harder for a new project to overrank it.

This type of approach could bring a synthesis with the various questions we pinpointed earlier, but by its very nature it would have to be applied to a specific case rather than being developed *in abstracto*. We hope that this will be the case in the years to come.

9.5. PROVISIONAL CONCLUSION

We feel we have raised some problems which are present in the minds of people who actually have to assist decision-makers in effective project appraisal.

We did not provide ready-made solutions to solve those problems, but only some directions along which further research and implementation could be considered. We hope it will stimulate discussion.

9.6. REFERENCES

Bertier, P. and Bouroche, J.M., *Approche Multicritère des Problèmes de Décision*, Collection AFCET, Hommes et Techniques, Paris, 1978.

Delft, A. van, and Nijkamp, P., A Multi-Objective Decision Model for Regional Development, Environmental Quality Control and Industrial Land Use, *Papers of the Regional Science Association*, vol.36, 1976, pp.35-38.

Fayette, J.R., Utilisation de la Programmation Linéaire à Plusieurs Fonctions d'Objectif dans la Planification, *Mondes en Developpement*, No. 16.

Geigch, J.P. van, *Applied General Systems Theory*, Harper and Row, New York, 1974.

Hill, M., A Goals-Achievement Matrix for Evaluating Alternative Plans, *Journal of the American Institute of Planners*, vol.36, 1968, pp.19-29.

Little, I.M.D. and Mirrlees, J., *Project Appraisal and Planning for Developing Countries*, Heineman Educational Books, London, 1974.

Ministère de la Coopération, *Analyse Critique des Méthodes d'Evaluation des Projets*, Paris, 1976.

Moscarola, J. and Roy, B., Procédure Automatique d'Examen de Dossiers Fondée sur une Segmentation Trichotomique en Présence de Critères Multiples, *RAIRO (vert)*, vol.11, no.2, 1977, pp.145-173.

Nijkamp, P., A Multicriteria Analysis for Project Evaluation, *Papers of the Regional Science Association*, vol.35, 1975, pp.87-111.

Nijkamp, P., Conflict Patterns and Compromise Solutions in Fuzzy Choice Theory, Research Memorandum 1978-7, Free University, Amsterdam, 1978a.

Nijkamp, P., A Theory of Displaced Ideals, Research Memorandum 1978-6, Free University, Amsterdam, 1978b.

Nijkamp, P. and Delft, A van, *Multi-Criteria Analysis and Regional Decision-Making*, Martinus Nijhoff, 1977.

Nijkamp, P. and Voogd, J.H., The Use of Multidimensional Scaling in Evaluation Procedures, *Planologisch Studiecentrum TNO*, Delft, 1978.

Paelinck, J.H.P., Qualitative Multiple Criteria Analysis Environmental Protection and Multiregional Development, *Papers of the Regional Science Association*, vol.36, 1976, pp.59-74.

Prou, C. and Chervel, M., *Etablissement des Programmes en Economies Sous-Développés: l'Etude des Grappes de Projets*, Coll. Statistiques et Programmes Economiques, Dunod, Paris, 1970.

Roy, B., Problems and Methods with Multiple Objective Functions, *Mathematical Programming*, vols. 1 and 2, November 1971, pp.239-266.

Roy, B., Critères Multiples et Modélisation des Préférences (l'Apport des Relations de Surclassement), *Rev. Eco. Po.* No. 1, 1974a.

Roy, B., La Modélisation des Préférences, Aspect Crucial de l'Aide à la Decision, *METRA*, vol.2, pp.135-153, 1979b.

Roy, B., Vers une Méthodologie Générale de l'Aide à la Décision, *METRA*, vol. XIV, No.3, 1975.

Squire, L. and Tak, H. van der, *The Economic Analysis of Projects*, The John Hopkins University Press, Baltimore, 1975.

C. SOCIOECONOMIC PROBLEMS

10. Energy Planning Using a Multiple Criteria Decision Method

S. Zionts and D. Deshpande

10.1. INTRODUCTION

This report describes the implementation and application of a multiple criteria decision-making method to problems of planning U.S. energy policy. The work was done at the School of Management, State University of New York at Buffalo in conjunction with Brookhaven National Laboratory (BNL). Several linear programming models have been developed at Brookhaven and applied to problems in energy planning for the U.S. Department of Energy (DOE). Since there are many conflicting objectives in these models, important trade-off decisions among objectives must be made. Our work employs a method developed specifically for solving linear programming problems involving several conflicting objectives (Zionts and Wallenius (1976)).

An earlier report (Zionts and Deshpande (1978)) described the first phase of our work, which implemented and used a method assuming a linear utility function. We have since implemented and applied the method using a concave utility function.

We first review what had previously been done at Brookhaven using linear programming energy planning models. Then we review the methodology employed, and describe our implementation of it on the Brookhaven computer. Finally we describe our experience with the program.

10.2. BACKGROUND

The Brookhaven Energy System Optimization Model (BESOM) (Cherniavsky (1974)), is a linear programming model of the national energy system. The model chooses, subject to technical constraints, which energy forms (e.g. electricity, oil, gas, coal) will be used to satisfy demands for energy services (e.g., space conditioning of households, vehicle miles, tons of steel produced). The optimization model contains energy balance equations plus detail on the utility sector load curve and technical constraints (relating, for example, to inherited capacity that will be present in a particular time frame). Earlier applications have included technology and scenario assessments usually with the objective of minimizing annualized supply-system cost. As indicated earlier, other criteria must be taken into account in order to achieve a balanced perspective on the energy system. Oil imports, environmental impacts, resource use and capital requirements are important factors in evaluating a particular case.

Multiple objective function analyses were performed with ERDA F-2 forecasts to determine a best case (Cherniavsky et al. (1977)). The six alternate objective functions selected for the study were:

(a) annualized system cost, including end-use device costs;

(b) oil imports;

(c) environmental index;

(d) resource use;

(e) capital in place, including end-use devices;

(f) annualized system cost, excluding end-use device costs.

10.2.1. *Original methodology*

Each of the objective functions was minimized in turn, and the levels of the other functions were observed. Pairs of alternate objective functions were then selected for trade-off analyses. Selection of pair members was based on importance of a parameter in policy analysis. Since minimization of one of a member pair is generally inconsistent with minimization of the other, trade-off analyses were performed by minimizing one objective function while requiring that the other not exceed a specified level. A series of different levels was used and the effects on the optimal solution (i.e. selection of energy forms, resource conversion processes, relative desirability of technologies as indicated by marginal values) were studied.

The behaviour of the functions under alternate objectives clearly indicated the existence of trade-offs between oil imports and capital installed, between oil imports and the environmental index, and between total cost and the environmental index. One would expect this to occur as a result of substitution of electricity for oil in the space heat and process heat sectors. Electrification is capital intensive, and, especially for coal steam plants, has far greater environmental impacts than direct oil use.

After making several tests and reviewing the results, a best case was chosen on a judgemental basis, without reference to any explicit utility function.

The above analysis was the departure point for our research. Our objective was to implement a particular method for helping a decision-maker to choose the 'best' levels of all objectives, on a systematic basis.

In the first phase the method for a linear utility function was to implement a particular method for helping a decision-maker to choose the 'best' levels of all objectives, on a systematic basis.

In the first phase the method for a linear utility function was implemented. Our experience with that method and program indicated that a linear utility function was not appropriate. A decision-maker's utility (at least those with whom we worked) seems to be nonlinear. Accordingly, we have now revised the program to allow for nonlinear utility functions. We have restricted the choice to concave functions of linear objectives that are to be maximized.

10.3. METHODOLODY

In this section we briefly describe the procedure employed for solving the multiple criteria linear programming problem. It was developed by Zionts and Wallenius (1976). We describe the method assuming a concave utility function. We assume a set of linear constraints as follows:

$$\begin{aligned} Ax &= b \\ Iu - Cx &\leq 0 \\ x &\geq 0, \quad u \text{ unrestricted in sign} \end{aligned} \tag{10.1}$$

x is the vector of decision variables, u is the vector of objectives, C is the matrix of objective functions, A is the matrix of coefficients, and b is the vector of constraint limits. All vectors and matrices are of appropriate order. The objective is to maximize a concave function of Cx. The procedure is as follows:

1. Choose an arbitrary vector $\lambda > 0$.
2. Solve the linear programming problem. Maximize $\lambda'u$ subject to the constraints in (10.1). Define the solution as the new solution. If there is no old solution, go to step 3. Otherwise, ask if the decision-maker prefers the new solution to the old solution. If yes, go to step 3; if no, choose a solution that was preferred to the old solution (in steps 5 or 6 of the last iteration) and designate it as the new solution; go to step 3.
3. Designate the new solution as the old solution. Identify all adjacent efficient extreme point solutions to the old solution. Indicate which of them the decision-maker may possibly prefer to the old solution on the basis of active previous responses. Call this set subset 1, and call the remaining adjacent solutions subset 2.
4. Ask the decision-maker to compare each of the solutions of subset 1, one at a time, with the old solution, and to indicate his preference. If he prefers any of the solutions to the old solution, go to step 6. Otherwise, go to step 5.
5. Ask the decision-maker to compare each of the solutions of subset 2, one at a time, with the old solution. If he does not prefer any of the solutions to the old solution, stop; the optimal solution is an efficient solution that is a convex combination of the old solution and solutions in subsets 1 and 2. Otherwise, delete the oldest set of responses and go to step 6.
6. Find a set of weights consistent with all current and active previous responses. If none exists, delete the oldest set of responses and repeat step 6. Otherwise, go to step 2.

The responses can be an expression of preference or the inability to express a preference. Our current practice is to ignore the responses of inability to express a preference.

Also, an adjacent efficient extreme point solution can be presented to the decision-maker in one of two ways: (1) in terms of the value of each objective function (as a 'scenario') or (2) in terms of the bundle of trade-offs available at the old solution, which lead to the adjacent solution. We use a scenario only when the two solutions (the old and the adjacent) are not very 'close' (on some predetermined basis) to each other: otherwise trade-offs are presented to the decision-maker.

In order to justify using a concave utility function we make three assumptions:

1. Continuity of the utility function.
2. Nonsatiability of objectives.
3. Non-increasing returns to scale.

We now elaborate on these assumptions. The first assumption needs no explanation. Regarding the second assumption, suppose u(x) is the utility function, where x is the vector of objectives. By nonsatiability we mean that other things equal, each objective is to be maximized: mathematically $\partial u/\partial x_i > 0$ for all i. This assumption alone assures us that by maximizing the true function u on a convex set, we will obtain an efficient or nondominated solution (thereby avoiding the problems of unconstrained maxima). Further, there exists a linear function, as well as nonlinear concave functions and other functions whose maxima correspond to the optimal solution. That the function u need not be concave is shown in Figure 10.1; a local optimum need not be globally optimal. All the functions have the property that no non-null vector in the (hyper) plane tangent to the surface of a utility function isoquant dominates nor is dominated by the null vector.

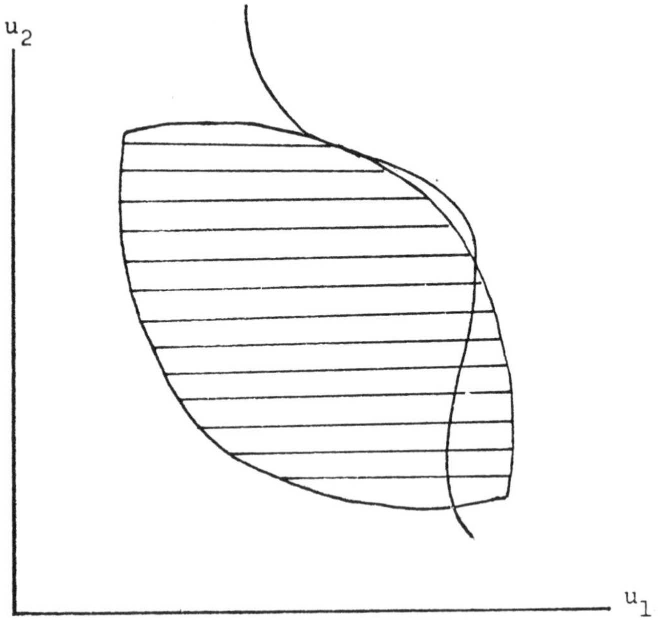

Figure 10.1. A graph of a nonsatiable function with local optimum on a convex set

To overcome the problem of local optima illustrated in Figure 10.1, we need a second order condition. The typical second order conditions associated with the Kuhn-Tucker conditions are not very useful, except in special circumstances. Therefore, we define a necessary and sufficient second order condition to justify the use of a concave utility function: that there are nonincreasing returns to scale. The way we accomplish this is to ask the decision-maker to say that given an incremental trade-off from a particular solution point, a second identical trade-off will *never* be more attractive than the first. This can be expressed in every-day terms in the following way. Let's assume a person does not like to eat liver. Then eating a second serving of liver cannot be less distasteful to him (i.e., more attractive) than eating the first serving of liver. To put it positively, assuming that a person likes ice cream, a second serving of ice cream consumed cannot be more attractive than the first serving of (the identical) ice cream. Though a rigorous testing of these second order conditions does not appear feasible, the decision-maker should be able to indicate in general terms if the conditions seem to hold. If they do hold, a concave utility function may be correctly assumed [1].

Assuming the second order conditions hold, optimality follows as with the general concave case of Zionts and Wallenius (1976).

We summarize the justification of the validation of concavity in the following theorem, which, though it must be known, we have not seen before. (Ginsberg (1973) and Newman (1969) develop various conditions for concavity, but none of theirs corresponds to ours).

Theorem [2]. A utility function to be maximized has nonincreasing returns to scale if and only if the utility function is concave. (By nonincreasing returns to scale, we mean that given a point of reference and two identical (arbitrary) vectors of changes in objectives from that point, and further that the first vector of change must be used before the second, the marginal utility of the second cannot exceed the marginal utility of the first).

Proof. The definition of concavity is that

$$f\,(\lambda x_1 + (1-\lambda)\,x_2) \geq \lambda f\,(x_1) + (1-\lambda)\,f\,(x_2) \qquad (10.2)$$

for $0 \leq \lambda \leq 1$ where x_1 and x_2 are two different vectors and f is the function. Define $\varepsilon \equiv x_2 - x_1$. To prove that nonincreasing returns to scale imply concavity, consider our point of reference x_1 and our arbitrary vector as $\varepsilon/2$. Using our definition of nonincreasing returns to scale, we may write

$$f\,(x_1 + \varepsilon/2 - f\,(x_1) \geq f\,(x_1 + \varepsilon) - f\,(x_1 + \varepsilon/2) \qquad (10.3)$$

which may be written as

$$f\,(x_1 + \varepsilon/2) \geq (f\,(x_1) + f\,(x_1 + \varepsilon))/2 \qquad (10.4)$$

which is the definition of concavity (10.2) for $\lambda = .5$. For any other λ, for example $(\lambda = .75)$, we may continue by induction by showing for example that $f\,(x_1 + .75\varepsilon) \geq (f\,(x_1 + .5\varepsilon) + f\,(x_1 + \varepsilon))/2 \geq .25f\,(x_1) + .75f\,(x_1 + \varepsilon)$. In the limit by this construction we may show the inequality (10.2) holds for all rational values of λ , $0 \leq \lambda \leq 1$. By continuity, it holds for all real values of λ as well. To prove that concavity implies nondecreasing returns to scale, we set $\lambda = .5$ in (10.2). By defining $x_2 = x_1 + \varepsilon$ (as above) we obtain expression (10.4), and by rearranging terms, we obtain expression (10.3). Now, since x_1 and x_2 may be chosen (or equivalently ε may be chosen) arbitrarily, expression (10.3) follows from concavity for all x_1 and ε , thereby proving that concavity implies nonincreasing returns to scale.

10.4. IMPLEMENTATION AND RESULTS

The program has been implemented on an interactive basis on the CDC 6600-7600 at the Brookhaven Laboratory. The interactive portion takes place on the 6600 and the linear programming problems are solved in batch mode on the 7600 using APEX. Under rather favorable operating conditions one iteration can be completed in a little less than an hour.

A flowchart of the procedure as implemented on the CDC 6600-7600 is shown in Figure 10.2. It is the same procedure described in the previous section. The program alternates between solutions to the composite linear programming problem described in step 2 of the procedure of section 3, and related information produced by APEX on the 7600 and the determination of questions and the interactive procedure on the 6600. In order to generate the necessary matrices of coefficients in APEX for use by our multiple criteria subroutines, we had to do several things, which would have been much easier had we developed the entire linear programming package as well. First, in order to obtain our matrix of trade-offs from APEX (as dexcribed in more detail in the appendix) we used the optimal basis for the composite linear programming problem and changed the objective function sequentially to each of the individual objective functions. Without performing any iterations we then computed the corresponding vector of evaluators or reduced costs. Each such row constitutes a row of our trade-off matrix. Second, in order to define all the adjacent extreme points to the current basic feasible solution, we used the cost ranging or sensitivity analysis feature of APEX. Then in the Fortran (6600) portion of the package, we are able to determine the efficient trade-off questions, and the corresponding adjacent solutions. This is done for two solutions each cycle, as described in the appendix.

We also use APEX to solve the small linear programming problems that determine the weights on the objective functions for the next composite functions.

The method has been used for several different problems. One of the problems was used for runs with Brookhaven personnel as decision-makers.

The first problem contained the following six objective functions:

a) Total systems cost

b) Unannualized capital cost with end-use devices

c) Annual consumption of refined oil, processed natural gas and low BTU gas

d) Annual consumption of clean and renewable energy sources (e.g., geothermal, solar, hydro, business and wind)

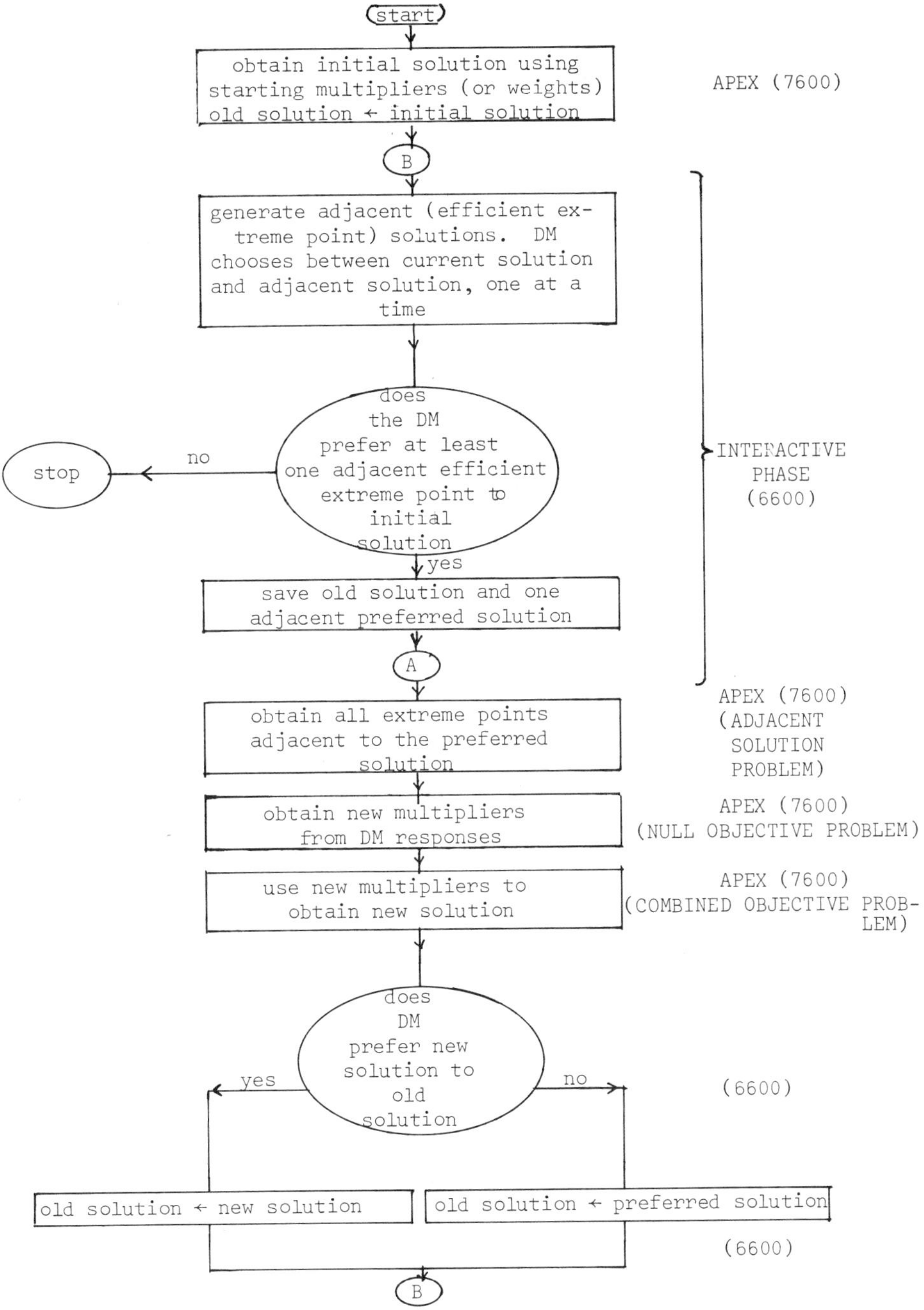

Figure 10.2. A flowchart of the procedure

e) Environmental index, a measure of pollution

f) Consumption of nuclear energy.

All the objectives, except the fourth, were to be minimized. The problem contained 481 constraints and 453 variables. It was used with four Brookhaven personnel serving as decision-makers. The number of interactive sessions required ranged from 8 to 14 and the number of questions from 43 to 63. The results are summarized below.

Table 10.1
A summary of tests with Brookhaven personnel

Decision-maker	Number of interactive sessions	Total number of questions	yes responses	no responses	I don't know responses
1	9	63	22	33	8
2	14	56	21	31	4
3	12	61	19	30	12
4	8	43	16	26	1

We asked each of the users to share us their feelings about the system; both good and bad. Our main conclusions are:

1. The method seems to perform well. Users find solutions they generally like. The number of questions and question sessions seem reasonable.

2. Although the computer system does not normally permit continuous solution of a problem, the quasi-batch mode of operation, whereby a user makes perhaps one or two runs a day, seems satisfactory.

3. The program seems to be relatively easy to understand and use. A number of users have used the program, with little or no difficulties. Several presentations at BNL on the use of the method have been well received.

4. One difficulty with the method has been that the concept of trade-offs is not always readily understood and appreciated by users. To overcome this difficulty, the program has been altered to give the user two feasible solutions (or scenarios) described in terms of objective function values. The user is asked to choose betwee them. However, sometimes two adjacent extreme points (projected into objective function space) may be extremely close or even identical because of degeneracy. In such instances, where solutions are said to be sufficiently close (as a function of a parameter in the program) we then revert back to presenting the questions in terms of trade-offs. The user must be sensitive to the changing nature of questions asked, even though the program output clearly indicates when a trade-off question is being posed.

5. In the course of problem solution with the method, some users complained about some of the objectives of this model. The model was an existing one and not one that had been set up specially for a study on which they were working. We encouraged them to change objectives, as appropriate, and to include objectives most meaningful from their perspective One objective, about which almost everyone complained was the environmental index, a measure of pollution. The index was not well

understood by most users. One person suggested that such an index could in fact be developed using our program. The user could use such a measure and then simply limit levels of certain pollutants, etc.

Other problems have also been solved using the approach. The results have generally been similar to those described above. The Brookhaven National Laboratory has indicated its interest in continuing to use the method in energy planning models, and we are working together in that regard. Some further details are described in the appendix.

A User's Manual (Deshpande and Zionts (1979)) as well as the program are available on request from BNL or from the authors.

Appendix

Some Special Concerns Involving the Use of APEX

USE OF APEX

The multiple objective linear programming is defined as follows:

$$\{ \max \; Cx \,|\, Ax = b, \quad x \geq 0, \quad x \in R^n, \quad b \in R^m \}$$

Let C be a $p \times n$ matrix. Let S be defined as the feasible region and E be the set of efficient points.

If $x = (x_B, x_N)$ is a basic feasible solution in S then the entire problem can be rewritten to correspond to this basic feasible solution. We then have (with B the basis, N the nonbasis, or B's complement with respect to A and C_B and C_N the corresponding submatrices of C) the following tableau.

$C_B B^{-1} b$	0	$C_B B^{-1} N - C_N$
$B^{-1} b$	I	$B^{-1} N$

The trade-off matrix is the matrix $C_B B^{-1} N - C_N$. From it we determine the efficient questions to be asked. Every column of the trade-off matrix is a potential question. The trade-off matrix is computed in APEX by taking the basis for the old solution and changing the objective function to each of the individual objective functions. No iterations are performed. We compute $C_B B^{-1} N - C_N$ where C_B and C_N are the coefficients of the objective function under consideration. For each objective, a row of the trade-off matrix is obtained.

Recall that in the procedure we also must have an adjacent solution preferred by the decision-maker as well as its trade-off matrix. We develop the two solutions in the same 7600 (APEX) session, in the second and every subsequent 7600 (APEX) session.

The above discussion assumes that we know the appropriate adjacent extreme point. In general, we must know all of the adjacent extreme point solutions. We develop them by performing a sensitivity analysis in terms of APEX. Simply, we ask the question what is the amount at which each nonbasic variable (variable x_j), considered separately, will enter the basis and which variable will leave the basis. The result is a vector, each entry (designate it as θ_j) corresponding to a nonbasic variable. To identify an adjacent extreme point in terms of its objective function levels, it is only necessary to multiply θ_j by the appropriate (i.e., the jth) column of the trade-off matrix and add it to the vector describing the old solution. The appropriate basis is described by starting with the old basis and then exchanging the departing variable and the entering variable.

10.5. NOTES

[1] If they do not hold, the assumption of a concave utility function will nonetheless yield a local optimum. Using different starting strategies, i.e., different starting sets of weights, may lead to different local optima which may or may not include the global optimum. The wisdom of doing this has yet to be explored.

[2] The authors wish to acknowledge discussions wiht and the suggestions of Dr. Sol Kaufman SUNYAB with reference to this result.

10.6. REFERENCES

Cherniavsky, Ellen A., "Brookhaven Energy System Optimization Model", Brookhaven National Laboratory Publication 19569, 1974.

Cherniavsky, Ellen A., Kydes, Andy S., and Davidoff Jack W., "Multiple-Objective Function Analysis of ERDA Forecase-2, Year 2000 Scenario", Brookhaven National Laboratory Publication 50685, 1977.

Deshpande, Dilip, and Zionts, Stanley, "User's Manual for the Zionts-Wallenius General Concave Multiple Criteria Method", Working Paper no.399, School of Management, State University of New York at Buffalo, 1979.

Ginsberg, William, "Concavity and Quasiconcavity in Economics", *Journal of Economic Therory 6,* 1973, pp.596-605.

Newman, Peter, "Some Properties of Concave Functions", *Journal of Economic Theory,* vol.1, 1969, pp.291-314.

Zionts, Stanley, and Deshpande, Dilip, "A Time Sharing Computer Programming Application of A Multiple Criteria Decision Method to Energy Planning - A Progress Report", in: Zionts, S. (ed.), *Multiple Criteria Problem Solving Proceedings, Buffalo, NY (U.S.A.),* Springer-Verlag, Heidelberg, 1978, pp.549-559.

Zionts, Stanley, and Wallenius, Jyrki, "An Interactive Programming Method for Solving the Multiple Criteria Problem", *Management Science,* vol.22, 1976, pp.652-663.

11 Hierarchical Multiobjective Models in a Spatial System

P. Nijkamp and P. Rietveld

11.1. INTRODUCTION

Multiregional policy analysis aims at providing tools for spatial conflict resolution. Harmonized planning strategies for a system divided into a set of subsystems (for example, districts within a metropolis, regions within a country, branches within an industry, sectors within a national economy, etc.) require methods for resolution of goal conflicts or interest conflicts emerging from the interdependence between the components of the system at hand. Hence, collective decision-making should guarantee an allocation of resources (money, commodities, investments, etc.) such that the ultimate state of the system reflects a meaningful compromise between the various policy options.

The complex interactions between both the components of the system and the policy or decision levels of the system can only be analysed in an appropriate way if insight is available into the structure of all systems components. This information comprises *inter alia*:

(a) *interdependencies* between the components of the system (for example, spillover effects and externalities);

(b) conflicts between various priorities, objectives or targets *within* one component of the system (for example, a friction between equity and efficiency at the *intra*regional level);

(c) *conflicts* between the priorities, objectives or targets set by the various components of the system at hand (for example, a competition between various cities for federal funds).

The information need related to (a) requires the construction and estimation of a *structure model*, which describes all interactions within and between the components of the system at hand (for example, an interregional model describing the functional economic relationships within and between regions of a national economy).

The policy conflicts inherent in (b) require the use of *multiobjective programming* theory in which a vector optimization problem reflects the conflicts between a set of different objectives (for example, the friction between the aim of a maximum production and a maximum environmental quality within an area).

Finally, the conflicts between the various components of the system require a co-ordinating mechanism at a higher level such that a meaningful compromise between the frictions at a lower level can be found (for example, the allocation of investment funds by a central government in order to stimulate the regional industrial growth potentials). The latter category of co-ordination problems within and between various policy levels is especially studied in the field of *multilevel programming theory*.

The interdependencies, interactions and causal-functional relationships within and between the components of a system are described by means of a model. This model and its side-conditions define the feasible area for both a multi-objective programming analysis and a multilevel programming analysis. *Multi-objective* programming aims at dealing with the multidimensional nature of choices and the conflictual options in real-world policy problems. *Multilevel* programming aims at concentrating on a co-ordination between different decision levels in order to avoid less efficient social choices. The present study aims at providing a synthesis between multi-objective and multilevel programming. This implies some sort of nested hierarchy problems between a co-ordination centre and the systems components. Thus, the assumption will be made that there are several decision units (in particular, regions) which are competing with respect to each other (*exterior conflicts* due to spatial spillovers and environmental externalities). Furthermore, the policies of the various systems components are to be co-ordinated by a central planning unit (either as a top-down (centralized) policy or as a bottom-up (decentralized) policy), especially because each component has its own interests (*multilevel conflicts*). Finally, each systems component is assumed to have a set of multiple conflicting objectives (*interior conflicts*).

In this paper, a brief introduction to multi-objective programming and multilevel programming will be given. Special attention will be paid to the co-ordination problems of a combined multi-objective-multilevel programming model. The computational aspects will also be discussed. The conflicts inherent in the possibility of forming coalitions among the parties will be treated as well. After a formal comprehensive analysis of the above-mentioned problems of conflict resolution, an empirical application will be presented which is based on a multiregional policy model incorporating *inter alia* pollution, employment and a two-level policy structure.

11.2. A MULTI-OBJECTIVE PROGRAMMING FRAMEWORK

The majority of traditional policy models is based on the assumption of individual decision units aiming at achieving a one-dimensional objective (revenues, utility, social welfare etc.). These policy analyses are often developed for a wonderland of no other decision units, while external spillover effects are frequently excluded by assumption.

Recently, however, there is a growing awareness of the existence and relevance of spillover effects, between both economic subjects and larger decision entities (such as regions or countries). A simultaneous analysis of all relevant policy objectives (implying a *multidimensional objective profile*) complicates the traditional policy and programming models to a considerable degree. In Figure 11.1 an illustrative representation of such a double multidimensional policy framework is given. This framework reflects the interdependencies and interactions among the various components of the policy structure at hand.

The various objective functions are denoted as $\omega_1, \omega_2, \ldots, \omega_J$. The picture from Figure 11.1 can easily be extended toward a three-level structure etc. This picture clearly reflects a double choice conflict, viz. between objectives and between systems components. The conflict between systems components is a result of (1) spillover effects between these

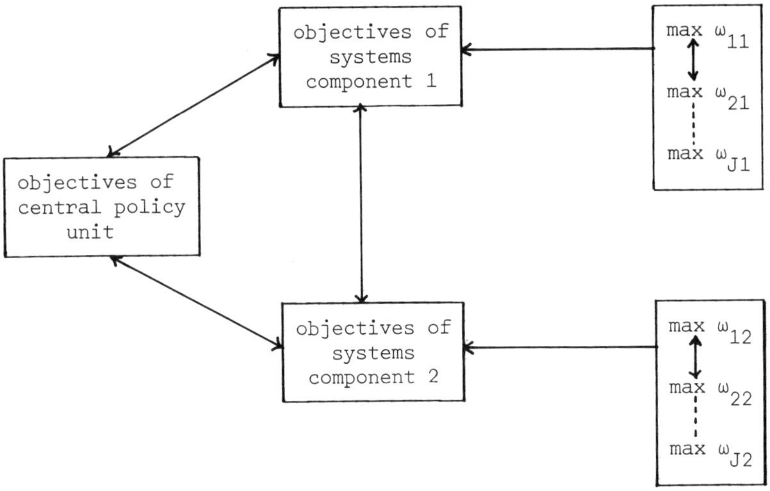

Figure 11.1. An illustrative picture of an integrated multidimensional policy framework

components (for example, spatial externalities and input-output linkages in a multiregional system) and (2) competition for scarce resources allocated by a higher decision or policy level. The goal conflicts emerge from the diverging nature of objectives within a certain systems component.

The presence of several competing *policy* units leads to an additional complication because it involves a double choice conflict. Formally, however, this problem can be described by adjusted multiobjective programming models.

In the present section, a multiregional system composed of R mutually dependent regions will be assumed; this interdependence emerges from spatial spillover effects. Each region is considered to be a spatially decentralized decision unit aiming at achieving a set of multiple objectives. Furthermore, there is a central decision or planning unit which attempts to co-ordinate the various regional decision strategies. Assuming J different objectives ($j=1,\dots,J$), R regions ($r=1,\dots,R$) and one central unit c, the following joint matrix Ω of objective functions for the total spatial system may be assumed:

$$\Omega = \left[\begin{array}{c|ccc} \omega_{1c} & \omega_{11} & \cdots & \omega_{1R} \\ \vdots & \vdots & & \vdots \\ \omega_{Jc} & \omega_{J1} & \cdots & \omega_{Jr} \end{array}\right] \tag{11.1}$$

where ω represents a certain objective function (production growth, environmental quality, equitable distribution, e.g.). Each objective function ω_{jr} is functionally determined by a set of state variables $\underline{s}_{jr}$, a set of instrument variables $\underline{t}_{jr}$, a set of external state and instrument variables $\underline{y}_{jr}$ (from surrounding regions) and a set of exogenous variables $\underline{e}_{jr}$:

$$\omega_{jr} = \omega_{jr}\,(\underline{s}_{jr}, \underline{t}_{jr}, \underline{y}_{jr}, \underline{e}_{jr}) \qquad (11.2)$$

The arguments of ω_{jr} are assumed to be related to each other by means of an underlying functional structure:

$$\underline{s}_{jr} = f\,(\underline{t}_{jr}, \underline{y}_{jr}, \underline{e}_{jr}) \qquad (11.3)$$

Then the multiobjective program of region r attempts to maximize ω_{jr} (j=1,...,J) subject to (11.3) and other side-conditions (inequalities e.g.).

The conflicts inherent in a separate optimization of the successive objective functions (either at an individual or at a regional scale) can be represented by means of the following pay-off matrix P (see also Nijkamp (1978)).

$$P = \begin{bmatrix} P_{cc} & P_{c1} & \cdots & P_{cR} \\ P_{1c} & P_{11} & \cdots & P_{1R} \\ \vdots & \vdots & \ddots & \\ P_{Rc} & P_{R1} & \cdots & P_{RR} \end{bmatrix} \qquad (11.4)$$

The elements on the main diagonal of (11.2) represent the absolute maxima of the corresponding functions. The block-diagonal matrices of (11.4) represent the *intra*regional conflicts: they represent the values of a certain objective function in a certain region r of the whole multiregional system when a competing objective function in region r is maximized. The off-diagonal blocks represent *inter*regional conflicts: they indicate the value of a certain objective function in region r when an objective function in another region is maximized.

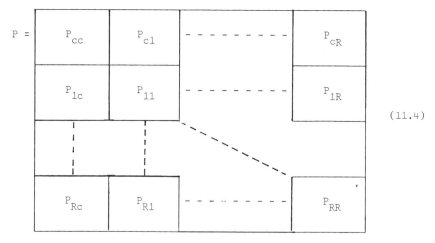

In the case of a centralized decision system, the central unit will indicate the limits within which the successive regional units have to achieve their objectives. In a decentralized system the successive regions will give signals to the central co-ordinating unit in order to reconcile the various interests. This situation implies an extension of traditional multi-objective programming: in addition to conflicts between objectives one has to deal with conflicts between regions (or decentralized decision units), so that a double choice problem arises; hence this relationship to multi-objective programming will be discussed later.

11.3. A SURVEY OF MULTILEVEL PROGRAMMING

Hierarchical or multilevel programming methods have been developed since the early sixties. These are capable of solving large scale programming problems by means of *decomposition*. The methods can also be used to study the *co-ordination* of the decisions of subdivisions by a central unit [1].

The idea of multilevel programming can be illustrated by means of the following linear programming problem:

$$\left.\begin{array}{llll} \max! & z=\underline{c}_1'\,\underline{x}_1 + \underline{c}_2'\,\underline{x}_2 + \ldots + \underline{c}_R'\,\underline{x}_R & & \\ \text{subject to:} & B_1\,\underline{x}_1 & \leq & \underline{b}_1 \\ & \quad B_2\,\underline{x}_2 & \leq & \underline{b}_2 \\ & \qquad\quad B_R\,\underline{x}_R & \leq & \underline{b}_R \\ & \underline{x}_r \geq \underline{o} \quad r=1,\ldots,R & & \end{array}\right\} \tag{11.5}$$

where $\underline{x}_r$ is the vector with instrumental and state variables of region r. The vector $\underline{x}_r$ has to satisfy a number of side-conditions denoted by $B_r\,\underline{x}_r \leq \underline{b}_r$. For the moment we assume that the regions have established an overall objective function $\omega_r = \underline{c}_r'\,\underline{x}_r$, where $\underline{c}_r$ is the vector with coefficients corresponding with $\underline{x}_r$. For the time being, we also assume that the central objective is the maximization of the sum of the regional objective functions.

Problem (11.5) is *separable*: the overall optimum can be attained when each region r solves its own decision problem:

$$\begin{array}{ll} \max! & \omega_r = \underline{c}_r'\,\underline{x}_r \\ \text{s.t.} & B_r\,\underline{x}_r \leq \underline{b}_r \\ & \underline{x}_r \geq \underline{o} \end{array} \tag{11.6}$$

In this case co-ordination is not necessary because of the lack of interdependencies between regions. When interdependencies are included in (11.5) by means of the additional constraints $\sum_r A_r\,\underline{x}_r \leqslant \underline{a}$, the whole situation changes. Different types of common constraints can be distinguished. They may pertain *inter alia* to [2]:

(1) common resources to be distributed among regions (manpower, capital, subsidies, funds);

(2) common tasks to be performed by the regions (provision of sufficient outputs);

(3) spill-over effects (immission of pollutants from surrounding regions).

Thus the central programming problem reads as:

$$\left.\begin{array}{llll}
\max! \; \underline{c}_1' \underline{x}_1 + \underline{c}_2' \underline{x}_2 + \ldots + \underline{c}_R' \underline{x}_R & & & \\
\text{s.t.} \; B_1 \underline{x}_1 & & \leq & \underline{b}_1 \\
\qquad B_2 \underline{x}_2 & & \leq & \underline{b}_2 \\
\qquad \qquad \ddots & & & \vdots \\
\qquad \qquad B_R \underline{x}_R & & \leq & \underline{b}_R \\
A_1 \underline{x}_1 + A_2 \underline{x}_2 + \ldots + A_R \underline{x}_R & & \leq & \underline{a} \\
\underline{x}_r \geq \underline{o} \quad , r=1,\ldots,R & & &
\end{array}\right\} \qquad (11.7)$$

Given these interdependencies, it is improbable that an unco-ordinated solution of the regional problems (11.6) will yield the optimal solution of (11.7). There are essentially two ways in which the centre can try to achieve such a co-ordination:

(a) it can impose additional *constraints* on problem (11.6) to ensure that the costs and benefits of the common constraints are distributed in such a way that the overall optimum will be reached;

(b) it can introduce *prices* into (11.6) to charge the regions for their use of the common resources.

Given the information contained in (11.7), it is not difficult to compute these constraints or prices. In most cases, however, this information on ($\underline{c}_r$, $\underline{b}_r$, B_r and A_r) is not completely known to the centre. In fact, this uncertainty about the structure of the decision problem is an essential characteristic of central planning problems.

It is an attractive property of multilevel programming methods that they explicitly recognize this uncertainty. They do not aim at finding an immediate solution by means of full information about the problem, but they aim at providing a stepwise approximation of the optimal solution by means of exchange of information between centre and subdivisions.

Various methods have been developed for such a communication process. They can be distinguished *inter alia* according to the following characteristics (cf. Kornai (1965) and Malinvaud (1972)):

(1) the nature of the indices generated by the centre;

(2) the way in which these indices have been computed;

(3) the nature of indices generated by the subdivisions;

(4) the way in which these indices have been computed;

(5) the termination rule;

(6) the way in which the final decision is formulated.

The two ways mentioned above to internalize the external effects into the subdivisional decision problems can be elaborated as follows:

A. Direct method (for example, Kornai (1965)).

This method is called direct because the centre directly distributes the common resources $\underline{a}$ among the subdivisions. The centre generates a provisional distribution of resources $(\underline{a}_1,\ldots,\underline{a}_r)$, satisfying $\sum_r \underline{a}_r = \underline{a}$). Each subdivision r solves:

$$\begin{aligned} &\max! \ \omega_r = \underline{c}'_r \underline{x}_r \\ &\text{s.t. } B_r \underline{x}_r \leq \underline{b}_r \\ &\qquad A_r \underline{x}_r \leq \underline{a}_r \\ &\qquad \underline{x}_r \geq \underline{o} \end{aligned} \tag{11.8}$$

and reports the shadow-prices $\underline{\pi}_r$ of the common resources back to the centre. Given this information about the prices, the centre revises the distribution of resources to increase the efficiency of the use of the common resources. When all shadow-prices $\underline{\pi}_r$ are equal (r=1,...,R), a redistribution does not increase efficiency, so that the optimum has been attained.

B. Indirect method (for example, Dantzig and Wolfe (1960)).

This method is called indirect because the centre computes the distribution of resources only after the optimal prices of these resources have been determined.

The centre starts with the generation of provisional prices $\underline{\pi}$ for the common resources. The subdivisions solve:

$$\begin{aligned} &\max! \ \underline{c}'_r \underline{x}_r - \underline{\pi}' A_r \underline{x}_r \\ &\text{s.t. } B_r \underline{x}_r \leq \underline{b}_r \\ &\qquad \underline{x} \geq \underline{o} \end{aligned} \tag{11.9}$$

and report back to the centre the optimal amounts $\underline{a}_r$ they need from $\underline{a}$. If $\sum_r \underline{a}_r = \underline{a}$, the overall optimum has been attained. If not, the centre has to revise the prices such that this equality can be reached ultimately.

The methods share the characteristic that the centre does not need to know anything about the A_r, B_r, $\underline{b}_r$, $\underline{c}_r$ at the start of the procedure. They differ with respect to the nature of the indices exchanged (see Figure 11.2).

In the next section we will give a more detailed description of the procedures to be used by the centre in order to guarantee a converging interaction in a series of steps.

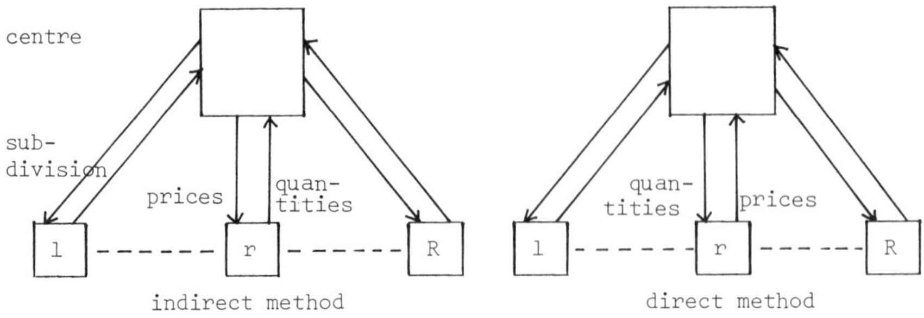

Figure 11.2. Exchange of indices between centre and subdivisions

11.4. COMPUTATIONAL ASPECTS OF MULTILEVEL PROGRAMMING

In the present section we shall first illustrate the Dantzig and Wolfe (1960) algorithm for the *indirect method*. Let S_r be the set of all $\underline{x}_r$ satisfying the constraints in (11.6):

$$S_r = \underline{x}_r \; \{B_r \underline{x}_r \leq \underline{b}_r \; ; \; \underline{x}_r \geq \underline{o}\} \tag{11.10}$$

The set S_r contains (say) K_r extreme points:

$\overset{+1}{\underline{x}_r}, \ldots, \overset{+K_r}{\underline{x}_r}$, which define the feasible area.

Let the matrix T_r be defined as:

$$T_r = \left(\overset{+1}{\underline{x}_r} , \overset{+2}{\underline{x}_r} , \ldots , \overset{+K_r}{\underline{x}_r} \right) \tag{11.11}$$

As S_r is a convex polyhedron, each element $\underline{x}_r$ of S_r can be written as a positive linear combination of the K_r extreme points:

$$\forall \underline{x}_r \in S_r \; \exists \; \underline{\mu}_r \; (\underline{\iota}' \underline{\mu}_r = 1, \; \underline{\mu}_r \geq \underline{0}) \text{ such that } \underline{x}_r = T_r \, \underline{\mu}_r$$

Consequently, (11.5) can be rewritten as:

$$\begin{aligned} &\max! \;\; \underline{c}_1' T_1 \underline{\mu}_1 + c_2' T_2 \underline{\mu}_2 + \ldots + \underline{c}_R' T_R \underline{\mu}_R \\ &\text{s.t.} \;\; A_1 T_1 \underline{\mu}_1 + A_2 T_2 \underline{\mu}_2 + \ldots + A_R T_R \underline{\mu}_R \leq \underline{a} \\ &\qquad \underline{\iota}' \underline{\mu}_r = 1 \qquad r=1,\ldots,R \\ &\qquad \underline{\mu}_r \geq \underline{0} \qquad r=1,\ldots,R \end{aligned} \tag{11.12}$$

The result of this reformulation is that (11.5) can be solved without explicit knowledge of $B_1,\ldots,B_R$, once the matrices $T_1,\ldots,T_R$ are known. Dantzig and Wolfe have developed an algorithm to determine a sufficiently large part of $T_1,\ldots,T_R$ to enable the computation of the optimum. Starting with one or some provisional solutions [3] of S_r, summarized in the matrix T_r^o, in each step i(i= 1,2,3..) a matrix T_r^i can be constructed by adding a new extreme solution $\underline{x}_r^{+i}$ of S_r to the matrix T_r^{i-1}. The solutions $\underline{x}_r^{+1}$ (r=1,...,R) can be found as follows:

(a) The centre solves (11.12) for T_r^{i-1}. It determines the shadow-prices of the common constraints and reports these prices to the subdivisions.

(b) The subdivisions solve (11.9) given $\underline{\pi}$ and report the optimal values of $\underline{x}_r$ to the centre.

(c) These solutions $\underline{x}_r$ are added as $\underline{x}_r^{+i}$ to the matrices T_r^{i-1}. If the central objective function cannot be increased, stop the procedure. Otherwise, set i=i+1 and return to (a).
The authors prove than when (11.12) is nondegenerate, this procedure will converge in a finite number of iterations.

The second part of this section is devoted to the *direct method* of multilevel planning. Given the initial distribution submitted to the subdivisions $(\underline{a}_1^o,\ldots,\underline{a}_R^o)$ and the prices $(\underline{\pi}_1^o,\ldots,\underline{\pi}_R^o)$ reported to the centre, there are several ways to generate a new distribution $(\underline{a}_1^1,\ldots,a_R^1)$ with a better overall performance.

We start with a very simple approach, developed by Schleicher (1971). It is based on the observation that when the price of resource k reported by region r and denoted by π_{kr}^i is larger than the corresponding price in region r' $(\pi_{kr'}^i)$, the overall performance of the system increases when $a_{kr'}$ is reduced in favour of a_{kr}. Thus the *direction* of redistribution can be determined. For the *size* of redistribution we introduce the variable q, indicating the step size.

We introduce the following criteria for a rule of redistribution:

(a) $\sum_r a_{kr}^i = a_k \quad , k=1,\ldots,K$

(b) if $\pi_{k1}^{i-1} = \ldots = \pi_{kR}^{i-1}$, then $(a_{k1}^{i-1},\ldots,a_{kR}^{i-1}) = (a_{k1}^i,\ldots,a_{kR}^i)$

(c) the $\underline{a}_r^i$ should lead to feasible solutions of (11.8) for r=1,...,R

(d) $z^i \geq z^{i-1}$

Consider (11.13) as a rule of redistribution [4]:

$$a_{kr}^i = a_{kr}^{i-1} + q \left\{\frac{\pi_{kr}^{i-1}}{\sum_r \pi_{kr}^{i-1}} - \frac{1}{R}\right\} |a_K| \tag{11.13}$$

It can easily be checked that (11.13) satisfies (a) and (b), while Schleicher shows that by an appropriate choice of the step size q, also (c) and (d) hold true. Obviously, when $\sum_r \pi_{kr}^{i-1} = 0$ there is no need for a redistribution. Schleicher proves that this procedure converges, though not necessarily in a finite number of steps.

Kornai (1965) formulates an alternative approach. He formulates the central decision problem in step i as:

$$\max! \sum_r \sum_k \pi_{rk}^{i-1} \; a_{rk}$$
$$\text{s.t.} \sum_r a_{rk} = a_k \qquad k=1,\ldots,K \tag{11.14}$$

Obviously, (11.14) may give rise to very extreme outcomes for the distribution of the a_k. When no nonnegativity conditions have been formulated for some of the a_{rk}, (11.14) may even become unbounded. Therefore, Kornai adds upper and lower bounds to (11.14), which can be revised in every step, but even then the outcomes of (11.14) may show considerable oscillations.

Therefore, some averaging procedure is introduced, so that the distribution of resources proposed in step i is a weighted mean of the solution of (11.14) and of the solutions in former steps. The algorithm can be proved to converge, but in general not in a finite number of steps.

The procedures implied by (11.13) and (11.14) share the characteristic that in step i a new distribution of resources in computed, given the information of step i-1, so that the information in the steps 1,...,i-2 remain unused. Ten Kate (1972) proposes an interesting approach related to (11.14), which explicitly uses the information in all preceding steps. A very interesting aspect of this procedure is its narrow relationship with the Dantzig-Wolfe algorithm. Essentially it is equivalent to the application of the Dantzig-Wolfe algorithm to the dual form of (11.7).

The procedure can be exposed as follows. Let $\underline{v}_r^i$ denote the vector with shadow-prices of the divisional constraints $B_r \underline{x}_r \leq \underline{b}_r$ in (11.8) in step i. Then $\eta_r^i = \underline{a}_r' \underline{v}_r^i$ represents the value of the divisional resources $\underline{a}_r$ in step i. The central problem in step i can be formulated as:

$$\max! \; z_c = \sum_r v_r$$
$$\text{s.t.} \; v_r \leq y^{i'} + \sum_k \pi_{kr}^{i'} \; a_{kr} \qquad i'=0,\ldots,i-1;\; r=1,\ldots,R \tag{11.15}$$
$$\sum_r a_{kr} = a_k \qquad k=1,\ldots,K$$

By means of (11.15) the common resources are redistributed in step i, given the information in all preceding steps. The relationship between (11.15) and Kornai's formulation (11.14) can be seen more clearly when (11.15) is reformulated as:

$$\max! \; z_c = \sum_r \left\{ \min_{i'=0,\ldots,i-1} \left(y_r^{i'} + \sum_k \pi_{kr}^{i'} \; a_{kr} \right) \right\}$$
$$\text{s.t.} \sum_r a_{kr} = a_k \qquad k=1,\ldots,K \tag{11.16}$$

We find that (11.14) and (11.16) are equivalent for i=1 [5]. When i > 1, (11.16) has the advantage above (11.14) that the objective function is concave rather than linear, which reduces the possibility that the optimum implies an extreme outcome.

It can be shown that the procedure converges in a finite number of steps. For the outcomes of the objective functions the following relationships can be established:

$$z_c^i \geq z_c^{i+1} \qquad i=1,2,3,\ldots$$

$$z^i = \sum_r \omega_r^i \leq z_c^i \qquad i=0,1,2,\ldots \tag{11.17}$$

Thus $\left\{z_c^1,\ z_c^2,\ldots,z_c^i\right\}$ forms a monotone nonincreasing series. Although it can be shown that the final value of z is larger than all the preceding ones, it cannot be shown that $\left\{z^o,\ z^1,\ldots,z^i\right\}$ is monotone nondecreasing. Temporarily, this series may show a decrease. Further information about these and other methods can be found in the Appendix.

11.5. HIERARCHICAL MULTI-OBJECTIVE PROGRAMMING

The hierarchical planning methods discussed above are based on the assumption that the central objective function z is simply the sum total of the regional objective functions ω_r. In practice, most authors appear to interpret z as the national product, which is indeed the sum of the regional products ω_r.

In this section we will deal with the question of how multilevel planning has to be organised when less rigid assumptions concerning the contents of the objective functions are formulated.

A first step might be a central objective function which is a weighted sum of the regional objective functions. For example, ω_r denotes regional pollution and $z = \Sigma\, \lambda_r\, \omega_r$ denotes the national damage produced by this pollution where λ_r is an index of the damage caused by one unit of pollution in region r. A brief inspection teaches that the algorithm dealt with in Section 11.4 can be maintained after minor modifications.

A more fundamental problem arises when the regional objective functions are considered to be essentially multi-objective in nature. Let $\underline{\omega}_r' = (\omega_{1r},\ldots,\omega_{jr})$ denote the vector with the performance of the J objectives in region r. The objectives depend on the instrument and state variables in the following way: $\underline{\omega}_r = C_r\, \underline{x}_r$. Suppose that the regions have formulated *a priori* vectors with weights $\underline{\lambda}_r$ to be attached to the $\underline{\omega}_r$'s. Then regional welfare can be directly measured as $\underline{\lambda}_r'\, C_r\, \underline{x}_r$. One should realize, however, that this is only one possible way to measure regional welfare. Any monotone increasing transformation such as $(a + b\, \underline{\lambda}_r'\, C_r\, \underline{x}_r)^c$ yields the same outcome for (11.9) and can also be conceived of as a measure of regional welfare (cf. Kapteyn (1977)).

The indeterminant nature of the welfare function also means that the dual variables $\underline{\pi}_r$ of (11.9) are not unique. Consequently, in direct methods where the regions specify the successive weights, the centre can only use the information from subdivisions in a meaningful way when it reaches agreement about the way in which regional welfare has to be measured.

A related problem arises in indirect methods. Say that the central objective function is: max! $\sum_{jr} \alpha_{jr} \omega_{jr}$, where α_{jr} is the weight attached by the centre to the j-th objective of region r. Application of the Dantzig-Wolfe method would mean that the dual variables $\underline{\pi}$ reported to the subdivisions appear in the following revised version of the objective function in (11.9):

$$\max! \ (a + b\ \underline{\lambda}' C_r \underline{x}_r)^c - \underline{\pi}\ A_r \underline{x}_r \tag{11.18}$$

which is again only meaningful when a common standard for regional and national welfare has been formulated.

Another severe problem with indirect methods is that the payment $\underline{\pi}' A_r \underline{x}_r$ for the use of scarce common resources $\underline{a}$ is very difficult to interpret in terms of welfare. Money is transferable, but welfare transfers are hard to imagine. Therefore, it can hardly be defended that (11.18) can be handled effectively by the subdivisions in a multi-objective context.

It is a well-known common feature of many multi-objective methods that they aim at analyzing alternatives in terms of the diverse objectives rather than in terms of unifying concepts such as utility and welfare. It may, therefore, be interesting to develop multilevel planning methods according to this principle. This would mean that the information produced no longer deals with dual variables reflecting the marginal *change in welfare* given a marginal change in resources. In the new context, the dual variables reflect the marginal *change in the various objectives*, given a marginal change in resources. Obviously, the number of prices to be calculated in this approach increases with a factor J.

We will develop this idea for the direct methods of multilevel planning. Consider the allocation problem for subdivisions:

$$\left.\begin{aligned} \max! \quad & \lambda_r' \underline{\omega}_r \\ \text{s.t.} \quad & \underline{\omega}_r = C_r \underline{x}_r \\ & B_r \underline{x}_r \leq \underline{b}_r \\ & A_r \underline{x}_r \leq \underline{a}_r \\ & \underline{x}_r \leq \underline{0} \end{aligned}\right\} \tag{11.19}$$

Instead of the vector of dual variables $\underline{\pi}_r' = (\pi_{1r},\ldots,\pi_{Kr})$ related to the K common resources, we compute now the matrix of dual variables Π_r with elements π_{jkr} reflecting the marginal change in objective j given a marginal change in resource k in region r. Unlike $\underline{\pi}_r$, the matrix Π_r cannot be derived directly from the Simplex tableau. A sensitivity analysis is needed to compute the matrix (cf. Wagner (1975), p.130). Since we know that $\pi_{kr} = \sum_j \lambda_{jr} \pi_{jkr}$, the J-th row of Π_r can be found directly when the preceding J-1 rows have been determined.

Schleicher's algorithm can be generalized for the multi-objective case in the following way. Let i denote the variables established in the i-th iteration. Then the redistribution of resources has to obey the following rule:

$$a_{kr}^{i} = a_{kr}^{i-1} + q \left(\frac{\sum_j \gamma_{jr} \pi_{jkr}}{\sum_r \sum_j \gamma_{jr} \pi_{jkr}^{i-1}} - \frac{1}{R} \right) \left| \sum_r a_{kr} \right| \tag{11.20}$$

where the γ_{jr} are the coefficients of the central objective function $\sum_{jr} \gamma_{jr} \omega_{jr}$.

Ten Kate's method to derive a new distribution of resources can be generalized as follows:

$$\begin{array}{lll} \max! & \sum_{jr} \gamma_{jr} \omega_{jr} & j=1,\ldots,J \\ \text{s.t.} & \omega_{jr}^{i} \leq \sum_k \pi_{jkr}^{i} a_{kr} + \eta_{jr}^{i} & r=1,\ldots,R \\ & \sum_r a_{kr} = a_k & i=0,1\ldots i-1 \end{array} \tag{11.21}$$

where η_{jr}^{i} denotes the contribution of the divisional resources in iteration i to the j-th objective. Note that $\sum_j \lambda_{jr} \eta_{jr}^{i} = \eta_r^{i}$.

The conclusion is that multilevel planning algorithms can be generalized for multi-objective problems, although it implies a heavier computational burden for both the centre and the subdivisions.

There are several directions for additional research. It might be interesting to extend the analysis for non-linear welfare functions. By means of goal programming, it is possible to introduce certain achievement standards for the objectives to be attained by all regions. Another possible specification of the central welfare function $\omega_c(\omega_{11},\ldots\omega_{J1},\ldots\omega_{1R},\ldots\omega_{JR})$ might be a separable one such as: $\omega_c = \omega_{c1}/\omega_{c2}$, where ω_{c1} indicates the welfare based on the national aggregate of the regional objectives, while ω_{c2} is an indicator of the multidimensional interregional inequalities (cf. Blommestein, Nijkamp and Rietveld (1979)).

It is also possible to abandon the use of welfare functions which are formulated *a priori*. Then interactive multi-objective decision methods are the appropriate tool. This would imply a double interaction: (1) between the centre and the subdivisions and (2) between the planning authorities and the analyst (see Figure 11.3).

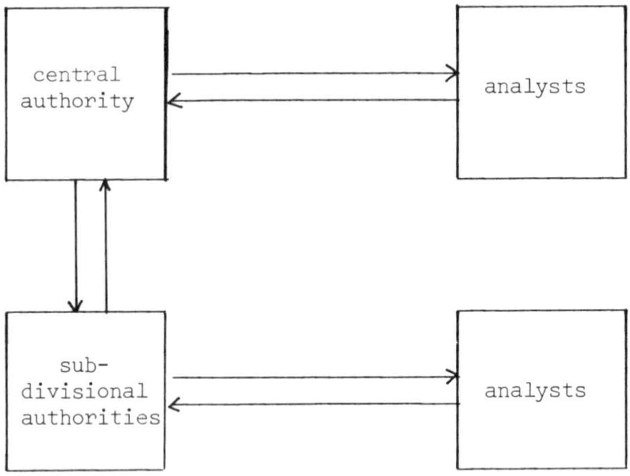

Figure 11.3. Interactions in a multilevel multi-objective planning pro-projects

Some of the multilevel planning methods discussed above will be applied to a numerical problem in the next section.

11.6. EMPIRICAL ILLUSTRATION

The application discussed here is a simple two-region model for the Netherlands. Consider an interregional input-output model with the following elements:

- 4 sectors : agriculture, industry, services, transport (s=1,...4);
- 2 regions : Rijnmond (the greater Rotterdam region) and the rest of the Netherlands (r=1,2);
- 2 objectives : maximization of regional income and minimization of regional pollution (j=1,2).

The following variables are distinguished:

$\underline{y}_r' = (y_{1r},\ldots,y_{4r})$: production levels in sectors 1,...4 in region r

e_r : emission of pollutants in region r

m_r : immission of pollutants in region r

$\underline{i}_r = (i_{ir},\ldots i_{4r})$: investments in sectors 1,...4 in region r.

The two objectives are:

max! $\omega_{1r} = \underline{c}_r' \underline{y}_r$ and min! $\omega_{2r} = m_r$, where $\underline{c}_r$ contains the value added coefficients in region r.

The model contains 11 *common constraints:*

1) There are 8 *input-output* relationships describing the intermediate deliveries between the 4 sectors in both regions:

$$\begin{bmatrix} -I+A_{11} & A_{12} \\ A_{21} & -I+A_{22} \end{bmatrix} \begin{bmatrix} \underline{y}_1 \\ \underline{y}_2 \end{bmatrix} \leq \underline{a}_1 \quad , \tag{11.22}$$

where the matrices A reflect the input-output matrices and where $-\underline{a}_1$ indicates the requirements for the final demand in the various sectors.

2) One constraint is imposed which reflects a limited amount a_2 for total *investments*:

$$\underline{\iota}'\underline{\iota}_1 + \underline{\iota}'\underline{\iota}_2 \leq a_2 \tag{11.23}$$

3) Two constraints describe the relationships between the *immission* of pollutants in a certain region and the *emission* in both regions:

$$\begin{aligned} m_1 - h_{11}\, e_1 - h_{21}\, e_2 &= 0 \\ m_2 - h_{12}\, e_1 - h_{22}\, e_2 &= 0 \end{aligned} \tag{11.24}$$

where the coefficients h denote the multiregional diffusion pattern of pollution.

In addition to these 11 constraints, there are for both regions 6 *divisional constraints*:

1) Four constraints concern the restricted amounts of *capital* for each sector:

$$\underline{y}_r - \hat{s}\, \underline{i}_r < \hat{s}\, \overline{\underline{K}}_r \tag{11.25}$$

where $\hat{s}$ is the diagonal matrix with capital productivities and $\overline{\underline{K}}_r$ the vector with the amounts of capital available at the beginning of the planning period.

2) One constraint has been imposed with respect to the limited amount of *labour* available:

$$\underline{\iota}'\, \hat{L}_r\, \underline{y}_r \leq b_{2r} \tag{11.26}$$

where $\hat{L}_r$ is the diagonal matrix with labour productivities and b_{2r} is the labour force in region r.

3) One relationship describes the links between the production levels in a region and the emission of pollution:

$$e_r - \underline{d}'_r\, \underline{y}_r = 0 \tag{11.27}$$

where $\underline{d}_r$ is a vector with emission coefficients. The values of the coefficients can be found in Mastenbroek and Nijkamp (1976).

First, this model has been used to test the speed of convergence of the multilevel planning methods. We have concentrated our attention on two direct methods, namely those proposed by Schleicher and Ten Kate, since so far no computational results of importance have been published for these methods (cf. Johansen (1978)). For this aim, it is not necessary to use the generalized multi-objective approach. Therefore we state that $\omega_r = \omega_{1r} - \omega_{2r}$, so that ω_r may be conceived of as the regional income corrected for the damage created by the immission of pollutants.

The results of Schleicher's method can be found in Table 11.1. For each iteration i and region r the division of the 11 common resources $\underline{a}_r$ has been printed as well as the shadow-prices $\underline{\pi}_r^i$ computed according to (11.9). There are several common constraints which show shadow-prices equal to zero in each iteration. Consequently, a revision of the distribution is superfluous in that case. Schleicher's method shows a steady but not a very fast growth of the regional objectives.

The same elements have also been depicted for Ten Kate's method (Table 11.2) [6]. Obviously, the latter is superior from the point of view of the speed of convergence. In no more than 8 iterations, the optimal distribution of resources has been attained.

11.7. CONCLUSION

Multilevel planning is an important concept for regional planning, since it explicitly recognizes that lack of information will induce communication in hierarchical networks. In this paper it has been shown that the range of multilevel planning methods can be extended when it is placed in the context of multi-objective decision methods, which means that uncertainties about priorities and conflicts between divergent objectives are taken into consideration.

11.8. APPENDIX

11.8.1. *A concise survey of multilevel planning methods*

Tables 11.3 and 11.4 contain a brief description of several important characteristics of 8 multilevel planning methods selected from the relevant literature. Methods 1-5 are direct, methods 6-8 are indirect. This table provides useful information for an evaluation of the methods. The following criteria are *inter alia* relevant for such an evaluation:

1. The amount of prior information necessary for the centre and the subdivisions to be able to start the procedure.
2. The complexity of the activities of the centre and the subdivisions to be performed in each step.
3. The size of the information streams per iteration.
4. The number of iterations.
5. The possibility to exclude misleading answers of the subdivisions.
6. The possibility to generalize the methods for multi-objective problems.

ad 1. Methods 5, 7 and 8 are less favourable than the other methods.

ad 2. Method 3 is less complex for the centre than the other methods.

ad 3. Indirect methods give rise to smaller amounts of information to be exchanged per iteration than direct methods.

ad 4. Methods 2, 5 nd 8 converge faster than the other methods.

ad 5. In methods 4 and 6 it appears to be unfavourable for the subdivisions to provide false information. The reason is that in these methods the distribution of resources is assumed to be given. For all other methods, the centre faces the problem that the subdivisions may try to obtain an extra large part of the common resources by giving misleading information.

ad 6. Direct methods are more suitable to deal with multi-objective problems than indirect methods.

Obviously, there is no method which dominates all other methods according to all criteria. In the set of direct methods, methods 2 and 3 seem to be more attractive than 1, 4 and 5. In the set of indirect methods, method 8 seems to be more appropriate than methods 6 and 7.

11.9. NOTES

[1] In this study the subdivisions are conceived of as regions. The concepts of multilevel planning can also be applied to other types of subdivisions such as sectors, faculties of a university, or the department of an organization or government.

[2] For ease of presentation $\underline{a}$ will, for each of the types, be called the vector with common resources.

[3] Some methods to generate feasible provisional solutions have been developed, but these will not be discussed in this context. We also will not deal with the problems arising when S_r is unbounded. For these technical aspects we refer to Dantzig (1963).

[4] Formula (11.13) may cause some minor problems, in particular when $a_k = 0$. In that case an appropriate positive number should be substituted for $|a_k|$ in (11.13). If side-conditions have been formulated for the a_{kr} (for example $a_{kr} \geq 0$), (11.13) can be adapted in a straightforward way. See Johansen (1978, p.156).

[5] This identity of (11.14) and (11.16) for i=1 implies that in the beginning of the iterative process, the Ten Kate method may have the same anomalies as Kornai's method, viz. rather extreme outcomes may be generated. Ten Kate shows that this can be remedied by the introduction of upper or lower bounds into (11.16). After a finite number of steps these bounds will become inactive constraints.

[6] A problem arising in all multilevel planning methods is that the division proposed by the centre may appear unfeasible for one or more subdivisions. In Ten Kate's approach this problem has been tackled as follows. If $\underline{a}_r^i$ yields an unfeasible solution, then a new proposal can be calculated as $q\,\underline{a}_r^i + (1-q)\,\underline{a}_r^{i-1}$ for $q < 1$. Reduce q stepwise until all divisional problems are feasible.

11.10. REFERENCES

Baumol, W.J. and Fabian, T., Decomposition, Pricing for Decentralization and External Economies, *Management Science*, vol.11, 1964, pp.1-32.

Blommestein, H.J., Nijkamp, P. and Rietveld, P., A Multivariate Analysis

i r	Common resources (k = 1, ... 11) 1	2	3	4	5	6	7	8	9	10	11	ω_r^i
1 1	-5.000	-80.000	-100.	-5.000	20.000	100.000	75.	5.000	200.000	4000.000	-6000.000	-279
	0.000	0.000	0.	0.000	0.000	0.000	0.	0.000	.206	-.024	.077	
1 2	1.000	50.000	35.	3.000	-50.000	-650.000	-550.	-20.000	550.000	-4000.000	6000.000	1024
	0.000	7.924	0.	165.979	0.000	0.000	0.	2.930	0.000	-.056	-.006	
2 1	-5.000	-87.500	-100.	-5.500	20.000	100.000	75.	1.250	387.500	4400.108	-4831.016	-332
	0.000	0.000	1.	.560	0.000	0.000	0.	245.208	0.000	-.024	.082	
2 2	1.000	57.500	35.	3.500	-50.000	-650.000	-550.	-16.250	362.500	-4400.108	4831.016	1206
	0.000	7.924	0.	165.979	0.000	0.000	0.	2.930	0.000	-.056	-.006	
3 1	-5.000	-95.000	-84.	-5.997	20.000	100.000	75.	4.911	387.500	4800.215	-3672.219	-81
	0.000	0.000	0.	0.000	0.000	0.000	0.	0.000	.206	-.024	.077	
3 2	1.000	65.000	19.	3.997	-50.000	-650.000	-550.	-19.911	362.500	-4800.215	3672.219	1368
	0.000	7.924	0.	165.979	0.000	0.000	0.	2.930	0.000	-.056	-.006	
4 1	-5.000	-102.500	-84.	-6.497	20.000	100.000	75.	1.161	575.000	5200.323	-2503.235	-166
	0.000	1.094	0.	0.000	0.000	0.000	0.	51.703	0.000	-.024	-.005	
4 2	1.000	72.500	19.	4.497	-50.000	-650.000	-550.	-16.161	175.000	-5200.323	2503.235	1550
	0.000	7.924	0.	165.979	0.000	0.000	0.	2.930	0.000	-.056	-.006	
5 1	-5.000	-105.340	-76.	-6.747	20.000	100.000	75.	2.835	575.000	5400.377	-2444.094	-91
	.018	1.141	0.	0.000	0.000	0.000	0.	48.958	.000	-.024	-.008	
5 2	1.000	75.340	11.	4.747	-50.000	-650.000	-550.	-17.835	175.000	-5400.377	2444.094	1621
	0.000	7.924	0.	165.979	0.000	0.000	0.	2.930	0.000	-.056	-.006	
6 1	-4.500	-108.147	-76.	-6.997	20.000	100.000	75.	4.499	668.750	5600.431	-2523.367	-60
	1.178	3.461	0.	.378	0.000	0.000	0.	0.000	.000	-.024	-.181	
6 2	.500	78.147	11.	4.997	-50.000	-650.000	-550.	-19.499	81.250	-5600.431	2523.367	1686
	332.705	0.000	0.	207.411	0.000	0.000	0.	3.266	0.000	-.100	-.006	

7 1	-4.748	-106.272	-76.	-7.121	20.000	100.000	75.	3.561	715.625	5753.877	-2757.327	-62
	.018	1.141	0.	0.000	0.000	0.000	0.	48.958	.000	-.024	-.008	
7 2	.748	76.272	11.	5.121	-50.000	-650.000	-550.	-18.561	34.375	-5753.877	2757.327	1706
	0.000	7.924	0.	165.979	0.000	0.000	0.	2.930	0.000	-.056	-.006	
8 1	-4.623	-106.973	-76.	-7.184	20.000	100.000	75.	3.977	739.062	5803.890	-2777.146	-44
	.018	1.141	0.	0.000	0.000	0.000	0.	48.958	.000	-.024	-.008	
8 2	.623	76.973	11.	5.184	-50.000	-650.000	-550.	-18.977	10.938	-5803.890	2777.146	1711
	0.000	0.000	144.	0.000	0.000	0.000	0.	.876	.040	.006	-.006	
9 1	-4.561	-106.505	-77.	-7.184	20.000	100.000	75.	4.203	727.344	5699.484	-2787.055	-34
	.420	1.945	0.	0.000	0.000	0.000	0.	0.000	.064	-.024	-.068	
9 2	.561	76.505	12.	5.184	-50.000	-650.000	-550.	-19.203	22.656	-5699.484	2787.055	1703
	0.000	7.777	0.	0.000	0.000	0.000	0.	.005	.115	-.074	-.006	
10 1	-4.529	-106.645	-77.	-7.184	20.000	100.000	75.	4.086	725.676	5715.417	-2813.253	-35
	.018	1.141	0.	0.000	0.000	0.000	0.	48.958	.000	-.024	-.008	
10 2	.529	76.645	12.	5.184	-50.000	-650.000	-550.	-19.086	24.324	-5715.417	2813.253	1705
	0.000	7.777	0.	0.000	0.000	0.000	0.	.005	.115	-.074	-.006	
11 1	-4.467	-106.994	-77.	-7.184	20.000	100.000	75.	4.320	713.957	5747.284	-2823.162	-35
	.420	1.945	0.	0.000	0.000	0.000	0.	0.000	.064	-.024	-.068	
11 2	.467	76.994	12.	5.184	-50.000	-650.000	-550.	-19.320	36.043	-5747.284	2823.162	1712
	0.000	7.777	0.	0.000	0.000	0.000	0.	.005	.115	-.074	-.006	

Table 11.1.
Results of Schleicher's method of direct distribution. For every iteration i and region r the distribution of resources $\underline{a}_r^i$ and the corresponding dual variables $\underline{\pi}_r^i$ have been depicted, respectively.

i r	Common resources (k = 1, ..., 11) 1	2	3	4	5	6	7	8	9	10	11	ω_r^i
1 1	-5.000	-80.000	-100.	-5.000	20.000	100.000	75.	5.000	200.000	4000.000	-6000.000	-279
	0.000	0.000	0.	0.000	0.000	0.000	0.	0.000	.206	-.024	.077	
1 2	1.000	50.000	35.	3.000	-50.000	-650.000	-550.	-20.000	550.000	-4000.000	6000.000	1024
	0.000	7.924	0.	165.979	0.000	0.000	0.	2.930	0.000	-.056	-.006	
2 1	-5.000	-146.667	-100.	-70.333	20.000	100.000	75.	2.778	444.444	6666.667	-3333.333	-164
	0.000	1.099	0.	0.000	0.000	0.000	0.	49.795	.001	-.024	-.005	
2 2	1.000	116.667	35.	68.333	-50.000	-650.000	-550.	-17.778	305.556	-6666.667	3333.333	2025
	0.000	0.000	0.	0.000	0.000	0.000	0.	0.000	.017	.080	-.006	
3 1	-5.000	-94.815	-100.	-70.333	20.000	100.000	75.	5.319	580.247	3703.704	-1851.852	-114
	1.178	3.461	0.	.378	0.000	0.000	0.	0.000	0.000	-.024	-.181	
3 2	1.000	64.815	35.	68.333	-50.000	-650.000	-550.	-20.319	169.753	-3703.704	1851.852	1487
	0.000	7.777	0.	0.000	0.000	0.000	0.	.005	.115	-.074	-.006	
4 1	-4.333	-184.938	-100.	-27.861	20.000	100.000	75.	5.281	693.416	2604.387	-3705.805	-52
	.420	1.945	0.	0.000	0.000	0.000	0.	0.000	.064	-.024	-.068	
4 2	.333	154.938	35.	25.861	-50.000	-650.000	-550.	-20.281	56.584	-2604.387	3705.805	1393
	0.000	0.000	0.	0.000	.241	.683	0.	0.000	.088	-.513	-.006	
5 1	-4.185	-187.077	-100.	-27.861	11.111	55.556	75.	5.281	718.564	3264.698	-4017.824	-51
	0.000	1.105	0.	0.000	0.000	0.000	0.	0.000	.097	-.024	-.006	
5 2	.185	157.077	35.	25.861	-41.111	-605.556	-550.	-20.281	31.436	-3264.698	4017.824	1617
	325.833	0.000	0.	0.000	0.000	0.000	0.	0.000	.135	-.119	-.006	

6	1	-5.756	-189.750	-100.	-27.861	11.111	55.556	75.	5.281	750.000	4090.086	-4053.145	-70
		0.000	1.105	0.	0.000	0.000	0.000	0.	0.000	.097	-.024	-.006	
6	2	1.756	159.750	35.	25.861	-41.111	-605.556	-550.	-20.281	0.000	-4090.086	4053.145	1926
		0.000	0.000	0.	0.000	0.000	0.000	0.	0.000	.135	-.119	-.006	
7	1	-5.756	-160.449	-100.	-27.861	11.111	55.556	75.	5.281	750.000	5571.812	-3653.699	-76
		.420	1.945	0.	0.000	0.000	0.000	0.	0.000	.064	-.024	-.068	
7	2	1.756	130.449	35.	25.861	-41.111	-605.556	-550.	-20.281	0.000	-5571.812	3653.699	2101
		0.000	7.672	0.	0.000	0.000	0.000	0.	0.000	.116	-.075	-.006	
8	1	-4.850	-160.933	-100.	-27.861	11.111	55.556	75.	5.281	750.000	5571.812	-3660.196	-76
		0.000	1.105	0.	0.000	0.000	0.000	0.	0.000	.097	-.024	-.006	
8	2	.850	130.933	35.	25.861	-41.111	-605.556	-550.	-20.281	0.000	-5571.812	3660.196	2105
		4.415	7.672	0.	0.000	0.000	0.000	0.	0.000	.116	-.075	-.006	

Table 11.2.
Results of Ten Kate's method of direct distribution. For every iteration i and region r the distribution of resources $\underline{a}_r^i$ and the corresponding dual variables $\underline{\pi}_r^i$ have been depicted, respectively.

Table 11.3.
Features of multilevel planning methods

method	nature of indices generated by centre	nature of indices generated by subdivision	relationship between objective function ω_c of centre and objective function ω_r of subdivisions
1. Kornai, 1965	quantities of resources and outputs	shadow-prices of central constraints	$\omega_c(\underline{x}_1,\ldots,\underline{x}_R) = \sum_r \omega_r(\underline{x}_r)$
2. Ten Kate, 1972	"	shadow-prices of central constraints; η_r	"
3. Schleicher, 1971	"	shadow-prices of central constraints	"
4. Malinvaud, 1972 (Section 8.4)	"	marginal rates of substitution	no objective specified for centre; the method aims at a Pareto-optimal equilibrium; the income distribution is assumed to be given.
5. Weitzman, 1970	unfeasible targets (outputs) and quota (resources)	an arbitrary feasible efficient combination of output and resources as well as the corresponding prices	no constraint on the specification of objective function ω_c
6. Malinvaud, 1972 (Section 8.3)	prices of outputs and resources	quantities demanded and supplied	see Malinvaud, 1972 (Section 8.4)
7. Malinvaud, 1972 (Section 8.5)	"	optimal technical coefficients, given the prices	see Weitzman, 1970
8. Dantzig & Wolfe, 1960		quantities demanded and supplied	$\omega_c(\underline{x}_1,\ldots,\underline{x}_R) = \sum_r \omega_r(\underline{x}_r)$

Table 11.4

Treatment of infomation in multilevel planning methods

way of producing information by centre	way of producing information by subdivision	information necessary for the centre to be able to start the iteration	information necessary for subdivision r to be able to start the iteration
1. solution of problems analogous to (11.14), followed by 'averaging' procedure	solution of the dual of (11.8), followed by an 'averaging' procedure	starting values of $\underline{a},\ldots,\underline{a}_R$; $\underline{a}$	$\underline{b}_r$, B_r ; objective function ω_r
2. solution of dual of Dantzig-Wolfe problem (11.15)	solution of the dual of (11.8)	"	"
3. direct redistribution of a_k on the basis of π_{kr}.	"	"	"
4. "	"	"	"
5. solution of problem similar to (11.15); the information contained in the matrices B_r can be approximated in an increasingly accurate way by means of the subdivision's responses	"	(over-optimistic) approximated values of B_r ; A_r; starting values of $\underline{a}_r$ (r=1,...,R)	$\underline{b}_r$; B_r
6. responses of the direct adjustment of prices, given revealed excess demand or supply	solution of (11.9)	$\underline{a}$; starting values of the prices $\underline{\pi}$	$\underline{b}_r$; B_r ; objective function ω_r
7. solution of the dual of a problem similar to (11.12); the information contained in the matrices B_r can be approximated in an increasingly accurate way by means of the subdivision's responses	"	$\underline{a}$; a combination of technical coefficients	$\underline{b}_r$; B_r ; objective function
8. solution of (11.12)	solution of (11.9)	$\underline{a}$; some starting values $\underline{x}_r^{+1}$ (r=1,..,R); $\underline{c}_r$,A_r(r=1,..R)	

of Spatial Inequalities, in W. Buhr and P. Friedrich (eds.), *Regional Development under Stagnation*, Nomos, Baden-Baden, 1979.
Dantzig, G., *Linear Programming and Extensions*, Princeton University Press, Princeton, 1963.
Dantzig, G. and Wolfe, P., The Decomposition Principle for Linear Programming, *Operations Research Quarterly*, vol.8, 1960, pp.101-111.
Davis, W. and Talavage, J., Three-Level Models for Hierarchical Coordination, *Omega*, vol.5,6, 1977, pp.709-720.
Johansen, L., *Lectures on Macroeconomic Planning*, (ch.2), North-Holland, Amsterdam, 1978.
Kapteyn, A., *A Theory of Preference Formation*, Pasmans, The Hague, 1977.
Kate, A. ten, Decomposition of Linear Programs by Direct Distribution, *Econometrica*, vol.40, 1972, pp.883-898.
Kornai, J., *Mathematical Planning of Structural Decisions*, North-Holland, Amsterdam, 1975.
Malinvaud, E. and Bacharach, M.O.L. (eds.), *Activity Analysis in the Theory of Growth and Planning*, MacMillan, London, 1967.
Malinvaud, E., Decentralized Procedures for Planning, in Malinvaud, E. and Bacharach, M.O.L. (eds.), 1967, pp.170-208.
Malinvaud, E., *Lectures on Microeconomic Theory*, North-Holland, Amsterdam, 1972.
Mastenbroek, A.P. and Nijkamp, P., A Spatial Environmental Model for an Optimal Allocation of Investments, in Nijkamp, P. (ed.), *Environmental Economics*, vol.2, Martinus Nijhoff, The Hague, 1976, pp.19-38.
Nijkamp, P., Competition among Regions and Environmental Quality, *Competition among Small Regions* in Buhr, W. and Friedrich, P. (eds.) Nomos Verlag, Baden-Baden, 1978, pp.153-171.
Schleicher, S., Decentralized Optimization of Linear Economic Systems with Minimum Information Exchange of the Subsystems, *Zeitschrift für Nationalökonomie*, vol.31, 1974, pp.33-44.
Wagner, H.M., *Principles of Operations Research*, Prentice Hall, London, 1975.
Weitzman, M., Iterative Multilevel Planning with Production Targets, *Econometrica*, vol.38, 1970, pp.50-65.

12 The Versatility Model in Decision Making under Uncertainty with Regard to Goals and Constraints

E. Werczberger

12.1. INTRODUCTION

This paper is concerned with decision-making when there is uncertainty with regard to the targets of the objectives or the parameter values of constraints. The criterion underlying the model presented is the versatility of the policies considered. Thus, the model evaluates policies in terms of the likelihood that they will be feasible and satisfactory for alternative possible futures, even though only limited information is available on goals and constraints.

The problem of uncertainty has, of course, always been one of the dominant problems in planning and decision-making, and several decision rules have been developed to deal with the problem. Basically, they fall into two classes: criteria which suggest definitions of the relevant payoff for the evaluation of alternative policies, and criteria which are concerned with their flexibility.

The first class of criteria includes, for example, all those approaches which are based on the expected value of the net benefits, using subjective estimates of probabilities (see e.g. Keeney and Raiffa (1976)). It also includes criteria based on game theory, such as the minimax, minimum regret, or Hurwicz criteria (see e.g., Baumol (1969)). A major difficulty is that all these decision rules usually require explicit consideration of every future state considered to be relevant. Given the limited resources available for design and analysis, proper assessment of the implications of each policy can be carried out only for a small number of the conceivable future developments. Obviously, the alternative chosen can then be efficient only in terms of the states analyzed. It may be totally inadequate in the event of developments not explicitly considered. The planner would then often be better advised to devote the resources available to a limited analysis of a more complete set of possible futures and their implications for goals and constraints.

Recently, more interest has been expressed in the second class of criteria - those which assess policy flexibility: the degree to which a policy can cope with, or can be adapted to an uncertain future. The flexibility criterion, for example, is concerned with multistage decision problems. It seeks to maximize the number of feasible policy sequences available for subsequent stages (Friend and Jessop (1969); Rosenhead et al. (1972); Pye (1978)). It is thus concerned with the size of the policy space, that is, the number of options remaining open after a decision has been made. However, since this approach does not differentiate between alternative options, equal importance is assigned to every feasible policy sequence. The criterion presumes thus that it is only the number of feasible options which concerns the decision-maker, and not their usefulness in the uncertain future.

In contrast, the maximum likelihood criterion, which was developed for multiobjective decision problems, identifies the solution which has the greatest probability of being optimal for a given set of alternative objective functions (Sengupta et al. (1974); Charnetski and Soland (1978; Werczberger (1978)). The decision criterion is the size of the objective function space for which a solution would be optimal. Uncertainty is assumed with regard to the weights which the decision-maker assigns to a set of objective functions.

The model presented in this paper suggests a related approach, based on the versatility criterion (Bonder (1978)). It is an attempt to enhance the versatility of the selected policy across the range of possible future developments, while ensuring an acceptable level of cost-effectiveness. Its objective is to ensure that the chosen alternative remains satisfactory for as many conceivable future developments as possible. It thus tries to maximize the set of acceptable futures. The idea behind this approach is that decision-makers are in many instances both satisficers and averse to risk taking; they may therefore prefer to maximize the probability of achieving a satisfactory level of goal achievement.

12.2. MATHEMATICAL EXPOSITION OF THE MODEL

12.2.1 *The set of feasible policies*

Consider the following problem. Assume a finite set of $\bar{p}$ alternative policies denoted by the subscript $p = 1, 2, \ldots, \bar{p}$. Each policy may involve several activities and can be fully described by a vector $\chi_p = (\chi_{p1}, \ldots \chi_{pd}, \ldots \chi_{p\bar{d}})$ whose $\bar{d}$ elements define the corresponding level for each of the activities.

Not all conceivable policies are feasible. The technical constraints given in (12.1) define the set of *feasible* policies as a function of the unknown future state f of the environment.

$$\Sigma_d \, a_{dj} \, \chi_{pd} + U_j = b_{fj} \quad \text{for all } j \qquad (12.1)$$

where b_{fj} is the right-hand coefficient of the jth constraint for state f and a_{dj} is the coefficient associated with the dth activity of the jth constraint. Furthermore, U_j is the nonnegative slack variable of the jth constraint; and χ_{pd} is the level of the dth activity for policy p. To simplify the exposition, the direction of the inequalities will throughout be taken to be such that the slack variables always have a positive sign.

A policy p is then feasible for state f if, after substitution of the values of χ_p, all equations of type (12.1) have nonnegative solutions for the corresponding slack variables U_j [1].

12.2.2 *Objectives*

The multiple objectives of the problem are defined by aspiration levels or targets for each goal dimension. These targets may also vary according to the state of the environment. Let $g = 1, \ldots \bar{g}$ be the subscripts identifying the $\bar{g}$ goals or objectives. The goal constraints are then given by the following expression:

$$\sum_d a_{dg} \chi_{pd} + U_g = b_{fg} \quad \text{for all } g \qquad (12.2)$$

where b_{fg} is the target of the gth objective for state f, a_{dg} is the coefficient for the dth activity of the gth goal, and U_g is the slack variable of the gth goal constraint.

12.2.3 *Acceptable solutions*

A solution which satisfies both the feasibility and the goal constraints will be called an *acceptable* solution. Moreover, as equations (12.1) and (12.2) are formally equivalent, no further distinction is made between feasibility and goal constraints, and the notation used in (12.1) is employed throughout.

Assume some policy p is acceptable for any state f that can be described by the right-hand parameter vector $b_f = (b_{f1}, \ldots b_{f\bar{j}})$. Substitution of χ_p and b_f into (12.1) yields, by definition, a nonnegative vector of slack variables U_j. Denote the set of possible future states f, i.e., vectors b_j for which χ_p is acceptable, by $\{b(p)\}$. This is the set of all possible vectors b_f whose substitution into (12.1) satisfies the corresponding constraints for policy p. Given our convention on the direction of the inequalities, $\{b(p)\}$ is the set of all vectors b_f whose elements satisfy $\Sigma_d a_{dj} \chi_{pd} \leq b_{fj}$ (see Figure 12.1).

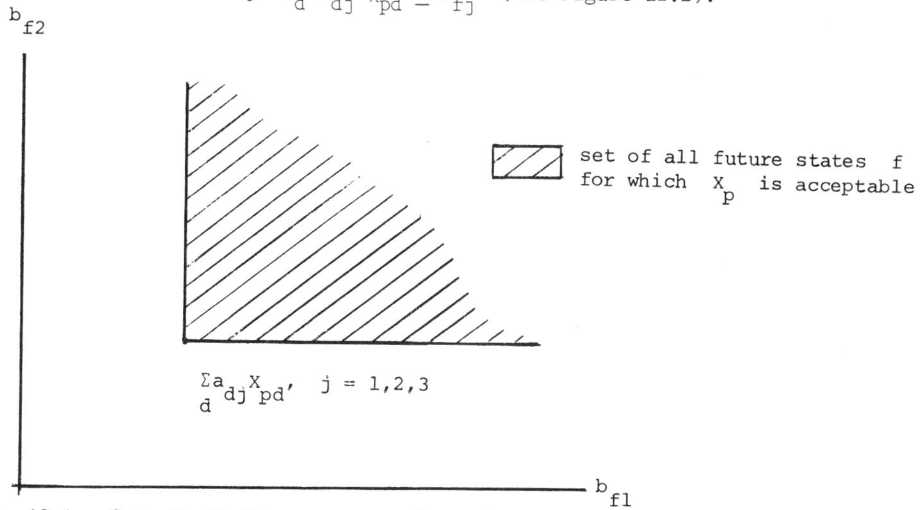

Figure 12.1. Set of all future states for which χ_p is acceptable

12.2.4 *Normal distribution of the* b_j *values*

Let us first assume that the density distribution of the elements of b_f is known. The total probability prob(p), that χ_p is acceptable then equals the product of the probabilities that each of the elements b_j is larger than $\Sigma_d a_{dj} \chi_{pd}$. Hence, prob(p) equals the integral of the probability density function over the set of b_f vectors which χ_p is acceptable.

For example, suppose that the elements of b_f are independent of each other and normally distributed with means $(\mu_1, \ldots \mu_{\bar{j}})$, and standard deviations $(\sigma_1, \ldots \sigma_{\bar{j}})$ [2]

Denote the normal probability density function for the jth element of the vector by $N(b_{jf}, \mu_j, \sigma_j)$. Then prob(p) is given by

$$\text{prob}(p) = \Pi_{j=1}^{\bar{j}} \left[\int_{\Sigma_d a_{dj} \chi_{pd}}^{\infty} N\,(b_{jf}, \mu_j, \sigma_j)\, db_j \right] \qquad (12.3)$$

The values of each integral are available from any table of the cumulative normal distribution, after normalizing the lower limits of integration e_j by calculating $e_j = (\Sigma_d a_{dj} \chi_{pd} - \mu_j)/\sigma_j$.

12.2.5 *The case of uncertainty*

In general, it is rather difficult to obtain meaningful estimates of the probability distribution of the vector b_f. However, it may be possible to define at least the set of possible right-hand coefficients {b}, which will be assumed to be closed, bounded, and convex. The decision problem is then one of uncertainty; although the set of possible states is taken to be known, their respective probabilities are not.

In multiple-criteria decision-making, the range of parameter values for which a solution is acceptable can be used as a measure of the importance of a target. The more important a goal (the greater the weight it has in the decision), the less the decision-maker will be willing to accept deviations from the corresponding target. Hence, for less important objectives, a greater range of aspiration levels may be acceptable than for the more crucial ones. Thus, the 'fuzziness' of the target definition would be inversely related to the priority assigned to the respective objective.

A given policy associated with the vector χ_p is acceptable for state f if, after substitution of χ_p, the following system of equations has a nonnegative solution for the slack variable U_j, $j = 1, \ldots \bar{j}$.

$$\Sigma_d a_{dj} \chi_{pd} + U_j = b_{fj} \mid b_f = (b_{f1}, \ldots b_{fj}, \ldots) \text{ and } b_f \in \{b\}, \quad \text{for all } j. \qquad (12.4)$$

$$U_j \geq 0$$

The set {b} and the vector χ_p thus implicitly define {b(p)}, the set of all possible states for which policy p is acceptable; hence, $\{b(p)\} \subset \{b\}$. Moreover, from the definition of {b} and from equation (12.4), it also follows that {b(p)} is a closed, bounded and convex polytope.

12.2.6 *The probability that a policy is acceptable*

The total probability of all states for which a policy p is acceptable is estimated using Laplace's criterion. This assumes equal probability for all possible states implying a rectangular probability density function over {b}. The probability that policy p is acceptable is then proportional to the hypervolume of {b(p)}.

The set of all possible states {b} has, of course, a probability of one. Therefore, prob(p), is proportionate to the ratio of the volume of {b(p)} to the volume of {b}. Denoting the hypervolume by Vol, we have

$$\text{prob}(p) = \text{Vol}\,\{b(p)\}/\text{Vol}\,\{b\} \qquad (12.5)$$

12.2.7 *A rectangular set {b}*

The simplest case arises when the boundaries of the set {b} are given as independent lower and upper limits for the right-hand parameter b_{fj} of each constraint. Let g_j be the lower limit for the parameter of the jth constraint, and h_j its upper limit. The hypervolume of b is then the product

$$\text{Vol}\,\{b\} = \Pi_j\,(h_j - g_i) \qquad (12.6)$$

To obtain the volume of {b(p)} determine first whether there is any state for which χ_p is acceptable, that is, whether χ_p satisfies the following constraints

$$g_j \leq \Sigma_d\, a_{dj}\, \chi_{pd} \leq h_j \quad \text{for all } j \qquad (12.7)$$

If it does, the volume of b(p) is given by

$$\text{Vol}\,\{b(p)\} = \Pi_j\,(h_j - \Sigma_d\, a_{dj}\, \chi_{pd}) \qquad (12.8)$$

If the slack variables of some constraints have a negative sign, the expression in parenthesis must, of course, be multiplied by -1.

12.2.8 *The set {b} is a general polytope*

If the extreme possible values of the right-hand parameters are mutually dependent, the limits may be defined as linear constraints, involving more than one parameter, such as

$$\Sigma_j\, w_{kj}\, B_j + V_k = c_k \quad \text{for all } k \qquad (12.9)$$

where k, $k = 1,\ldots \bar{k}$ denotes the kth constraint, B_j the right-hand parameter which is now a variable, w_{kj} is the coefficient for the kth

constraint and the jth right-hand parameter, V_k is the slack variable and c_k the constant of the constraint. This definition implies that the set {b} is an $\bar{s}$ dimensional polytope, where $\bar{s} \leq \bar{j}$.

Schlafli (1958) suggests calculating the volume of an n-dimensional polytope by breaking it down into n-dimensional pyramids. The volume of each such pyramid equals the product of its height, and the hypervolume of its (n-1) dimensional basis multiplied by the factor (1/n). The hypervolume of each basis is then further decomposed into a set of (n-1) dimensional pyramids, etc., until $n = 2$. The resulting algorithm yields accurate results; but, except for very small problems, it is very inefficient. For calculating the volume, therefore numerical integration is required because the boundaries of the polytopes are defined by hyperplanes.

The proposed algorithm, based on the Monte Carlo method, is briefly described below. Further discussion is provided in the appendix. A computerized version is available from the author upon request.

First, an arbitrary point ξ in the interior of {b(p)} is selected as the origin of a spherical coordinate system. Denote the radial distance from ξ by ρ , and the vector of angular coordinates by ϕ . Any possible vector of right-hand coefficient $b_f \in$ {b} such as in equation (12.4) can then be represented as

$$b_f = \xi + \rho\delta_\phi \tag{12.10}$$

where $\bar{s}$ is the dimension of {b} , and where $\delta_\phi = (\delta_{\phi 1}, \ldots \delta_{\phi \bar{s}})$ denotes the unit vector through the origin ξ whose angular coordinates are ϕ. To simplify the terminology, the ray coinciding with δ_ϕ will be denoted by its angle ϕ.

Since only the ratio of the hypervolumes is required and not their absolute values, it is sufficient to explicitly integrate in the radial direction. Instead of integrating in the angular directions, a sample of rays is constructed through ξ into every direction within the set of {b}. On any ray ϕ, integration in the radial direction can be carried out explicitly over the interval between ξ and the intersections of ϕ with the boundaries of the polytopes {b} and {b(p)} respectively. The ratio of the sum of the integrals over the two polytopes can then be used as an estimate of the ratio of their hypervolumes. Thus, given a random sample of rays of size $\bar{\phi}$, the following expression approximates prob(p), (Charnetski (1978)).

$$\text{prob}(p) = \Sigma_{\phi=1}^{\bar{\phi}} (\lambda_{\phi p})^{\bar{s}} / \Sigma_{\phi=1}^{\bar{\phi}} (\gamma_\phi)^{\bar{s}} \tag{12.11}$$

where γ_ϕ and $\lambda_{\phi p}$ are the upper limits of integration used for the estimates of the volumes of {b} and {b(p)} respectively. These limits are the distances from ξ of the intersection of the ray ϕ with the boundaries of the polytopes. Since ξ is an interior point of {b(p)}, the ray ϕ intersects the boundaries of the two polytopes only once, and the lower limits of integration are zero.

The proposed algorithm can be summarized by the following seven steps:

1. Select a point ξ interior to $\{b(p)\}$ as origin for the rays.
2. Construct a random half ray through ξ in direction ϕ within $\{b(p)\}$.
3. Calculate the limits of integration γ_{ϕ} and $\lambda_{\phi p}$.
4. Use equation (12.11) to compute the contribution of the ray ϕ to the estimate of the hypervolume ratio for policy p.
5. Repeat from step 2 until desired accuracy is reached.
6. Repeat procedure for next policy.
7. Select the policy with the highest probability to be acceptable.

12.2.7 *An illustrative example*

The following is a highly simplified example intended to illustrate the model's potential application. Imagine a planning agency in Israel faced with the task to compare alternative plans for the physical rehabilitation and renewal of a residential neighbourhood. Usually much of the final information on needs, budgets and objectives, becomes available only at later stages in the planning process. However, postponing the decision on the program inevitably causes delay in implementation, which for many reasons may be highly undersirable. Therefore the planning agency may prefer to select at an early stage a program which is very likely to meet the needs and constraints even if in the end it will turn out to be suboptimum.

Assume then a neighbourhood of 400 households living in blocks of four apartments each. The dwelling units are very small, having a floor area of only 42 sq. m. Moreover, they are badly deteriorated, but most of the apartments can be rehabilitated. The resident population consists of several groups: old couples for which the dwelling size is adequate, families with children and very large households with seven or more persons living in very crowded conditions. The accepted policy is to provide housing for all families in the neighbourhood itself. In addition, there are a number of young couples, for whom dwellings should be provided in the area.

Activities considered (see Table 12.1) include remodelling of the apartments, joining of two apartments and for very large families, addition of a room to two joined apartments. Alternatively, the houses can be demolished either for the constructions of row houses for large households or for apartment blocks with 16 dwelling units each.

Table 12.1. Activities considered

X_1 = Rehabilitation of one dwelling unit for an elderly family without children.

X_2 = Joining and remodelling of two apartments for a young couple.

X_3 = Joining and remodelling of two apartments for a resident family with children.

X_4 = Joining and remodelling of two apartments and addition of one room for a large household.

X_5 = Demolition of an old dwelling unit.

X_6 = Construction of an economy row house for a large household.

X_7 = Construction of an apartment for a young couple in an apartment block of 16 units.

X_8 = Construction of an apartment for a resident family with children in an apartment block of 16 units.

There are a number of constraints which limit the set of acceptable policies (see Table 12.2). These reflect the supply of and the demand for housing and land, the budget available for the implementation of the program and various housing policy targets.

Table 12.2. Constraints

1. *Supply of dwelling units in the neighbourhood* must be greater than or equal to the number of units demolished, rehabilitated and joined to larger apartments.

$$X_1 + 2X_2 + 2X_3 + 2X_4 + 2X_5 \leq b_1 = 400 \text{ d.u.}$$

2. *Vacant Land supply* must be greater than or equal to the area of land used for construction minus the area of land vacated by demolition.

$$-.1X_5 + .25X_6 \; .07X_7 + .07X_8 \leq b_2 = 22 \text{ sq. m.}$$

3. *Housing needs of local residents* must be met in the neighbourhood through rehabilitation, remodelling and new construction.

$$X_1 + X_3 + X_4 + X_6 + X_8 \geq b_3 = 400 \text{ d.u.}$$

4. *Expansion of apartments* is only possible at the ground level. Hence, their number must be less than or equal half to the number of apartments not demolished.

$$-.5X_1 - X_2 - X_3 + X_4 \leq 0$$

5. *Housing target for young couples*

$$X_2 + X_7 \geq b_5$$

6. *Housing target for very large households*

$$X_4 + X_6 \geq b_6$$

7. *Housing target for families with children*

$$X_3 + X_8 \geq b_7$$

8. Budget constraint (in IL. 1000)

$$200X_1 + 500X_2 + 500X_3 + 700X_4 + 10X_5 + 1200X_6 + 900X_7 + 900X_8 \leq b_8$$

9. *Estimate of amount of demolition* necessary because of

$$X_5 \geq b_9$$

For some of the constraints, only ranges can be obtained on the possible parameter values (see Table 12.3). Examples are the budget constraints, housing targets and the number of dwellings which must be demolished. In addition, policy guidelines exist for the desired proportion between the housing targets for very large households, young couples and families with children. The need to define ranges of acceptable values for constraints parameters is due to prevailing uncertainty with regard to existing conditions, future policy and objectives.

Table 12.3. Constraints on possible parameter values

1.	Housing target for young couples	:	$180 \leq b_5 \leq 230$
2.	Housing target for very large households	:	$30 \leq b_6 \leq 60$
3.	Housing target for families with children	:	$150 \leq b_7 \leq 175$
4.	Budget constraint	:	$405{,}000 \leq b_8 \leq 440{,}000$
5.	Proportion of housing target for young couples to target for large households	:	$b_5 - 2b_6 \geq 0$
6.	Proportion of housing target for young couples to target of families with children	:	$b_5 - b_7 \leq 0$

Suppose that several alternative programs have been suggested. These might, for example, be based on architectural design criteria. Suppose also the suggestions are equivalent in their quality. Thus the versatility of a given program for possible development may be considered a plausible choice criterion. We consider here three such alternative designs each of which implies a somewhat different program and is defined by a vector of activity levels.

P_1 = (200, 25, 25, 25, 50, 20, 175, 130)
P_2 = (180, 0, 50, 45, 30, 0, 220, 125)
P_3 = (180, 0, 40, 55, 30, 0, 220, 135)

The probabilities associated with each policy are respectively

prob(P_1) = 42.8 Prob(P_2) = 40.0 prob(P_3) = 20.0

The time required for a solution on a DCD 6600 computer for a problem of this size is 16 sec CPU time per policy using 10,000 rays.

We conclude that policy 1 is the most preferred one. However, the advantage compared with policy 2 is probably negligible.

12.3. DISCUSSION

The following concluding paragraphs analyze the utility function underlying the model and its relationship to alternative decision criteria.

The decision-maker for whom this model is pertinent would evidently have to be a satisficer with regard to his substantive objectives. If an objective has been attained, its marginal utility falls to zero. Moreover, a solution is acceptable only if it achieves all objectives, so that satisficing pertains to the target set as a whole, and not only to individual goal constraints.

In contrast to goal programming and discrepancy analysis, the model ignores the amount by which a solution falls short of the targets, as the major concern is the probability that a given policy will be acceptable. On the other hand, with regard to the probability of success (i.e., the acceptability of the chosen solution) the decision-maker is assumed to be a maximizer. The solution selected is that which has the highest probability of being feasible and attaining all targets.

The explicit consideration of the probability of success suggests greater optimism toward risk than that implied by the minimax criterion. The latter seeks the policy which achieves the highest guaranteed level of goal achievement for any possible development. It is consequently very sensitive to extremely unfavorable events which may be unlikely but not impossible. This guaranteed minimum target level is the endogenous variable. In the present model, the desired minimum level of goal achievement is exogenous. The decision criterion is the probability by which this level can be attained. The minimax criterion can then be interpreted as a limiting case of the versatility criterion, in which the aspiration level is attained with probability of one, and this for a single objective.

The determination of target values is inevitably arbitrary. Therefore, it will often be useful to perform a sensitivity analysis by evaluating the relationship between the targets set and the probability that the given policy will be acceptable. For this purpose, aspiration levels are changed in small steps within the relevant range and the probability that the given policy will be acceptable is calculated for each case. The decision-maker can then apply his judgement on the trade-off between target values and probability of success in selecting the optimum solution.

If the versatility criterion is applied in a large number of choices, it should maximize the number of acceptable outcomes, which is equivalent to the average rate of success in decision-making. In contrast, the expected value criterion maximizes the average pay-off; it therefore requires that different objectives be commensurate, i.e. measurable by a common unit, such as money or utils. As the versatility criterion maximizes the probability of acceptable outcomes rather than average pay-off, it requires no such "conversion". It is thus more suitable for multiple criteria analysis.

12.4. APPENDIX: THE ALGORITHM FOR THE HYPERVOLUME RATIO WHEN {b} IS A POLYTOPE

The following is a more detailed description of the major stages of the algorithm for the computation of the hypervolume ratio for policy p when the boundaries of {b} are given by a set of linear constraints.

12.4.1 *Selection of a point* ξ *interior to the polytope* $\{b(p)\}$

First an arbitrary β on the boundary of $\{b(p)\}$ must be identified. For this, solve an LP which uses equation systems (4) and (9) as the constraint set, and an arbitrary objective function. Redistributing and collecting the constants to the right yields

$$- B_j + U_j = - \Sigma_d \, a_{dg} \, x_{pd} \qquad \text{for all } g \qquad \text{(A.1a)}$$

$$\Sigma_j \, w_{kj} \, B_j + V_j = c_{jk} \qquad \text{for all } k \qquad \text{(A.1b)}$$

Any feasible basis thus obtained can be used for the desired vertex β.

Next, seek a point ξ which is interior to $\{b(p)\}$ and close to its center. For that purpose identify all vertices v_i of the polytope $\{b(p)\}$ which are adjacent to β. For each v_i calculate the unit vector u_i which has the same direction as the arc connecting β and v_i. Construct a random sample of rays through β into $\{b\}$. A slightly biased sample can be obtained by taking random numbers between 0 and 1 for each ray $\bar{j}$ and normalizing them to sum to 1. These are used as weights to form a vector ψ, as a weighted sum of the unit vectors u_i. For each random ray ψ, calculate the distance ρ_ψ on the ray between β and the boundary of $\{b\}$ (Charnetski (1978)), defined by the hyperplane k of equation system (12.9).

$$\rho_\psi = \min \{(c_k - \Sigma_s w_{ks} \beta_s) / (\Sigma_s w_{ks} d_{\psi s}) ;$$

for

$$\Sigma_s w_{ks} \beta_s < 0, \Sigma_s w_{ks} d_{\psi s} > 0 \} \qquad (A.2)$$

(If the two right-hand coefficients are not satisfied, ignore distance ρ_ψ since ray ψ does not intersect the hyperplane k). A reasonable estimate of ξ is obtained by constructing a ray ψ_ξ a weighted sum of all sample rays, using the length ρ_ψ of the rays as weights. The midpoint of ψ_ξ is used for ξ.

$$\xi = \beta + (\rho_{\psi max} \delta_{\psi max} 0.5) \qquad (A.3)$$

12.4.2 *Construction of random half rays through* ξ

Using the Gram-Schmidt procedure, for example, construct a set of $\bar{s}$ ortho-normal vectors which span the space of $\{b\}$. If the number of vectors thus obtained equals the number of constraints of type (12.1), it will be more convenient to use the unit vectors of the coordinate system.

For each ray ϕ, select a random vector consisting of $\bar{s}$ random numbers between 0 and 1, and subtract 0.5 from each element. Discard vectors which are not contained by the hypersphere whose radius equals 0.5, i.e. for which the sum of the squares of the elements is not less or equal $(\frac{1}{2})^2$. Normalize the resulting vector to obtain unit length and use its coordinates as weights to construct δ_ϕ, a weighted sum of the ortho-normal vectors spanning $\{b\}$.

12.4.3 *The limits of integration*

To obtain the upper limits of integration of any ray ϕ, calculate the distances between ξ and the intersections of the ray with the hyperplanes bounding the polytopes $\{b\}$ and $\{b(p)\}$ respectively. The distance $d_\phi(k)$ along ray ϕ between ξ and the kth hyperplane is, as before,

$$d_\phi(k) = \{(c_k - \Sigma_w w_{kj} \xi_j) / (\Sigma_w w_{kj} \delta_{\phi j});$$

for

$$\Sigma w_{kj} \xi_j < 0 , \Sigma_j w_{kj} \delta_{\phi j} > 0\} \qquad (A.4)$$

where ξ_s is the sth element of ξ. (If the two side conditions are not satisfied, the respective distance $d_\phi(k)$ can again be ignored since ϕ does not intersect the hyperplane k).

The upper limit of integration along ray ϕ in {b} is

$$\gamma_\phi = \min_{k\epsilon\{b\}} \{d_\phi(k)\} \qquad (A.5)$$

where $k\epsilon\{b\}$ means that yperplane k is one of the hyperplanes bounding {b}. For the upper limit of integration in {b(p)}, use

$$\gamma_{\phi\rho} = \min_{k\epsilon\{b(p)\}} \{d_\phi(k)\} \qquad (A.6)$$

where $k\epsilon\{b(p)\}$ expresses that hyperplane k is an element of the set of hyperplanes bounding {b(p)}.

12.4.4 *The contribution of the ray to the estimate of the hypervolume ratio*

Given the upper limits of integration, calculate the contribution of ray ϕ to the estimate of the hypervolume ratio of every policy, using equation (12.11). The total probability that policy p is acceptable equals the ratio of the sum of the integrals along each ray for {b(p)} and {b}.

12.4.5 *Size of the sample*

The procedure outlined in this algorithm requires a considerable number of rays. The largest example calculated until now had seven dimensions. With 15,000 rays, the error obtained amounted to less than .020 per cent of the total volume. However, with an increase in the number of dimensions, the size of the sample required for the same accuracy seems to grow arithmetically.

12.5. NOTES

[1] If some constraint has an equal sign, its right-hand parameter must be the same for all future states. Otherwise no policy will have a nonzero probability of being acceptable.

[2] Such estimates may be available from statistical analysis or from subjective judgements; e.g. Waber (1963) suggests obtaining three estimates for each such variable: the two extreme values, (a, b) between which about 95% of the values are expected, and the most likely value (c). If the distribution is normal, the estimates for the mean would then be (a + 4c + b)/6, and for the standard deviation (a + b)/4.

12.6. REFERENCES

Baumol, W.J., *Economics Theory and Operations Analysis*, Prentice Hall, Englewood Cliffs, 1965.

Ben Shahar, M., Mazar, A., and Pines, D., Town Planning and Welfare Maximization: a Methodological Approach, *Regional Studies* 3, 1969, pp.105-113.

Bonder, Changing the Future of O.R., presented at the IFORS 8th Triennial Conference on Operations Research, Toronto, Canada, June 1978.

Charnetski, J.R., and Soland, R.M., Statistical Measures for Linear functions on Polytopes, *Operations Research*, vol.24, no.1, 1976, pp.201-204.

Charnetski, J.R., and Soland, R.M., Multiple Attribute Decision-Making with Partial Information. The Comparative Hypervolume Criterion, *Naval Research Logistics Quarterly*, 1978.

Friend, J.K., and Jessop, *Local Government and Strategic Choice*, Tavistock, London, 1969.

Keeney, R.D., and Raiffa, H., *Decision Analysis*, Addison Wesley, 1976, Reading, Mass.

Pye, R., A Formal Decision - Theoretic Approach to Feasibility and Robustness, *Journal of the Operations Research Society*, vol.29, no.3, 1978, pp.205-227.

Rosenhead, J.V.et al., Robustness and Optimality as Criteria for Strategic Decisions, *Operations Research Quarterly*, vol.23, 1972, pp.413-431.

Schläfli, L. (1858) Lehre von den linearen Kontinnen, in *Gesammelte Mathematische Abhandlungen*, Birkhauser, Basel, 1950, pp.177-193.

Sengupta, S.S., Podrebarac, M.L., and Fernando, T.D.M., Probabilities of Optima in Multi-Objective Linear Programming, in Cochrane, J.L., and Zeleny, M. (eds.), *Multiple Criteria Decision-Making*, University of South Carolina Press, Columbia, S.C., 1973.

Waber, R.K., Planning with the Program Evaluation and Review Technique (PERT), Industrielle Organization, 1963.

Werczberger, E., Multi-Objective Linear Programming with Ordinal Ranking of Objective Functions, presented at the VIII IFORS Conference in Toronto: W.P. 50, Center for Urban and Regional Studies, Tel-Aviv University, Tel-Aviv, 1978.

Acknowledgements

Financial support for the research reported in this paper has been obtained from the Israel Academy of Sciences and is gratefully acknowledged. I would also like to extend my particular thanks to G. Matiowitz, who programmed the algorithm.

13 Hierarchical-Multiobjective Framework for Large Scale Systems

Y. Y. Haimes and K. Tarvainen

13.1 INTRODUCTION

Two major attributes characterize most large-scale systems. These are: (a) a large number of components (subsystems), which are coupled with one another and which can be effectively related (modelled and optimized) via a hierarchical structures of layers, levels and echelons; and (b) a set of multi-objective functions (often noncommensurable), which represents the most meaningful way to model the inherent goals and objectives of the system. Systems such as water and land resources, energy, transportation, and other civil systems are often characterized by complexity, a large number of variables and multiple objectives, and several levels of decision-making. Integrating the hierarchical and multi-objective approaches should yield a powerful generalized framework for modelling and optimizing large-scale systems. Furthermore, the hierarchical-multiobjective framework, which combines and builds on the strengths of the two separate approaches, should provide the analyst with a modelling and optimization framework that is more responsive to the real attributes of these complex and large-scale systems.

13.2 HIERARCHICAL APPROACH

A necessary condition for the successful use of systems methodologies for any given problem is the ability to develop a (mathematical) model responsive to and accountable for the various systems objectives, constraints, and input-output, causal relationships. Only at this stage is the solution of the model -the optimization phase -meaningful and potentially implementable.

Each optimization technique provides a way to solve a certain class of mathematical models. Often, much of a model's utility is lost when it must be adapted to fit an optimization technique. This loss usually involves simplification of the model to the extent that the simplified model may not be sufficiently accurate in portraying the real system.

The modelling of large-scale and comprehensive problems in a way amenable to efficient overall solution strategies is an intricate task. The availability of flexible approaches and philosophies, such as the hierarchical-multilevel approach, as an aid to modelling and studying smaller subsystems for an ultimate, optimal solution to the whole system, makes this task both feasible and tractable. Fundamental to the hierarchical modelling of a total complex system is the development of new models and/or the modification, utilization and coördination of existing models for various subsystems.

The hierarchical approach possesses many important attributes for both modelling and optimization. First, the hierarchical approach is a philosophy rather than a rigid methodology. This philosophy recognizes that large-scale systems have most of these characteristics (see Haimes (1977)):

(i) multiple non-commensurable objectives, as well as multiple decision-makers;

(ii) large number of variables and parameters;

(iii) large number of coupled components (subsystems);

(iv) input-output causal relationships that are non-linear (often a combination of continuous, discrete and 0- 1 decisions); dynamic (time dependent); non-deterministic with high elements of risk and uncertainties; and incorporate distributed parameters;

(v) variable portions of the system (problem) inappropriate to quantitative modelling analysis.

Simple methodologies are likely to fall short of successfully modelling and optimizing large-scale systems with the above characteristics. What is needed is an approach capable of utilizing the best attributes of existing methodologies. The concept of the hierarchical approach is based upon both the decomposition of large and complex systems, and the subsequent modelling of these systems into 'independent' subsystems. By utilizing the concepts of levels, strata, layers, and echelons, such a decentralized approach enables the system analyst to understand and interpret the behavior of the subsystems at a lower level; and, therefore, to transmit the information obtained to fewer subsystems at a higher level. Whenever more decentralization is needed, the system is further decomposed. This decomposition is often accomplished by introducing new variables, often called 'pseudo variables', into the system. Each subsystem is then separately and independently optimized. In this process, different optimization techniques may be applied, depending upon the nature of the subsystem models, as well as upon the objectives and constraints of the subsystems. This operation is termed a first or lower-level solution. The subsystems are joined by coupling variables, which are manipulated at a second or higher-level of the hierarchical structure, in order to arrive at the optimal solution of the entire system. One way to achieve subsystem "independence" is by first relaxing one or more of the necessary conditions for optimality; and then satisfying these conditions at a higher level.

In order to illustrate the hierarchical approach, consider a company with N departments. Each department has a manager who reports to the president of the company. The objective of the i-th manager is to maximize the performance of his department. The president may maximize the performance of the entire company by imposing, for example, internal prices for transactions between the department products or services. The company's overall optimal policy is, thus, achieved through an iterative procedure. The separate optimization of each individual department does not necessarily imply the overall maximization of the company's performance, unless the performance of each department is properly coordinated at a higher level (i.e., by the president), and certain mathematical criteria are achieved (see Lasdon (1970) and Haimes (1977)).

13.2.1 *Attributes of decomposition and multilevel optimization*

Decomposition and multilevel optimization have several significant advantages over conventional optimization methods. In the solution of large-scale complex optimization problems, decomposition and multilevel optimization attributes generally yield to (see Haimes (1977)):

(i) conceptual simplification of complex systems;
(ii) reduction in dimensionality;
(iii) simple programming and computational procedures;
(iv) more realistic system models;
(v) permissible interactions among subsystems;
(vi) applicability to both static and dynamic systems;
(vii) applicability of different optimization techniques to different subsystems;
(viii) broader use of existing models (modularity);
(ix) economic interpretation of the coupling variables;
(x) applicability to multiobjective analysis.

13.2.2 *Overlapping coordination*

In the modelling process of large-scale and complex systems, more than one mathematical model is likely to emerge-each focusing on a specific aspect of the system, yet all regarded as acceptable representations of the system. This phenomenon is particularly common in hierarchical-multiobjective modelling, where more than one decomposition approach may be both feasible and desirable. Consequently, the decomposition of a system often presents the modeller with the dilemma of what the subsystems should be. For example, an economic system may be decomposed according to the various functions of the system, or along hydrologic or even political boundaries. If several aspects of the system are to be dealt with (e.g., the geographic regions and activity sectors of an economic system), it may be advantageous to consider several decompositions.

To further illustrate, suppose a given system naturally decomposes into either geographic regions or activity sectors (functional decomposition). Clearly, these two decompositions overlap if each geographic region involves more than one activity, or if each activity is distributed over more than one geographic region. It can be assumed that each geographic region, or each activity sector has its own agent, who is responsible for that region or sector. Each activity agent, then, overlaps several regional agents; or, conversely, as depicted in Figures 13.1 and 13.2.

The integration of all these decompositions can then be coordinated via the overlapping coordination approach (See Haimes and Macko (1973), Macko and Haimes (1978), Mendu (1978), Sung (1978) and Mendu, Haimes and Macko (1980)). The following situation can, then, be investigated: Suppose that the sole objective of the system is to maximize a given overall benefit, and that each agent makes his/her own decisions independently of the other agents. An objective is to devise a structure in which:

(i) each individual agent's decision is feasible in the overall system, and
(ii) information exchange between regional agents and activity agents leads to a sequence of decisions that increases overall benefit and converges to the optimum.

In summary, overlapping coordination of two or more hierarchical modelling structures has the following important attributes:

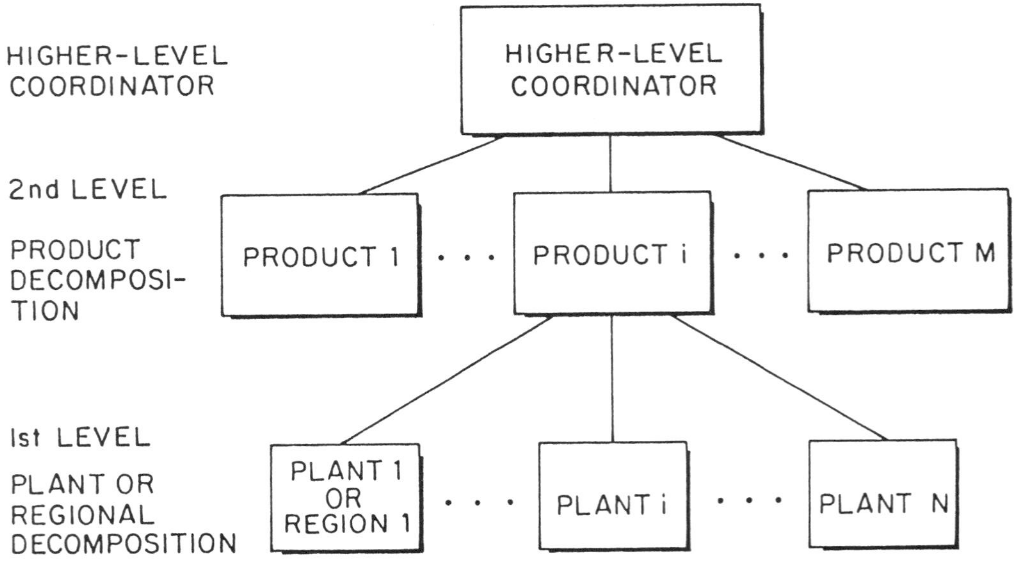

Figure 13.1. Overlapping hierarchical-multiobjective structures

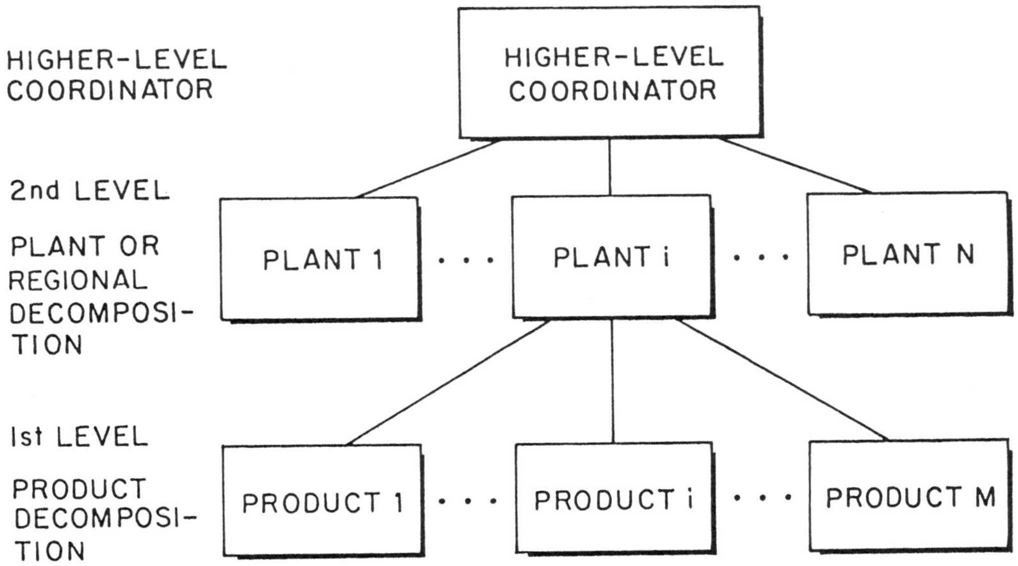

Figure 13.2. Overlapping hierarchical-multiobjective structures

(i) adds flexibility in modelling;

(ii) yields more realistic models by increasing the responsiveness of the model structures to the organizational, political, technical, financial and historical realities;

(iii) increases the responsiveness of model structures to available data.

13.3. MULTIOBJECTIVE APPROACH

A recent trend in systems analysis has been to consider models which have more than one objective function. This trend is especially important in the modelling and optimization of large-scale systems, where there tend to be several conflicting and noncommensurable objectives. For example, one may wish to maximize both economic efficiency-measured in monetary units - and reduction of flood damage - measured in acres of flooded land or probability of assurance. Traditionally, only one objective - economic efficiency - has been considered. Other objectives have been included either as constraints, or as somehow commensurate with the primary objective. However, contemporary society places increasing importance on nonpecuniary objectives -difficult, if not actually impossible, to quantify monetarily.

13.3.1 *The surrogate worth trade-off (SWT) method*

Fundamental to multiobjective analysis is the Pareto optimum concept also known as a non-inferior solution. Qualitatively, a non-inferior solution of a multiobjective problem is one in which any improvement of one objective function can be achieved only at the expense the degradation of another.

To define a non-inferior solution mathematically, consider the following multiobjective optimization problem, also known as a vector optimization problem:

Minimize

$$\{f_1(\underline{x}), f_2(\underline{x}), \ldots, f_n(\underline{x})\} \qquad (13.1)$$

$$\underline{x} \in X$$

where $\underline{x}$ is the N-dimensional vector of decision variables

$g_i(\underline{x}) \leq 0$ is the $\underline{ith}$ constraint

X is the set of all feasible solutions

$$X = \{\underline{x} | g_i(\underline{x}) \leq 0, \quad 1 = 1,2,\ldots,m\}$$

Definition: A decision vector $\underline{x}^*$ is said to be a non-inferior solution to the problem posed by the systems (13.1) if, and only if, there does not exist another $\underline{\bar{x}}$ so that $f_j(\underline{\bar{x}}) \leq f_j(\underline{x}^*)$, $j = 1,2,\ldots,n$, with strict inequality holding for at least one j. Figure 13.3 depicts non-inferior solutions.

A basic goal of the SWT method is to develop a set of Pareto optimal solutions and their corresponding trade-offs, and then to arrive at the decision-maker's preferences. Of course, as a first step, this procedure requires specifying the relationship between each objective and its corresponding decision variables.

The trade-off values between the ith and the jth objective functions are denoted by λ_{ij}. These λ_{ij}'s are generated by the SWT method, and have been shown to satisfy the following relationships:

$$\lambda_{ij} = -\frac{\partial f_i(\underline{x})}{\partial f_j(\underline{x})}, \quad i \neq j, \quad i,j = 1, 2, \ldots, n \tag{13.2}$$

where

$f_i(\underline{x})$	is the ith objective function
$f_j(\underline{x})$	is the jth objective function
λ_{ij}	is the trade-off function
$\lambda_{ij} > 0$	is a sufficient condition for non-inferior solutions

Note that it is sufficient to generate only one row vector of the trade-off matrix, e.g. $\lambda_{12}, \lambda_{13}, \ldots, \lambda_{1n}$, and to derive all other trade-offs from this vector using the following relationship:

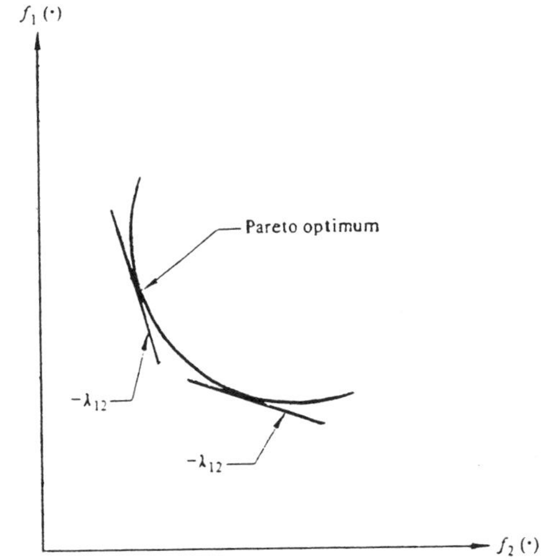

Figure 13.3 Pareto optimal solutions and respective trade-offs.

It is important to note that the trade-off function λ_{ij} is obtained for any two noncommensurate functions. For example, let the units of $f_i(\underline{x})$ be \$, and the units of $f_j(\underline{x})$ be flooded acres or probability of assurance. Then the units of λ_{ij} are in \$/acre or \$/assurance level. It is also important to note that the analyses here are conducted in the objective-function space, $f_1(\underline{x}), \ldots, f_n(\underline{x})$, and not in the decision space $x_1, \ldots, x_N$. This method, of course, has a clear advantage, since typically $N >> n$. (One may have 100 or 1,000 decisions with three to 10 objective functions.)

As a final step, the set of trade-offs can be transformed to yield their relationship with the decision variables. Assuming that certain (mathematical) properties of the trade-offs are satisfied, this transformation can be shown to exist. At this point, the decision-maker is, again, brought into the analysis. Given the attainment levels of all objectives, the decision-maker needs only establish his/her preferences concerning the trade-offs between them. In other words, for a given set of circumstances, is the marginal change in one objective (expressed by the trade-off ratio) more or less desirable than a unit change in the other? The objective here is to locate the set of trade-offs yielding indifference to that question; i.e., that set to which the decision-maker's response is 'neither more nor less desirable.'

The Surrogate Worth function will be used to deduce this indifference set. By assigning an ordinal ranking to the estimated desirability of each of the trade-off ratios, a Surrogate Worth function directly related to the trade-off ratios can be derived. For example, with zero selected as signifying indifference, a scale from -10 to +10 can be used. A +10 would indicate that the marginal change given by a particular trade-off ratio is very desirable, and -10 would indicate the opposite extreme. The procedure may then be defined for each trade-off ratio. If a Surrogate Worth of zero were consistently assigned to indicate indifference, the set of optimum trade-off ratios would then correspond to those simultaneously equating the Surrogate Worth functions to zero. This indifference solution is often referred to as 'the best-compromise solution' or 'the preferred solution'.

The SWT method would also appear useful for examining political decision systems. One of the most important requirements of decision-making for complex systems is that the evaluation of the political consequences of any recommended course of action becomes the responsibility and prerogative of the decision-maker(s), not of the analyst.

An important characteristic of the SWT method is that it properly leaves to the specialized analysts the quantitative-predictive (scientific) aspects of evaluation, but clearly gives decision-maker(s) the responsibility for evaluating the merits of improving any one objective at the expense of any other-given the associated quantitative levels of achievement of all objectives. Because of this characteristic, the SWT method lends itself well either to simulating the likely outcome of the multiple-member decision process (given the characteristics of each DM), or to assisting the multiple-member decision group in identifying and focusing efficiently on the issues implicit in the problem's structure, and within the public constituency.

A detailed discussion of the SWT method is available elsewhere, and, therefore, is presented only in brief overview here (see Haimes (1977)):

(i) The SWT method is capable of generating all needed non-inferior solutions to a vector optimization problem.

(ii) The method generates the trade-offs between any two objective functions, based on the duality theory of non-linear programming. The trade-off function between the ith and jth objective functions, λ_{ij}, is explicity evaluated and is equivalent to

$$-\frac{\delta f_i}{\delta f_j}.$$

(iii) The decision-maker interacts with the systems analyst and the mathematical model, at a general and very moderate level. Interaction is accommodated through the generation of the Surrogate Worth functions, which relate the decision-maker's preferences to the non-inferior solutions through the trade-off functions. These preferences are constructed in the objective function space (more familiar and meaningful to the decision-makers), and then transferred to the decision space. This procedure is particularly important, since the dimensionality of the objective function space is often smaller than that of the decision space. These preferences yield an indifference band in which the decision-maker is indifferent to any further trade-off among the objectives.

(iv) The SWT method provides for the quantitative analysis of noncommensurable objective functions.

(v) The method is well suited to the analysis and optimization of multiobjective functions with multiple decision-makers.

13.3.2 *Multiobjective Statistical Method (MSM)*

The Multiobjective Statistical Method (MSM) is an integration of a statistical procedure for assigning joint probalilities to stochastic events (e.g. rainfall and river stage events), and a multiobjective optimization procedure using the Surrogate Worth Trade-off (SWT) method coördinated into a computer package. A computer program implementing the MSM has been developed for interior drainage systems and fully tested in the Moline area using the U.S. Army Corps of Engineers, Rock Island District's Computer System (See Haimes, Loparo, Olenik, and Nanda (1980)).

An outline of the key features of MSM may be stated as follows:

(i) Problem definition;

a) Identify the decision vector $\underline{x}$ and the appropriate finite decision space X.

b) Identify the pertinent random variables $\underline{r}$. Obtain data to evaluate probabilities associated with $\underline{r}$.

c) Given a set of verbal objectives, quantify them in terms of a set of state variables $\underline{y}$, i.e., $f = \underline{f}(y)$.

d) Obtain a method (simulation or other) to express the state vector $\underline{y}$ in terms of the decision vector $\underline{x}$ and the random vector $\underline{r}$, i.e., $\underline{y} = \underline{y}(\underline{x}, \underline{r})$.

e) Problem statement is now:

$$\min \underline{f}(\underline{y}(\underline{x}, \underline{r}))$$

$$\underline{x} \in X$$

subject to system's constraints.

(ii) Conversion of probabilistic problem to deterministic problem:

a) Place limits on ranges of random variables $\underline{r}$.

b) Choose number of discrete levels of each component of $\underline{r}$ and discretize accordingly into $\underline{r}_d$ intervals.

c) Define random events spanning intervals of $\underline{r}_d$.

d) Calculate the appropriate probabilities of random events.

e) Determine the expected value of objective functions for a given value of the decision vector, using the appropriate probabilities: $[\tilde{f}(\hat{x}) \equiv E(f(\hat{x}))]$.

f) Through curve-fitting of a set of points $\{\hat{x}, f(\hat{x})\}$ or via explicit dependence on $\underline{x}$, determine $\underline{\tilde{f}}(\underline{x})$.

g) Problem statement is now:

$$\min \ \underline{\tilde{f}}(\underline{x})$$

$$\underline{x} \in X$$

subject to system's contraints.

(iii) Apply the SWT method to the expected value problem (g) to determine the 'optimal' decision vector $\underline{x}^*$.

Figure 13.4 is a schematic diagram of the MSM.

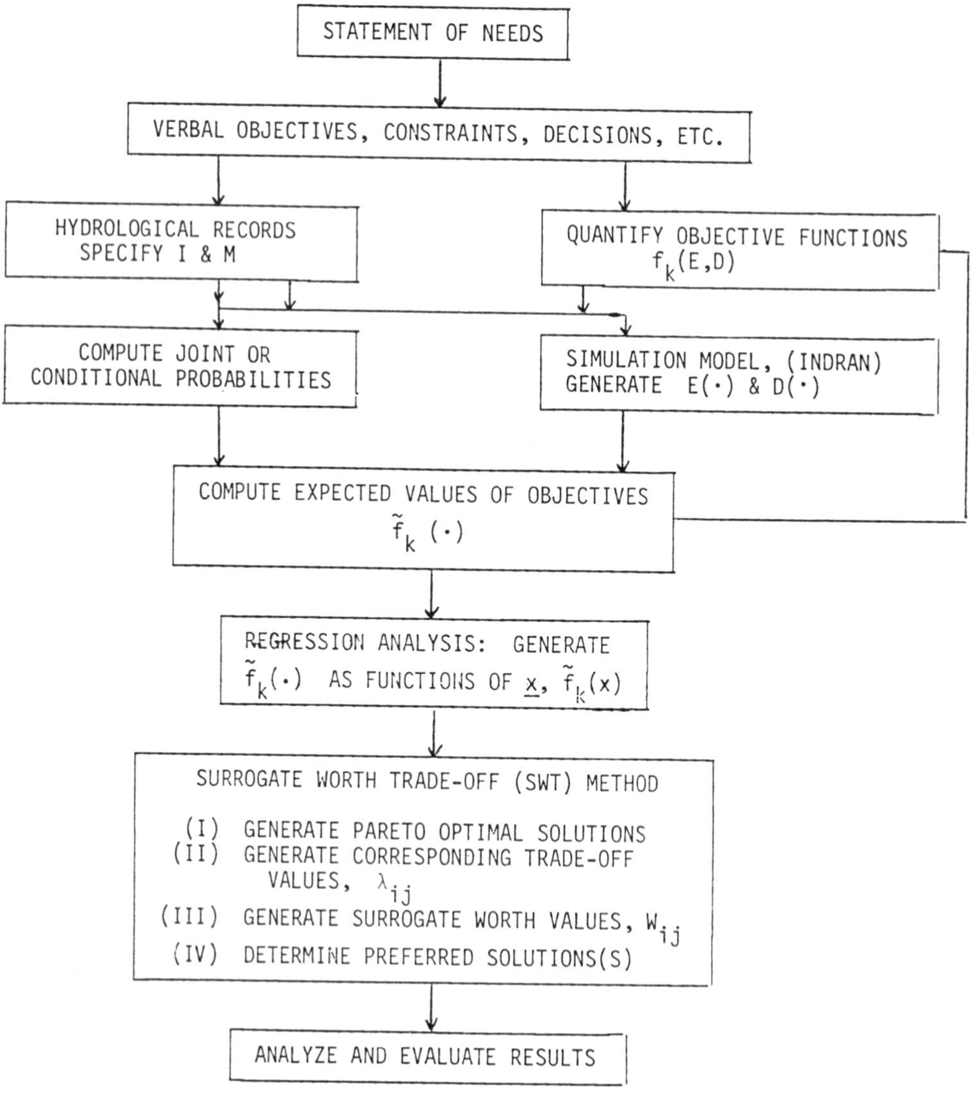

Figure 13.4. Schematic diagram of the multiobjective statistical method (msm)

13.4. HIERARCHICAL-MULTIOBJECTIVE APPROACH

Higher-level co-ordination among the various subsystems in hierarchical structures has commonly been achieved through commensuration of the subsystem's objectives, and subsequent application of single objective optimization techniques. A superior modelling and optimization process involves the integration of the hierarchical and multiobjective approaches into a unified framework. This framework combines the strengths of both. The flexibility of hierarchical-multiobjective structures makes the modelling process more realistic and understandable to the decision-makers- the ultimate users of these models. The notion of a single 'optimal' solution generated in a single-objective model (the cause of both scepticism and dismay among executives and decision-makers) is replaced with the more realistic concept of Pareto optimality and associated trade-offs.

The integration of the hierarchical and multi-objective approaches may, thus, result in a hierarchy of noncommensurable objectives at various levels. A four-level, hierarchical-multiobjective structure, for example, may have four levels of objectives and subjectives (see Figure 13.5.). This is, indeed, the actual situation in most, if not all, large-scale systems.

Co-ordination among several objectives at a higher level, and the corresponding sub-objectives at a lower level in the hierarchy represents the core of the hierarchical-multiobjective framework. The fundamental issue here is to harmonize often competing and conflicting objectives and sub-objectives at the various levels.

Two basic hierarchical-multiobjective structures may be thus identified:

(i) Single-objective functions are associated with lower-level subsystems, and multiple-objective functions are associated with the highest level of the hierarchical structure.

(ii) Multiple-objective functions are associated with some or all of the lower-level subsystems, as well as with the highest level of the hierarchical structure.

<u>Note</u>: The case where the multiple-objective functions are associated with the lower-level subsystems but a single objective function associated with the highest level of the hierarchical structure seems unrealistic at this stage; however, its merit should be investigated as well. Case (ii) is more general, and the others can be viewed as special cases.

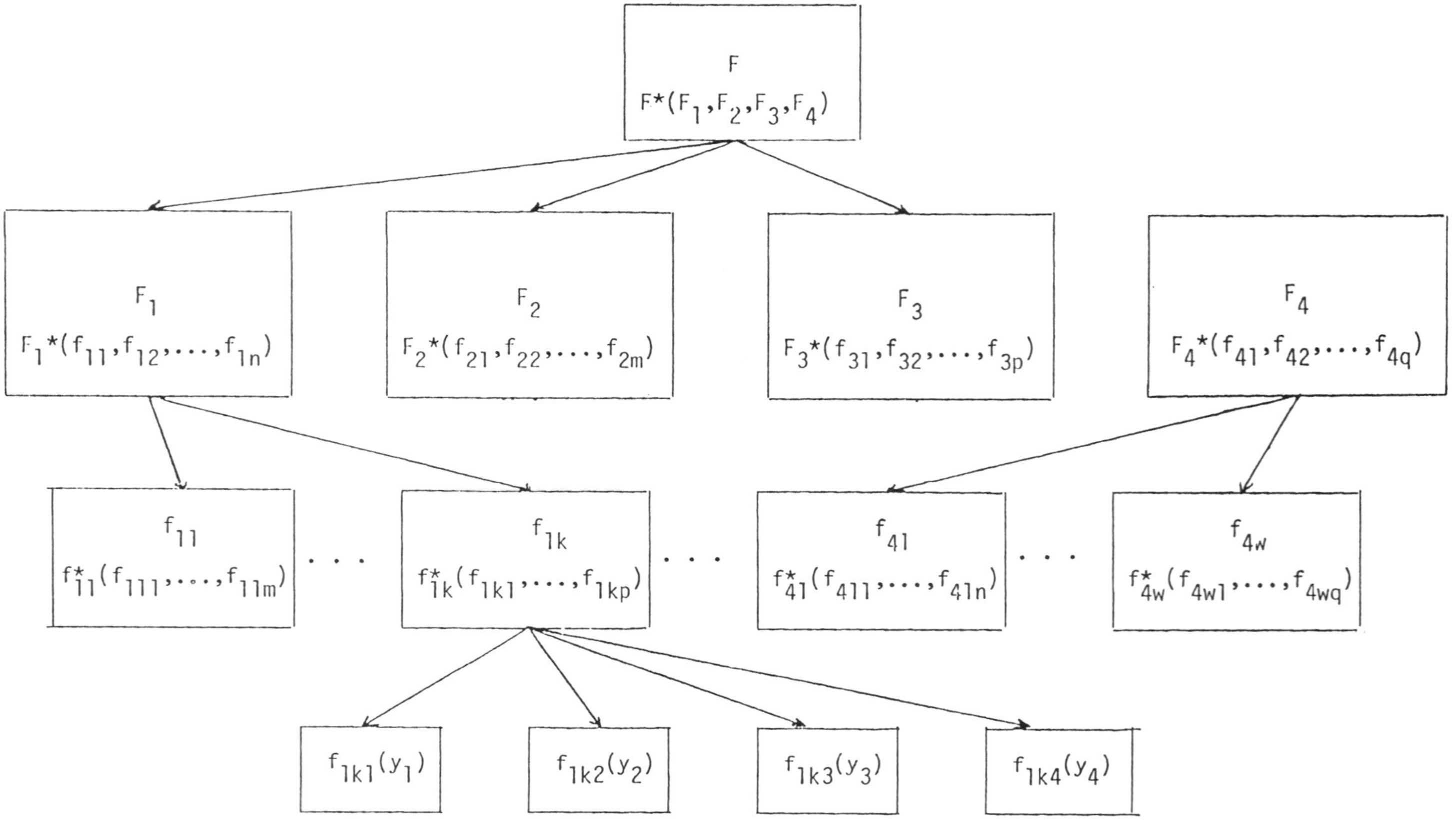

Figure 13.5. Coordination of hierarchical-multiobjective framework

13.5. CO-ORDINATION OF HIERARCHICAL-MULTIOBJECTIVE STRUCTURES

13.5.1. *Problem definition*

Consider a system consisting of N intercoupled subsystems. In each subsystem i = 1,..., N let

y_i = output vector of subsystem i

x_i = input vector of subsystem i from other subsystems

m_i = decision vector of subsystem i

$f^i = (f^i_1, f^i_2, \ldots, f^i_{n_i})^T$ = objective vector of subsystem i

n_i = the number of objectives of subsystem i.

Each subsystem's output is a function of its input from other subsystems and of its decision variables:

$$y_i = H_i(x_i, m_i) \qquad i = 1, \ldots, N \qquad (13.3)$$

This relationship is usually given via several system equations. To develop decompositions, it is enough to deal with (13.3); in applying results, (13.3) is just replaced with these systems equations.

Each subsystem has constraints given by vector valued g_i-functions:

$$g_i(x_i, m_i, y_i) \leq 0 \qquad i = 1, \ldots, N \qquad (13.4)$$

Here, for brevity, equality constraints (e.g., r = 0) are transferred to inequality constraints ($r \leq 0$, $-r \leq 0$).

The couplings between subsystems can be presented concisely, as follows:

$$x_i = \sum_{j=1} C_{ij}y_j, \qquad i = 1, \ldots, N \qquad (13.5)$$

where C_{ij}'s (i, j = 1, ..., N) are matrices with only zero and one as elements. Usually, coupling matrices are such that, when x_i's k-th component is connected with y_i's 1-th component, then C_{ij}'s (k, 1)-element is one and others, as well, other elements of C_{it}'s ($t \neq j$) are zero. In what follows, this is not necessary; C_{ij}'s may be any constant matrices. Thus, any linear operations on the subsystems outputs can be imbedded in C_{ij}-matrices.

The coupled system may have global constraints that are here assumed to be of separable form:

$$\sum_{i=1}^{N} q_i(x_i, m_i, y_i) \leq 0 \qquad (13.6)$$

where q_i's (i = 1, ..., N) are vector valued functions. For example, when some subsystems have cost as an objective, a constraint for the total cost can be presented in this form.

The subsystems' objectives are functions of subsystem variables:

$$f_j^i = f_j^i(x_i, m_i, y_i), \qquad i = 1, \ldots, N; \quad j = 1, \ldots, n_i. \qquad (13.7)$$

In a general case, the whole system's objective vector does not consist of all f_j^i's, and one could call f_j^i's subgoals or indicators. For example, when some subsystems have cost as an objective, the total system's one objective, total cost, is a sum of these subsystem's cost objectives. So, when denoting $f = (f^1, f^2, \ldots, f^N)^T$ = vector of all subsystem objectives, we take $F = (F_1(f), \ldots, F_n(f))^T$ = the system objective vector where n = the number of the overall system's objectives.

In summary, the problem is as follows (when minimizing has been assumed a goal):

$$\min \begin{bmatrix} F_1(f^1, \ldots, f^N) \\ \cdot \\ \cdot \\ \cdot \\ F_n(f^1, \ldots, f^N) \end{bmatrix} \qquad (13.8)$$

where $f^i = (f_1^i(x_i, m_i, y_i), \ldots, f_{n_i}^i(x_i, m_i, y_i))^T$, i = 1, ..., N, subject to

$$y_i = H_i(x_i, m_i) \qquad i = 1, \ldots, N \qquad (13.9)$$

$$g_i(x_i, m_i, y_i) \leq 0 \qquad i = 1, \ldots, N \qquad (13.10)$$

$$x_i = \sum_{j=1}^{N} C_{ij} y_j \qquad i = 1, \ldots, N \qquad (13.11)$$

$$\sum_{i=1}^{N} q_i(x_i, m_i, y_i) \leq 0. \qquad (13.12)$$

This is an integrated problem formulation that can be solved in interaction with a decision-maker who articulates preferences for the objectives.

It is possible to decompose this problem into N multiobjective subproblems, and a co-ordination problem such that, when the same decision-maker solves these problems, the answer will be the same as by the integrated solution. This form of problem analysis is a natural basis for developing decomposition methods, and also serves as a basis for justifying schemes where subproblems are, in fact, solved by different decision-makers.

In the following discussion, several hierarchical schemes will be presented without derivations (see Tarvainen and Haimes (1980a, 1980b)).

13.5.2. *Trade-off notions*

The following discussion expresses preferences for objectives in terms of trade-offs. Note, however, that multi-objective optimization methods not using trade-offs explicitly can be used in solving subproblems presented later - if they can be modified in ways that correspond to modifications presented in context of trade-offs.

Let F_1 be a prime objective; between it and other objectives we have:

$$\lambda_{1i}^{*}(f) = \text{indifferent, acceptable trade-off between } F_1 \text{ and } F_i \text{ at } f, \qquad i = 2, \ldots, n \qquad (13.13)$$

Note that the indifferent value of the trade-offs, $\lambda_{1i}^{*}(f)$, is determined via an interaction with the decision-maker(s). This process is an integral part of the SWT method. For simplicity in notation, however, the superscript (*) will be deleted in the following discussion.

For notational purposes, we define a n-dimensional vector called trade-off vector and denoted by $\lambda(f) = (\lambda_1, (f), \ldots, \lambda_n(f))$ - so that

$$\lambda(f) = [1, \lambda_{12}(f), \ldots, \lambda_{1n}(f)]^T \qquad (13.14)$$

In the multilevel schemes to follow, so-called internal trade-off vectors, denoted by λ^i, are used in subsystems. They are determined by:

$$\lambda^i(f) = \left(\sum_{k=1}^{n} \lambda_k(f) \frac{\partial F_k}{\partial f^i}(f) \right)^T, \qquad i = 1, \ldots, N \qquad (13.15)$$

(A derivative of a scalar with respect to a vector is in this presentation a row vector; e.g., $\partial F_1/\partial f^1 = (\partial F_1/\partial f_1^1, \ldots, \partial F_1/\partial f_{n_1}^1)$.)

Furthermore, we define scaled internal trade-off vectors. We assume that, in each $\lambda^i(f)$, there is at least one nonzero (for all values of f) component; and, without loss of generality, we take it to be the first one, denoted by $\lambda_1^i(f)$. The scaled internal trade-off vectors, denoted by λ_s^i's, are given by dividing internal trade-off vectors by their first component, or:

$$\lambda^i(f) = \lambda_1^i(f)\, \lambda_s^i(f), \qquad i = 1, \ldots, N \qquad (13.16)$$

(Note: the subscript s denotes this scaling; it is not a component index.)

In the following, until Section 13.5.4., it is assumed that λ_s^1 depend, in fact, only on f^i, i = 1, ..., N; and so we denote these vectors by $\lambda_s^i(f^i)$. According to the notation in (13.14), the components of these vectors are denoted as follows:

$$\lambda_s^i(f^i) = [1, \lambda_{12}^i(f^i), \ldots, \lambda_{1n_i}^i(f^i)]^T, \quad i = 1, \ldots, N \qquad (13.17)$$

Finally, we define:

$$\lambda^{k\ell}(f) = \frac{\lambda_1^{\ell}(f)}{\lambda_1^{k}(f)} \quad \text{for} \quad k, \ell = 1, \ldots, N \tag{13.18}$$

and call this trade-off between subsystems k and ℓ, for short; in fact, the first objectives are in question.

Note that in (13.18), $\lambda^{k\ell}(f)$ denotes the trade-off between the first objective functions of subsystems k and ℓ. For simplicity in notation, the respective subscripts are eliminated. For a general case, the trade-off between the i-th objective of subsystem k and the j-th objective of subsystem ℓ should be denoted by $\lambda_{ij}^{k\ell}(f)$.

We take the r-th subsystem ($r \in \{1, \ldots, N\}$) as a reference, and deal with trade-offs λ^{ri}, $i = 1, \ldots, N$. The other trade-offs are determined by these trade-offs using (13.18). Note that, by (13.8) $\lambda^{rr} = 1$.

When applying multilevel methods, trade-offs are evaluated only at some points; so the trade-off functions and F_i's ($i = 1, \ldots, n$) need not be explicitly known.

In the following two main methods, the feasible and non-feasible, will be presented (Haimes 1977).

13.5.3. *Feasible methods*

The idea of feasible methods in single objective optimization is to fix variables that are common to two or more subsystems, and next to optimize the cost function with respect to the other variables. Because of the fixing, the optimization decomposes trivially into separate subsystem optimizations. The fixed variables are changed, and new subsystem optimizations are carried out; this change continues until an optimum is also achieved with respect to the fixed variables.

This idea can be applied also to the multiobjective case. In the following, we describe briefly two different schemes.

In the first, less general scheme, it is assumed that the global constraints (13.6) are not active, or equivalently, $q_i \equiv 0$, $i = 1, \ldots, N$, as in the following.

For the first scheme, the number of variables is reduced--substituting x_i's, $i = 1, \ldots, N$, from the coupling equations (13.11) to other expressions.

Now only y_i's are variables appearing in several subsystems, and are taken as co-ordination parameters. We denote the vector of co-ordination parameters by

$$p = (y_1, \ldots, y_N). \tag{13.19}$$

The objective vectors are, after substitution of x_i's, denoted by:

$$f^i(m_i, p) = f^i\left(\sum_{i=1}^{N} C_{ij}\, y_j, m_i, y_i\right), \quad i = 1, \ldots, N \tag{13.20}$$

The constraints for subsystems are presented compactly by the following constraint sets:

$$R_i = \left\{(m_i, p) \mid y_i = H_i\left(\sum_{j=1}^{N} C_{ij}\, y_j, m_i\right),\ g_i\left(\sum_{j=1}^{N} C_{ij}\, y_j, m_i, y_i\right) \leq 0\right\} \quad , \quad i = 1, \ldots, N \quad (13.21)$$

In the first scheme, it is assumed that, for every p given by the upper level, there is in the i-th subsystem m_i satisfying subsystem constraints; that is, $(m_i, p) \in R_i$; $i = 1, \ldots, N$.

The first scheme is summarized in Figure 13.6. First, the upper level guesses a value for p. Then the N subsystems solve the multicriteria problems depicted in the picture. Note that, in general, f^i's are vectors just as we have, in the use of language, presupposed. Note, however, that the treatment is easily modified to concern one or more subsystems with only one objective.

The subsystems solve the multiobjective problems using the internal trade-off vectors λ_s^i ; $i = 1, \ldots, N$ (13.17). The actual multiobjective solution technique applied to a subsystem need not be one using explicit trade-offs. Nonetheless the technique used shall have implicit

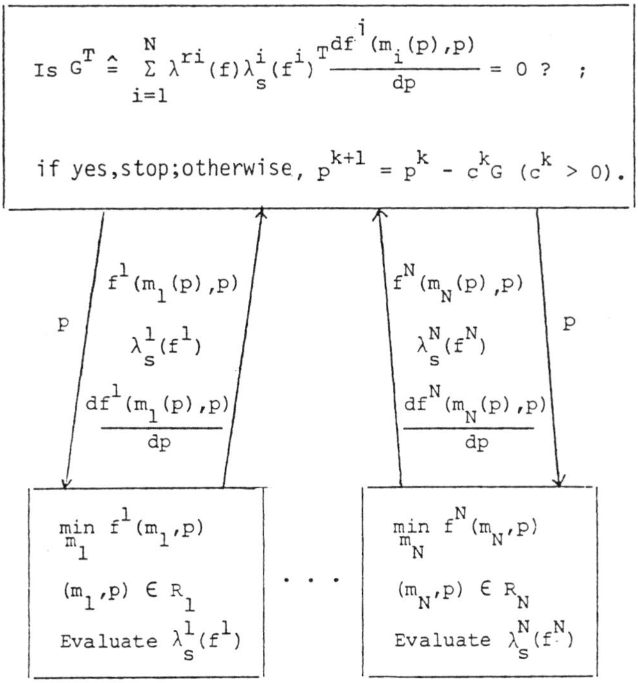

Figure 13.6. Feasible method, scheme 1.

trade-offs that relate to the overall problems, trade-offs (possibly, implicit, too), as λ^i relates to λ in (13.15). However, for the upper level, the trade-offs at the reached preferred subsystem solutions, denoted by $m_i(p)$ $(i = 1, \ldots, N)$, must be evaluated.

The subsystems evaluate also the derivatives $df^i(m_i(p), p)/dp$, $i = 1, \ldots, N$, which are assumed to exist in this scheme. These can be evaluated, e.g., numerically by perturbating p . They can be figured out either directly, or by the right-hand-side of the equation

$$\frac{df^i(m_i(p), p)}{dp} = \frac{\partial f^i(m_i(p), p)}{\partial m_i} \frac{\partial m_i}{\partial p} + \frac{\partial f^i(m_i(p), p)}{\partial p} \qquad (13.22)$$

For the upper level, also, the preferred values of objectives are, in a general case, needed to evaluate λ^{ri}'s , $i = 1, \ldots, N$ (13.18).

The upper level checks whether $G = 0$ (see Figure 13.6). If $G = 0$, the overall preferred solution has been reached; if not, the co-ordinator changes the value according to the equation in Figure 13.6 , where k is an iteration index.

In the second, more general scheme (Figure 13.7) (which is basically a counterpart of the single objective method in Brosilow, Lasdon, and Pearson (1965), the problem (13.8), ..., (13.12) is first modified replacing (13.10) by an equivalent set of equations:

$$q_i(x_i, m_i, y_i) = \ell_i \quad , \qquad i = 1, \ldots, N \qquad (13.23)$$

$$\sum_{i=1}^{N} \ell_i \leq 0 \quad , \qquad (13.24)$$

where ℓ_i's , $i = 1, \ldots, N$, are now additional decision variables, of the same dimension as q_i's.

Now the variables $y_1, \ldots, y_N$, $\ell_1, \ldots, \ell_N$ are taken as co-ordination parameters. When some values are given to them at the beginning of the k-th iteration $(k = 1, 2, \ldots)$, corresponding values for x_i's are calculated according to the coupling equations: $x_i^k = \sum_{j=1}^{N} C_{ij} y_j^k$, $i = 1, \ldots, N$. As in the first scheme, we are left in each subsystem with a multiobjective problem with respect to m_i and with the same trade-off vector λ_s^i . For $i = 1, \ldots, N$ these subproblems are:

$$\min_{m_i} \begin{bmatrix} f_1^i(x_i^k, m_i, y_i^k) \\ \cdot \\ \cdot \\ \cdot \\ f_{n_i}^i(x_i^k, m_i, y_i^k) \end{bmatrix} \qquad (13.25)$$

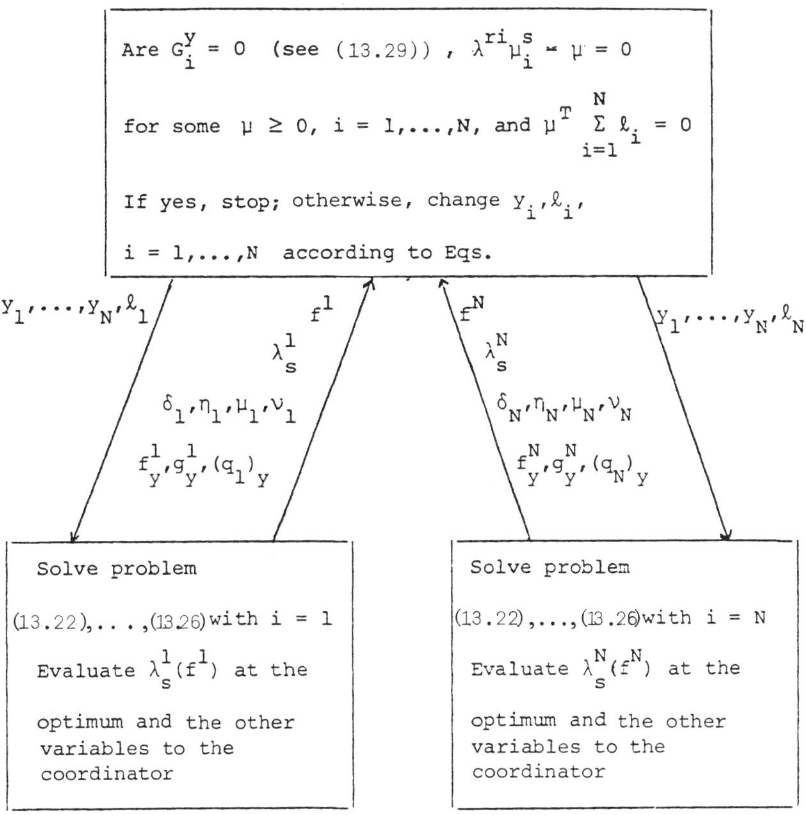

Figure 13.7. Feasible method, scheme 2

Subject to:

$$y_i^k = H_i (x_i^k, m_i) \tag{13.26}$$

$$g_i (x_i^k, m_i, y_i^k) \leq 0 \tag{13.27}$$

$$q_i (x_i^k, m_i, y_i^k) = \ell_i^k \tag{13.28}$$

with a trade-off vector

$$\lambda_s^i (f^i (x_i^k, m_i, y_i^k)) \tag{13.29}$$

After a subsystem i has solved its multiobjective problem, it solves constraint multipliers, δ_i, η_i, μ_i from the following linear equation, $i = 1, \ldots, N$, where all functions are evaluated at the preferred solution reached in the optimization of the k-th iteration:

$$(\lambda_s^i(f^i))^T \frac{\partial f^i}{\partial m_i} + \delta_i^T \frac{\partial H_i}{\partial m_i} + \eta_i^T \frac{\partial g_i}{\partial m_i} + \mu_i^T \frac{\partial q_i}{\partial m_i} = 0 \tag{13.30}$$

If we assume that, for each i, the constraints H_i, g_i, and q_i do not contain altogether more components than m_i, there are unique solutions to (13.30).

Next, ν_i multipliers are solved (directly after evaluating the derivatives) from the following $(i = 1, \ldots, N)$ equations, where functions are evaluated at the same values as in (13.30).

$$(\lambda_s^i(f^i))^T \frac{\partial f^i}{\partial x_i} + \delta_i^T \frac{\partial H_i}{\partial x_i} + \eta_i^T \frac{g_i}{x_i} - \nu_i^T + \mu_i^T \frac{\partial q_i}{\partial x_i} = 0 \tag{13.31}$$

Note that these multipliers are usual Lagrange multipliers if $\eta_i = 1$. In that case, an optimation technique may give them directly, when the problem is reformulated such that in (13.25), ..., (13.29), x^k is replaced by x, and a new equation $-x = -x^k$ is added. Also, when we have a multiobjective subproblem, we get in using the SWT method, in some cases, the multipliers directly (cf. Chankong and Haimes (1978)).

After this, the subsystems evaluate $\partial f^i/\partial y_i$, $\partial g_i/\partial y_i$, and $\partial q_i/\partial y_i$ at the preferred solution in question; in Figure 13.7 partial derivates are indicated by subscripts.

At the upper level, it is checked whether the following equations hold for $i = 1, \ldots, N$:

$$(G_i^y)^T \triangleq (\lambda_s^i(f^i))^T \frac{\partial f^i}{\partial y_i} - \delta_i^T + \eta_i^T \frac{\partial g_i}{\partial y_i} + \sum_{k=1}^{N} \frac{\lambda^{rk}}{\lambda^{ri}} \nu_k^T C_{ki} + \mu_i^T \frac{q_i}{y_i} = 0 \tag{13.32}$$

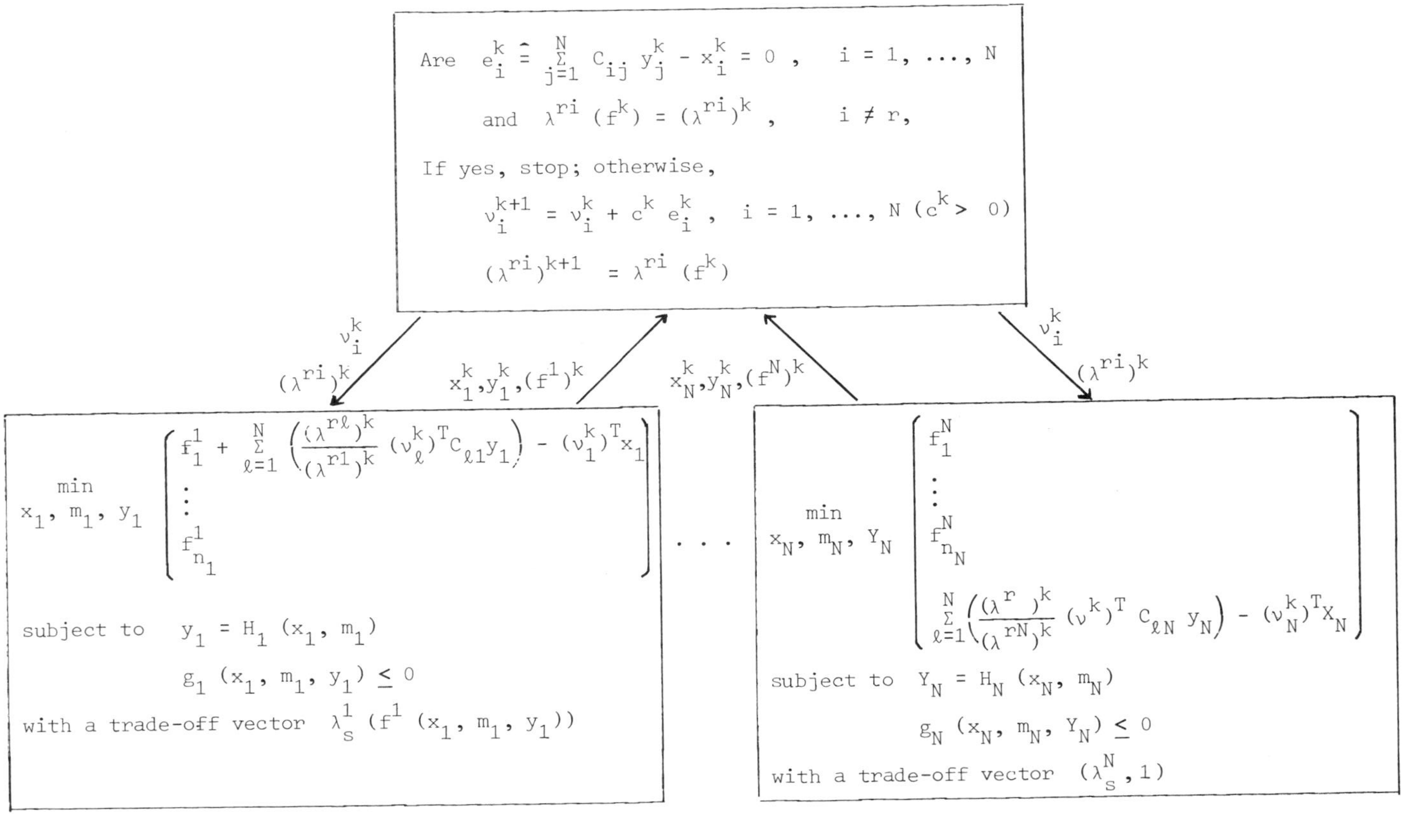

Figure 13.8. Non-feasible method with two different subproblem formulations, one coordination algorithm, $q_i \equiv 0$, $i = 1, \ldots, N$.

$$\lambda^{ri} \mu_i - \mu = 0 \qquad \text{for some} \qquad \mu \geq 0 \tag{13.33}$$

$$\mu^T \sum_{i=1}^{N} \ell_i^k = 0 \tag{13.34}$$

If (13.32), ..., (13.34) are not satisfied, the values of y_i, ℓ_i $(i = 1, \ldots, N)$ are changed. In general, this procedure is a difficult task, owing to the constraints that the new values should satisfy. In this sheme, a new direction $d = (\Delta y_i, \ldots, \Delta y_N, \Delta\ell_1, \ldots, \Delta\ell_N)$ is selected; and the movement of the coordination parameter in this direction is determined, more or less, by trial and error. When d is a direction vector, it is usually normalized so that $\|d\| = 1$ (Euclidean norm). Here, as usually operant in feasible methods, d is normalized by a more practical ℓ_∞ norm; that is,

$$-1 \leq \Delta y_i \leq 1 , \quad -1 \leq \Delta\ell_i \leq 1 , \quad i = 1, \ldots, N \tag{13.35}$$

In a first-order accuracy, d and corresponding changes in other variables have to satisfy:

$$\Delta y_i = \frac{\partial H_i}{\partial x_i} \Delta x_i + \frac{\partial H_i}{\partial m_i} \Delta m_i , \qquad i = 1, \ldots, N \tag{13.36}$$

$$\frac{\partial g_{ik}}{x_i} \Delta x_i + \frac{\partial g_{ik}}{\partial m_i} \Delta m_i + \frac{\partial g_{ik}}{\partial y_k} \Delta y_i = 0 , \quad k \in \{k | g_{ik} = 0\},$$
$$i = 1, \ldots, N \tag{13.37}$$

$$\Delta x_i = \sum_{j=1}^{N} C_{ij} \Delta y_j , \qquad i = 1, \ldots, N \tag{13.38}$$

$$\frac{\partial q_i}{\partial x_i} \Delta x_i + \frac{\partial q_i}{\partial m_i} \Delta m_i + \frac{\partial q_i}{\partial y_i} \Delta y_i = \Delta\ell_i , \quad i = 1, \ldots, N \tag{13.39}$$

$$\sum_{i=1}^{N} \Delta\ell_i = 0 , \qquad \text{if} \qquad \mathop{\Delta}_{i=1}^{N} \ell_i = 0 \tag{13.40}$$

In the scheme a new direction is determined as a $(\Delta y_1, \ldots, \Delta y_N, \Delta\ell_1, \ldots, \Delta\ell_N)$ that minimizes

$$\sum_{j=1}^{N} (G_i^y)^T \lambda^{ri} \Delta y_i - \sum_{i=1}^{N} \lambda^{ri} \eta_i^T \left(\frac{\partial g_i}{\partial x_i} \Delta x_i + \frac{\partial g_i}{\partial m_i} \Delta m_i + \frac{\partial g_i}{\partial y_i} \Delta y_i \right)$$
$$- \sum_{i=1}^{N} \lambda^{ri} \mu_i^T \Delta\ell_i \tag{13.41}$$

subject to (13.35), ..., (13.40) . Here G_i^y is given in (13.32).

The minimum of (13.41) will be negative, and we can determine the optimal movement in the optimal direction given by this linear problem, so that we stop when expression (13.41), where Δ variables are the same as in the optimal direction but other variables are evaluated at the point in question; or we stop when a constraint is met. All this, provided that the optimal direction is feasible. That is, there is at least a small movement into that direction leading to a point satisfying all constraints. If this is not the case (and, often, even if it were, to prevent jamming in the numerical calculations), modifications like in the feasible methods of single optimization theory must be made (Cf. Zoutendijk (1960), Polak (1971), Geoffrion (1972)).

13.5.4. *Non-feasible methods*

Figure 13.8. depicts the non-feasible method in the case $q_i \equiv 0$ $(i = 1, \ldots, N)$; a more general case with q_i's nonzero is handled in a similar way.

As coordination paramters we have now ν_i's, $i = 1, \ldots, N$, λ^{ri}'s , $i \neq r$. (We know that $\lambda^{rr} = 1$; other λ^{ri}'s may be also constant, in which case they need not to be iterated by the upper level).

In Figure 13.8., two subproblem formulation possibilities are presented. They differ only in that either may be more suitable for making correspondent modifications in a specific method not using explicit trade-offs.

In the left-hand alternative in Figure 13.8., there is an additional term in the first objective. Note, however, that the acceptable trade-offs are evaluated using λ^1_s $(f^1$ $(x_1, m_1, y_1))$-- that is, using the values of not modified objectives.

In the second alternative, we have an additional objective which has a constant trade-off 1 with the first objective. Other trade-offs are given by the internal trade-off vector.

At the upper level, a check is made on whether the coupling constraints (13.11) are satisfied and whether the λ^{ri}'s guessed correspond to the values of objectives given by the subsystem solutions. If not, new values are given in a scheme, according to equations in the Figure 13.8.

The non-feasible method presupposes some convexity properties, similar to non-feasible methods in single objective theory. In this case, the conditions are more complex due to trade-off functions. Because these functions are often not known before the interaction with a decisonmaker, the conditions as such are not always usable.

13.5.5. *Trade-offs depending on objectives in other subsystems*

When the trade-offs used in subsystems depend on objectives outside the subsystem in question, we may proceed exactly in the same manner as in the non-feasible method with respect to λ^{ri}'s . That is, for a trade-off that depends on outside objectives, a value is guessed at the beginning of the process. Once all subsystem optimizations are carried out, we check if the value guessed corresponds to the values of objectives. If not, a new value - equal to the value of the trade-off at the latest values of objectives - is assigned. We can use, as always in these kinds of iterations, a smoothing formula, if divergence is noticed. That is, in the case of λ^{ri}'s in Figure 13.8, we use the following updating equation:

$$(\lambda^{ri})^{k+1} = c_\lambda\,(\lambda^{ri})^i + (1 - c_\lambda)\,\lambda^{ri}\,(f^k) \tag{13.42}$$

where c_λ is a constant such that $0 \leq c_\lambda < 1$.

In the non-feasible method where there is also an iteration with respect to the coupling equations, it may be necessary, in order to guarantee convergence not to change trade-offs under iteration in every iteration round.

Alternatively, we can take the objectives from other subsystems that affect a trade-off as additional coordination parameters. That is, if e.g., an objective, $f_j^i\,(z_i)$, affects a trade-off in subsystem $k \neq i$, we take a coordination parameter α . For each value of α , we have a constraint $f_j^i\,(z_i) = \alpha$ in the i-th subsystem and when evaluating the trade-off in question in the i-th subsystem the value of α is used for the objective $f_j^i\,(z_i)$. In the feasible method, this modification is directly implemented. In the non-feasible method we change the value of α , just as in the feasible method. So, in effect, the non-feasible method will be a mixed method. This way of handling such trade-offs is the same as in the single objective case the handling of so-called non-separable problems (see, for example, Singh and Titli (1978)).

13.5.6. *Example*

13.5.6.1 *Problem formulation*

Consider the following multiobjective problem, which is depicted in Figure 13.9.

$$\min \begin{bmatrix} F_1 \\ F_2 \end{bmatrix} \quad \text{with} \quad \begin{aligned} F_1 &= .5f_1^1 + f_1^2 \\ F_2 &= f_2^1 \end{aligned} \tag{13.43}$$

where

$$f_1^1 = m_{11}^2 + m_{12}^2 + x_1^2 \tag{13.44a}$$

$$f_2^1 = m_{11} + x_1 \tag{13.44b}$$

$$f_1^2 = m_{21}^2 + m_{22}^2 + y_2^2 \tag{13.44c}$$

subject to

$$x_1 = y_2 \tag{13.44d}$$

$$y_2 = m_{21} + m_{22} \tag{13.44e}$$

In the following, this problem is solved using the non-feasible method explained in Section 13.5.4. The feasible method could be used as well.

To solve a multiobjective problem, a decision-maker is needed. For our purpose of demonstrating hierarchical-multiobjective solution structures, we assume a mathematical model for the decision-maker. Specifically in this example we assume that the acceptable trade-off between the two

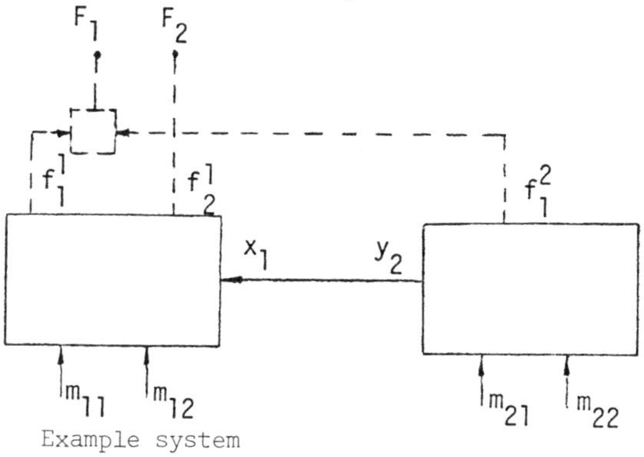

Figure 13.9. Example system

objectives is the following:

$$\lambda_{12}^{*} (f) = 1 + f_2^1 \tag{13.45}$$

Thus, the trade-off vector defined in (13.14) is

$$\lambda (f) = [\lambda_1(f), \lambda_2(f)]^T = [1, 1 + f_2^1]^T \tag{13.46}$$

In practice preferences evolve during the interaction between the analysts and decision-makers, and they are evaluated at some specified values of the objective functions. An indifference band corresponding to acceptable trade-offs and preferred solutions may exist (see Section 13.3.1). However, for our illustrative purposes, the existence of a unique preferred solution will be assumed.

This multiobjective example problem is solved twice - with and without decomposition.

13.5.6.2. *Integrated solution*

Eliminating the constraints (13.44d, 13.44e) by direct substitutions yields:

$$\min_{Z} \begin{bmatrix} G(Z) \\ F_1(Z) \\ \vdots \\ F_r(Z) \end{bmatrix}$$

where

$$G(Z) = Z^T AZ + b^T Z \tag{13.47a}$$

$$F_1(Z) = C_1^T Z + d_1$$

$$\vdots$$

$$F_r(Z) = C_r^T Z = d_r$$

with

$$\lambda = (1, \alpha_1^T F + \beta_1, \ldots, \alpha_r^T F + \beta_r)^T \tag{13.47b}$$

where λ is the trade-off vector and where $F = (F_1(Z), \ldots, F_r(Z))^T$; Z, b, c_i's, α_i's are vectors, a positive definite matrix, d_i's, β_i's scalars.

An analytical solution is derived by following the SWT method. Let:

$$C^T = \begin{bmatrix} C_1^T \\ \vdots \\ C_r^T \end{bmatrix}, \quad d = \begin{bmatrix} d_1 \\ \vdots \\ d_r \end{bmatrix}, \quad \alpha = \begin{bmatrix} \alpha_1^T \\ \vdots \\ \alpha_r^T \end{bmatrix}, \quad \beta = \begin{bmatrix} \beta_1 \\ \vdots \\ \beta_r \end{bmatrix}, \quad \varepsilon = \begin{bmatrix} \varepsilon_1 \\ \vdots \\ \varepsilon_r \end{bmatrix} \tag{13.48}$$

Using the ε-constant approach, a single-objective problem with constraints is formulated (see Haimes et al. (1971) and Haimes (1977)):

$$\min_Z \; Z^T AZ + b^T Z \tag{13.48a}$$

subject to

$$C^T Z + d \leq \varepsilon \tag{13.48b}$$

where ε is a vector of values of the respective objective functions viewed as constraints in the SWT formulation. The Lagrangian for this problem is

$$L = Z^T AZ + b^T Z + \lambda_E^T (-\varepsilon + C_Z^T + d) \tag{13.48c}$$

where λ_E is a vector of Lagrange multipliers. Assuming the existence of A^{-1} , the condition $L_Z = 0$ yields

$$Z = -\tfrac{1}{2} A^{-1} (C \lambda_E + b) \tag{13.49}$$

Assuming that λ_E has strictly positive components, (13.48b) becomes an equality; then substituting (13.47) into it yields:

$$C^T A^{-1} C\lambda_E = - C^T A^{-1} b + 2d - 2 \varepsilon \tag{13.49a}$$

According to (13.47b), at the preferred solution, ε and λ_E are related such that

$$\lambda_E = \alpha \varepsilon + \beta \tag{13.49b}$$

Substituting (13.49b) into (13.49a) yields:

$$\varepsilon = (2I + C^T A^{-1} C\alpha)^{-1} (2d - C^T A^{-1} (C\beta + b)) \tag{13.49c}$$

where I is an identity matrix and the existence of the inverse components of (13.49c) is assumed.

Substituting the value of ε from (13.49c) into (13.49b) yields λ_E. Checking the positivity of λ_E, (13.49) yields the preferred decision vector, Z^0.

In our example, we have:

$$Z = \begin{bmatrix} m_{11} \\ m_{12} \\ m_{21} \\ m_{22} \end{bmatrix} , \qquad A = \begin{bmatrix} .5 & 0 & 0 & 0 \\ 0 & .5 & 0 & 0 \\ 0 & 0 & 2.5 & 1.5 \\ 0 & 0 & 1.5 & 2.5 \end{bmatrix}$$

$$b = 0 , \ c^T = [\, 1 \ \ 0 \ \ 1 \ \ 1 \,] , \ d = 0 , \ \alpha = 1 , \ \beta = 1$$

Applying (13.49) yields:

$$Z^0 = \begin{bmatrix} m_{11} \\ m_{12} \\ m_{21} \\ m_{22} \end{bmatrix} = \begin{bmatrix} -.4444 \\ 0 \\ -.1111 \\ -.1111 \end{bmatrix}$$

And, from (13.44), (13.43) :

$$f_1^1 = .2716 , \quad f_2^1 = F_2 = -.6667 , \quad f_1^2 = .0741 ,$$

$$F_1 = .3457 , \quad \lambda_E = \lambda_{12} = .4444 .$$

Next, the problem (13.43), (13.44) is solved using a non-feasible method.

5.6.3. *Non-feasible scheme*

First, the trade-off vectors to be used in the subsystems are evaluated according to (13.15), using the trade-off vector (13.46).

$$\lambda^1(f) = \left[\lambda_1 \left\{\frac{\partial F_1}{\partial f_1^1} , \frac{\partial F_1}{\partial f_2^1}\right\} + \lambda_2 \left\{\frac{\partial F_2}{\partial f_1^1} , \frac{\partial F_2}{\partial f_2^1}\right\}\right]^T$$

$$= \left[.5 , 1 + f_2^1\right]^T , \qquad (13.50)$$

$$\lambda^2(f) = \lambda_1 \frac{\partial F_1}{\partial f_1^2} + \lambda_2 \frac{\partial F_2}{\partial f_1^2} = 1 . \qquad (13.51)$$

Therefore, the scaled internal trade-off vectors (13.16) are:

$$\lambda_s^1 = [\, 1 , 2 + 2 f_2^1 \,]^T , \qquad (13.52)$$

$$\lambda_s^2 = 1 . \qquad (13.53)$$

As a reference subsystem we can take the first one: $r = 1$. And we have (13.18)

$$\lambda^{12} = \lambda_1^2 / \lambda_2^1 = 2$$

In practice, λ^i's are evaluated according to (13.15) pointwise, when they are needed in the multicriteria method used, such as the SWT method. Furthermore, F_i's need not be known analytically.

The methodology depicted in Figure 13.8. is foolowed in the subproblem formulation, where ν_1 is the coordination parameter.

Subproblem 1.

Following is the formulation of subproblem 1 (note that $C_{11} = C_{21} = C_{22} = 0$, $C_{12} = 1$).

$$\min_{m_{11},\, m_{12},\, x_1} \begin{bmatrix} f_1^1 - \nu_1^k x_1 \\ f_2^1 \end{bmatrix}$$

with a trade-off vector $\lambda_s^1 (f) = [1 , 2 + 2 f_2^1]^T$.

This problem is of the general form (13.47) with

$$Z = \begin{bmatrix} m_{11} \\ m_{12} \\ x_1 \end{bmatrix} , \quad A = \begin{bmatrix} 1 & 0 & 0 \\ 0 & 1 & 0 \\ 0 & 0 & 1 \end{bmatrix} , \quad b = \begin{bmatrix} 0 \\ 0 \\ -\nu_1^k \end{bmatrix}$$

$$c^T = [1 \ 0 \ 1] , \quad d = 0 , \quad \alpha = 2 , \quad \beta = 2 .$$

Applying (13.49) yields:

$$Z^0 = \begin{bmatrix} m_{11}^k \\ m_{12}^k \\ x_1^k \end{bmatrix} = \begin{bmatrix} -.3333 & -.3333\nu_1^k \\ 0 & \\ -.3333 & +.3333\nu_1^k \end{bmatrix} \quad \begin{matrix} (13.54a) \\ (13.54b) \\ (13.54c) \end{matrix}$$

Subproblem 2.

The same formulation as above is used for subproblem 2. In this case, there is only one objective. Terms associated with other objectives are vacuous; and we are left with the following ordinary optimization problem:

$$\min_{m_{21},\, m_{22},\, y_1} \quad f_2^1 + 2\, \nu_1^k\, y_1$$

subject to $y_1 = m_{21} + m_{22}$.

This is a simple single-objective problem with the following solution:

$$m_{21}^k = -.3333\nu_1^k \tag{13.55a}$$

$$m_{22}^k = -.3333\nu_1^k \tag{13.55b}$$

$$y_1^k = -.6667\nu_1^k \tag{13.55c}$$

Coordination

The task of the coordinator is to determine a ν_1^k such that $y_2^k - x_1^k = 0$. In this case, the coordination can be solved analytically. Let ν_1^0 denote the solution. It satisfies (cf. (13.54c), (13.55c)) the following equation:

$$-.6667\nu_1^0 + .3333 - .3333\nu_1^0 = 0 ,$$

or, $\nu_1^0 = .3333$.

The corresponding subproblem solutions are given by (13.54), (13.55), and they are commensurate with the integrated solution of section 13.5.6.2.

In practice, coordination is generally performed iteratively. Consider the algorithm given in Figure 13.8; inthis cae:

$$\nu_1^{k+1} = \nu_1^k + c^k (y_2^k - x_1^k) = \nu_1^k + c^k (.3333 - \nu_1^k) \tag{13.56}$$

Assuming $c^k = c =$ constant; then we have an ordinary difference equation for ν_1^k . It is easily seen that $\nu_1^k \to \nu_1^0$, as $k \to \infty$, whenever $0 < c < 2$. Thus, for these values of c , this coordination algorithm works. In practice, the values of c^k are tuned on the basis of the observed convergence.

13.6. CONCLUSION

Even with this very simple example problem, which illustrates the non-feasible method, a reduction in dimensionality is achieved. In the integrated solution, there are four decision variables, where a four by four matrix (Z) has to be inverted - the inversion is the major computer load in the analytical method used. In the multilevel solution the largest subproblem has no more than three decision variables. It is readily seen how decomposition in large scale problems with several decision variables may significantly reduce the analyst's work.

For a decision-maker, decomposition may reduce the number of objectives to be dealt with. In this example, one subproblem was a single-objective problem. More generally, a problem with several objectives may be reduced to a set of problems with fewer respective objectives.

There is a feature, not present in this example, which may counteract computer load benefits. Similar to the single objective case, the number of iterations in the hierarchical-multiobjective case may grow large. For these cases, suboptimal stopping rules are of importance.

13.7. NOTES

(1) For a more comprehensive discussion on the hierarchical approach, the reader is referred to Mesarovic, Macko, and Takahara (1970), Lefkowitz (1966), Lasdon (1970), Wismer (1971), Himmelblau (1973), Haimes and Macko (1973), Macko and Haimes (1978), Haimes (1973, 1975, 1977), Olenik and Haimes (1979), and Mendu, Haimes, and Macko (1979), and Tarvainen and Haimes (1980 a,b).

(2) The Surrogate Worth Trade-off (SWT) method was first developed by Haimes and Hall (1974). Additional material on the SWT method and its extensions can be found in Haimes, Hall and Freedman (1975), Hall and Haimes (1976), Haimes and Hall (1975), Haimes (1977), Cohon and Marks (1975), Chankong (1976), Chankong and Haimes (1978), Haimes and Chankong (1979), Haimes and Hall (1978), and Haimes (1979).

13.8. REFERENCES

Brosilow, C.B., Lasdon, L., and Pearson, J.D., Feasible Optimization Methods for Interconnected Systems, 1967 JACC Conference, June 22 - 25, R.P.I., Troy, New York, 1965.

Chankong, V., and Haimes, Y.Y., The Interactive Surrogate Worth Trade-off (ISWT) Method for Multiobjective Decision-Making, *Multi-Criteria Problem Solving,* Stanley Zoints, Editor, Springer-Verlag, New York, 1978.

Cohon, J.L., and Marks, D.H., A Review and Evaluation of Multiobjective Programming Techniques, *Water Resources Res.,* 11, no.2, April 1975, pp.208-220.

Geoffrion, A.M., and Hogan, W.W., Coordination of Two-Level Organizations with Multiple Objectives, in *Techniques of Optimization,* Balakrishnan, A.V., Editor, Academic Press, New York, 1972, pp.455-466.

Haimes, Y.Y., Lasdon, L.S., and Wismer, D.A., On the Bicriterion Formulation of the Integrated System Identification and System Optimization, *IEEE Transactions on Systems Man and Cybernetics,* SMC-1, 1971, pp. 296-297.

Haimes, Y.Y., Decomposition and Multilevel Approach in the Modelling and Management of Water Resources Systems, in *Decomposition of Large-Scale Problems,* Himmelblau, D., Editor, North-Holland Elsevier, Amsterdam, The Netherlands, 1973, pp.347-368.

Haimes, Y.Y., and Macko, D., Hierarchical Structures in Water Resources Systems Management, *IEEE-Systems Man and Cybernetics,* vol.SMC-3, no.4, 1973, pp.396-402.

Haimes, Y.Y., and Hall, W.A., Multiobjective in Water Resources Systems Analysis: The Surrogate Worth Trade-off Method, *Water Resources Research,* vol.10, no.2, August 1974, pp.614-624.

Haimes, Y.Y., and Hall, W.A., Analysis of Multiple Objectives in Water Quality, *Journal, ASCE, Hydraulics Division,* vol.101, no.HY4, April, 1975, pp.387-400.

Haimes, Y.Y., Hall, W.A., and Freedman, H.T., *Multiobjective Optimization in Water Resources Systems: The Surrogate Worth Trade-off Method,* Elsevier Scientific Publishing Company, The Netherlands, 1975.

Haimes, Y.Y., *Hierarchical Analyses of Water Resources Systems: Modelling and Optimization of Large-Scale Systems,* McGraw-Hill International Book Company, New York, 1977.

Haimes, Y.Y., and Hall, W.A., Sensitivity, Responsivity, Stability and Irreversibility as Multiple Objectives in Civil Systems, *Advances in Water Resources,* vol.1, no.2, 1978.

Haimes, Y.Y., Large-Scale Water Resources Systems, in *Handbook of Large-Scale Systems Engineering Applications*, Singh, M., And Titli, A., Editors, North-Holland Publishing Company, 1979.
Haimes, Y.Y., and Chankong, V., Kuhn-Tucker Multipliers as Trade-offs in Multiobjective Decision-Making Analysis, *Automatica*, vol.15, no.1, 1979, pp.59-72.
Haimes, Y.Y., Loparo, K.A. Olenik, S.C., and Nauda, S.K., Multiobjective Statistical Method (MSM) for Interior Drainage Systems, *Water Resources Research*, 1980 (in press).
Hall, W.A., and Haimes, Y.Y., The Surrogate Worth Trade-off Method with Multiple Decision-Makers, in *Multiple Criteria Decision-Making: Kyoto, 1975*, Zeleny, M., Editor, Springer-Verlag, Inc., New York, 1976, pp.207-233.
Himmelblau, D.M. (editor), Decomposition of Large-Scale Problems, American Elseview, New York, 1973.
Lasdon, L., *Optimization Theory for Large Systems*, MacMillan, London, 1970.
Lefkowitz, I., Multilevel Approach Applied to Control System Design, Trans. ASME, vol.88D, 1966.
Macko, D., and Haimes, Y.Y., Overlapping Coordination of Hierarchical Structures, *IEEE Transactions on Systems, Man and Cybernetics*, vol. SMC-8, no.10, Oct. 1978, pp.745-751.
Mendu, S.R., Applicability of Overlapping Coordination for Linear Hierarchical Structures, Master Thesis, Department of Systems Engineering, Case Institute of Technology, Case Western Reserve University, Cleveland, Ohio, 1978.
Mendu, S.R., Haimes, Y.Y., and Macko, D., Computational Aspects of Overlapping Coordination Methodology for Linear Hierarchical Systems, *IEEE Transactions on Systems Man and Cybernetics*, 1980 (in press).
Mesarovic, M.D., Macko, D., and Takahara, Y., *Theory of Hierarchical Systems*, Academic Press, New York, 1970.
Olenik, S.C., and Haimes, Y.Y., A Hierarchical-Multiobjective Method for Water Resources Planning, *IEEE Transactions on Systems Man and Cybernetics*, vol.SMC-9, no.9, 1979.
Polak, E., *Computational Methods in Optimization*, Academic Press, New York, 1971.
Singh, M.G., and Titli, A., (editors), *Handbook of Large-Scale Systems Engineering Applications*, North-Holland Publishing Company, 1979.
Singh, M.G., and Titli, A., *System-Decomposition, Optimization and Control*, Pergamon Press, Oxford, 1978.
Sung, Kai, Multiobjective Optimization and Hierarchical Overlapping coordination in Water Resources Systems, Ph.D. Dissertation, Department of Systems Engineering, Case Institute of Technology, Case Western Reserve University, Cleveland, Ohio, 1978.
Tarvainen, K., and Haimes, Y.Y., Basic Hierarchical Multiobjective Optimization Techniques, Case Western Reserve University, Cleveland, Ohio, Rep. no.SED-WRR-1-80, 1980a.
Tarvainen, K., and Haimes, Y.Y., Coordination of Hierarchical Multiobjective Systems: Theory and Methodology, Case Western Reserve University, Cleveland Ohio, Rep. no.SED-WRR-2-80. Also submitted for publication, 1980b.
Wismer, D.A., (editor), *Optimization Methods for Large Scale Systems ... with Applications*, McGraw-Hill Book Company, New York, 1971.
Zoutendijk, G., *Methods of Feasible Directions*, Elsevier Publishing Co., Amsterdam, 1960.

ACKNOWLEDGMENTS

The authors thank Drs. I. Lefkowitz and M.A.H. Ruffner for their contributions. Current support for this work is provided by the United States Department of Ene-gy, Contract no. EC-77-S-01-2124, under the project title, "Modelling and Synthesis of Energy Storage Devices in Power Systems", and by the National Science Foundation, Grant no. ENG79-03605, under the project title, "The Integration of the Hierarchical and Multiobjective Approaches".

D. SPECIFIC METHODS

14 Multistage Decision Problems with Multiple Criteria

P. L. Yu and L. Seiford

14.1. INTRODUCTION

Consider a serial production process in which the production divisions are interrelated such that the input of one division is the output of its previous division. Both *cost* and *quality* are important to management. This yields an example of a finite stage multiple criteria (cost and quality) decision problem. One criterion finite stage decision problems (finite stage dynamic programming) have been explored in the literature. For instance see Nemhauser (1966). In this chapter we shall address multiple criteria finite stage problems.

In contrast to single stage multicriteria problems (see those articles in Cochrane and Zeleny (1973), Starr and Zeleny (1977), Zeleny (1976) and Zionts (1978)), the transition of the state variables is a very important factor in general finite stage problems. Although finite stage problems can be converted into large one stage problems, the intuitive meaning of the models will disappear and the computation will become unyielding.

In contrast to the infinite stage single criterion problem (for instance see Leitmann (1976) and Leitmann and Marzollo (1975), the use of a single operator is usually not assumed in finite stage problems. For example, addition might be followed by multiplication in combining the returns from preceding stages. This added versatility is necessary to model many problems.

Since there is no universally accepted solution concept for multicriteria problems and since domination structures and nondominated solutions (see Yu (1973, 1974)) can be used to unify existing solution concepts, we shall focus on domination structures and nondominated solutions in Section 14.3. Necessary and sufficient conditions for such a scheme to work will also be reported. To facilitate our presentation, in the next section we shall describe a general framework for multicriteria finite stage problems and briefly introduce the concepts of domination structures and nondominated solutions which, in general, do not require transitivity. An example will be given in Section 14.4 and some research problems will be described in the conclusion (Section 14.5).

Before we close this section, the following related articles are worth mentioning. Mitten (1974) describes a method for solving finite stage problems where the preference structure over the policies can be represented by a *complete weak ordering*. His results generalize traditional dynamic programming with real valued preferences. Sobel (1975) extends Mitten's results to infinite horizon problems and discusses value and policy improvement techniques. The results of Mitten (1974) and Sobel (1975) are not applicable to most multicriteria problems. Both assume a complete and transitive preference relation. The preference relation induced by Pareto optimality is *not* complete and transitive; that more general preference relations fail to be transitive is well-known. Brown and Strauch (1965) consider dynamic programming problems in which the return space is a conditionally complete associative multiplicative lattice. They assume that the *same associative* operation is used to combine the returns from successive stages. Such assumptions limit the utility of their results. Many frequently encountered problems require operators which are not associative and/or which vary from stage to stage. In Henig's dissertation (1978), Denardo's results (1967) are elegantly extended to multicriteria problems. While Henig's results are not directly related to the current report, they nevertheless are an important part of multicriteria dynamic programming, especially in the value and policy improvement techniques for infinite stage problems.

14.2. FORMULATION AND PRELIMINARY RESULTS

Let us consider the serial decision problems depicted in Figure 14.1.

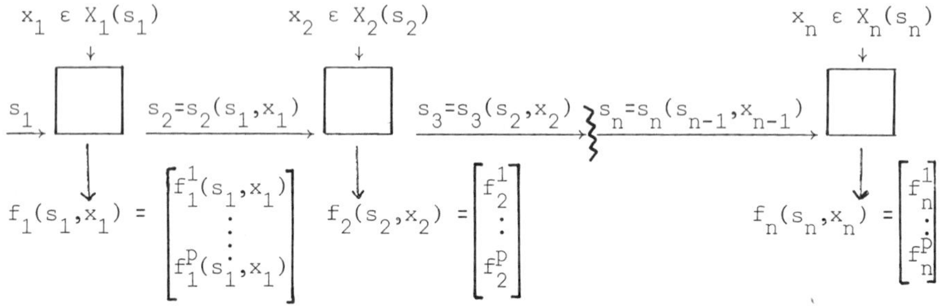

Figure 14.1. A number of serial decision problems

The decision variable is $x = (x_1,\ldots,x_n)$ with each $x_t \in X_t\ (s_t)$.
The state variables $\{s_t\}$ are generated by:

$$s_{t+1} = s_{t+1}\ (s_t,\ x_t) \qquad t=1,\ldots,n-1 \tag{14.1}$$

where $x_t \in X_t\ (s_t)$.
Note that $X_t\ (s_t)$ is a set which specifies the set of alternatives when the state s_t is reached. The sequence $\{s_t\}$ generated serially by $\{x_t\}$ is a *path* in the state space. The familiar constraints in mathematical programming such as $\sum_j s_j \geqq c$, $\pi_j\ g_j\ (x_j) \geqq c$ or $\max_j \{g_j(x_j)\} \geqq c$ can be converted to the above serial formulation (see Chapters II, III of Nemhauser (1966)).

The only deviation from traditional finite stage dynamic programming in this note is that at each stage t there are p-criteria $(f_t^1,\ldots,f_t^p)^T$ $p \geqq 1$. In a serial production process, the criteria at each stage could be *cost* and *quality*. The overall measurement in terms of criteria i is denoted by $F^i\ (f_1^i(x_1),\ldots,f_n^i(x_n))$, $i=1,\ldots,p$. Thus, for our example F^1 would be the overall cost (a function of the cost for each stage) and F^2 would be the overall quality.

For convenience, the following notation will be used:

$$f^i = (f_1^i(s_1,x_1),\ldots,f_n^i(s_n,x_n))$$

$$f_t = (f_t^1(s_t,x_t),\ldots,f_t^p(s_t,x_t))^T \quad \text{and}$$

$$F = (F^1,\ldots,F^p)^T .$$

Note that the superscript is used for the criteria index, and the subscript is for the stage index of the decision variables and their related contributions.

The decision problem with which we are faced is to find an x which satisfies constraints (14.1) and which is *good* in view of the criteria F. We shall briefly describe the concept of domination structures and nondominated solutions to facilitate our latter discussion (see Yu (1973, 1974) for a more thorough discussion).

Let X, called the *decision space*, be the totality of all x satisfying (14.1); and let $Y = \{F(x) \mid x \in X\}$ be the *criteria space*.

Suppose that $y^1, y^2 \in Y$ and y^1 is preferred to y^2, denoted by $y^1 \succ y^2$. We can think of this preference as occurring because of the factor $d = y^2 - y^1$. Suppose that $y^1 \succ y^1 + \lambda d$ for all $\lambda > 0$, $\lambda \in R^1$. Then d is called a *domination factor* for y^1. The set of all domination factors for y^1 is denoted by $D(y^1)$. The family $\mathcal{D} = \{D(y) \mid y \in Y\}$ is called the *domination structure* for our decision problem (for example, with Pareto optimality D(y) is the constant domination cone $\Lambda^{\leq} \equiv \{d \mid d \leq 0\}$). Note that transitivity is not required in domination structures.

Definition 2.1. Given $y^1, y^2 \in Y$, y^2 is *dominated* by y^1 iff $y^2 \in y^1 + D(y^1)$. y^1 is *nondominated* iff y^1 is not dominated by any other $y \in Y$. That is, there is no $y \in Y \setminus \{y^1\}$ such that $y^1 \in y + D(y)$. The set of all nondominated solutions in Y will be denoted by $N[Y|\mathcal{D}]$, its corresponding solutions in X will be denoted by $N[X|\mathcal{D}]$. That is, $N[X|\mathcal{D}] = \{x \in X \mid F(x) \in N[Y|\mathcal{D}]\}$. When $\mathcal{D}$ is clear from the context we shall denote the above sets by N[Y] and N[X] respectively. When no confusion can occur the term *N-points* will mean points of N[Y] or N[X]. One of the important tasks in solving multicriteria problems is to locate all relevant N-points.

14.3. DECOMPOSITION OF SERIAL SYSTEMS

In this section, conditions for decomposing serial systems for stage-wise computation will be described in order that dynamic programming can be extended to the multicriteria case. These conditions are separability, monotonicity, and nondominance boundedness.

Definition 3.1. (separability). The vector criteria F is *separable* if there exist vector functions $\{g_t \mid t=1,\ldots,n-1\}$, each $g_t: R^{2p} \longrightarrow R^p$ such that:

$$F = g_1(f_1(s_1,x_1),\ g_2(f_2(s_2,x_2),\ g_3(\ldots g_{n-2}(f_{n-2}(s_{n-2},x_{n-2}), \tag{14.2}$$

$$g_{n-1}(f_{n-1}(s_{n-1},x_{n-1}),f_n(s_n,x_n)))\ldots)))$$

When no confusion occurs, (14.2) will be written as:

$$F = f_1(s_1,x_1) \circ f_2(s_2,x_2) \circ \ldots \circ f_n(s_n,x_n) \tag{14.3}$$

Observe that each 'o' represents a vector operator which may contain different operations in its components and may vary from stage to stage.

Example 3.1. Consider a three stage production process with cost and quality as the two criteria, i.e. p=2. (i) Let $F^1(x_1,x_2,x_3) = \sum_{t=1}^{3} f_t^1(x_t)$ and $F^2(x_1,x_2,x_3) = \max_t \{f_t^2(x_t)\}$. (The total cost is the sum of the costs incurred at each stage and the total 'quality' is the max of the individual 'qualities' at each stage.) Then $F = (F^1,F^2)^T$ is separable. (Note $F^2(x_1,x_2,x_n) = \max \{f_1^2(x_2), \max \{f_2^2(x_2)\ ,\ f_3^2(x_3)\}\})$. The vector operator 'o' represents addition in the first component and 'max' in the second component, i.e., $g_1(f_1,g_2) = \begin{Bmatrix} f_1^1 + g_2^1 \\ \max \{f_1^2,g_2^2\} \end{Bmatrix}$

(ii) Let $F = (F^1,\ F^2)^T$ with $F^1 = f_1^1(x_1)f_2^1(x_2) + f_3^1(x_3)$ and $F^2 = f_1^2(x_1) + f_2^2\ (x_2)\ f_3^2\ (x_3)$. Then F is not separable (since F^1 cannot be represented as a function $g_1(f_1,g_2(f_2,f_3))$.

Now suppose that F is separable. Recall that there are n-stages, the (input) state variable is s_n for the nth stage and N[Y] is the set of all N-points of Y with domination structure *D*. A dynamic programming scheme for the multicriteria problem may be described as:

$$\text{Define } Z_n\ (s_n) = \cup\{f_n(s_n,x_n) \mid x_n \in X_n\ (s_n)\} \tag{14.4}$$

For t=n,n-1,...,2, the following are backwardly and recursively defined:

$$N_t(s_t) = N(Z_t(s_t)) \tag{14.5}$$

$$Z_{t-1}(s_{t-1}) = \cup\ \{f_{t-1}\ (s_{t-1},x_{t-1}) \circ N_t(s_t) \mid x_{t-1} \in X_{t-1}(s_{t-1}) \tag{14.6}$$

where

$$f_{t-1}(s_{t-1},x_{t-1}) \circ N_t(s_t) = \{f_{t-1}(s_{t-1}),x_{t-1}) \circ z_t \mid z_t \in N_t(s_t)$$

and s_{t-1}, x_{t-1}, s_t satisfy (14.1).

Recursively, $N_1(s_1)$ can be computed. Note that the computation process (14.4) - (14.6) for $N_1(s_1)$ is similar to that of dynamic programming.

For each stage, instead of maximization or minimization, we compute the set of N-points. In order to see this point, define the *attainable set* from s_t, $t = 1, \ldots, n$, recursively and backwardly as follows:

$$A(s_n) = \cup \{f_n(s_n, x_n) \mid x_n \in X_n(s_n)\} \tag{14.7}$$

for $t = n, n-1, \ldots, 2$

$$A(s_{t-1}) = \cup \{f_{t-1}(s_{t-1}, x_{t-1}) \circ A(s_t(s_{t-1}, x_{t-1})) \mid x_{t-1} \in X_{t-1}(s_{t-1})\} \tag{14.8}$$

where $f_{t-1}(s_{t-1}, x_{t-1}) \circ A(s_t) = \{f_{t-1}(s_{t-1}, x_{t-1}) \circ z_t \mid z_t \in A(s_t)\}$ (14.9)

and s_{t-1}, x_{t-1}, s_t satisfy (14.1) .

From (14.4) - (14.6) and (14.7) - (14.9), it is seen that:

$$Z_t(s_t) \subset A(s_t) \quad \text{for } t = 1, \ldots, n, \quad \text{and } Y = A(s_1) \ .$$

The immediate question is what is the relationship between $N_1(s_1) = N(Z_1(s_1))$ obtained by (14.4) - (14.6) and $N(A(s_1))$? Specifically, under what conditions does $N[Y] = N_1(s_1)$? First we introduce,

Definition 3.2. (Monotonicity). A separable multicriteria objective function $F = f_1 \circ f_2 \circ \ldots \circ f_n$ is monotonic with respect to D iff $z_{t+1} > z'_{t+1}$ and $z_{t+1}, z'_{t+1} \in A(s_{t+1}(s_t, x_t))$ imply that:

$$f_t(s_t, x_t) \circ z_{t+1} > f_t(s_t, x_t) \circ z'_{t+1} \ .$$

Note that the above monotonicity is similar to that of Mitten (1974).

Theorem 3.1. Suppose that F is separable (Definition 3.1.) and that the monotonicity condition (of Definition 3.2.) is satisfied. Then $N[Y] \subset N_1(s_1)$.

Proof. Let $y \in N[Y]$ and y be the outcome of $x = (x_1, \ldots, x_n) \in X$. Thus $y = f_1(s_1, x_1) \circ \ldots \circ f_n(s_n, x_n)$ and s_t satisfies (14.1), $t = 1, \ldots, n$. For simplicity, let $y_t = f_t(s_t, x_t)$. Note that, by definition $y_n \in Z_n(s_n) = A(s_n)$. Suppose that $y \notin N_1(s_1)$. Let $\bar{k}$ be the largest index such that $y_{\bar{k}} \circ y_{\bar{k}+1} \circ \ldots \circ y_n \in Z_{\bar{k}}(s_{\bar{k}}) \setminus N_{\bar{k}}(s_{\bar{k}})$. (Note that $1 \leq \bar{k} \leq n$.) Then there exists $z_{\bar{k}} \circ z_{\bar{k}+1} \circ \ldots \circ z_n \in Z_{\bar{k}}(s_{\bar{k}}) \subset A(s_{\bar{k}})$ and $z_{\bar{k}} \circ \ldots \circ z_n > y_{\bar{k}} \circ \ldots \circ y_n$. Hence by monotonicity,

$$(y_1 \circ \ldots \circ y_{\bar{k}-1} \circ z_{\bar{k}} \circ \ldots \circ z_n) > (y_1 \circ \ldots \circ y_{\bar{k}-1} \circ y_{\bar{k}} \circ \ldots \circ y_n) = y$$

which leads to a contradiction. Q.E.D.

Remark 3.1. Theorem 3.1. states that when monotonicity is satisfied $N_1(s_1)$ contains $N[Y]$. Thus $N[Y]$ can be approximated by $N_1(s_1)$.

A further condition is needed to ensure $N[Y] = N_1(s_1)$.

Definition 3.3. The decision problem is *nondominance bounded* if for each $y \in Y$ either y is nondominated or it is dominated by a nondominated point in Y.

Note that in the abstract, the preference over Y is nondominance bounded if $Y \subset \cup \{y + D(y) \mid y \in N[Y]\}$. Some discussion along this line can be found in Hartley (1978) and Yu (1974). For instance, if Y is compact and $D(y)$ is a constant closed convex cone, then the problem is nondominance bounded. Thus, if the domination structure is Pareto, a sufficient condition for nondominance boundedness is a compact criteria space.

Theorem 3.2. Suppose that F is separable and that the monotonicity of Definition 3.2. and the nondominance boundedness of Definition 3.3. are satisfied. Then $N_1(s_1) \subset N[Y]$.

Proof. Assume the contrary. Let $y^o \in N_1(s_1) \setminus N[Y]$. By nondominance boundedness, there exists $y' \in N[Y]$ such that $y' > y^o$. However, by Theorem 3.1., $y' \in N_1(s_1) \subset Z_1(s_1)$. Since $y^o \in N_1(s_1)$, y' cannot dominate y^o. This leads to a contradiction. Q.E.D.

The following example shows that nondominance boundedness cannot relaxed in Theorem 3.2.

Example 3.1. In a two stage problem (see also Figure 14.2), let $X_1(s_1) = \{x_{11}, x_{12}\}$, $f_1(s_1, x_{1i}) = y_{1i}$, $i = 1, 2$.

$$s_2(s_1, x_{1i}) = s_{2i}, \quad i = 1, 2 .$$

$$X_2(s_{21}) = \{x^1_{21}, x^2_{21}\} \text{ with } f_2(s_{21}, x^k_{21}) = y^k_{21}, \quad k = 1, 2 .$$

$$X_2(s_{22}) = \{x_{22}\} \text{ and } f_2(s_{22}, x_{22}) = y_{22} .$$

Let $y_{11} \circ y^k_{21} = y^k_{21}$.

$$y_{12} \circ y_{22} = y_{22} .$$

Then with the domination structure in Figure 14.3, we have:

$$Z_2(s_{21}) = \{y^1_{21}, y^2_{21}\}$$

$$N_2(s_{21}) = \{y^2_{21}\}$$

$$Z_2(s_{22}) = \{y_{22}\} = N_2(s_{22})$$

$$Z_1(s_1) = \{y^2_{21}, y_{22}\} = N_1(s_1) .$$

But, $Y = \{y^1_{21}, y^2_{21}, y_{22}\}$ and $N[Y] = \{y^2_{21}\}$.

Thus, $N[Y] \subsetneq N_1(s_1)$.

Observe that y_{22} is not nondominance bounded. It is dominated only by y^1_{21} which is a D-point.

Remark: The conclusion $N[Y] = N_1(s_1)$ will actually hold under a weaker monotonicity condition if we require nondominance boundedness at

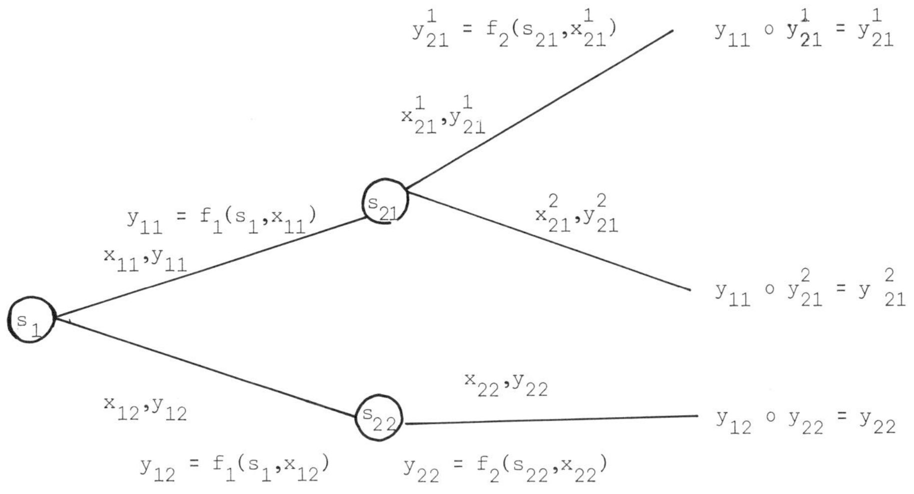

Figure 14.2. Numerical example

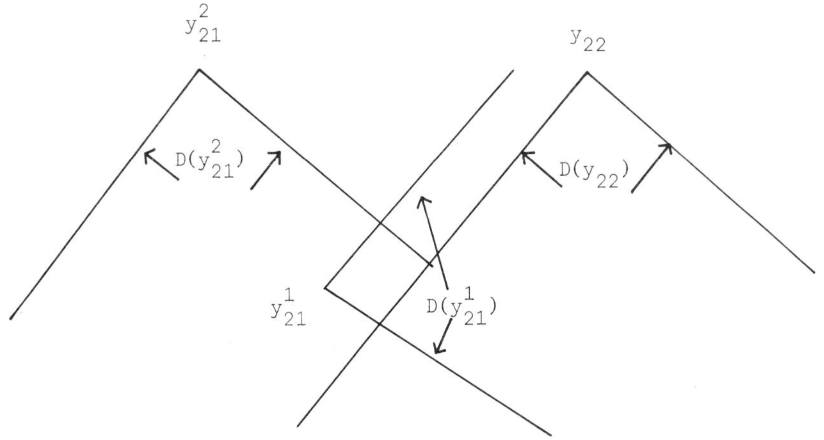

Figure 14.3. Domination structure of Example 3.1

each stage. Specifically, a separable multicriteria objective function $F = f_1 \circ f_2 \circ \ldots \circ f_n$ is weakly monotonic with respect to D iff $z_{k+1} > z'_{k+1}$ and $z_{k+1}, z'_{k+1} \in A(s_{k+1}(s_k, x_k))$ imply that either

$$f_k(s_k, x_k) \circ z_{k+1} > f_k(s_k, x_k) \circ z'_{k+1}$$

or $$f_k(s_k, x_k) \circ z_{k+1} = f_k(s_k, x_k) \circ z'_{k+1}$$

It can then be shown that if F is a separable weakly monotonic multicriterion objective function and $A(s_k)$ is nondominance bounded for each s_k, $k = 1, \ldots, n$, then $N[Y] = N_1(s_1)$.

14.4. AN EXAMPLE

Consider a three stage production process for which there are five discrete units of a resource available to be allocated among the three stages. The decision to allocate x_i units to stage i results in a revenue, f_i^1, and a measure of quality, f_i^2, which can be interpreted as the probability of failure (or defects). We wish to maximize the total revenue and minimize the maximum probability of failure.

To be more specific, we want to determine the set of N-points of:

$$F = \begin{bmatrix} f^1 \\ f^2 \end{bmatrix} = \begin{bmatrix} 15x_1 + 10x_2 + 20x_3 \\ \max\{.3^{x_1}, .6^{x_2}, .4^{x_3}\} \end{bmatrix}$$

subject to: $\sum_{i=1}^{3} x_i = 5$, $x_i \geq 0$, x_i integer, $i = 1, 2, 3$.

Thus we have the following two criteria three stage decision problem:

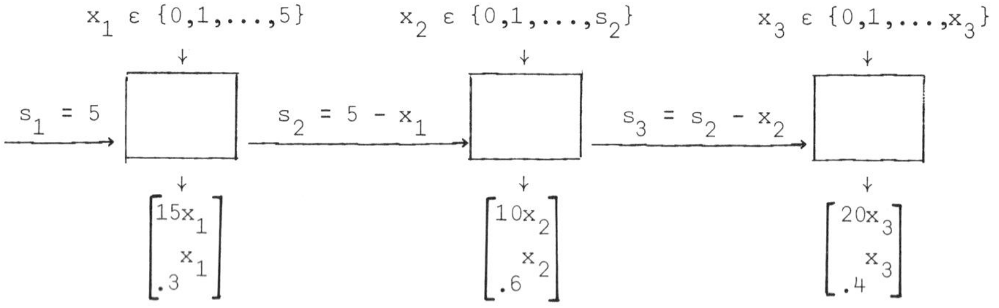

The domination structure for our problem is the constant domination cone $\Lambda = \{d \in R^2 \mid d_1 \leq 0, d_2 \geq 0, d \neq 0\}$. The multicriteria objective function F is weakly monotonic and separable; 'o' represents the vector operator which contains addition in its first component and 'max' in its second component. Furthermore, since nondominance boundedness holds at each stage we have $N[Y] = N_1(s_1)$. To determine $N_1(s_1)$ we proceed sequentially as follows:

s_3	Z_3 (s_3)	N_3 (s_3)
5	{(0,1), (20,.4), (40,.16), (60,.06), (80,.03), (100,.01)}	(100,.01)
4	{(0,1), (20,.4), (40,.16), (60,.06), (80,.03)}	(80,.03)
3	{(0,1), (20,.4), (40,.16), (60,.06)}	(60,.06)
2	{(0,1), (20,.4), (40,.16)}	(40,.16)
1	{(0,1), (20,.4)}	(20,.4)
0	{(0,1)}	(0,1)

Similarly

s_2	N_2 (s_2)
5	{(100,1), (90,.6), (80,.36), (70,.22), (60,.4)}
4	{(80,1), (70,.6), (60,.36), (50,.4)}
3	{(60,1), (50,.6), (40,.4)}
2	{(40,1), (30,.6)}
1	{(20,1)}
0	{(0,1)}

and N_1 $(s_1 = 5)$ = {(100,1), (85,.6), (75,.36)}
which correspond to the decisions $x = (0, 0, 5)$, $x = (1, 1, 3)$ and $x = (1, 2, 2)$ respectively.

14.5. FURTHER COMMENTS AND CONCLUSION

We have shown that when separability and monotonicity are satisfied the set of all nondominated solutions can be approximated by the solution set $N_1(s_1)$ obtained by a dynamic programming approach. Furthermore, if nondominance boundedness is also satisfied then this solution set is nondominated, i.e., the approximation is exact. Monotonicity and nondominance boundedness are frequently satisfied in applications. However, separability may not be satisfied.

In computing nondominated solutions, linear combinations of the criteria (that is $\sum_i \lambda_i F^i$, $\lambda_i \in R^1$) become important in forming a new criterion or constraints for the computation (see for instance, Yu (1974) for details). Unless each F^i is linear or additive, $\sum_i \lambda_i F^i$ will make separability invalid. Thus it would be difficult to compute N-points by first forming $\sum_i \lambda_i F^i$ i.e., reducing the multicriteria return function to a single criterion return function and then applying traditional dynamic programming. Such a difficulty does not occur, however, in our multicriteria dynamic programming formulation, since at each stage we work with the return function in its multiple criteria form.

Several research problems remain to be answered. For instance, in computing $N_k(s_k)$ $k = 1, \ldots, n$, it is desirable to have *cone convexity*.

(See Yu (1974).) If each F^i is additive in its components, f^i_j, which are convex, and each $X_j(s_j)$ is convex, then $Z_k(s_k)$ will be cone convex. This will simplify the computation. What conditions will preserve the cone convexity of $Z_k(s_k)$, $k = 1, \ldots, n$ under backward induction? Since our main interest is in $N_1(s_1)$ (to locate $N[Y]$), not all $N_k(s_k)$ ($k = 1, \ldots, n$, for all possible s_k) are needed. Is there any way to determine which $N_k(s_k)$ are necessary? In the absence of nondominance boundedness, $N_1(s_1)$ could be used as an approximation of $N[Y]$ (see Remark 3.1). Under what conditions is the approximation close, i.e., the 'error' $N_1(s_1)$ $N[Y]$ is 'small'? Finally, if the form of F or f_j is changed, what is the impact on $N_1(s_1)$?

14.6. REFERENCES

Brown, T.A. and Strauch, R.E., Dynamic Programming in Multiplicative Lattices, *Journal of Mathematical Analysis and Applications*, vol.12, no.2, 1965, pp.364-370.

Cochrane, J.L. and Zeleny, M., (eds.), *Multiple Criteria Decision Making*, University of South Carolina Press, Columbia, South Carolina, 1973.

Denardo, E.V., Contraction Mapping in the Theory Underlying Dynamic Programming, *SIAM Review*, vol.9, no.2, 1967, pp.165-177.

Hartley, R., On Cone-Efficiency, Cone-Convexity and Cone-Compactness, *SIAM, Journal on Applied Mathematics*, vol.34, no.2, 1978, pp. 211-222.

Henig, M.I., *Multicriteria Dynamic Programming*, Ph.D. Dissertation, Yale University, May, 1978.

Leitmann, G., (ed.), *Multicriteria Decision Making and Differential Games*, Plenum Press, New York, 1976.

Leitmann, G. and Marzollo, A., (eds.), *Multicriteria Decision Making*, CISM Courses and Lectures No. 211, Springer-Verlag, Wien-New York, 1975.

Mitten, L.G., Preference Order Dynamic Programming, *Management Science*, vol.21, no.1, 1974, pp.43-46.

Nemhauser, G.L., *Introduction to Dynamic Programming*, John Wiley and Sons, New York, 1966.

Sobel, M.J., *Ordinal Dynamic Programming*, *Management Science*, vol.21, no.9, 1975, pp.967-975.

Starr, M.K. and Zeleny, M., (eds.), *Multiple Criteria Decision Making*, Studies in the Management Sciences, vol.6, North-Holland, New York, 1977.

Yu, P.L., Introduction to Domination Structures in Multicriteria Decision Problems, in *Multiple Criteria Decision Making*, Cockrane, J.L. and Zeleny, M., (eds.), University of South Carolina Press, Columbia, South Carolina, 1973.

Yu, P.L., Cone-Convexity, Cone Extreme Points and Nondominated Solutions in Decision Problems with Multiobjectives, *Journal of Optimization Theory and Applications*, vol.14, 1974.

Zeleny, M., (ed.), *Multiple Criteria Decision Making, Kyoto, 1975*, Springer-Verlag Lecture Notes in Economics and Mathematical Systems, no.123, 1976.

Zionts, S., (ed.), *Multiple Criteria Problem Solving*, Springer-Verlag Lecture Notes in Economics and Mathematical Systems, no.155, Springer-Verlag, Wien-New York, 1978.

15 A Multicriteria Analysis for Trichotomic Segmentation Problems

B. Roy

15.1. DECISION AID AND TRICHOTOMIC SEGMENTATION

The classical scientific procedures used in making (or justifying) decisions are usually based on the elaboration of a unique criterion of choice and the search for an optimal solution of this criterion, relative to a previously defined set of mutually incompatible solutions. The decision aid procedure dealt with in this article departs from this traditional optimisation problem formulation. This traditional formulation proves to be ill-adapted to problems in which a decision-maker, who increasingly becomes acquainted with objects or individuals (for example, through dossiers, observations or discussions), must make a decision on the legitimacy or advisability of their assigment to a particular category or segment. These categories are defined according to the ulterior treatment to which the objects or individuals thus assigned would be submitted. This will be the case, for example, in granting credit, adopting a therapeutic treatment, according promotion or a diploma, launching a new product or research project, etc.

In this article we will confine ourselves to three mutually excluding categories or segments (trichotomic segmentation). These three categories however cannot be chosen arbitrarily. Two extremely simplified examples will help us to make this point more precise.

First of all, let us consider the case of credit demanding dossiers presented to a financing organization. Confronted with a particular dossier, the person in charge may either make a positive decision (credit is granted), or a negative decision (credit is refused), or delay making a decision (the dossier is considered insufficient and returned for additional information). Consider now the case of a patient and a therapeutic treatment appropriate to a particular diagnosis. From the initial information on this patient the treatment is judged <u>a priori</u> as being possible. The doctor with this, and if necessary complementary information, will have a choice between three possibilities of the same nature as those precedent: either he accepts the treatment as being appropriate to the patient's condition, or he rejects it as being ill-adapted or risky (this implies that other treatments are taken into consideration), or he is of the opinion that he can and must wait for the results of complementary examinations before making a decision on the advisability of the treatment.

It must be pointed out right from the start that in this type of problem, the decision-maker must take into account diverse factors not always quantifiable and even sometimes subjective. When his calculations are based on numerical data, he must take into account the margin of error that is likely to affect this data. Finally, certain information may be completely missing, and obtaining it may be problematical, time-consuming or costly. In these circumstances and because of the repetitive character of this type of decision, the decision-maker may wish to employ a procedure which recommends the assignment of the particular object or individual to one of three possible categories. It then remains for him to confirm or revise this assignment. The aid provided by such a procedure will obviously be more helpful when the proposed assignments are accompanied by some justification, and the assignment to the class involving a return for additional information has some indication of orientation of the search for such information.

This type of problem has been considered by several authors working in different fields, particularly by Altman (1978), Benayoun and Boulier (1972), Bernard and Besson (1971), Bouroche and Curvalle (1974), Caisse Nationale des Marchés (1973), Levasseur, Hargaine, Schlosser and Vernimmen (1972), Michel (1974) and Pandey and Chawdhary (1973). It seems to us however that none of them, at least to our knowledge, have proposed a procedure giving a solution of a sufficiently general bearing.

After giving in Section 15.2 a more rigorous and complete formulation of the problem, we propose in Section 15.3 a procedure that can be used in different circumstances. Before the conclusion, a numerical example is presented in Section 15.4.

15.2. PROBLEM FORMULATION

15.2.1. *Mono-criterion approach*

We consider objects or individuals denoted by a_i examined in sequence before making a decision. This decision relates to the execution of a precise action (monetary payment, application of a therapy, awarding a diploma, execution of a job, etc). The decision may take one of three possible forms:

- a_i is assigned to category K^+ : positive decision accepting the particular action,
- a_i is assigned to category K^- : negative decision rejecting the particular action,
- a_i is assigned to category $K^?$: awaiting a decision, i.e. delay in order to obtain additional information.

Let us suppose that the formalizable data chosen for use in a decision aid procedure can, in an intelligible and aignificant way, be summarized by a unique criterion g. This criterion may be a financial ratio (acceptance of a credit demand), a weighted mean of evaluations (awarding a diploma), etc. Such a criterion allows each a_i to be characterized by a number $g(a_i)$. This criterion can be defined in such a way that the greater the value of $g(a_i)$ the greater is the legitimacy or advisability of the particular action.

In these circumstances, the higher values of $g(a_i)$ justify assigning a_i to K^+ and the lower values assigning it to K^-. Because of hypotheses which imply using such a criterion g, and also because of the inprecision or uncertainty affecting certain of the elements used in calculating the value $g(a_i)$, it might seem quite arbitrary to wish to define a norm such that every value of the criterion above it implies acceptance and every value below it rejection. In many cases it is more realistic to define :

- on the one hand, an upper limit b fixing the smallest value of $g(a_i)$ for which it appears legitimate or advisable to assign a_i to category K^+;

- on the other hand, a lower limit c ($c < b$) fixing the largest value of $g(a_i)$ for which it appears legitimate or advisable to assign a_i to category K^-.

Once such limits have been defined, it is clear that a_i is assigned to category $K^?$ if and only if :

$c < g(a_i) < b$ (zone where the criterion is inconclusive).

The principal obstacles to this mono-criterion approach lie in fixing the limits b and c and elaborating a unique criterion g.

15.2.2. *Multi-criteria approach*

Let us now suppose that the elements likely to influence the decision lead to a consideration of not one but several criteria denoted by g_j $j = 1, \ldots, n$.

As before, each of these criteria is defined in such a way that the greater the value of $g_j(a_i)$ the more the particular action appears legitimate or advisable from the point of view of those phenomena summarized by this criterion.

Each criterion corresponds to a particular significant feature of the decision. Thus, in the credit demand example several ratios might be necessary in order to represent the diverse aspects of the demander's financial situation. Similarly, in the example relating to a therapeutic treatment, to one or more laboratory results or clinical examinations we might add a (possibly several) criterion (criteria) to appraise the gravity of the injuries (in the short, medium or long term) incurred by the patient to whom this treatment is applied when there is an error in the diagnosis. Not only does each criterion possess, for the same reasons as before, an inconclusive zone, but in addition the degree of inconclusivity is limited by the nature and bearing of the data thus integrated.

Thus, the value of each criterion may contribute to orientating the decision. However there is no reason why these criteria should be independent. In fact just the opposite. But the relationship between them is likely to be so complex that it might appear fruitless to wish to analyse it. Obviously, the positive decision may not be restricted to cases where each of the n criteria attain a sufficiently high value to justify acceptance. On the contrary, the fact that one of the criteria attains a high value - regardless of the values taken by the other $n - 1$ criteria - is not necessarily sufficient to imply acceptance. Finally, the approach involving a determination of trade-offs between criteria (based on the idea that decreasing the criterion g_1 by one unit might be compensated by increasing the criterion g_j by a given amount) hardly appears to us realistic in this kind of problem.

In many cases, the objects or individuals which would involve making a correct positive decision may be of different types. According to their financial situation, their socio-professional status, it might be pertinent to distinguish between certain populations of credit demanders judged worthy of confidence. Similarly, a therapeutic treatment might be considered appropriate to several forms of the same illness, and perhaps to more than one illness.

The preceding considerations explain why we cannot in general, be contented with a generalization of the mono-criterion approach with n pairs of limits (upper and lower). Each of these limits is related to a particular criterion and each criterion is considered independent of the other $n - 1$. Fixing the lower and upper limits for a given criterion has in fact only any significance relative to the values fixed for the other $n - 1$ criteria. Thus it is necessary to reason globally on the set of n criteria. We may then wish to define a first combination of n coherent upper limits $b_1^1, \ldots, b_n^1$ forming a vector $\underline{b}^1$ referred to as the *upper* profile. By definition, this corresponds to a class of objects or individuals for which in normal circumstances a positive decision would be made. Associated with the objects or individuals in this class is a vector $g(a_i)$ whose components are equal, to the corresponding components of the vector $\underline{b}^1$ (in the following paragraph we will see what almost really means). In the same way and for the same class of objects or individuals we may define a lower profile $\underline{c}^1$. By means of an appropriate typology for the populations of objects or individuals under consideration, we can define other coherent combinations of values giving two sets of vectors $B = \{\underline{b}^1, \underline{b}^2, \ldots\}$ and $C = \{\underline{c}^1, \underline{c}^2, \ldots\}$ between which there exists a natural bijection. Each of these vectors plays the role of limiting profiles for acceptance and rejection.

Once the sets B and C have been defined, the next problem is the choice of an assignment procedure (the case $n = 1$ (mono-criterion) poses no problem). We will study this problem in the following section.

15.3 A GENERAL PROCEDURE

15.3.1 *The guiding line*

Consider the case of an object or individual characterized by a vector $g(a_i)$ such that there exists an upper profile $\underline{b}^h$ satisfying $\underline{g}(a_i) \geq \underline{b}^h$ (inequality satisfied by corresponding components). This justifies the hypothesis that a_i belongs to a well-defined type of population and that the procedure must recommend a positive decision. In the same way, if $\underline{g}(a_i) \leqq \underline{c}^k$ or $\underline{c}^k \leqq \underline{g}(a_i) \leqq \underline{b}^k$, the decision to recommend is straightforward.

Obviously it is not always as simple as this, either because of the complexity of the phenomena difficult to apprehend with the chosen typology, or because the criteria are imperfect or the data only approximate.

Recall that a positive decision remains justified if the inequalities $g_j(a_i) \geqq b_j^h$ are slightly contradicted for some of the n values of j. The comparison of a vector $\underline{g}(a_i)$ with an upper profile (or a lower profile) implies avoiding nuances in the meanings of 'true or false'. For this reason we propose to use the concept of degree of outranking (cf.15.3.2.) which is based on the notion of a fuzzy binary relation. This leads (in order to be able to distinguish between slight differences) to a first number obtained by trying to situate $\underline{g}(a_i)$ in relation to the considered profile and a second number obtained by trying to situate the profile in relation to $\underline{g}(a_i)$.

The systematic comparison of $\underline{g}(a_i)$ with p profiles of B and p profiles of C results in four p values. It is then straightforward, by means of a decision tree (cf. 15.3.3) , to use these p values to recommend a suitable assignment of a_i to one of the three categories K^+, K^- and $K^?$. In the last case, we may use the configuration of these four p values to orientate the search for complementary information.

15.3.2. *The concept of degree of credibility of outranking*

Let us consider a problem involving five criteria whose values are expressed as percentages $(0 \leqq g_j(a_i) \leqq 100)$. Let:

$\underline{b}^h = (75, 75, 50, 50, 50)$ and $\underline{c} = (50, 50, 50, 50, 50)$.

We can always define two objects or individuals b^h and c^h such that :

$\underline{g}(b^h) = \underline{b}^h$ and $\underline{g}(c^h) = \underline{c}^h$.

Let us now consider an arbitrary object or individual a_i. Obviously we ignore whether or not it comes from the type of population which has served to define the profiles $\underline{b}^h$ and $\underline{c}^h$. Nevertheless, we may wonder whether the comparison of the vector $g(a_i)$ with the profile $\underline{b}^h$ allows us to provide clear and positive proof favorable to the assignment of a_i to K^+, which is at least as convincing as that justifying the tangential assignment of b^h to the same class. If this is the case, as for example with (85, 72, 65, 65, 65), we say that a_i *outranks* b^h. If, on the other hand, it is obvious that the evidence is less significant, as for example with (60, 60, 53, 52, 50) or even (60, 85, 45, 60, 50), we say that a_i does not outrank b^h.

Unfortunately there may be certain objects or individuals for which it appears quite arbitrary to reply to this question of the outranking of b^h in terms of true or false. When the answer is ambiguous, as for example with (85, 70, 65, 47, 47), we may seek to translate by a number $d(a_i, b^h)$ the more or less high credibility or validity of outranking. This number is by definition, the degree of credibility of outranking of

b^h by a_i. For an outranking conclusively validated, we will put $d(a_i, b^h) = 1$. For no outranking, again conclusively validated, we will put $d(a_i, b^h) = 0$.

Now reversing the order and considering the arguments which make $\underline{b}^h$ an upper profile (delimiting an inferior limit of acceptance), it is not without interest to examine the outranking of a_i by b^h. Therefore we obtain a degree of credibility $d(b^h, a_i)$ equal to 1 if the assignment of b^h to K^+ appears (in relation to the quality and nature of the data) at least as well justified as the assignment of a_i to the same class. When this is not the case $d(b^h, a_i) = 0$. Note that although in many instances $d(a_i, b^h) = 1$ goes hand in hand with $d(b^h, a_i) = 0$, it is not necessarily always the case. If, compared to b^h, the evidence in favour of assigning a_i to K^+ is not as conclusive, $d(a_i, b^h) = d(b^h, a_i) = 1$. If however a_i apparently belongs to a type of population fundamentally different from that serving to fix the profile $\underline{b}^h$, we may well end up with $d(a_i, b^h) = d(b^h, a_i) = 0$ (total absence of outranking).

The formulae enabling a degree of credibility of outranking to be calculated from two particular vectors (and should the occasion arise from additional information relative to the discriminant power of the criteria and their importance) should be adapted to the circumstances of the problem in question. You will find in Roy (1977, 1978) the general principles on which these formulae may be established.

Everything that we have said in relation to the upper profile $\underline{b}^h$ transposes in an obvious way to the lower profile $\underline{c}^h$. This transposition involves an object or individual c^h such that $\underline{g}(c^h) = \underline{c}^h$. Here we are concerned with the class K^-, but we must take care since if we wish to conserve the same language and formula to define the degree of credibility of outranking, the meaning must be reversed : the higher the value of $d(a_i, c^h)$, the less justified (with reference to $\underline{c}^h$) we are in assigning a_i to the category K^- (and inversely for $d(c^h, a_i)$).

15.3.3. *Decision tree*

Given a_i, once the four series of p numbers :

$$d(a_i, b^h),\ d(b^h, a_i),\ d(a_i, c^h),\ d(c^h, a_i),\ h = 1, \ldots, p$$

have been calculated, it may well be that the decision to recommend is obvious. If, for example, the numbers in the first and last series are close to 0, and those of the other two close to 1, then it goes without saying that a_i is assigned to the class $K^?$. Nevertheless, the multiplicity of cases to consider is very large even p is small. Furthermore there exist litigious cases. In order to resolve them it is important to take into consideration the consequences of accepting an action when it should have been rejected, rejecting it when it should have been accepted, as well as the disadvantages (delay, cost, etc) that returning for additional information implies.

From the above , it is possible to construct a decision tree to serve as a guide in the examination of the four series of p numbers to recommend a decision. The examination of a particular path must allow the decision-maker to understand the *raison d'être* of this proposition. Admittedly, the decision tree is not self imposing and on each occasion it must be defined in relation to the circumstances of the particular problem.

Finally, let us note that such a tree may advantageously bring into play some or all of the four following quantities :

$$\max_{b \in B} d(a,b) = d(a,\hat{b}) \qquad \max_{c \in C} d(c,a) = d(\hat{c},a)$$

$$\max_{b \in B-\{\hat{b}\}} d(b,a) = d(b^*,a) \qquad \max_{c \in C-\{\hat{c}\}} d(a,c) = d(a,c^*)$$

The comparison of the values assumed by these quantities with certain thresholds determines the path through the tree. The figure below represents such a tree with four thresholds (β, γ, β', γ'). These thresholds must be fixed by taking into consideration the consequences and disadvantages cited above.

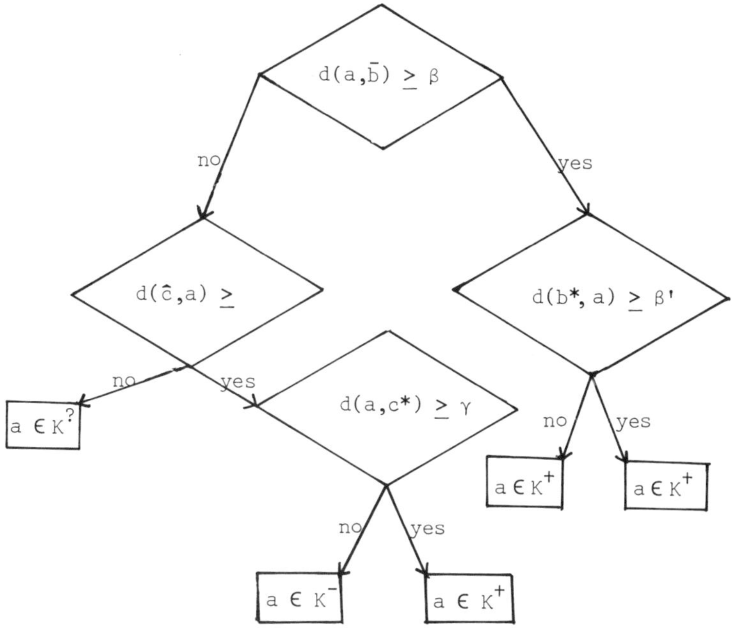

Figure 15.1. Example of a decision tree.

15.4 NUMERICAL EXAMPLE

Let us consider once again the example introduced above involving five criteria. These criteria are of equal importance and assume values between 0 and 100. Suppose that only two upper profiles and two lower profiles have been retained:

$$\underline{b}^1 = (75, 75, 50, 50, 50),\ \underline{b}^2 = (50, 50, 70, 70, 70)$$
$$\underline{c}^1 = (50, 50, 50, 50, 50),\ \underline{c}^2 = (50, 50, 30, 70, 50)$$

We will consider successively six objects or individuals characterized by the following values of the five criteria :

$$\underline{g}(a_1) = (72, 73, 54, 50, 50),\ \underline{g}(a_2) = (50, 50, 60, 70, 70)$$
$$\underline{g}(a_3) = (72, 73, 30, 70, 55),\ \underline{g}(a_4) = (60, 60, 30, 70, 24)$$
$$\underline{g}(a_5) = (60, 60, 60, 50, 12),\ \underline{g}(a_6) = (50, 50, 40, 58, 50)$$

Let us suppose that a difference of 5% on any criterion cannot be considered as being significant, whilst a margin of 15% is significant beyond all question. Suppose also that, on this basis, a formula defining the degree of credibility of outranking resulted in the data reproduced in Table 15. 1. Let us determine the decision rule Figure 15. 1 leads to when it is applied to the data in this table, by setting :

$$\beta = 0,9 \quad \beta' = 0,8 \quad \gamma = 0,8 \quad \gamma' = 0,7$$

(These thresholds and the values assumed by the six objects on the given criteria have been chosen to illustrate the use of the procedure in certain particularly litigious cases regarding the hypotheses introduced).

Apart from some insignificant differences, $g(a_1)$ can be considered as being equivalent to the upper profile $\underline{b}^1$. This is indicated by the following values in Table 15.1 :

$$d(a_1,b^1) = 1,\ d(b^1,a_1) = 1$$

It seems normal to accept a_1. This is precisely what the decision tree of Figure 15.1 recommends, since :

$$d(a_1,\hat{b}) = 1 > \beta \text{ and } d(b^*,a_1) = 0,22 < \beta'$$

We arrive at the same conclusion with a_2, since :

$$d(a_2,\hat{b}) = 0,90 = \beta \text{ and } d(b^*,a_2) = 0 < \beta'$$

The fact that $d(a_2,\hat{b})$ is equal to the threshold β indicated that the acceptance of a_2 is obtained by more delicate conditions than for a_1. This is because $g_3(a_2) = 60$, whereas $g_3(b^2) = 70$: $\underline{g}(a_2)$ is still assimilated into the upper profile $\underline{b}^2$, but the margin of ten points is the maximum margin consistent with such an assimilation and only on the condition that, on all the other criteria, the evaluations on the object or individual concerned were at least equal to those of the profile.

The four objects or individuals are such that $d(a,\hat{b}) < \beta$. Since $g_3(a_3) = 30$, a_3 cannot be considered as outranking b^2. However neither c^1 nor c^2 outrank it. Therefore we are justified in neither accepting nor rejecting it. It appears that the procedure leads to recommend assigning it to $K^?$ and in so doing without the necessity of being too close to the thresholds.

The fact that γ is significantly less than β indicates a decision to be less cautious in rejecting than accepting. This explains the asymmetry of the conclusions relative to a_3 and a_4. For a_4 :

$$d(\hat{c},a_4) = 0,80 = \gamma \text{ and } d(a_4,c^*) = 0 < \gamma'$$

which leads to rejection and not to adjournment as would be the case with $\beta = \gamma = 0,9$. We are then still however in an undetermined position (equality with the threshold).

Like a_4, a_5 assumes a value on the fifth criterion clearly worse than the one justifying acceptance or even delay for additional information. The decision tree however suggests an assignment to $K^?$. This is due to the fact that, unlike a_4 which can be considered as belonging to the second type of population with a high degree of credibility of outranking of a_4 by c^2, a_5 is not easily comparable with either of the limiting profiles and may be suspected as not belonging to any of considered populations.

For the same reason a_6 is assigned to the category $K^?$. However, the path which leads to it in the tree of Figure 15.1 is quite different. Here we note that if the outranking of a_6 by c^1 is very credible (0,94), the credibility of outranking of c^2 by a_6 is far from being negligible (0,86). a^6 is therefore in an ambiguous position between the two types of populations : the first, in itself, would justify rejection, but the second incites us to try to obtain additional information.

Before leaving this example, it may be interesting to compare conclusions obtained from adopting the criterion :

$$\sigma(a_i) = g_1(a_i) + \ldots + g_5(a_i)$$

with the mono-criterion approach described in paragraph 2.1. The criterion σ assigns the same value 2,50 to the lower profiles which can be taken as the lower norm. The choice of the upper norm is more delicate since :

$$\sigma(b^1) = 3,00 \quad \sigma(b^2) = 3,10$$

Let us arbitrarily choose a value 3,05 for the upper norm.

Table 15.2 allows us to compare the conclusions obtained from such an approach with those obtained above. The differences (3 times out of 6)

Table 15.1
Examples of values of the degree of credibility of outranking intervening in the proposed procedure

object or individual		b^1	b^2	c^1	c^2
a_1	$d(a_1, x) =$	1,00	0,40	1,00	0,80
	$d(x, a_1) =$	1,00	0,22	0,22	0,01

object or individual		b^1	b^2	c^1	c^2
a_2	$d(a_2, x) =$	0,00	0,90	1,00	1,00
	$d(x, a_2) =$	0,00	1,00	0,00	0,00

object or individual		b^1	b^2	c^1	c^2
a_3	$d(a_3, x) =$	0,80	0,00	0,80	1,00
	$d(x, a_3) =$	0,80	0,22	0,06	0,22

object or individual		b^1	b^2	c^1	c^2
a_4	$d(a_4, x) =$	0,00	0,00	0,00	0,00
	$d(x, a_4) =$	0,80	0,80	0,60	0,80

object or individual		b^1	b^2	c^1	c^2
a_5	$d(a_5, x) =$	0,00	0,00	0,00	0,00
	$d(x, a_5) =$	0,90	0,90	0,70	0,00

object or individual		b^1	b^2	c^1	c^2
a_6	$d(a_6, x) =$	0,00	0,00	0,90	0,86
	$d(x, a_6) =$	0,94	1,00	0,94	0,90

are explained by the fact that the criterion of the sum does not take into account the non-significant character of small variations and allows weak values on certain criteria to be compensated by strong values on others. It follows that, in the problem considered, it does not constitute a good instrument for decision aid.

Table 15.2.
Comparison of mono-criterion approach with multi-criterion approach

	$\sigma(a_i)$	MONO-CRITERION APPROACH	MULTI-CRITERION APPROACH
a_1	2,99	delay	acceptance (non-tangential)
a_2	3,05	acceptance	acceptance (tangential)
a_3	3,00	delay	delay (non-tangential)
a_4	2,44	rejection	rejection (tangential)
a_5	2,42	rejection	delay (non-tangential)
a_6	2,48	rejection	delay (non-tangential)

15.5 CONCLUSION

The decision to which the procedure leads must be considered as a suggestion made to the decision-maker (financier, doctor, jury, etc). In particular it may be that, when an object or individual a_i is assigned to $K^?$, an examination of the data or the degrees of credibility of different outrankings leads the decision-maker to the conviction that a positive or negative decision is perfectly justified. When this is not the case, he is quite right to expect the procedure to help him orientate the search for additional information.

In many real life situations, the problem formulation presented in Section 15.3.2 may appear too simple. The trichotomic segmentation neglects the fact that rejecting a particular action might imply choosing between other actions or even (which is just about the same thing) accepting a particular action and in doing so excluding all others which can be envisaged *a priori*. This is the case in the problem of choice of therapy, for example. Certainly problems of this type may be tackled using more complex procedures, but such procedures are the result of a type of approach similar to that presented above.

In particular, we may try to progressively restrict the set of *a priori* possible actions (the therapies, for example) by separately applying to each one of these actions a procedure of the type considered above. Difficulty arises from the fact that there is nothing to guarantee (because of imperfect data, simplifying hypotheses, approximate criteria and typologies) a sufficient coherence of the set of conclusions obtained (for a given object or individual) from trichotomic classifications carried out in sequence or parallel. The contraction of the set of possible actions must be effected by taking into account the seriousness of a positive decision in favour of an action other than the correct one. This aspect of the problem intervenes, as we have seen above, at two levels : on the one hand in the list of criteria g_j considered, and on the other in fixing thresholds such as β and γ. When several actions are in competition, the modelling of this degree of seriousness of an error, as the decision-maker sees it, may pose quite delicate problems (cf. Alperovitch (1979)). Its integration into decision aid may imply a high level of complexity.

15.6. REFERENCES

Alperovitch, A., Assesment of Cost of a Diagnostic Error - Methodology and Preliminary Results, Proceedings of the Working Conference on Evaluation of Efficacy of Medical Action, Bordeaux, May 1979, North-Holland, Amsterdam.

Altman, E.I., Financial Ratios, Discriminant Analysis and the Prediction of Corporate Bankruptcy, Journal of Finance, September 1978.

Benayoun, R. and Boulier,C., Approches Rationelles dans la Question du Personnel, Réflexions et Expériences, Monographies AFCET, Paris, Dunod, 1972.

Bernard, G. and Besson, M.L., Douze Méthodes d'Analyse Multicritères, RAIRO, 5e année, no. V-3, 1971.

Bouroche, J.M. and Curvalle B., La Recherche Documentaire par Voisinage, RAIRO, VI, January 1974, pp. 65 - 96.

Caisse Nationale des Marchés, Méthode de Décision Multicritère Appliquée à l'Evaluation de l'Enterprise, Bulletin de la Caisse Nationale des Marchés, no 58, ler trimestre 1973.

Levasseur, M. Hargaine, M. Schlosser, M. and Vernimmen, P., Attribution Automatisée des Crédits à la Consommation, Banque, no 308, June 1972.

Michel, J., La Sélection des Projets de Programmation d'Architecture Nouvelle, Actes du séminaire "Aide à la Décision", AFCET, Paris, May 1974.

Pandey, R.J. and Chawchary, A.K., Single Sampling Plan by Attributes with Three Decision Criteria, Sankhya : The Indian Journal of Statistics - Series B, 1973, pp. 265 - 278.

Roy, B., Partial Preference Analysis and Decision-Aid : the Fuzzy Outranking Relation Concept, in Conflicting Objectives in Decisions, edited by David E. Bell, Ralph L. Keeney and Howard Raiffa, John Wiley, 1977.

Roy, B., ELECTRE III : un Algorithme de Classements Fondé sur une Représentation Floue des Préférences en Présence de Critères Multiples, Cahiers du Centre d'Etudes de Recherche Opérationnelle, Vol. 20, no. 1, 1978.

16 Postefficient Sensitivity Analysis in Linear Vector-maximum Problems

T. Gal

16.1. INTRODUCTION

Consider the linear vectormaximum problem (LVMP)

$$\max_{x \in X} \quad Z(x) = C^T x \tag{16.1}$$

where $C = (c^1, \ldots, c^k, \ldots, c^K) \quad c^k \in R^M$,

$Z(x) = (z_1(x), \ldots, z_k(x), \ldots, z_K(x))^T$,

$z_k(x) = (c^k)^T x$ the k-th objective function,

$X = \{x \in R^M \mid Ax = b, x \geq 0\}$, $A = (a^1, \ldots, a^M)$, $a^j \in R^m$, $b \in R^m$.

Suppose that (16.1) is solved in the sense to determine the set of all efficient solutions by any method (cf. e.g. Gal (1977), Isermann (1977) and references quoted therein), i.e. the set

$$E = \{\bar{x} \in X \mid \nexists\, x \in X: C^T x \geq C^T \bar{x} \quad \text{and} \quad C^T x \neq C^T \bar{x}\} \tag{16.2}$$

As is indicated by several authors (cf. e.g. Kornbluth (1975), Roy (1976)) in the framework of a bargaining procedure for finding a compromise solution $x \in E$ it might be of interest to investigate the influences of changing some of the initial data on E. This is an investigation which is quite analogous to various postoptimal analyses such as sensitivity analysis in linear programming (LP).

Therefore, regarding an LVMP we call such kind of investigations postefficient sensitivity analysis.

16.2. POSTEFFICIENT SENSITIVITY ANALYSIS WITH RESPECT TO C

In the postoptimal sensitivity analysis to an LP-problem the imperative is to find the region of changes of some initial data such that the found optimal basis remains optimal. In analogy, the postefficient analysis to an LVMP with respect to C is to determine the region of changes of C such that the found set E does not change.

Introduce

$$C(\omega) = C + \bar{C}\,\omega_D \tag{16.3}$$

where $\bar{C}$ is an (M , K) constant matrix and

$$\omega_D = \begin{bmatrix} \omega_1, & \dots, & 0 \\ \cdot & \cdot\ \cdot\ \cdot & \cdot \\ 0, & \dots, & \omega_K \end{bmatrix} \tag{16.4}$$

is a diagonal matrix the main elements of which define the parameter vector

$$\omega = (\omega_1, \dots, \omega_K)^T ,$$

which represents the changes of the initial elements c_j^k of C .

Suppose that the set E to the LVMP (16.1) is determined. Denote by $E(Z(\omega))$ the set of all efficient solutions to (16.1) with respect to (16.3) and define

$$E(Z(0)) := E \quad , \tag{16.5}$$

i.e. with $\omega = 0$ the original problem is considered.

The imperative for the postefficient sensitivity analysis to an LVMP with respect to C can then be formulated as follows:

Determine a region $\Omega \subset R^K$ of admissible parameters, such that for all $\omega \in \Omega$ the set E to (16.1) does not change, i.e.

$$E(Z(\omega)) = E \quad \text{for all} \quad \omega \in \Omega \quad . \tag{16.6}$$

Obviously, $X(\omega) = X$ for all $\omega \in R^K$.

What remains to solve is the problem to determine the region Ω . In order to make the answer more understandable, we shall use a small illustrative example.

Consider the LVMP

$$\max_{x \in X} \begin{cases} z_1(x) = -2x_1 + x_2 \\ z_2(x) = 2x_1 + x_2 \\ z_3(x) = x_1 + 2x_2 \end{cases} \tag{16.7}$$

$$\begin{aligned} X = \{x \in R^6 \mid\ & x_1 + x_2 - x_3 = 4 \ ; \ -2x_1 + 3x_2 + x_4 = 7 \ ; \\ & 2x_1 + 3x_2 + x_5 = 23 \ ; \quad x_1 - 2x_2 + x_6 = 1 \ ; \\ & x_j \geq 0 , \quad j = 1(1)6 \quad \} \end{aligned} \tag{16.8}$$

The matrix C is in our case the matrix

$$C = \begin{bmatrix} -2 & 2 & 1 \\ 1 & 1 & 2 \\ 0 & 0 & 0 \\ 0 & 0 & 0 \\ 0 & 0 & 0 \\ 0 & 0 & 0 \end{bmatrix} , \quad \text{i.e.} \quad \begin{aligned} c^1 &= (-2, 1, 0, 0, 0, 0)^T \\ c^2 &= (\ 2, 1, 0, 0, 0, 0)^T \\ c^3 &= (\ 1, 2, 0, 0, 0, 0)^T \end{aligned}$$

Denote by x^s an efficient basic feasible solution to (16.1) and by $\gamma(x^s, x^{s'})$, $s \neq s'$, the edge of X which joins x^s and $x^{s'}$, $x^{s'} \in E$. Then the set E to (16.7) as determined by any method is the set

$$E = \gamma(x^2, x^3) \cup \gamma(x^3, x^4) ,$$

where

$$x^2 = (7, 3, 6, 12, 0, 0)^T , \quad x^3 = (4, 5, 5, 0, 0, 7)^T ,$$
$$x^4 = (1, 3, 0, 0, 12, 6)^T .$$

For the sake of simplicity introduce a scalar parameter ω and define

$$\bar{C} = \begin{bmatrix} 1 & -1 & 1 \\ -1 & -1 & 1 \\ 0 & 0 & 0 \\ 0 & 0 & 0 \\ 0 & 0 & 0 \\ 0 & 0 & 0 \end{bmatrix}$$

so that (16.7) becomes

$$\max_{x \in X} Z(x,\omega) = \begin{aligned} z_1(x,\omega) &= (-2 + \omega)x_1 + (1 - \omega)x_2 \\ z_2(x,\omega) &= (\ 2 - \omega)x_1 + (1 - \omega)x_2 \\ z_3(x,\omega) &= (\ 1 + \omega)x_1 + (2 + \omega)x_2 \end{aligned} \tag{16.9}$$

Denote by

$${}^s\Delta c^k_k = (c^k_B)^T\, B_s^{-1}\, a^j - c^k_j \tag{16.10}$$

the j-th element of c^k as transformed into basis B_s, i.e. the criterion row for $z_k(x)$, and by

$${}^s\Delta \bar{c}^k_j = (\bar{c}^k_B)^T\, B_s^{-1}\, a^j - \bar{c}^k_j \tag{16.11}$$

the j-th element of the k-th row of matric $\bar{C}$ as transformed into basis B_s.

The simplex tableau associated with x^s or with B_s can then be schematically represented as shown in Figure 16.1.

	$x_{j_{m+1}}$ ... x_{j_M}	$^s b$
x_{j_1} ⋮ x_{j_m}	$B_s^{-1}A$	$B_s^{-1}b$
$^s\Delta c_j^1$ ⋮ $^s\Delta c_j^K$	$C_B^T B_s^{-1} A - C^T$	$C_B^T\ ^s b$
$^s\Delta \bar{c}_j^{1}$ ⋮ $^s\Delta \bar{c}_j^{k}$	$\bar{C}_B^T B_s^{-1} A - \bar{C}^T$	$\bar{C}_B^T\ ^s b$

Figure 16.1. Simplex tableau associated with x^s.

In our example the simplex tableau associated with e.g. x^2 is represented in Figure 16.2.

	x_5	x_5	^2b
x_2	1/7	-2/7	3
x_4	1/7	12/7	12
x_3	3/7	1/7	6
x_1	2/7	3/7	7
$^2\Delta c_j^1$	-3/7	-8/7	-11
$^2\Delta c_j^2$	5/7	4/7	17
$^2\Delta c_j^3$	4/7	-1/7	13
$^2\Delta \bar{c}_j^{1}$	1/7	5/7	4
$^2\Delta \bar{c}_j^{2}$	-3/7	-1/7	-10
$^2\Delta \bar{c}_j^{3}$	3/7	1/7	10

Figure 16.2. Simplex tableau associated with x^2.

In Gal (1977) it is shown how to determine whether a solution x^s is an efficient point and which of the edges of X incident with x^s are efficient. This procedure is called the efficiency test and uses the connection between the LVMP (1.1) and the multiparametric LP problem

$$\max_{x \in X} \; z(x,t) = (Ct)^T x, \qquad t > 0 , \qquad t \in R^K \tag{16.12}$$

as has been established by Focke (1973). With respect to B_s the problem which has to be solved as the efficiency test consists of solving the following LP problems:

$$\min \; \xi_j$$

s.t.

$$\begin{aligned} &- \sum_{k=1}^{K} {}^{s}\Delta c_j^k t_k + \xi_j = 0 \quad \text{for all nonbasic } j\text{'s} , \\ &\sum_{k=1}^{K} t_k = 1 , \quad t_k \geq 0 \quad k , \quad \xi_j \geq 0 , \forall j , \end{aligned} \tag{16.13}$$

where the minimum of ξ_j is sought only if in the jth column of $B_s^{-1}A$ there exists a positive element. The corresponding subset of the nonbasic j's is denoted by P_s . Denote further by $\bar{P}_s \subseteq P_s$ the set of indices j such that for each $j \in \bar{P}_s$ the min $\xi_j = 0$ and ξ_j is nonbasic variable. This means that to x^s an efficient neighbour $x^{s'}$ is found along with the corresponding efficient edge $\gamma(x^s, x^{s'})$.

In our example the efficiency test with respect to x^2 consists of solving the LP problems:

$$\min \; \xi_j , \quad j \in P_s = \{5 , 6\} ,$$

s.t.

$$\begin{aligned} (3/7)t_1 - (5/7)t_2 - (4/7)t_3 + \xi_5 &= 0 , \\ (8/7)t_1 - (4/7)t_2 - (1/7)t_3 + \xi_6 &= 0 , \\ t_1 + t_2 + t_3 &= 1 , \\ t_k \geq 0 , \quad k = 1, 2, 3, \quad \xi_j \geq 0 , \quad j &= 5 , 6 \end{aligned} \tag{16.14}$$

Solving these problems would show that $\min \xi_5 > 0$ and $\min \xi_6 = 0$, what implies $\bar{P}_2 = \{6\}$. Consequently, $\gamma(x^2, x^3) \subseteq E$.

Introducing ω according to (16.3) the efficiency test with respect to x^s becomes

$$\min \; \xi_j , \quad j \in P_s ,$$

s.t.

$$- \sum_{k=1}^{K} {}^{s}\Delta c_j^k(\omega_k) + \xi_j = 0 \quad \text{for all nonbasic } j\text{'s}$$

$$\sum_{k=1}^{K} t_k = 1 \ , \qquad (16.15)$$

$$t_k \geq 0 \ \forall \ k \ , \quad \xi_j \geq 0 \ , \forall j \quad ,$$

where ${}^{s}\Delta c_j^k \ (\omega_k)$ are linear functions in ω of the form

$$ {}^{s}\Delta c_j^k \ (\omega_k) = {}^{s}\Delta c_j^k + {}^{s}\Delta c_j^{-k} \ \omega_k \qquad (16.16)$$

Let us state that (16.15) is a problem with parameters in the "technological matrix". This implies that solving (16.15) we obtain rational functions in ω (cf. Gal (1979), pp.249-272).

In our example the efficiency test with respect to x^2 and with regard to ω consists of solving the problems

$$\min \xi_j \ , \quad j \in P_2 = \{5 \ , 6\} \quad ,$$

s.t.

$$(\tfrac{3}{7} - \tfrac{1}{7}\ \omega)\ t_1 + (- \tfrac{5}{7} + \tfrac{3}{7}\ \omega)\ t_2 + (- \tfrac{4}{7} - \tfrac{3}{7}\ \omega)\ t_3 + \xi_5 = 0 \ ,$$

$$(\tfrac{8}{7} - \tfrac{5}{7}\ \omega)\ t_1 + (- \tfrac{4}{7} + \tfrac{1}{7}\ \omega)\ t_2 = (\ \tfrac{1}{7} - \tfrac{1}{7}\ \omega)\ t_3 + \xi_6 = 0 \ , \qquad (16.17)$$

$$t_1 + t_2 + t_3 = 1 \ ,$$

$$t_k \geq 0 \ , \quad k = 1, 2, 3, \quad \xi_j \geq 0 \ , \ j = 5 \ , 6 \qquad .$$

The imperative for the postefficient sensitivity analysis to an LVMP implies that we have to determine a region Ω_s for ω such that for all $\omega \in \Omega_s$ the corresponding efficiency test provides the same results as without ω .

In our example this means: solving (16.17) the results must be again $\min \xi_5 > 0$, $\min \xi_6 = 0$.

In order to show what this problem consists of we shall solve (16 . 7) . In Figure 16.3 the corresponding solution is presented.

	t_2	ξ_6	
ξ_5	$\frac{-\ 1\ -\ 2\omega}{3}$	$-\ \frac{2}{3}$	$\frac{1\ -\ \omega}{3}$
t_1	$\frac{5\ -\ 2\omega}{12\ -\ 6}$	$\frac{7}{12\ -\ 6\omega}$	$\frac{4\ -\ \omega}{12\ -\ 6}$
t_2	$\frac{7\ -\ 4\omega}{12\ -\ 6}$	$\frac{-7}{12\ -\ 6\omega}$	$\frac{8\ -\ 5\omega}{12\ -\ 6}$

Figure 16.3. Solution of the efficiency test with respect to x^2 and ω .

Set $\omega = 0$; from Figure 16.3 it is seen that $\min \xi_5 = 1/3 > 0$ because all the elements in the corresponding row are nonpositive (cf. e.g. Gal (1979), Chapter 2), $t_1 = 1/3 > 0$, $t_2 = 2/3 > 0$ and there exists $t > 0$ satisfying (16.14). Moreover, $\min \xi_6 = 0$ because ξ_6 is nonbasic variable. In order to maintain $x^2 \in E$ and x^3 being a neighboring efficient solution of x^2 along with $\gamma(x^2, x^3) \subseteq E$, the above conditions must hold with ω either.

Let us call "the dual condition" the condition that all elements are nonpositive in the row ξ_j , i.e. in the row in which ξ_j stands as basic variable and $\min \xi_j > 0$. The "primal condition" is obvious: the values of the basic t_k's as well as those of the basic ξ_j's must remain strictly positive. Hence, in our example from Figure 16.3 we have:

The "dual condition":

$$\frac{-1-2\omega}{3} \leq 0 \quad ;$$

the "primal condition":

$$\xi_5(\omega) = \frac{1-\omega}{3} > 0 \ , \quad t_1(\omega) = \frac{4-\omega}{12-6} > 0 \ , \quad t_2(\omega) = \frac{8-5\omega}{12-6\omega} > 0 \ .$$

Obviously, the values of ω satisfying the above conditions will not influence the property of the initial x^2 in the sense that $x^2 \in E$, $\gamma(x^2, x^3) \subseteq E$ and there are no more efficient neighboring solutions of x^2 .

Solving the above system of inequalities we obtain

$$\Omega_s = [-0.5 \, ; 1) \ .$$

Before we proceed further in solving the question how to determine Ω let us introduce the following notion:
A solution x^s is called a non-invariant solution iff $\bar{P}_s \subset P_s$. It is called an invariant solution iff $\bar{P}_s = P_s$.

Thus, a non-invariant solution has at least one neighboring solution $x^{s'}$ such that $\lambda(x^s, x^{s'}) \subseteq E$. In our example x^2 is such a non-invariant solution. An invariant solution x^s has the property that all its neighbors along with the corresponding edges belong to E . In our example x^3 is an invariant solution.

It is clear that the 'dual condition' is sensible only for non-invariant solutions.

In Figure 16.4 the solution to the efficiency test with respect to x^3 and ω is represented.

		t_3	ξ_4	
(i)	t_2	$\frac{7 - 4\omega}{12 - 6\omega}$	$\frac{2}{2 - \omega}$	$\frac{8 - 5\omega}{12 - 6\omega}$
	ξ_5	$-\frac{1}{3}$	1	$\frac{1 -}{3}$
	t_1	$\frac{5 - 2\omega}{12 - 6\omega}$	$\frac{-2}{2 - \omega}$	$\frac{4 - \omega}{12 - 6\omega}$
		t_3	ξ_5	
(ii)	t_2	$\frac{11 - 4}{12 - 6}$	$\frac{-2}{2 - \omega}$	$\frac{4 - \omega}{12 - 6\omega}$
	ξ_4	$-\frac{1}{3}$	1	$\frac{1 - \omega}{3}$
	t_1	$\frac{1 - 2\omega}{12 - 6\omega}$	$\frac{2}{2 - \omega}$	$\frac{8 - 5\omega}{12 - 6\omega}$

Figure 16.4. Solution of the efficiency test with respect to x^3 and ω.

Incidentally, setting $\omega = 0$ we can see that $\min \xi_5 = \min \xi_4 = 0$, hence $\bar{P}_3 = P_3$ and x^3 is invariant. This means that $\gamma(x^3, x^2) \subseteq E$, $\gamma(x^3, x^4) \subseteq E$, i.e. all neighbors of x^3 along with the corresponding edges belong to E.

The admissible values of ω result from the inequalities ('primal' conditions only):

$$t_2(\omega) = \frac{8 - 5\omega}{12 - 6\omega} > 0 \; ; \; \xi_5(\omega) = \frac{1 - \omega}{3} > 0 \; ; \; t_1(\omega) = \frac{4 - \omega}{12 - 6\omega} > 0 \; ;$$

and

$$t_2(\omega) = \frac{4 - \omega}{12 - 6\omega} > 0 \; ; \; \xi_4(\omega) = \frac{1 - \omega}{3} > 0 \; ; \; t_1(\omega) = \frac{8 - 5\omega}{12 - 6\omega} > 0 \; .$$

Solving these systems of inequalities, we obtain

$$\Omega_3 = (-\infty, 1{,}6) \cup (4, +\infty) \; .$$

Compare Ω_2 with Ω_3. Obviously using the values $\omega \in \Omega_3$ which do not belong to Ω_2 the solution x^2 would become nonefficient.

Clearly, x^2 and x^3 along with the corresponding edge remain efficient for all $\omega \in \Omega_2 \cap \Omega_3$. This must be, however, valid for Ω_s for all s, s', $s \neq s'$, such that $x^s \in E$, $x^{s'} \in E$ and $\gamma(x^s, x^{s'}) \subseteq E$. Hence,

$$\Omega = \bigcap_{s=1}^{S} \Omega_s \; ,$$

where S is the number of all basic efficient solutions.

Considering again our example, we would find that $x^4 \in E$ is non-invariant and that $\Omega_4 = [-0,5 ; 1)$. Hence

$$\Omega = \bigcap_{s=2}^{S} \Omega_s = [-0,5 ; 1) \quad .$$

The 'classical' or 'direct' postefficient sensitivity analysis, in analogy with the postoptimal analysis in LP problems, investigates the case

$$c_j^k(\omega) = c_j^k + \omega \quad \text{for } j \text{ and } k \text{ fixed,}$$

or for k fixed .

The above considerations and results are formally described and proved in Gal and Leberling (1976).

Now let us add a note in connection with compromise solutions. Suppose a compromise solution $x^K \in E$ is determined and a postefficient sensitivity analysis with respect to C is of interest. Since the whole set E does not matter, the region Ω for ω can be obviously determined as

$$\Omega' = \bigcap_{s=1}^{S'} \Omega_s \quad ,$$

where S' is the number of all neighboring efficient solutions of x^K .

Suppose $x^* \in E$ is a nonbasic compromise solution. If in such a case a postefficient sensitivity analysis with respect to C is of interest, the set Ω'' of admissible parameters can be defined as

$$\Omega'' = \bigcap_{s=1}^{S''} \Omega_s \quad ,$$

where S'' is the number of all basic efficient solutions which determine the hyperplane (edge) to which x^* belongs.

16.3. POSTEFFICIENT SENSITIVITY ANALYSIS WITH RESPECT TO B.

Unfortunately, in the case of changing elements of b in an LVMP (16.1) the imperative for to determine the corresponding region of admissible parameters cannot be "... such that E does not change" as it is in the case of canging C. The reason for this is that with changes in b set X changes and by this set E changes as well.

In order to construct conditions which define the admissible parameter region we introduce the following notion:

The structure G(E) of the set E of all efficient solutions to a given LVMP (16.1) is defined by the set of all basic efficient solutions x^s , the corresponding efficient edges $\gamma(x^s , x^{s'})$ and by the efficient faces.

In Figure 16.5 a three-dimensional set X is represented. The thick lines represent the efficient edges, the shadowed areas the efficient faces. The structure G(E) in this case is defined by the solutions x^s, $s = 1(1)8$, by the corresponding (thick) edges $\gamma(x^s , x^{s'})$ and by the faces defined by the solutions x^s , $s = 1(1)5$ and $x^{s'}$, $s' = 3, 4, 6, 7$.

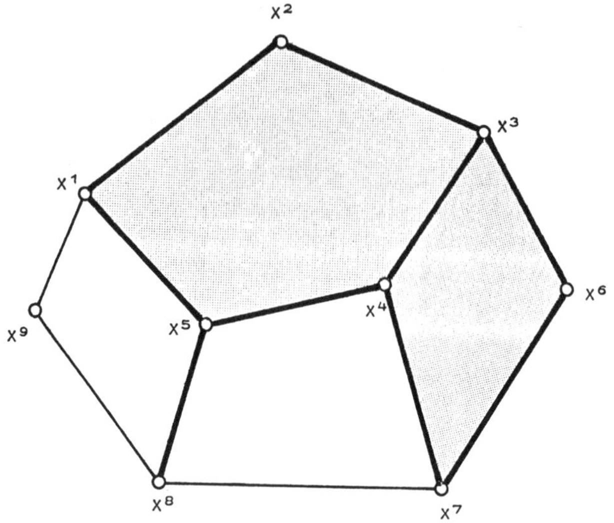

Figure 16.5. Example of a three-dimensional set X.

Consider

$$b(\lambda) = b + L\lambda , \tag{16.18}$$

where L is an (m , V) constant matrix, $\lambda \in R^V$ is a parameter vector. Denote by E(X (λ)) the set of all efficient solutions to (16.1) with respect to (16.18) and define

$$E(X(0)) := E . \tag{16.19}$$

Denote further by G(E (λ)) the structure of E with respect to (16.18) and define

$$G(E(0)) := G(E) . \tag{16.20}$$

The imperative for the postefficient sensitivity analysis with respect to b can then be formulated as follows:

Determine a region $\Lambda \subseteq R^V$ of admissible parameters λ such that the structure of the set of all efficient solutions does not change, i.e.

$$G(E(\lambda)) = G(E) \quad \text{for all } \lambda \in \Lambda . \tag{16.21}$$

Obviously, $C(\lambda) = C$ for all $\lambda \in R^V$.

What remains to show is how to determine Λ . For this we use again our illustrative example from Section 16.2. For the sake of simplicity we shall agian consider a scalar parameter λ only. Let

$$b(\lambda) = b + \bar{b}\lambda , \quad \text{where } \bar{b} = (2 , -3 , -1 , 3)^T ,$$

i.e.

$$\max_{x \in X(\lambda)} Z(x) , \tag{16.22}$$

where $Z(x)$ is given as in the initial example and $X(\lambda)$ is defined by the constraints

$$
\begin{aligned}
x_1 + x_2 - x_3 &= 4 + 2\lambda \\
-2x_1 + 3x_2 + x_4 &= 7 + 3\lambda \\
2x_1 + 3x_2 + x_5 &= 23 - \lambda \\
x_1 - 2x_2 + x_6 &= 1 + 3\lambda \\
x_j \geq 0 \quad , \quad j &= 1(1)6 \quad .
\end{aligned}
$$

Consider Figure 16.2 and enlarge the corresponding tableau by the column $B_2^{-1}\bar{b} = {}^2\bar{b} = (-1, 2, -2, 1)^T$.

Considering the solution x^2 as if it was an optimal solution to an LP problem, a 'normal' sensitivity analysis provides

$$
\begin{aligned}
\underline{\lambda} &= \max\{-12/2\ , -7/1\} = -6 \\
\lambda &= \min\{\ 3/1\ ,\ 6/2\} = \quad 3 \quad ,
\end{aligned}
$$

i.e. the critical region $[-6\ , 3]$ would result. If we would however choose $\bar{\lambda} = 3$, the initial set X reduces to $X(\bar{\lambda})$, which is a single point (cf. Figure 16.6, where X is drawn in terms of x_1, x_2 , whereas $x_3, \ldots, x_6$ are slack variables).

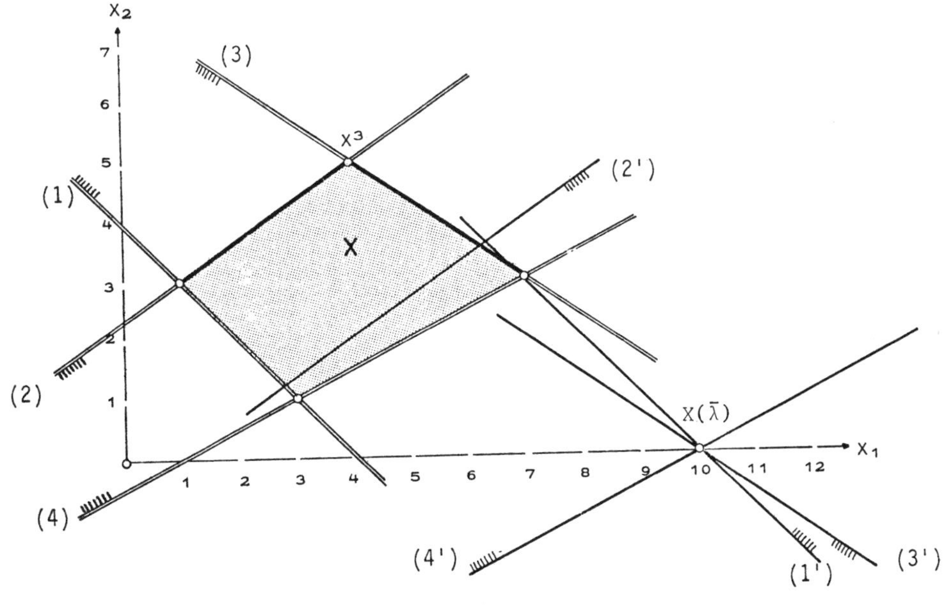

Figure 16.6. The initial constraints are labeled by figures in parentheses, the constraints which correspond to $\bar{\lambda}$ are labeled with the figures primed.

Hence, setting $\lambda = \bar{\lambda}$, the structure $G(E)$ of the set E changed. It is seen (cf. Figure 16.6) that setting $\lambda = \bar{\lambda} - \varepsilon$, $\varepsilon > 0$ sufficiently small, the structure $G(E)$ would not change. Thus the region of λ resulting from a 'normal' postoptimal sensitivity analysis should not be taken as a closed set but as an open set.

Consider an efficient solution x^s associated with the basis B_s . As is well known from the sensitivity analysis in LP (cf. Gal (1979)), the critical region for λ is defined by

$$- B_s^{-1}L\lambda \leq B_s^{-1}b \qquad \text{or} \qquad -{}^sL\lambda \leq {}^sb \quad .$$

This (convex) set is obviously closed. Therefore, in the postefficient sensitivity analysis to an LVMP with respect to b the critical region associated with x^s is defined by

$$\Lambda_s := \{\lambda \in R^V \mid - {}^sL\lambda < {}^sb\} \quad . \tag{16.23}$$

In our example we then have $\Lambda_2 = (-6 , 3)$.

Consider now x^3 ; here ${}^3\bar{b} = (-2/3 , 7/6 , 11/6 , 1/2)^T$, so that $\underline{\lambda} = -30/11$ and $\bar{\lambda} = 15/2$, hence $\Lambda_3 = (-30/11 , 7.5)$.

Comparing Λ_2 with Λ_3 it is clear that choosing $\lambda \in (-6 , -30/11)$ or $\lambda \in (3 , 7.5)$ the structure $G(E)$ would change. Therefore, we may choose λ only from the intersection of Λ_2 and Λ_3 .

Recall that Λ is the set of all admissible parameters. Then, in general, obviously

$$\Lambda = \bigcap_{s=1}^{S} \Lambda_s \tag{16.24}$$

where S is the number of all efficient basic solutions ot (16.1) with respect to (16.18).

Suppose $x^K \in E$ is a compromise solution and some kind of postefficient sensitivity analysis with respect to b is of interest. By 'some kind' we mean the possibility of defining matrix L or vector $\bar{b}$. Unfortunately, in this case we cannot proceed as we did in the case of changing C . Up till now it is not fully clarified how to proceed exactly in such a case, especially because the corresponding theory is not completely finished yet.

It should be noted that some considerations for the general theory for the postefficient sensitivity analysis can be found in Gal and Leberling (1976).

16.4. REFERENCES

Focke, J., Vektormaximumprobleme und parametrische Optimierung, *Math. O.F. Stat.*, vol.4, 1973, pp.365-369.

Gal, T., A General Method for Determining the Set of all Efficient Solutions to a Linear Vectormaximum Problem, *Eur. J. of OR*, vol.1, 1977, pp. 307-322.

Gal, T., *Postoptimal Analyses, Parametric Programming and Related Topics*, McGraw Hill, New York, 1979.

Gal, T., and Leberling, H., Relaxation Analysis in Vectorvalued Optimization, Working Paper no. 76/15, University of Aachen, 1976.

Isermann, H., The Enumeration of the Set of all Efficient Solutions for a Linear Multiple Objective Program, *Oper. Res. Quart.*, vol.28, 1977, pp.711-725.

Kornbluth, J.S.H., Duality, Indifference and Sensitivity Analysis, *Oper. Res. Quart.*, vol.25, 1975, pp.599-614.

Roy, B., From Optimization on a Fixed Set to Multicriteria Decision Aid, In: *Proc. on Multiple Criteria Decision Making,* M. Zeleny, ed., Springer: Berlin, 1976, pp.283-286.